THE JEWISH FAMILY

Traditional Jewish family law has persevered for hundreds of years, and rules covering marriage, the raising of children, and divorce are well established; yet pressures from modern society are causing long-held views to be re-examined. *The Jewish Family: Between Family Law and Contract Law* examines the tenets of Jewish family law in light of new attitudes concerning the role of women, assisted reproduction technologies, and prenuptial agreements. It explores, through interdisciplinary research combining the legal aspects of family law and contract law, how the Jewish family can cope with both old and modern obstacles and challenges. It focuses on the nexus of Jewish family law and contract law to propose how "freedom of contract" can be part of how family law can be interpreted. *The Jewish Family* will appeal to practitioners, activists, academic researchers, and laymen, readers who are interested in the fields of law, theology, and social science.

YEHEZKEL MARGALIT is a senior lecturer at Netanya Academic College in Israel.

CAMBRIDGE STUDIES IN LAW AND JUDAISM

The law and religion movement is a growing field dedicated to studying the religious dimensions of law, the legal dimensions of religion, and the interaction of legal and religious ideas, institutions, norms and practices. *Cambridge Studies in Law and Judaism* cultivates scholarship on Jewish topics in law and religion including translations, historical accounts of the foundations of the Jewish legal system, and innovative comparative studies. Its mission is to break new ground in studying what Jewish law has, can, and should offer to public, private, penal, and procedural law and legal theory.

The Jewish Family

BETWEEN FAMILY LAW AND CONTRACT LAW

YEHEZKEL MARGALIT
Netanya Academic College

CAMBRIDGE
UNIVERSITY PRESS

CAMBRIDGE
UNIVERSITY PRESS

University Printing House, Cambridge CB2 8BS, United Kingdom

One Liberty Plaza, 20th Floor, New York, NY 10006, USA

477 Williamstown Road, Port Melbourne, VIC 3207, Australia

314–321, 3rd Floor, Plot 3, Splendor Forum, Jasola District Centre, New Delhi – 110025, India

79 Anson Road, #06–04/06, Singapore 079906

Cambridge University Press is part of the University of Cambridge.

It furthers the University's mission by disseminating knowledge in the pursuit of education, learning, and research at the highest international levels of excellence.

www.cambridge.org
Information on this title: www.cambridge.org/9781107163409
DOI: 10.1017/9781316681350

First published 2017

Printed in the United Kingdom by Clays, St Ives plc

A catalogue record for this publication is available from the British Library.

Library of Congress Cataloging-in-Publication Data
NAMES: Margalit, Yehezkel, author.
TITLE: The Jewish family : between family law and contract law / Yehezkel Margalit, Netanya Academic College.
DESCRIPTION: Cambridge [UK] ; New York : Cambridge University Press, 2017. | Includes bibliographical references and index.
IDENTIFIERS: LCCN 2017031854 | ISBN 9781107163409 (Hardback)
SUBJECTS: LCSH: Domestic relations (Jewish law) | Marriage (Jewish law) | Prenuptial agreements (Jewish law) | Agunahs. | Parent and child (Jewish law)
CLASSIFICATION: LCC KBM531 .M37 2017 | DDC 296.7/4–dc23
LC record available at https://lccn.loc.gov/2017031854

ISBN 978-1-107-16340-9 Hardback

Contents

Preface

This book deals with the nexus of Jewish contract law and Jewish family law and their potential mutual influence. The essence of the research explores whether and to what extent there is considerable halakhic room for the usage of ancient and modern contractual devices and doctrines to privately regulate the Jewish family. Whereas Jewish law regulates comprehensively and thoroughly both the spousal and parental relations, it is necessary to discuss whether and to what extent there is freedom of contract to privately regulate the various angles of those relations. The subject of the research is mainly the horizontal relationship between spouses, but it also discusses the vertical relationship between parent and child. The research draws upon material from the biblical period and concludes with current analysis and materials. It focuses mainly on the Mishnah and the Talmud periods onward. This book discusses mainly Jewish law, which I prefer for several reasons to call *halakhah* and which stands at the crossroads of theology and law, but it also engages with modern civil law.

This is especially true in the last chapter of the book, Chapter 5, where one can find discussions of the most cutting-edge legal-ethical dilemmas in the field of advanced biomedical innovations regarding who should be determined as the legal parent of a child conceived through artificial means. The methodology of the research is taken mainly from the halakhic dogmatic method but often also applies the historical method; it is thus an example of Professor Menahem Elon's combined historical-dogmatic standpoint. This book concludes the results of my writings over the last decade in both Jewish and civil law. The research commenced with my MA thesis, "Public Regulation and Private Agreement of Spousal Conjugal Privileges in Jewish Law," which was published in 2006. This was followed in 2011 with the publication of my PhD dissertation, "Determining Legal Parentage by Agreement." Following these two major research projects, I developed my thinking in over twenty publications in various law reviews in the United States as well as in Israel, drawing it together in this book.

Acknowledgments

First and foremost, I am grateful to my MA thesis and PhD dissertation supervisors: Professor Berachyahu Lifshitz, former dean of the Hebrew University Faculty of Law, and Professor Shahar Lifshitz, current Faculty of Law dean at Bar-Ilan University. Both of them are world-renowned experts in family and contract law, respectively in the halakhic and civil aspects. I warmly thank them for opening the gate for me to the scholarly research of these developing and challenging fields. Professor Shahar Lifshitz has been my mentor throughout.

The first chapters of this book were written during the years I served as a research associate at the Agunah Research Unit at the Centre for Jewish Studies, University of Manchester, U.K. I am grateful to Professor Bernard S. Jackson, the director of this challenging project, for his encouragement and financial support while writing these chapters. I wrote this book as faculty and Senior Lecturer at Netanya Academic College. I am sincerely thankful to the college and to Professor Sinai Deutch, currently Senior Vice President, Director, and Dean of the Law School, for the generous grant to publish it. The preparation and publication of the work was supported also by the Memorial Foundation for Jewish Culture. There is no doubt that without these meaningful grants, this book would not have been published.

Thanks also to dayyan Ronnie Warburg for carefully reading the entire manuscript and giving me knowledgeable and thorough comments. Special thanks are due to my colleagues Professor Israel Z. Gilat, and Professor Pamela Laufer-Ukeles who provided me with helpful comments while I was writing this book. Thanks are also due to Mr. Uri Yamin, who helped me identify and read various Islamic sources in the original while writing the fourth chapter. I am grateful also to Mrs. Chava Cassel for her enormous assistance in the linguistic editing of the book. Mrs. Cassel thoroughly and critically edited the manuscript and made many essential and important comments regarding substantial concerns. Finally, I want to thank Rabbi Avishai Elboim, Director of the Rambam Library in Tel Aviv, Israel, for his efficient and prompt assistance in finding any missing rare bibliographical information.

During the last decade, while writing this book, I spent huge amounts of time at both the Judaica Library and the Law Library at Bar-Ilan University. I am grateful for the help of the library staff. I would like to thank my dear parents, Shlomo and Chana Margalit, and my in-laws, Shmuel and Chana Burkash, who have served me as second parents, and my children – Shira, Hallel, Yehonatan-Zvi, and Eitan-Reuven – who taught me throughout the years how deep and meaningful the parent–child bond can be. Finally, I want to thank from the depths of the heart my beloved wife, Hagit, who over the last few decades has proven to me how enormous and experiential true spousal love can be.

Introduction

One of the most fascinating issues in every legal system is the nexus of contract law and family law and their potential mutual influence. On the one hand, one can contemplate using contractual devices and doctrines to achieve a more flexible and nuanced regulation of the various issues arising in family law instead of the rigid and determined regulation by public policy-inspired statute. On the other hand, it is possible to explore whether and the extent to which family law assists in the validation of different (family) agreements and contracts. In scholarly literature, one can find in the last decades writing regarding the expanding influence of civil contract law on modern family law.[1] This book focuses mainly on regulating some aspects of marital status. By way of example, it uses various spousal agreements, such as prenuptial and postnuptial agreements, divorce agreements, cohabitation agreements, and even agreements between same-sex partners.

Similarly, in the field of parent–child relationships, this book includes discussions of various co-parenting agreements.[2] In the modern era, "nontraditional" families, in both the spousal and the parental contexts, urgently require the provision of such agreements since their relationships are not recognized by their jurisdictions as a married couple. The unique interplay between greater social openness and rapid biomedical developments in the field of reproduction enables reproduction in almost every family structure, with large numbers of

[1] *See, e.g.*, SHAHAR LIFSHITZ, CONTRACTUAL REGULATION OF SPOUSAL RELATIONSHIP IN CIVIL LAW 263 n.2 (PhD thesis, Bar-Ilan University, 2002) (Heb.); ibid, *The Regulation of the Spousal Contract in the Israeli Law – First Outline*, 4 KIRYAT HAMISHPAT 271 (2004–05) (Heb.).

[2] *See* Charles P. Kindregan, *Collaborative Reproduction and Rethinking Parentage*, 21 J. AM. ACAD. MATRIMONIAL L. 43 (2008); Bix Brian, *Domestic Agreements*, 35 HOFSTRA L. REV. 1753 (2007); Katherine M. Swift, *Parenting Agreements, The Potential Power of Contract, and the Limits of Family Law*, 34 FLA. ST. U. L. REV. 913 (2007).

children being born using nontraditional means.[3] Consequently, the need to contractually regulate the relationship between all the parties to those enterprises has been accelerated.

There is much less academic discussion concerning the potential influence of various family law doctrines and principles on the regulation of modern contractual devices and doctrines.[4] Modern contract theory has been regarded as much more sensitive and potentially even more humane than classical contract theory is.[5] There is a stark contrast between contracts regulating family settlements and contracts governed by classical contract theory, which holds that any given contracting parties are rational and reasonable enough for signing the best contract for them[6] – and therefore "Qui dit contractual, dit juste"[7] – and they must fulfill their contractual obligations. This is true even though there might be various problems concerning the formation and operation of a contract, such as unequal bargaining power of the contracting parties, a change of heart, changed circumstances, and other cognitive obstacles for properly foreseeing the future at the moment of signing the contract.

Likewise, both the rabbinic and the scholarly literature[8] have not dealt extensively enough with the possible influence of contractual devices and doctrines on the

3 *See* recently Yehezkel Margalit, *Dying to Be a Father – About the Appropriate Normative Limits on the Use of the Will of the Deceased to Reproduce after His Death* ch. 1 (on file with author) (Heb.).

4 For seminal academic writings regarding the modern/neoclassical contract doctrine, see Ian Ayres, *Valuing Modern Contract Scholarship*, 112 YALE L.J. 881 (2003); Morton J. Horwitz, THE TRANSFORMATION OF AMERICAN LAW, 1780–1860 (1997); GOOD FAITH AND FAULT IN CONTRACT LAW 7–12 (Jack Beatson & Daniel Friedmann eds., 1995); Jay M. Feinman, *The Significance of Contract Theory*, 58 U. CIN. L. REV. 1283 (1990); Ian R. Macneil, THE NEW SOCIAL CONTRACT: AN INQUIRY INTO MODERN CONTRACTUAL RELATIONS (1980).

5 *See, e.g.*, Elizabeth S. Scott & Robert E. Scott, *From Contract to Status: Collaboration and the Evolution of Novel Family Relationships*, 115 COLUM. L. REV. 293 (2015) passim; Yehezkel Margalit, *In Defense of Surrogacy Agreements: A Modern Contract Law Perspective*, 20 WM. & MARY J. WOMEN & L. 423 (2014) passim; Allen M. Parkman, *The Contractual Alternative to Marriage*, 32 N. KY. L. REV. 125 (2005); Robert Leckey, *Relational Contract and Other Models of Marriage*, 40 OSGOODE HALL L.J. 1 (2002); John Wightman, *Intimate Relationships, Relational Contract Theory, and the Reach of Contract*, 8 FEMINIST LEGAL STUD. 93 (2000); Elizabeth S. Scott & Robert E. Scott, *Marriage as Relational Contract*, 84 VA. L. REV. 1225 (1998).

6 *See* Ian R. Macneil, *Contracts: Adjustment of Long-Term Economic Relations under Classical, Neoclassical and Relational Contract Law*, 72 NW. U. L. REV. 854 (1978); Michel Rosenfeld, *Contract and Justice: The Relation between Classical Contract Law and Social Contract Theory*, 70 IOWA L. REV. 769 (1985); Kevin M. Teeven, *A History of Legislative Reform of the Common Law of Contract*, 26 U. TOL. L. REV. 35 (1994); PATRICK S. ATIYAH, AN INTRODUCTION TO THE LAW OF CONTRACT 7 (1995); Melvin A. Eisenberg, *Why There Is No Law of Relational Contracts*, 94 NW. U. L. REV. 805 (2000).

7 For this legal doctrine, see Louise Rolland, *Qui dit contractual, dit juste (Fouillee) . . . en trois petits bonds, a reculons*, 51 MCGILL L.J. 765 (2005–06).

8 For a general discussion of the Jewish contract law, see Menachem Elon, *Contract* in THE PRINCIPLES OF JEWISH LAW 246–56 (Menachem Elon ed., 1975); LEVINE AARON, FREE ENTERPRISE AND JEWISH LAW: ASPECTS OF JEWISH BUSINESS ETHICS 33–57 (1980). For a discussion of the general difficulty to formulate contemporary contract that can be reconciled

regulation of Jewish family law, mainly in finding a viable solution to the problem of the *agunah* (Jewish chained woman), as is discussed extensively in the outset of the third chapter of this book. These discussions revolve around contractual devices and doctrines that are based on contractual agreements per se and are included in prenuptial agreements and a commitment to grant a *get* (religious divorce) and in different contractual doctrines such as conditional marriage, mistaken marriage, and so on. If those contractual solutions are accepted as a viable alternative for the acute need of receiving the *get*, one may properly cope with the heart-wrenching case of the *agunah*.

Besides the complexities arising because of the status of marriage, discussed above, there is an urgent need for further discussion regarding the regulation of different financial aspects arising from the spouses' use of an explicit or implicit contract.[9] These discussions should be much easier from halakhic perspective since they deal only with the monetary angles of spousal life, such as mutually agreeing upon egalitarian or contractual ownership and distribution of the family assets. In addition, these private agreements may enable the spouses to mutually agree upon increasing, decreasing, or even absolutely abolishing gender halakhic obligations, such as contractual agreements to exempt or obligate the husband to pay the wife's maintenance and/or the child support or to waive the husband's right to inherit his wife. It is my opinion that these important and substantial contractual devices have not received the attention they deserve in either the halakhic or the scholarly literature. This lacuna will be filled with the theoretical and practical conclusions of this book.

THE STRUCTURE OF THIS WORK

The main theme of this book is exploring the potential influence of halakhic contract law on halakhic family law in both spousal and parent–child relationships. In Chapter 1, I initiate the discussion of the use of contractual devices to privately regulate the various halakhic spousal obligations that derive from the status of being married according to "the law of Moses and Israel" (*kedat Mosheh veYisrael*).

with the rigid halakhic restrictions, see the following Hebrew references: David Bass, *Contracts According to Dine Torah*, 1 KETER 17 (1996); Benjamin Porat, *The Law of Fraudulent Prices – Fundamentals, Principles and Values*, 4 KETER 292 (2004); DEFECTIVE CONTRACTS (Nahum Rakover ed., 2011); REMEDIES FOR BREACH OF CONTRACT (Nahum Rakover ed., to be published); and the various articles in the periodical 4 MISHPETEI ERETZ (2016).

9 For example, ARIEL ROSEN-ZVI, THE LAW OF MATRIMONIAL PROPERTY (1982) (Heb.) has dealt extensively with regulating the monetary spousal relationship via contractual devices in both *halakhah* and civil law. *See*, respectively, ibid, at 124–27, 132, 222, 339, and 349–50, and in the index, s.v. "contract law" (*hozim*). For a discussion of the various spousal monetary agreements and waving away the various *ketubah* stipulations, see, respectively, BENZION SCHERESCHEWSKY, FAMILY LAW IN ISRAEL 98, 157, 164, and 101–02 (4th ed., 1993) (Heb.) and more recently BENZION SCHERESCHEWSKY & MICHAEL CORINALDI, FAMILY LAW IN ISRAEL vol. 1, 225–78 (2015) (Heb.).

Recently there has been an increase in academic and rabbinical literature dealing with various aspects of the approach of Jewish law to marital relations between spouses, discussions that until not long ago took place only in private. Jewish law regulates this relationship in a most comprehensive manner, in accordance with the concept of *halakhah*. This is different to civil law, which in liberal modern systems avoids legal involvement in this intimate relationship. The halakhic term used for regulating this relationship is the commandment/duty of *onah*.

In this chapter, I seek to discuss anew the traditional determination that sees the element of *onah* in Jewish marriages as mandatory, a rigid halakhic and basic obligation owed by a husband to his wife, from which a man cannot be exempted either by mutual agreement between the parties or by a unilateral stipulation on his part. This traditional approach is expressed in the determination of the Babylonian Talmud, which chose the element of *onah* as the prototype for any attempt to stipulate with regard to an obligation that originates from the Torah. Any such stipulation will be void since it comes within the category of "one who stipulates about what is written in the Torah"; thus *rishonim* (early rabbis) insisted that *onah* is the "essence of matrimony" and "the essence of Torah marriage" and that "marital relations are the essence of marriage from the Torah." This chapter reexamines this traditional approach, seeking to illuminate the dispositive foundations of the elements of *onah* – whether by imposing a condition in the *kiddushin* (Jewish betrothal) and thus negating the obligation of *onah* or by permitting the wife to renounce her *onah* rights or giving her permission to violate her *onah* right.

The discussion in Chapter 2 is a direct continuation of the conclusions of Chapter 1, focusing only on the possible private regulation of the marital relations between spouses by consent. The discussion in Chapter 1 highlights the essential differences between the Babylonian Talmud, which rejects from the outset almost any private agreement regarding this intimate relationship, and the Palestinian Talmud, which is much more flexible and enables this type of spousal agreement. In this chapter I examine whether there exists only one essential difference in the Talmudic points of view regarding conjugal relations or whether there is a much more comprehensive and meaningful gap in the Talmud's outlook. Recently there has been considerable interest also in the contractual aspects of the relationship between spouses in both *halakhah* and civil law. In *halakhah* the discussion is primarily concerned with the limits of freedom of contract. In other words, the question is to what extent a couple married under Jewish law can use a contract to regulate their financial relations at the commencement of their married life. These halakhic contracts are generally called prenuptial agreements.

In this chapter I am interested in reconsidering the extent of "freedom of contract" in Talmudic family law in light of the special approach found in the Palestinian Talmud and contrast it with that of the Babylonian Talmud. I devote most of the discussion to those components dealing with matters of ritual (*issura*), issues that are not specifically financial from a pure halakhic point of view but that are connected to Jewish marriage. Among the subjects discussed besides the husband's duties regarding *onah* are the possibility of limiting through contracts obligations and privileges resulting from marital status, such as the husband's obligation to pay the basic *ketubah* sum and his right to inherit his deceased wife's estate. The special approach found in the Palestinian Talmud permits a much wider and more flexible approach to the freedom of contract than that of the Babylonian Talmud. In the light of this approach, Chapter 2 is primarily concerned with the dogmatic basis for the woman's right to initiate a divorce because she hates her husband based on prior agreement at the time of the marriage, a condition that was common in Palestine during the period of the Palestinian Talmud.

After concluding in the first two chapters that indeed we have an explicit contradiction between the two Talmuds and there is an essential gap in their perspectives regarding the limits of freedom of contract for couples who wish to marry according to the law of Moses and Israel, I seek in Chapter 3 to take the issue one step further and explore whether it is possible to practically use one of the available contractual devices as a possible solution for the heart-wrenching case of the *agunah*. In the modern era, there have been a number of suggestions for halakhic solutions for the problem of the *agunah*. Those solutions are based on contractual agreements per se and are included in prenuptial agreements and a commitment to grant a *get* and in different contractual doctrines such as conditional marriage, mistaken marriage, and so on. The use of doctrinal contracts that lead to conditional marriage is rejected first because of the Amoraic rejection of conditional marriage and second because they are not in accordance with Torah law.

My intention in this chapter is to negate these two claims. I cite both early and recent halakhic authorities, which put forward the opinion that since we have unified the two stages *kiddushin* and *nissuin* (Jewish marriage), any condition laid down with regard to *kiddushin* is also applicable to *nissuin*. Furthermore, it is my intention to demonstrate a principle, which was accepted by early authorities, that all halakhic marriages are basically conditional. I also attempt to extract samples from Tannaitic and Amoraic levels of the Mishnah and Talmud that include different preconditions in marriage and to show that they could even be considered conditional marriages. There are thus early halakhic precedents for the use of conditions in Jewish marriage, as has been suggested as a contemporary solution for the problems of the *agunah*. At the Tannaitic level, I examine the following conditions: the wife having no outstanding vows or blemishes prior to the marriage, the marriage being subject to the consent of a third party, and the postponement of the *kiddushin* until entry under the marriage canopy. At the Amoraic level, I consider the following conditions: the wife having no outstanding vows or blemishes prior to the marriage and the Palestinian *simphon*.

In Chapter 4, which is consequent upon the discussion in Chapter 3, I present a little-known potential halakhic solution to the problem of the *agunah* – that of temporary marriage. I consider its roots and the different applications of this solution in Talmudic sources, in both the Palestinian Talmud and the Babylonian Talmud, where there is a more detailed discussion. An example of the Babylonian application of this solution is the cry by important Babylonian *amoraim* – "Who will be mine for a day?" In this case, some of the halakhic authorities rule that there is no necessity for a *get* in order to terminate the marriage. I consider the early halakhic rulings in this case and the modern version of this suggestion, which was also rejected by modern halakhic authorities. I also undertake a comparative study of a possible parallel to this unique marriage – the Shi'ite temporary marriage, which is intentionally restricted to an agreed period of time and does not require divorce to annul it. I conclude the discussion by revealing the possible common roots of the Talmudic temporary marriage and Shi'ite temporary marriage in ancient Persian law.

Recent decades have borne witness to dramatic changes in the institutions of family and parenthood. Various sociological changes, however, have brought about rapid and major changes to the definitions of family, partnership, parenthood, and parent–child relations. As if this were not enough, advances in modern medicine have intensified the ability to separate sexuality, fertility, and parenthood. There is a dramatic increase today in the number of couples and parents who seek to acquire parental status, along with all the rights and responsibilities inherent therein, by means of a varying set of contracts and agreements. It is imperative, therefore, to bridge the gap created between the current family structure and existing normative law. The problem is that legislators and judges consistently choose to confer traditional public-regulatory arrangements on these kinds of relationships and usually do not permit private arrangements, nor do they recognize the validity of these agreements and contracts.

In the concluding chapter, Chapter 5, I examine the regulation of these matters from the point of view of civil family law in comparison with *halakhah*. My intention is to compare the legal and bioethical frameworks in both systems in some detail, focusing on the question of the appropriate place and extent of the freedom of contract with respect to bringing children into the world in a nontraditional manner, and to deal with the possibility of establishing parenthood by agreement. I examine this question in the following test cases: sperm and ova donations, surrogate agreements, and disposition agreements pertaining to the use of frozen embryos. After exploring the main themes of *halakhah* and the civil law, I try to find a compromise between those two contradictory approaches and open the question of whether we are on the way to establishing halakhic parenthood by agreement.

METHODOLOGY

I chose to write this book almost entirely from the standpoint of the dogmatic method of halakhic research. This method, in contrast to the historical method,[10]

10 For a seminal writing in the historic method of halakhic research, see Shalom Albeck, *Law and History in Halakhic Research*, in MODERN RESEARCH IN JEWISH LAW 1 (Bernard S. Jackson ed.,

focuses the discussion only on exploring the legal/halakhic aspects of the relevant sources without any connection to the broad historical background, which would look at where and when they were written.[11] It should be emphasized that numerous prominent halakhic scholars have chosen the dogmatic method of halakhic research as the preferred one.[12] Moreover, many students of Professor Menahem Elon have criticized his two-headed method, the historical-dogmatic standpoint, and have argued that the dogmatic method is a much superior one.[13] I use this method in writing the vast majority of the research in front of us.

In addition, the research was based, *inter alia*, on Talmudic research[14] by using the accepted philological devices in the realm of the Talmudic law's research.[15] In this context, it is noteworthy that in translating the Babylonian Talmud texts, I constantly used the Online Soncino Babylonian Talmud Translation, http://ancientworldonline.blogspot.co.il/2012/01/online-soncino-babylonian-talmud.html. That is the best and most accepted English translation, as far as I know. Therefore, I have quoted it verbatim without making any corrections, omissions, or additions. The Palestinian Talmud translation is well known for its lack of

1980) and the various researches of Chaim Soloveitchik. For supporting Albeck's method, see Baruch Shiber, *The Albeck System in Talmudic Research*, in MODERN RESEARCH IN JEWISH LAW 112 (Bernard S. Jackson ed., 1980). *See also* Peretz Segal, *Jewish Law during the Tannaitic Period*, in AN INTRODUCTION TO THE HISTORY AND SOURCES OF JEWISH LAW 101, 137 (Neil S. Hecht et al. eds., 1996).

11 *See* MENAHEM ELON, JEWISH LAW: HISTORY, SOURCES, PRINCIPLES (Bernard Auerbach & Melvin J. Sykes trans., 1994); ibid, JEWISH LAW CASES AND MATERIALS (1999), and more specifically ibid, *More about Research into Jewish Law*, in MODERN RESEARCH IN JEWISH LAW 66 (Bernard S. Jackson ed., 1980). For the historical-dogmatic standpoint of his research books, see Ze'ev W. Folk, *What Is "Jewish Law"? A Review of Jewish Law: History, Sources, Principles-Ha-Mishpat Ha-Ivri by Elon Menachem. Jewish Publication Society*, 1994, 11(2) J.L. & RELIGION 835 (1994). For other possible methods of halakhic research, see Izhak Englard, *Research in Jewish Law – Its Nature and Function*, in MODERN RESEARCH IN JEWISH LAW 21 (Bernard S. Jackson ed., 1980); Haim H. Cohn, *The Methodology of Jewish Law – A Secularist View*, in MODERN RESEARCH IN JEWISH LAW 123 (Bernard S. Jackson ed., 1980); BOAZ COHEN, JEWISH AND ROMAN LAW: A COMPARATIVE STUDY vol. 1, vii–xxvii (1966).

12 Such as ELIAV SHOCHETMAN, ILLEGAL ACT IN JEWISH LAW 17–21 (1981) (Heb.), who states in the preface to his book that he uses the dogmatic method.

13 *See, e.g.*, the prefaces of the following dissertations: BERACHYAHU LIFSHITZ, ONE DOES NOT RECEIVE BOTH THE DEATH PENALTY AND PAYMENT 1–11 (PhD thesis, Hebrew University, 1979) (Heb.); SHALOM LERNER, ELEMENTS OF THE LAW OF PLEDGES IN JEWISH LAW 13–17 (PhD thesis, Hebrew University, 1980) (Heb.).

14 *See* a similar statement in the outset of SHMUEL SHILO, DINA DE-MALKHUTA DINA – THE LAW OF THE STATE IS LAW 1 (1974) (Heb.). For the historical-dogmatic standpoint of this book, see Peter Elman, *Dina de-Malkhuta Dina (The Law of the State Is Law). By Shilo S. [Academic Press, Jerusalem, 1974, 511]*, 11 ISRAEL L. REV. 133 (1976).

15 It should be noted that Berachyahu Lifshitz, who supports the usage of the Talmudic research's method in researching the Jewish law, has made a similar statement in the outset of his dissertation; *see* LIFSHITZ, *supra* note 13. Similarly, the periodical DINE ISRAEL has dedicated an entire gate for the various angles of this method; *see* 20–21 DINE ISRAEL 437–589 (2000–01) (Heb.) ("Talmudic Law").

reliable comprehensive scientific translation. I preferred to use Heinrich W. Guggenheimer's translation[16] in the hope that it is much better than Jacob Neusner's translation.[17]

Although the vast majority of this book is based on the dogmatic method, from time to time I also use the historical method. I enumerate some sociological-historical reasons for explaining the gap between the two different Talmuds' perspectives regarding the available freedom of contract in privately regulating the spousal relationship as a deviation from the rigid public regulation of familial relations. For example, using the historical method may greatly assist us in explaining the pattern of freedom of contract in the Palestinian Talmud, which allows us to introduce conditions with regard to different aspects of a couple's intimate relations – the conditions of the *ketubah*, the husband's inheriting his wife's property, and the possibility of the wife initiating divorce proceedings are extensively explored in Chapter 2. The historical method proposes that this Palestinian wide freedom of contract was aimed primarily at alleviating the heavy halakhic spousal economic burden.

Thus, on the one hand, the groom may decrease the expenses he is required to pay to his bride when marrying her, such as imposing in the marriage contract the condition that he will be exempt from paying for her clothing and food or by reducing his payment of her basic *ketubah* sum (*ikkar ketubah*). On the other hand, the bride also may impose a stipulation that waives her groom's right to inherit her property. This double and urgent necessity was crucial especially in Palestine due to the tough economic situation in the era of the Mishnah and the Talmud.[18] We have several testimonies, the earliest of which date back to the Tannaitic period, that teach us how much the severe economic situation influenced ancient Palestinian family law. One prominent example is found in the deed of R. Tarfon, a late first-century CE sage and priest[19] who betrothed 300 women in order to feed them

[16] *See* TALMUD YERUSHALMI: EDITION, TRANSLATION, AND COMMENTARY (Heinrich W. Guggenheimer ed., 1999–2012).

[17] *See* THE TALMUD OF THE LAND OF ISRAEL: A PRELIMINARY TRANSLATION AND EXPLANATION (Jacob Neusner trans., 1982). For an evaluation of Neusner's work, see Tirzah Meacham, *Review: Neusner's "Talmud of the Land of Israel,"* 77(1) JEWISH Q. REV. 74 (1986).

[18] For the possible effect of the severe economic situation in ancient Palestine on the prevailing usage of imposing a condition in the marriage contract, see YITZHAK D. GILAT, STUDIES IN THE DEVELOPMENT OF THE HALAKHA 240–43 (1992) (Heb.) and the references he enumerated. For a general historical overview of this miserable situation, see GEDALIAH ALON, THE JEWS IN THEIR LAND IN THE TALMUDIC AGE, 70–640 CE, vol. 2, 66–69, 182–93 (1961) (Heb.); AVRAHAM BUCHLER, STUDIES IN THE PERIOD OF THE MISHNAH AND TALMUD 113–37 (Ben-Zion Segal trans., 1968) (Heb.). For describing the severe economic situation already in the third century, see, e.g., Saul Liberman, *Palestine in the Third and Fourth Centuries*, 36 JEWISH Q. REV. 329 (1945–46); Dov Herman, *The Historical Background of Halakhot Praising the Nocturnal Study of Torah*, 6 SIDRA: A JOURNAL FOR THE STUDY OF RABBINIC LITERATURE 31, 37 n.28 (1990) (Heb.).

[19] For discussing this vague action, see Ben Zion Rosenfeld & Haim Perlmutter, *"Who Is Rich"? The Rich in Roman Palestine 70–250 C.E.*, 6(2) J. ANCIENT JUDAISM 275, 284 (2015). For possible testimonies that R. Tarfon was indeed a priest, see, e.g., Rashi, in his commentary to BT *Kiddushin* 71a, s.v. *"ahar ahi"*; PT *Yoma* 1:1 (38:4).

priestly tithes during a drought year.[20] He had explicitly stipulated that all of them would be permitted to eat the priestly food from the very moment of their betrothal;[21] nonetheless, it was obvious that it was only a fictional act and he never seriously intended to marry them.[22]

Similarly, the historical method may claim that the Palestinian Talmud enables the woman to unilaterally initiate divorce proceedings against her husband, as is extensively explored in Chapter 2, following the massive Hellenistic influence on this Talmud. This foreign conceptualization of the marriage is much more egalitarian while treating the spousal relationship as a full partnership in all aspects of the family; their aim was that it should lead to egalitarian and harmonic relations. It is reasonable to assume that the Hellenistic approach is the source of or at least the inspiration for the Talmud's unique approach that enables a woman to unilaterally initiate divorce in accordance with an explicit stipulation that was agreed upon to this effect in the marriage contract, even if her husband strongly opposes the divorce.[23]

[20] *See* Tosefta *Ketobut* (Liberman ed.) 5:1. For the parallels, see PT *Yevamot* 4:11 (6:2). *Midrash Shir Ha-Shirim* 6:2 (Greenhot ed.).

[21] For additional Palestinian evidence that documents the ability of a man to betroth a wife and impose a condition with her that she will be permitted to eat priestly tithes from the very first moment of their betrothal, see PT *Nedarim* 10:4 (42:1); PT *Ketobut* 11:1 (34:2).

[22] *See* Enoch Albeck, *Betrothal and Betrothal Writs*, in STUDIES IN MEMORY OF MOSES SCHORR, 1874–1941, 12 (Louis Ginzberg et al. eds., 1944) (Heb.).

[23] For the Hellenistic conceptualization of the marriage, see the references enumerated by ADIEL SCHREMER, MALE AND FEMALE HE CREATED THEM: JEWISH MARRIAGE IN THE LATE SECOND TEMPLE, MISHNAH AND TALMUD PERIODS 302–04 (2003) (Heb.). Similarly, I want to shed a light upon the wide freedom that had been given in Roman law to both the bride and the groom in enabling them to unilaterally initiate divorce proceedings against their spouse (at least until the Constantinus Christian legislation at the year 331; *see* Codex Theodosianus 3.16.1). This important ancient jurisdiction may have massively influenced the Palestinian Talmud's unique approach that enables a woman to unilaterally initiate divorce in accordance with an explicit stipulation that was agreed upon to this effect in the marriage contract, even if her husband strongly opposes the divorce. It is noteworthy that the prevailing opinion in the Talmudic research dated this Talmud at the latest to the year 360–70, *see* Yaakov Sussmann, *And Again to Yerushalmi Neziqin*, in TALMUDIC STUDIES vol. 1, 55, 103 (David Rosenthal & Yaakov Sussmann eds., 1990) (Heb.). Moreover, even Christian legislation did not absolutely abolish the ability of the woman to initiate her divorce but only imposed legal sanctions on such a woman. It is safe to assume that the Palestinian Jews, who were living in Palestine under the Roman Empire, were enormously influenced by the perception that even a wife is eligible to unilaterally initiate a divorce.

1

Regulating Marital Relations between Spouses by Consent

INTRODUCTION

In this chapter, I discuss the possibility of private ordering and the limits of freedom of contract for couples who wish to marry according to "the law of Moses and Israel" (*kedat Mosheh veYisrael*) as a means of mutually regulating their sexual relationship. But first I present a brief background summary of this issue in both Jewish and civil law. The issue of the rebellious wife (*moredet*)[1] who refuses to have a sexual relationship with her husband, usually claiming that "he is repulsive to me" (*mais alay/me'is 'alay*)[2] and therefore demanding a divorce, has been discussed extensively both in rabbinic and academic literature.[3]

But recently we have witnessed an increase in academic and rabbinical literature dealing with various aspects of the approach of Jewish law to the spouses' marital relations, discussions that until recently took place only behind closed doors.

1 *See* SHLOMO RISKIN, WOMEN AND JEWISH DIVORCE: THE REBELLIOUS WIFE, THE AGUNAH AND THE RIGHT OF WOMEN TO INITIATE DIVORCE IN JEWISH LAW, A HALAKHIC SOLUTION 31–32 (1989); ELIMELECH WESTREICH, TRANSITIONS IN THE LEGAL STATUS OF THE WIFE IN JEWISH LAW: A JOURNEY AMONG TRADITIONS (2002) (Heb.); AVISHALOM WESTREICH, TALMUD-BASED SOLUTIONS TO THE PROBLEM OF THE AGUNAH 4–24 (2012); BERNARD S. JACKSON ET AL., AGUNAH: THE MANCHESTER ANALYSIS passim (2011), http://static1.1.sqspcdn.com/static/f/784513/11612882/1302166384333/BSJ+ARU+Final+v2.pdf?token=RSyrg%2F9cedI5z83pXkaDqfKWoZQ%3D.

2 For a discussion of this claim and the great weight it carried in early *halakhah*, see the references listed *infra* note 3.

3 For seminal rabbinic writings, see AVRAHAM HOROWITZ, KONTRAS HA-BIRURIM (1975); RAPHAEL A. BEN SIMEON, BAT NAAVAT HA-MARDUT (2000). For a discussion of academic articles, see the following in Hebrew: Moshe Schapiro, *Divorce on Grounds of Revulsion*, 2 DINE ISRAEL 117 (1971); Razon Arussi, *The Ethnic Factor in Rabbinical Decision-Making – Enforcement of Divorce on the Ground of Revulsion in the Yemenite Community*, 10–11 DINE ISRAEL 125 (1981–83); BENZION SCHERESCHEWSKY, FAMILY LAW IN ISRAEL 185–203 (4th ed., 1993); Avishalom Westreich, *"Such Coercion Never Occurred to the Sages" (Nachmanides, Ketubot 63b) – Divorce Compulsion in the Mishnaic and Talmudic Laws of the Rebellious Wife*, 25(2) BAR-ILAN L. STUD. 563 (2009).

Thus, nowadays one may find lively discussions of the halakhic implications of engaging in a sexual relationship before marriage[4] and after the marriage has been dissolved;[5] the legitimacy of a sexual relationship as singles without marriage;[6] marital rape;[7] and so on. Similarly, the issue of the couple's marital relations being regulated by Jewish law has been discussed in several rabbinic and secular articles[8] and includes the appropriate intention that the couple should have when engaging in sexual relations.[9] The general perception of sexuality in *halakhah* and the place of the evil inclination (*yetzer hara*) are also dealt with extensively in numerous books[10] and

[4] *See, e.g.*, the following: Israel M. Lau, *The Halakhic Ramifications of Sexual Relationships before Marriage*, 27 TORAH SHE-BE'ALPE 84 (1986) (Heb.); JENNIE ROSENFELD & DAVID S. RIBNER, THE NEWLYWED'S GUIDE TO PHYSICAL INTIMACY (2011).

[5] This is the issue of the "old *get*" (*get yashan*). There is a dispute among the *tannaim* with regard to a couple that engages in sexual relations after the *get* – bill of divorce – has been obtained, as to whether a new *get* is required, out of the halakhic concern that the divorcee may have again become the wife of her ex-husband via this sexual act. *See* Mishnah *Gittin* 8:4; BT *Gittin* 79b. For a summary regarding a *get yashan*, see TALMUDIC ENCYCLOPEDIA vol. 5, 688 (Shlomo Zevin et al. eds., 1976) (Heb.). *See also* Rabbinical Court (Beer Sheva) 1086905/2 Anonymous v. Anonymous (unpublished, Nov. 23, 2016).

[6] *See* in the scholarly literature GETSEL ELLINSON, NON-HALAKHIC MARRIAGE: A STUDY OF THE RABBINIC SOURCES (1975) (Heb.). The issue most discussed is the comparison between the ancient *pilegesh* and cohabitation without marriage in modern times and the precise relationship between them. In any event, the common denominator in both cases is engaging in a sexual relationship without officially being married according to *halakhah*. See the recent highly debated series of articles listed in Chapter 4 of this book, n.46.

[7] For a discussion of the halakhic perspective, see Nahum Rakover, *Coercive Marital Relations between a Man and His Wife*, 6–7 SHNATON HA-MISHPAT HA-IVRI 295, 299 (1979–80) (Heb.), www.mishpativri.org.il/researches/mekorotalimut.htm; Yigal Tzfira, *Coercive Sexual Relationships*, 24 TECHUMIN 222 (2004) (Heb.). For a discussion from the perspective of civil law, see DIANA E. H. RUSSELL, RAPE IN MARRIAGE (1982); Irene Hanson Frieze, *Investigating the Causes and Consequences of Marital Rape*, 8(3) SIGNS 532 (1983); Jill Elaine Hasday, *Contest and Consent: A Legal History of Marital Rape*, 88 CAL. L. REV. 1375 (2000).

[8] For rabbinic writings, see the following in Hebrew: Moshe Ehrenreich, *The Onah Obligation: An Ordinary Obligation or the Essence of the Marriage*, 2 HEMDAT HA'ARETZ 42 (2002); Shagar, *Mitzvat Onah*, in AND HE NAMED THEM ADAM: LOVE AND RELATIONSHIPS FROM A NEW JEWISH POINT OF VIEW 193 (Zohar Maor ed., 2005) (Heb.). For academic writing, see YEHEZKEL MARGALIT, PUBLIC REGULATION AND PRIVATE AGREEMENT ABOUT SPOUSAL CONJUGAL PRIVILEGES IN JEWISH LAW (LLM thesis, Bar-Ilan University, 2006) (Heb.) (hereinafter MARGALIT, PUBLIC REGULATION). For an initial and brief discussion of the dispositive elements of the *onah* obligation, see Yehezkel Margalit, *On the Dispositive Foundations of the Obligation of Spousal Conjugal Relations in Jewish Law*, 18 JEWISH L. ASS'N STUD 161 (2008) (hereinafter Margalit, *On the Dispositive*).

[9] For a discussion of the appropriate intention, see Jeremy Cohen, *Intention in Sexual Relations According to Twelfth- and Thirteenth-Century Rabbinical Opinion*, 13 TEUDAH 155 (1997) (Heb.).

[10] *See* DANIEL BOYARIN, CARNAL ISRAEL: READING SEX IN TALMUDIC CULTURE (1995); ibid, UNHEROIC CONDUCT: THE RISE OF HETEROSEXUALITY AND THE INVENTION OF THE JEWISH MAN (1997); DAVID BIALE, EROS AND THE JEWS: FROM BIBLICAL ISRAEL TO CONTEMPORARY AMERICA (1997); SEXUALITY AND THE FAMILY IN HISTORY: COLLECTED ESSAYS (Israel Bartal & Isaiah Gafni eds., 1998) (Heb.); ISHAY ROSEN-ZVI, DEMONIC DESIRES: "YETZER HARA" AND THE PROBLEM OF EVIL IN LATE ANTIQUITY (2011).

articles.[11] My objective in this chapter is to explore the halakhic public regulation of spousal marital relations, as distinct from the procreational aspect of the first commandment to be fruitful and multiply, which is discussed in Chapter 5.[12] Differentiating between these two commandments – the obligation of sexual relations and the obligation to procreate – has three main implications.

First, the vast majority of *poskim* (halakhic decisors)[13] contend that the *onah* obligation (the husband's conjugal obligations to his wife) is independent of the possibility of the wife conceiving as a result of the sexual relations. Therefore, the conjugal obligation applies even if the wife is barren, pregnant, or postmenopausal and thus unlikely to conceive.[14] A further aspect of this distinction is that a husband who has already fulfilled the commandment to procreate must continue to carry out his *onah* obligation toward his wife even when the couple is beyond reproductive age and there is no possibility of her conceiving.[15] Second, as I soon discuss at length, a husband and wife may mutually waive the *onah* obligation, or alternatively, the wife may renounce this right, whereas refraining from fulfilling the commandment to procreate is prohibited. Third, because the *onah* obligation is unrelated to the commandment to procreate, the husband may fulfill this obligation without engaging in full sexual relations.

Since, on the one hand, the *onah* obligation need not result in procreation and its outcome is not important, the husband may fulfill his obligation toward his wife by means of such physical intimacies as kissing and hugging, without engaging in full sexual relations.[16] On the other hand, the commandment to procreate, to be fruitful

[11] For a discussion of the general Jewish attitude towards sexuality, see SHMUEL BOTEACH, KOSHER SEX (1998); STEPHEN G. POST, ENCYCLOPEDIA OF BIOETHICS, s.v. "sexuality, Judaism" (2004). *See also* JEWISH EXPLORATIONS OF SEXUALITY (Jonathan Magonet ed., 1995); YAKIR ENGLANDER, SEXUALITY AND THE BODY IN THE NEW RELIGIOUS ZIONIST (2015). For a discussion of a comparative study of Christianity's approach to the procreation aspect of sexuality, which is beyond the scope of the present discussion, see JEREMY COHEN, "BE FERTILE AND INCREASE, FILL THE EARTH AND MASTER IT": THE ANCIENT AND MEDIEVAL CAREER OF A BIBLICAL TEXT (1989).

[12] *See* PT *Ketubot* 5:7. For a discussion of the centrality and importance of this commandment, see RONIT IRSHAI, FERTILITY AND JEWISH LAW: FEMINIST PERSPECTIVES ON ORTHODOX RESPONSA LITERATURE 225 (Joel A. Linsider trans., 2012) and the other references listed in Chapter 5 of this book, n.9. There is a clear dichotomy among *poskim* with respect to the commandment regarding the spousal sexual relationship and the commandment regarding its procreational implications, which are actually two separate and independent commandments. *See, e.g.*, the commentary Maggid Mishneh on Maimonides, *Ishut* 15:1.

[13] *See* Eliya Rabbah, *Orach Chaim* 240b; Leket Yosher, *Orach Chaim* 46; Afikei Meginim, *Orach Chaim* 240a.

[14] Maimonides, *Ishut* 15:1.

[15] MOSHE FEINSTEIN, RESP. IGROT MOSHE *Even ha-Ezer* vol. 1 ch. 102 (1959).

[16] This distinction has already been discussed by several prominent *aharonim*, such as HAIM BEN MORDEHAI SOFER, RESP. MAHANE HAIM *Orach Chaim* vol. 2 ch. 41, 129 (1963); AVRAHAM S. BEN MOSHE, RESP. KTAV SOFER *Even ha-Ezer* ch. 102 (1960); Rabbinical Court (Tel Aviv-Jaffa) 4237/1952 Anonymous v. Anonymous 1 PDR 340, 344 (unpublished, 1953); AVROHOM Y. KARELITZ (HAZON ISH) & YAAKOV KANIEVSKY, HOLY LETTERS FROM THE OUTSTANDING RABBIS OF THE GENERATION 8 (1968) (Heb.).

and multiply, necessitates the possibility of impregnating the wife, which cannot occur without full sexual relations.[17] I wish to suggest a meta-halakhic explanation for those two separate obligations in terms of two goals of marriage: (1) love, partnership, and spousal relations, which are embodied in the *onah* obligation; and (2) creating a legal mechanism for begetting and raising legitimate children, as is explored in Chapter 5 of this book and which is reflected in the procreation obligation.[18]

This chapter focuses solely on exploring the scope of the husband's obligation to have marital relations with his wife and not on the mirror image, the wife's obligation toward her husband. It should be noted, however, that there is no explicit mention of the wife's obligation in either the Bible or the Talmud. It is deduced only from a discussion in Tractate *Nedarim* that a woman cannot refuse to allow her husband to cohabit with her, as she is under obligation to him in this regard according to *halakhah*. In other words, any attempt on her apart to circumvent her obligation by means of an oath that the husband is not allowed to enjoy having marital relations with her is invalid because of her obligation to him.[19] The only possible solution for her to circumvent her obligation is for her to vow not to allow herself to enjoy having marital relations with her husband, and if the husband wishes to have conjugal relations with her, he must first annul her vow. Several *rishonim* (early halakhic authorities) pointed out that the bride's obligation toward the groom regarding their conjugal relations is a direct derivative of the Jewish *nissuin* and the spousal relationship (*zikat ishut*).[20]

In addition, there is a widely accepted understanding among the *aharonim* (later halakhic authorities), such as Naftali Z. Berlin of Volozhin, that the obligation of a wife to her husband means that she is obligated to have sexual relations only with him and not with strangers.[21] It should be noted that several scholars as well argue that obviously the bride is not literally "enslaved" to her husband. They prove this by the fact that the entire monetary "transaction" in the *kiddushin* ceremony involves a minimal sum of money (*shve pruta*) that the groom gives the bride. The fact that the transaction involves the minimum available coin clearly reflects the symbolic nature

[17] For a discussion of this view, see, e.g., Yosef C. ben Eliyahu, Resp. Rav Pealim *Orach Chaim* vol. 3 ch. 10 (1980); Avraham Z. ben Eliezer Perlemuter, Resp. Damesek Eliezer *Even ha-Ezer* ch. 92 (1905). For a summary of the opinions of *poskim* concerning this point, see Otzar ha-Poskim vol. 20, 40a–b (2001).

[18] *See* Yosef B. Soloveitchik, *The Marriage*, in Family Redeemed: Essays on Family Relationships 31 (David Shatz & Joel B. Wolowelsky eds., 2000).

[19] BT *Nedarim* 81b, and compare with the parallels in BT *Nedarim* 15b; BT *Ketubot* 71b.

[20] For this obligation that is a derivative of the Jewish *nissuin*, see Novellae of Ha-Rashba on Tractate *Nedarim* 15b, s.v. "*ve'amar Rav Kahana*"; Commentary of Avraham Min HaHar ibid, s.v. "*vechi ha*" (1962).

[21] *See* Naftali Z. Berlin, Resp. Meshiv Davar vol. 4 ch. 35 (1968). *See also* Novellae of Ha-Rashba on Tractate *Gittin* 75a, s.v. "*tmiaa*"; Chaim Sofer, Resp. Machne Chaim *Even ha-Ezer* vol. 2 ch. 44, s.v. "*vegam mesvara*" (1963); Yosef S. Natanson, Resp. Shoel Umeshiv 3rd ed., vol. 3 ch. 9 (1973); Ben-Zion M. Uziel, Resp. Mishpatei Uziel *Even ha-Ezer* vol. 5 ch. 49 (1964); Kopel Kahana, The Theory of Marriage in Jewish Law 101–23 (1962).

of the "transaction" and "acquisition," indicating that the wife is not an acquisition of goods by the husband in the usual sense of a transaction for the acquisition of goods.[22]

The husband's obligation to have conjugal relations with his wife is anchored in the *onah* commandment. As I prove shortly, the traditional halakhic determination sees the element of *onah* as mandatory, a rigid halakhic and basic obligation owed by a husband to his wife, from which the husband cannot be exempted, either by mutual agreement between the parties or by a unilateral stipulation on his part. This traditional approach is expressed in the determination of the Babylonian Talmud, which chose the *onah* as the prototype for any attempt to stipulate with regard to an obligation that originates in the Torah. Any such stipulation will be void since it comes within the category of "one who stipulates about what is written in the Torah." Perceiving the *onah* obligation as one of the three basic Torah obligations of a husband to his wife is a well-accepted premise in the Talmud, as expressed in the following discussion in the Babylonian Talmud:

> Rav Adda the son of Rav Ika replied: When we say that where a stipulation is made to break an injunction laid down in the Torah the condition is void, we refer for instance to a stipulation to withhold the food, raiment and marriage duty (conjugal rights/*onah*) [of a married woman], where it is the man who nullifies the injunction.[23]

Indeed, anyone familiar with the halakhic world has encountered the widely accepted halakhic theme, which I discuss shortly and which is reflected in the Babylonian Talmud, that the *onah* obligation in the traditional Jewish marriage is regarded as a prototype of an obligation written in the Torah. As such, it is rigid, has several binding aspects, and is not simply a dispositive obligation. Therefore, any attempt to stipulate in its regard is doomed to failure from the outset.

This premise was reinforced particularly during the time of the *rishonim*, many of whom pointed out the centrality and importance of the *onah* obligation in explaining why any attempt to waive it is void, since it is the heart of any Jewish marriage: *onah* is the "essence of matrimony," "the essence of Torah marriage," "marital relations are the essence of marriage from the Torah." In addition, this understanding is anchored in the authoritative halakhic codices, both the Mishneh Torah of Maimonides and the *Shulhan Arukh*,[24] that any attempt to waive this obligation is rejected from the outset, including a unilateral stipulation by the husband to exempt himself from the *onah* obligation. But, in my opinion, an in-depth and thorough rereading of the halakhic literature throughout the generations, including both the

[22] For a discussion of the various aspects of this symbolic "acquisition," see Hanoch Albeck, The Six Orders of the Mishnah Seder Nashim *Kiddushin* 1:1 (2d ed., 1955) (Heb.). For a more extensive discussion of these aspects, see Yaakov Neubauer, The History of Marriage Laws in Bible and Talmud (1994) (Heb.).

[23] BT *Gittin* 84b.

[24] *See*, respectively, Maimonides, *Ishut* 6:9–10; *Shulhan Arukh Even ha-Ezer* 38:5.

Tannaitic and Amoraic literature and particularly the Palestinian Talmud and medieval literature, will yield a far more complex picture. This different and suprising picture could challenge the stable halakhic premise that the *onah* obligation is a binding and unchangeable one.

I have devoted the first section of this chapter to a brief exploration of the main difference between Jewish law and civil law with respect to regulating a couple's marital relations: *halakhah* regards itself as a jurisdiction that regulates all aspects of the relationship, including intimate marital relations, whereas civil law prefers to minimize the regulation of intimate spousal relations. In the second section, I examine the various binding aspects of the *onah* obligation, which suggests that the halakhic obligation is inflexible, deriving from the status of marriage as a religious institution. This approach would *prima facie* block any possibility of private contractual arrangements in its regard. In the third section, which is the core of this chapter, I attempt to illuminate the various dispositive aspects of the *onah* obligation found in the early sources. These aspects form a basis for giving a married couple a measure of contractual freedom to make private contractual arrangements for regulating their intimate relations. This review of early sources demonstrates that there are considerable differences of opinions with regard to the possibility of using private rather than public means to regulate intimate relations between a couple.

While the Babylonian Talmud is consistent with the halakhic approach that views the duty of *onah* as a fixed, inflexible, binding duty that is not subject to private stipulation, the approach of the Palestinian Talmud is different, regarding it as an area that may be governed by free contractual agreements. Just as the monetary aspects of the marital bond are subject to change by mutual agreement, the intimate relationship between a couple may also be changed by mutual agreement. In the fourth section, I examine another possible halakhic device, which while not entirely uprooting the *onah* obligation, enables the wife to waive this right by giving the husband a dispensation temporarily or permanently not to perform this obligation. Afterward, in the fifth section, I discuss the halakhic foundations of the possibility that a wife give special permission to her husband to refrain from fulfilling his *onah* obligation in a prenuptial agreement that they sign before the wedding or even in a postnuptial agreement after the wedding.

1 THE DIFFERENCE BETWEEN *HALAKHAH* AND CIVIL LAW

One of the most basic and central differences between *halakhah* and modern, liberal civil law is conceptualizing the relationship between a person and his or her sovereign in totally different rhetoric. Whereas Jewish law structures the relationship between an individual and his or her Creator in terms of duties, civil law conceptualizes the relationship between individuals, or between individuals and a sovereign in terms of rights. To put it differently, in *halakhah* people ask themselves what are their duties in this world, whereas in civil law people primarily have rights and the role of the law is to protect their human rights.[25] Likewise, conjugal relations and the consequent procreation and raising of children are referred to as halakhic obligations that are binding upon all Jews, apart from certain exceptions. Civil law, on the other hand, views the family cell from the perspective of the individual, with the institution of marriage being primarily a human institution, based on an autonomous relationship between two equal individuals. Because of this approach, the possibility of marrying and dissolving the marriage is regarded as one of the most basic rights in the Western world.

But in spite of the dramatic change in the approach of the civil courts in the last decade, and their growing recognition of the different contracts that couples may sign, they still obstinately refuse to address agreements or contracts dealing with a couple's intimate relations and the resulting fertility issues. This approach can be deduced from various incidental remarks in judgments handed down in the United States[26] that clearly indicate the extent to which the courts appear to avoid any involvement in such matters.[27] Indeed, I have found it difficult to find precedents in legal databases for the use of contracts to govern conjugal relations, thus confirming Laura P. Graham's claim[28] that she found very few precedents in this regard in the United States. There are also few academic discussions on this subject.[29] In this

[25] *See* Moshe Silberg's seminal article, *Law and Morals in Jewish Jurisprudence*, 75 Harv. L. Rev. 306, 311 (1961) ("the law itself does not only order relationships between man and man but also between man and God. The system in its entirety is religious in origin and therefore involves obligations to God."). *See also* Pamela Laufer-Ukeles, *Gestation: Work for Hire or the Essence of Motherhood? A Comparative Legal Analysis*, 9 Duke J. Gender L. & Pol'y 91, 125–26 (2002); Margalit, *On the Dispositive*, *supra* note 8, at 164–66.

[26] *See* Casey v. Planned Parenthood, 112 S. Ct. 2791 (1992).

[27] For academic discussions of the rights of the prisoner to intimate relations and artificial insemination and the right of the state to limit these privileges for security reasons, and so on, see, e.g., Adam M. Breault, *"Onan's Transgression": The Continuing Legal Battle over Prisoners' Procreation Rights*, 66 Albany L. Rev. 289 (2002); Richard Guidice, *Procreation and the Prisoner: Does the Right to Procreate Survive Incarceration and Do Legitimate Penological Interests Justify Restrictions on the Exercise of the Right?*, 29 Fordham Urban L.J. 2277 (2002); Rachel Roth, *No New Babies?: Gender Inequality and Reproductive Control in the Criminal Justice and Prison Systems*, 12 Am. U. J. Gender Soc. Pol'y & L. 391 (2004).

[28] *See* Laura P. Graham, *The Uniform Premarital Agreement Act and Modern Social Policy: The Enforceability of Premarital Agreements Regulating the Ongoing Marriage*, 28 Wake Forest L. Rev. 1037 (1993). Professor Graham cites only one ruling, which deals with the husband's claim that he does not have to pay alimony to his former wife, as she violated their contract dealing with the frequency of intimate relations; *see* Favrot v. Barnes, 332 So. 2d 873 (La. Ct. App. 1976).

[29] To the best of my knowledge, there are very few scholarly articles that deal with the regulation of intimate relations between spouses. *See* the following seminal works: Gregg Temple, *Freedom of Contract and Intimate Relationships*, 8 Harv. J.L. & Pub. Pol'y 121 (1985); Lenore J. Weitzman, The Marriage Contract: Spouses, Lovers, and the Law ch. 10 (1987); Laurence Drew Borten, *Sex, Procreation, and the State Interest in Marriage*, 102(4) Columbia L. Rev. 1089 (2002); Joline F. Sikaitis, *A New Form of Family Planning? The Enforceability of No-Child Provisions in Prenuptial Agreements*, 54 Cath. U. L. Rev. 335 (2004); Kaiponanea T. Matsumura, *Public Policing of Intimate Agreements*, 25 Yale J.L. & Feminism 159 (2013).

chapter, I explore *halakhah*'s comprehensive and thorough public regulation of marital relations, but first I begin by shedding light upon the binding aspects of the intimate spousal relationship, at least as regards the husband's obligation toward his wife.

2 THE BINDING ASPECTS OF THE HUSBAND'S CONJUGAL DUTY

Elsewhere[30] I have pointed out that *halakhah* regulates intimate relations narrowly, obligating the husband to have sexual intercourse with his wife. The halakhic requirements are fixed and inflexible and are treated as an absolute legal "debt" that must be "paid" at clear, rigid, and fixed times, as in any other legal debt.[31] The etymology of the Hebrew word "*onah*" means both a fixed time and torture, implying that the husband must fix times (*onah*) for intercourse, or alternatively, that the husband may not torture his wife by denying her intimate relations. The frequency of intercourse is a function of the husband's occupation and the amount of time he spends at home, as determined in the Mishnah in *Ketubot* 5:6:

> The times for conjugal duty prescribed in the Torah are: for men of independence, every day; for laborers, twice a week; for ass drivers, once a week; for camel drivers, once in thirty days; for sailors, once in six months. These are the rulings of R. Eliezer.[32]

This Tannaitic source formally and rigidly regulates the frequency of a husband's halakhic obligation to engage in conjugal relations with his wife. However, these are also flexible determinations that depend upon the husband's occupation and the amount of time he spends at home. All men in a particular category are totally obligated to this specific frequency of marital relations with their wives. The continuation of the Mishnah reveals additional aspects of the *onah* obligation that are incumbent upon the husband as strict, binding obligations, allowing no freedom of action for the couple to make special conditions, and certainly not allowing the couple to refrain from sexual intercourse. The Mishnah commences by negating the right of the husband to make an oath denying his wife any benefit from him, which of course includes sexual relations. The Mishnah then establishes the maximum period that a husband may deny his wife sexual relations before he is forced to divorce her and pay her the full sum written in the *ketubah*. Finally, the Mishnah also establishes a maximum period that a husband may be away from home without

[30] *See* Margalit, *On the Dispositive*, *supra* note 8, at 167–70 and more extensively in MARGALIT, PUBLIC REGULATION, *supra* note 8.

[31] For a discussion of an ethical approach toward this obligation, see *Tur*, *Orach Chaim* 240:1. I assume that the *Tur*'s source is the commentary of Rabbeinu Yonah ben Avraham of Gerona on Mishnah *Avot* 2:12.

[32] For more information on the frequency of the *onah* obligation for different occupations, see MARGALIT, PUBLIC REGULATION, *supra* note 8, at 45–57.

his wife's permission. That is, the length of time the husband may be away from home and thus not carry out his *onah* obligation toward his wife:

> If a man forbade himself by vow to have intercourse with his wife, Beth Shammai ruled: [she must consent to the deprivation for] two weeks; Beth Hillel ruled: [only for] one week. Students may go away to study the Torah, without the permission [of their wives for a period of] thirty days.[33]

In my opinion, one may infer from this dispute and from other Tannaitic sources that it is normative for a husband to *a priori* vow not to have intercourse with his wife. The above-mentioned dispute revolves only around the question of the maximum period of time a man may vow not to have intercourse with his wife. Beth Hillel maintains that it should be no longer than one week, but Beth Shammai disagrees and extends the time to two weeks. In any event, all agree that if the husband abstains for a longer period of time, he should be coerced to divorce his wife and pay her the marriage settlement in her *ketubah*. The following Talmudic source also teaches us about *halakhah*'s rigid approach to the *onah* obligation. It states in BT *Ketubot* 62b that a women is presumed to always prefer a husband who stays at home with her, and thus carries out his *onah* obligations, to a husband who is often away from home and does not carry out his *onah* obligations. This is true even when the absent husband is making a lot of money:

> Said Rabbah son of R. Hanan to Abaye: What [is the law where] an ass-driver becomes a camel-driver? – The other replied: A woman prefers one Kab with frivolity to ten Kab with abstinence.[34]

Thus, without mutual spousal agreement and/or the wife's permission, or her renouncing her conjugal right, it is forbidden to even partially reduce her full conjugal right, even if the husband is earning much more money. The Talmud makes a presumption that is relevant to all women – their preference that their husbands spend more time at home rather than earn more money.

To summarize this section, it may be deduced from several Talmudic discussions that halakhic marital relations are a rigid obligation of a husband to his wife. They are thus a binding and not only dispositive element of everyday Jewish spousal life. By contrast, I now explore other Tannaitic and Amoraic sources that offer a totally different understanding of the *onah* obligation and view it as a purely dispositive one. These surprising discussions indicate that there is room in *halakhah* for private ordering of marital relations, and the frequency of these relations may be changed and reduced or even totally eliminated, in stark contrast to the sources presented in this section and to *halakhah*.

[33] Mishnah *Ketubot* ibid. For more information about overriding the *onah* obligation by means of different sorts of oaths, see Margalit, Public Regulation, *supra* note 8, at 15–27.

[34] *See* extensively Margalit, Public Regulation, *supra* note 8, at 15–27, 27–39, 39–45.

3 "CONDITIONAL" MARRIAGE – "YOU ARE BETROTHED TO ME ON CONDITION THAT YOU HAVE NO CLAIMS OF CONJUGAL RIGHTS"

3.1 *The Tannaitic Period – Is This Indeed a Condition That Is Contrary to Torah Law?*

Even if we follow the generally accepted opinion in rabbinic literature that the *onah* obligation is a biblical obligation, there are discussions in a number of Tannaitic sources as to whether, in certain contexts, one can make conditions that depart from Torah law. Below is a Tannaitic source that is cited in the Babylonian Talmud and deals with a dispute between R. Meir and R. Judah regarding which of a husband's obligations to his wife are subject to negotiation and may even be nullified:

> If one says to a woman, "Behold, thou art betrothed unto me on condition that thou hast upon me no claims of sustenance, raiment and conjugal rights," she is betrothed, but the condition is null; this is R. Meir's view. R. Judah said: In respect of money matters, his condition is valid.[35]

The dispute between R. Meir and R. Judah regarding the possibility of making conditions regarding clothing and food, which are financial matters, is obvious, since the dispute revolves around the question of whether one may or may not make conditions with respect to financial conditions that are not in accordance with a Torah ruling. I present an analysis of R. Judah's position with regard to the validity of conditions relating to the *onah* obligation, since in all the citations in the Babylonian Talmud of this major Tannaitic dispute (*Kiddushin* 19b; *Bava Metzia* 51b, 94a; *Bava Batra* 126b), R. Judah's position is unclear, and we do not know what his opinion is regarding the possibility of making conditions with regard to this obligation. There are halakhic authorities who claim that R. Judah's position of "[i]n respect of money matters, his condition is valid" (*bedavar shebemamon tnao kayam*) shows that he distinguishes between financial conditions – "clothing and food" – where he differs from R. Meir, and holds that the conditions are valid, but that he does not regard the *onah* obligation as a financial matter. We can accept this position of the halakhic authorities that R. Judah does not regard the *onah* obligation as a financial matter since if R. Judah had been of the opinion that the *onah* obligation too is a financial matter and the husband may indeed make conditions in its regard, it would have been sufficient for him to state only "his condition is valid" (*tnao kayam*).[36]

The widely accepted opinion, anchored in the authoritative halakhic codices, as mentioned above,[37] follows the approach of R. Judah that the *onah* is a binding

[35] BT *Bava Metzia* 94a and in the parallel sources.

[36] *See, e.g.*, the commentary Parashat ha-Melekh on Maimonides, *Ishut* 6:10; OVADIA HADAYA, RESP. YASKIL AVDI *Even ha-Ezer* vol. 7 ch. 20 (1931).

[37] *See* the sources listed in *supra* note 24.

element of the Jewish marriage and is an unchangeable obligation. However, the Torah may be succinct in one place and more expansive in another place. The answer to our investigation of what exactly is R. Judah's opinion may be found in the wording of the text of the Tosefta in *Kiddushin*:

> [If he says] "I hereby betroth you ... on condition that if I die you shall not be subject to levirate marriage," she is betrothed, and the condition is void, as he has contracted out of a Law contained in the Torah, and when anyone stipulates out of a Law contained in the Torah, the condition is void. [If he says] "on condition that you have no claim against me for food, clothing, or conjugal rights," she is betrothed, and the condition is valid. This is the principle: Contracting out of a Law contained in the Torah as to a monetary matter is valid, but as to a nonmonetary matter is void.[38]

This Tosefta compares and contrasts a condition whose aim is to save a woman from a levirate marriage should her husband die without children – a condition that is invalid because it contradicts a Torah law and seeks to nullify the law of a levirate marriage – with a condition that aims to exempt a husband from his obligations of food, clothing, and *onah*, a condition that may be upheld because it does not contradict a Torah law. In other words, the Tosefta's approach is not in accordance with the generally accepted halakhic opinion, including that of the *amoraim* in the Babylonian Talmud, which regards the attempt to cancel the *onah* obligation as an example of a condition that contradicts a Torah law and presents an opposing approach.

According to the Tosefta, not only is the *onah* obligation not included among the conditions that contradict Torah laws, but also it is presented as a different case, which is specifically excluded from that category. From the combination of the two rulings in the Tosefta and the fact that they are presented together, we can assume that in R. Judah's opinion, which is presented without attribution in the second part of the Tosefta, and in light of the internal explanation of the Tannaitic sources attributed to R. Judah, the *onah* obligation is a dispositive obligation, and making conditions with regard to this obligation is as valid as making conditions with regard

38 Tosefta *Kiddushin* (Lieberman edition) 3, 7–8. The Tosefta's version, which appears in the text above, is the version of the passage in the Erfurt manuscript of the Tosefta and in the printed editions. Early rabbinic authorities who accept this version of the text include HAIM BEN IZHAK, OR ZARUA Piske *Bava Metzia* vol. 3, 301 (1862). The parallel source in PT *Bava Metzia* 7:7 (11c) omits the words "and the condition is valid," and they are also omitted in the Leiden manuscript. However, both SAUL LIEBERMAN & ELIEZER S. ROSENTHAL, YERUSHALMI NEZIQIN 71 (2008) (Heb.) and J. N. Epstein, *Sefer Ha-Ma'asim Li-Vnei Eretz Yisrael*, 1 TARBIZ 33, 40 (1930) (Heb.) support the version presented in the text. For other documentation of this version, see SAUL LIEBERMAN, TOSEFTA KI-FSHUTAH: A COMPREHENSIVE COMMENTARY ON THE TOSEFTA TRACTATE KIDDUSHIN 947 n.27 *(1973)*. For an academic discussion of this important source, see Bernard S. Jackson, Mishpat Ivri, Halakhah and Legal Philosophy: Agunah and the Theory of "Legal Sources," *1* JEWISH STUDIES, AN INTERNET JOURNAL 69, 88 *(2002)*; *ibid*, Agunah and the Problem of Authority: Directions for Future Research, *1* MELILAH 1, 8 (2004); JACKSON ET AL., *supra* note 1, at 64–65.

to food and clothing. To summarize, the question of whether it is possible to waive the husband's *onah* obligation toward his wife is disputed by the Tosefta, and there definitely is not a consensus that it is a binding element regarding which no conditions may be made.

3.2 *The Amoraic Period – Is* Onah *a Dispositive Obligation?*

3.2.1 The Discussions in the Palestinian Talmud

After establishing that in Tannaitic sources the *onah* obligation is regarded as dispositive and not binding, I wish to demonstrate that there is a disagreement between the two Talmuds on this issue, and in contrast to the accepted halakhic opinion based upon the Babylonian Talmud, the Palestinian Talmud and apparently the Palestinian Midrash, Bereshit (Genesis) Rabbah,[39] follow the approach of the Tosefta, as they generally do. Indeed, an examination of the relevant references in the Palestinian Talmud reveals that in one case, the Talmud cites the Tosefta, and in two other cases, it applies this unusual approach as normative. I begin my discussion with the source in the Palestinian Talmud that is based on the Mishnah in *Bava Metzia* 7:11, the same Mishnah that serves as the basis for determining that the laws of guardianship of objects rest on dispositive principles. The guardian is entitled to establish the level of guardianship of the object for which he is responsible and to use the appropriate category from the categories defined in the Torah.[40] The uniqueness of this source is that anonymously and unanimously it dictates the basic theme of our entire discussion – that in nonmonetary matters, any stipulation against what is written in the Torah is invalid, which is mentioned elsewhere only in the name of Rabban Shimon ben Gamliel.[41] The text in the Palestinian Talmud regarding the above Mishnah reads as follows:

[39] It should be mentioned that Midrash Bereshit (Genesis) Rabbah, which was redacted after the redacting of the Palestinian Talmud (apparently toward the end of the fifth century CE) is an early midrashic work originating in Palestine, *see* YONAH FRANKEL, THE WAYS OF THE MIDRASH AND THE AGGADAH vol. 1, 6–7 in the introduction (1991) (Heb.). Rashi, in his commentary to the Pentateuch (Genesis, 47, 2), calls this Midrash, "*agadat Erez-Israel*"; ZECHARIAH FRANKEL, INTRODUCTION TO THE JERUSALEM TALMUD 51, 2 (1967) (Heb.) commented that many of the "*aggadot*"" that appear in the Palestinian Talmud appear in the midrashic works, especially in Bereshit Rabbah. This is also the opinion of HANOCH ALBECK in the introduction to GENESIS RABBAH 67 (1965) (Heb.). He claims that the redactor of Bereshit Rabbah relied heavily on the Palestinian Talmud. I can therefore conclude that there is an additional early source that demonstrates that the tradition in Palestine was to recognize conditions that nullified the various obligations incumbent upon the husband, including the duty of *onah*.

[40] For a more extensive discussion of the possibility of a guardian fixing and/or changing the level of his or her guardianship, see BARUCH KAHANE, BAILMENT LAW (1998) (Heb.).

[41] Mishnah *Ketubot* 9:1.

> The stipulation of anybody who stipulates against what is written in the Torah, etc. It was stated: "The stipulation of anybody who stipulates against what is written in the Torah, monetary stipulations are valid, non-monetary stipulations are invalid." How is this? If one said to a woman: be preliminarily married to me on condition that you have no claim on me for sustenance, clothing, and marital relations,[42] she is preliminarily married [and his stipulation is valid.[43] on condition that] if I die you shall not be obligated for levirate marriage,[44] she is preliminarily married[45] but his stipulation is invalid.[46]

This appears to be a direct quotation of the Tosefta in *Kiddushin*, except for the fact that the examples are presented in reverse order – food, clothing, and *onah* appearing before levirate marriage. Similarly, the assumption underlying another discussion in the Palestinian Talmud reflects the same notion, that normatively speaking the husband has the legal capacity to make conditions with regard to his *onah* obligation, and even totally annul it, in the same way that he may make conditions with regard to his monetary, food, and clothing obligations. The Mishnah in *Ketubot* 5:7 maintains, "If a wife rebels against her husband, her *ketubah* may be reduced by seven *denarii* a week. ... Similarly, if a husband rebels against his wife, an addition of three *denarii* a week is made to her *ketubah*." This Mishnah lays down that a wife who rebels and refuses to have intercourse with her husband is fined seven *denarii*, to be taken out of her *ketubah* each week, whereas a husband who refuses to have intercourse with his wife must add three *denarii* to the *ketubah* each week.

42 In the edition of the Palestinian Talmud by Lieberman & Rosenthal, *supra* note 38, the text reads "not sustenance and not clothing and not marital relations," an addition that was probably added to emphasize that the husband was exempt from these three elements or because of the influence of the parallels in the Palestinian Talmud, such as PT *Kiddushin* 1:2 (59c), PT *Ketubot* 5:8 (30b), and the version in Sefer Ha-Ma'asim, *supra* note 38.

43 In Ms. Leiden, and in the Venetian editions, the words "and his stipulation is valid" (*vetna'o kayam*) are missing. But, Lieberman & Rosenthal, as well as the version of Sefer Ha-Ma'asim, *supra* note 38, support this addition, as does Zeev W. Rabinovitz, Notes and Comments on Yerushalmi 493 (1940) (Heb.).

44 *See* the relevant discussions by Yom Tov Ishbili (Ritba) in his novellae on *Ketubot, Bava Metziah*, and *Bava Batra* and in Resp. Ritba ch. 117 (1959). In the scholarly literature, Lieberman, *supra* note 38, suggested that Ritba did not give his own opinion but copied this version from an unknown earlier commentator. For a discussion of the limits of spousal freedom of contract regarding the stipulation that their marriage will be a temporary one, such as the stipulation that if the husband dies, the bride will not be subject to a levirate marriage, see extensively in Chapter 4 of this book.

45 In Ms. Leiden, the word/s "she is divorced" (*megoreshet*) was/were wrongly corrected by the copyist or by some other anonymous person. (Lieberman assumes that this change was made by the copyist.) However, this is actually a wrong version that does not fit the context. In fact, it was eventually replaced with the appropriate word/s "she is married" (*mekudeshet*), as in Lieberman & Rosenthal's edition of the Palestinian Talmud, *supra* note 38. For other documentation of the correct version "she is married" (*mekudeshet*), see Shimon ben Tzemach Duran, Resp. Tashbetz vol. 2 ch. 17, s.v "*tshuva pliaa*" (1998).

46 PT *Ketubot* 7:7 (11c).

We thus are presented with an approach whereby a husband can make conditions regarding his *onah* obligation or even nullify it, in the same way that he can make conditions or nullify his monetary obligations of food and clothing. The Palestinian Talmud in *Ketubot* 5:8 presents R. Yosi bar Hanina's explanation that because a wife must undertake seven different household tasks, she therefore pays a fine of seven *denarii* per week, whereas the rebellious husband who does not fulfill his three obligations to his wife (food, clothing, and *onah*) pays three *denarii* per week. The Palestinian Talmud finds this approach problematic and asks what would happen in the case of a couple who did not have these obligations. For example, if the wife brought female slaves to do the housework or the husband had already nullified his three obligations, would we not fine them, and if not, "what is the point of the rabbinical decree?"

> Think of it (*agah atzmecha*),[47] if she brought him slaves, she is not obligated for anything! Think of it, if he stipulated [that he is not obligated for] either *se'er*, or dress, or *onah*,[48] he is not obligated for anything![49]

This basic assumption also appears in the Palestinian Talmud in *Kiddushin* 1:2 (59c), but first with an objection to this approach:[50]

> But did we not state: A person may marry a woman and stipulate with her that she have no claim on him for food, clothing, or marital relations? One understands food and clothing. But are marital relations not a personal matter? Hiyya bar Ada said, explain it for an underage girl.

[47] Incidentally, it should be noted that in the Palestinian Talmud, the term "consider" (*agah atzmecha*) generally appears in the imperative form; *see* Alexander Kohut, Arukh ha-Shalem vol. 4, 108, entry "*yga*" (1955). However, in our context, it would be more appropriate to translate the term as an expression of surprise and not as a command or explanation, as pointed out by Leib Moskovitz in The Terminology of the Yerushalmi: The Principal Terms, in the entry "*agah atzmecha*"(2009). The first explanation of the term is appropriate in most cases.

[48] Meiri, Beit Ha-Behirah in his commentary on the Mishnah in BT *Ketubot* 63a writes that "*onah*" should be omitted from this passage since it was written here by mistake following the general discussion of the rebellious husband, which is generally associated with the sexual relationship.

[49] This passage from the Palestinian Talmud was cited in Teshuvot Hakhmei Provence ch. 73 (Avraham Sofer ed., 1967) with a minor change.

[50] Yissachar Tamar, Aley Tamar on Seder Nezikin 406, s.v. "*beonah*" (1983) suggests that since tractates *Bava Kama, Bava Metziah,* and *Bava Batra* in the Palestinian Talmud were written and redacted differently from the other tractates in the Palestinian Talmud, as concluded by various Talmudic researchers such as Yaakov Zussman, Moshe Assis, and others. It is suggested that this may be another contradiction in the redacting of Tractate Nezikin and the redacting of the other tractates of the Palestinian Talmud. For academic support for this claim, see Saul Lieberman, The Talmud of Caesarea (1931) (Heb.). Clearly it is difficult to reconcile this explanation with the above-mentioned discussion in PT *Ketubot,* or perhaps it is another example of "contradictory discussions" (*sugyot muhlafot*), which will be discussed in Chapter 3 of this book, n.113.

The question in the Palestinian Talmud is based on a Tannaitic source that assumes the validity of making conditions regarding *onah*. The Talmud expresses surprise because *onah* is a physical rather than a financial obligation, and as such, any condition would be invalid. R. Hiyya bar Ada's response is that we are discussing a minor – that is, we must limit the application of the Palestinian Talmud's determination that making conditions is normative and that we may make conditions with regard to *onah*. Commentators on the Palestinian Talmud and many later halakhic authorities[51] reached the conclusion that in the case of a wife who is an adult, the husband would have no right to make conditions regarding *onah*, whereas in the case of a minor, who would not be harmed by the condition, the husband may make conditions or nullify his obligation.

Pinhas Halevi Horowitz (rabbi and Talmudist, 1731–1805)[52] objects to this approach for several reasons and reaches the opposite conclusion: an adult wife may nullify her *onah* rights, and all the discussions in the Palestinian Talmud refer to an adult who is capable of nullifying her rights to *onah*. The Tannaitic source, which rejects the possibility of making such a condition, is dealing with a minor, since her father is not allowed to agree to such a condition, as the Torah has given him no such right.[53] A compromise opinion can be found in the commentary *Parashat ha-Melekh* on Maimonides, *Ishut* 6:10, which supports the first interpretation, that it is possible to stipulate regarding the conjugal right of a minor, but apparently restricts it and determines that when she becomes an adult, this stipulation is no longer valid.

[51] This is in accordance with the opinion of the author of Korban ha-Edah (David ben Naphtali Fränkel, 1704–62). *See* his commentary to the discussion in *Kiddushin*, s.v. "*u-meshane*." This is also the opinion of the author of Mishne la-Melekh (*Ishut*, 15:1) (Judah ben Samuel Rosanes, 1657–1727). The author of Pnei Moshe (Moshe ben Shimon Margalit, 1710–80) presents a similar view in his commentary, ibid, s.v. "*tipater*," that a minor is not concerned with her *onah*, and many modern rabbinic authorities concur. *See, e.g.*, ELAZAR M. M. SHACH, AVI EZRI *Ishut* 6:10 (2d ed., 1967). SHLOMO BEN ISRAEL COHEN, RESP. BINYAN SHELOMO *Even ha-Ezer* vol. 2 ch. 4 (1992) writes that a minor who is not negatively affected would waive her *onah* rights willingly, whereas if an adult says that she agrees to waive her husband's obligation, we suspect that she is embarrassed in his presence and is not agreeing wholeheartedly. HADAYA, *supra* note 36, presents a more extreme approach: in the case of a minor who is not concerned about *onah* and would not be distressed by the loss of her right to *onah*, the husband has no obligation of *onah*. However, in the case of an adult who enjoys *onah*, the husband is obligated and cannot waive this right regardless of whether this would distress his wife.

[52] *See* PINHAS HALEVI HOROWITZ, HAHAFLAA last section, 69, 6 (1860) and ibid, HA-MAQNE *Kiddushin* 19b paragraph beginning "*batos*" (1962).

[53] *See, e.g.*, YONATHAN AIIBISHITZ, BNEI AHUVA *Ishut* 6:10 (1965). Meir Simcha of Dvinsk, in his commentary *Or Sameach on Maimonides*, ibid, discusses this point in his emendations to the Palestinian Talmud in the passage "and these are the words of the living God and the Palestinian Talmud is true for those who understand." SHMUEL HA-LEVI WOZNER, RESP. SHEVET HA-LEVI *Even ha-Ezer* vol. 6 ch. 212 (2002) also adopts this approach, as does SHIMON M. DISKIN, MASSAT HA-MELEKH on *Kiddushin* 331 (1998), that specifically in the case of a minor whose father agreed to the limiting conditions regarding *onah*, the conditions are valid, whereas an adult woman who agrees to release her husband from the obligation of *onah* is not agreeing wholeheartedly.

Mention should be made of the group of medieval halakhic authorities who adopted the Palestinian Talmud's position that the *onah* obligation is dispositive and the parties may agree to conditions that change the obligation or even nullify it. Among others, I would mention Ritba (Yom Tov ben Avraham Ishbili, 1250–1320),[54] who posits that the *onah* obligation is dispositive and subject to conditions – basing himself primarily on the Palestinian Talmud's approach, which I have discussed in depth. Second, the Babylonian Talmud, in a discussion in *Bava Kama* 93a, is also of the opinion that bodily discomfort and pain can be translated into financial terms, and since we are discussing a woman's discomfort and pleasure, and since she is permitted to make conditions or nullify the obligation, the husband may also make conditions and nullify the obligation. This opinion is cited in the name of Ritba in the commentary *Mordekhai* on BT *Bava Metzia*,[55] by Yosef Kolon (Maharik), root (*shoresh*) 10, and other early halakhic authorities[56] raised this unique opinion in their response. This major difference of opinion was best summarized in Mishneh la-Melekh (*Ishut* 6:10):

> We would summarize the opinions of Rashi, the Tosafists, Maimonides, Ran, Tur, and Rabenu Yeruham, that conditions regarding the obligation of *onah* are invalid, whereas Rabbenu Tam, Mordekhai and Ritba believe that one may make conditions with regard to *onah* just as one does regarding sustenance and clothing, and their source is the Palestinian Talmud as we have shown.

In light of the various above-mentioned discussions in the Palestinian Talmud, it is safe to infer that the Palestinian Talmud has a unique overall approach to the *onah* obligation, regarding it as dispositive and not binding. In addition, since the discussion in *Ketubot* deals with a bride who is no longer a minor, who stipulates with her groom that she is willing to forgo her conjugal right in their future spousal life,

54 *See* his commentary to the various discussions in the Talmud, e.g., BT *Bava Metzia* 51a, s.v. "*Rabbi Yehudah*"; BT *Kiddushin* 19b in the paragraph beginning "*Rabbi Yehudah.*"

55 Chapter 369, as well as in *Ketubot* chapter 313, where he states that the husband's conditions regarding *onah* are valid; however, the author of Bach (Joel ben Samuel Sirkis, 1561–1640) in his commentary (ibid, letter *kaf*) omitted the word *onah* and ignored the unconventional approach to the subject found in Mordekhai.

56 It is conceivable that according to an early edition of Rashi (cited in Shita Mekubetzet to *Ketubot* 56a), a woman is not very willing to waive her *onah*, but should she agree to do so, her agreement is valid. R. Elhanan holds a similar opinion (Tosafists, ibid, s.v. "*harei zu*"). Thus, if the husband uses the formula "I want you to release me from the *onah* obligation," the condition is valid. The author of Parashat ha-Melekh (*Ishut*, 6:10) concluded that *onah* is a dispositive element from the words of the author of Sefer ha-Itur, who after presenting the dispute between R. Meir and R. Judah, quoted the Palestinian Talmud, which supports the possibility that *onah* can be subject to stipulation. However, there is another opinion by Yizhak ben Abba Mari, Sefer ha-Itur letter *kuf*, on *Kiddushin* 79a (Rabbi Yonah's edition, 1874), in which he quotes R. Judah's opinion without making any comment of his own, suggesting that he does not believe that *onah* is a financial matter. For a full discussion of this approach and the views of other halakhic authorities, see Mishneh la-Melekh and Bnei Ahuva on Maimonides (ibid).

we should support the second interpretation – that only an adult wife can waive her *onah* right. Thus, in my opinion, the most reasonable interpretation of all the discussions in the Palestinian Talmud, but obviously not the only one, is that a groom may impose a condition with his bride concerning her *onah* only when she is an adult, because only then does she have the authority to renounce this basic spousal right. But, in the case of a minor girl, neither she nor her father have the authority to forgo her bodily discomfort, since the "ownership" of the father over his minor daughter is only with regard to her monetary rights but not her bodily discomfort.[57]

3.2.2 The Discussions in the Babylonian Talmud

As mentioned earlier, the traditional view is that the Babylonian Talmud rejects the possibility of stipulating with regard to the *onah* obligation. It is assumed that according to the Babylonian Talmud, the Tannaitic dispute in the Tosefta in *Kiddushin* relates only to financial matters – clothing and food – but *prima facie*, all agree that the *onah* obligation is not subject to stipulation. However, a more thorough rereading of all the relevant sources in the Babylonian Talmud that discuss this Tannaitic dispute[58] reveals a different picture, that in fact there is no decisive support for this traditional premise. The discussions in the Babylonian Talmud address only the general framework of the dispute between R. Meir and R. Judah over the validity of stipulating with regard to monetary matters that contradict Torah law. But, as far as I know, the Babylonian Talmud has never extensively discussed whether R. Judah indeed defines the *onah* obligation as a monetary obligation. There is no positive assertion in the Babylonian Talmud, or even an incidental remark, that R. Judah does not regard the *onah* obligation as a monetary obligation and therefore cannot be waived. Moreover, to the best of my knowledge, the only discussion in the Babylonian Talmud that is related to the subject is an incidental statement in a discussion of the various conditions that the husband may impose in a *get*, as was discussed earlier in this chapter.[59]

In my opinion, even this incidental discussion cannot serve as a cornerstone for any systematic Babylonian perspective concerning the *onah* obligation, since even this source deals only generally with the limits of the halakhic premise of "one who stipulates about what is written in the Torah." Although actually a very important discussion, even this single Amoraic source does not provide us with any positive evidence that according to R. Judah, the *onah* obligation is binding and not

57 For a discussion of a similar approach, see MALKIEL Z. TENENBUM, RESP. DIVREI MALKIEL vol. 1 ch. 96 letters (*otiot*) 4–7 (1970). It should be noted that the Palestinian Talmud's usual meaning of "*tipater*" is not consistent with my suggested interpretation of the word for our discussion; *see* MOSKOVITZ, *supra* note 47, at the entry "*tipater*."

58 *See* the parallels in BT *Kiddushin* 19b; BT *Bava Metzia* 51b, 94a; BT *Bava Batra* 126b.

59 BT *Gittin* 84b. *See* our discussion in *supra* note 23 and the accompanying text.

dispositive. On the contrary, it is entirely possible that the statement of Rav Adda, the son of Rav Ika – "When we say that where a stipulation is made to break an injunction laid down in the Torah, the condition is void" – is relevant only to R. Meir. Moreover, the Babylonian Talmud's sweeping inclusion of all three elements of food, clothing, and *onah* within the category of "one who stipulates about what is written in the Torah" can teach us that indeed this is the opinion of R. Meir and not R. Judah, an opinion that was rejected, and we can learn nothing from it regarding the subject of our discussion.

In spite of the innovative conclusion that the *onah* obligation is a dispositive obligation and not a binding one, for the purposes of our discussion I will accept the traditional premise that the Babylonian Talmud rejects from the outset any stipulation regarding the *onah* obligation. I will now suggest a new explanation for the different approaches of the Babylonian and Palestinian Talmuds, based on their different understandings of the Jewish institution of marriage.[60]

3.3 *The Essence of the Jewish Marriage – Conjugal Relations or Business Partnership?*

Elsewhere[61] I have suggested two possible explanations of the principle of "one who stipulates about what is written in the Torah." Based on my first explanation – that there is no freedom of contract to change any existing halakhic institution – according to the Palestinian Talmud's perspective, the *onah* obligation may be defined as a dispositive obligation, and therefore negotiable, like all the other monetary spousal obligations that are subject to stipulation or renouncing. According to the view of the Palestinian Talmud, the *onah* obligation is not an intrinsic element of the Jewish marriage but a consequent obligation that is only a by-product of it, similar to the husband's obligations to provide clothing and food.[62] In other words, based on my above interpretation, any spousal element that is not defined as an intrinsic element of the Jewish marriage, but only a consequent obligation, should be regarded as a "monetary element." It should be emphasized that this is not the widely accepted business definition of a monetary element that may be redeemed or traded but a more narrow meaning of a dispositive element that is changeable due to the fact that it is not inherent to the biblical marriage and therefore not included in the concept of "one who stipulates about what is written in the Torah." In my opinion, this explanation may be taken one step further, to a

60 The possible explanations regarding the different views of the two Talmuds have been extensively discussed elsewhere; *see* Margalit, Public Regulation, *supra* note 8, at 73–77.

61 *See* also the discussion in Chapter 3 of this book, n.32, and more extensively in Margalit, Public Regulation, *supra* note 8, at 81–89.

62 It should be noted that the basic outcome of the Jewish marital status, aside from the husband's *onah* obligation, is that the wife is prohibited from having sexual relations with another man and is permitted to have intimate relations only with her husband.

much more innovative explanation of the different perspectives of the two Talmuds, which derive from two different meta-halakhic understandings of the Jewish marriage and its essence.

The Palestinian Talmud's approach to the *onah* obligation is a derivative of a more general premise that various elements of the spousal obligations may be defined as dispositive elements and as "monetary" obligations. Thus, all of them are subject to stipulation, and they do not fall under the category of "one who stipulates about what is written in the Torah." In my opinion, according to the Palestinian Talmud's point of view, and in stark contrast to the accepted Babylonian and halakhic perspective, the role of conjugal relations in the Jewish marriage, while obviously an important and central part of it, is not the essence of the marriage but is on par with all the other monetary obligations of the husband to his wife, which derive from their status of being married according to the law of Moses and Israel (*kedat Mosheh veYisrael*).[63]

Thus, even the *onah* obligation is only a by-product of the Jewish marriage that is imposed on the husband in the same way as his obligations regarding clothing and food.[64] If my interpretation is correct, perhaps we can now more easily explain the pattern of freedom of contract in the Palestinian Talmud, which allows us to introduce conditions with regard to different aspects of a couple's intimate relations, the conditions of the *ketubah*, the husband's inheriting his wife, and the possibility of the wife initiating divorce proceedings.[65] Since from its perspective, all such conditions are defined as monetary elements, they are subject to stipulation. By contrast, the view of the Babylonian Talmud, followed by the authoritative halakhic codices, perceives the *onah* obligation as a nonmonetary element that is inherent to the Jewish marriage; therefore, any freedom of contract in its regard is rejected from the outset and even more so if we hold that the *onah* obligation has biblical roots.[66]

[63] For a discussion and conceptualizion of marriage as an economic partnership, see Moshe D. Her, *Marriage from a Socio-Economic Halakhic Perspective*, in MISHPAHOT BEIT YISRAEL 37 (1976) (Heb.). For an overview of the various views of marriage as reflected in the Talmuds and the extent to which the Jewish perception has been influenced by non-Jewish views, see KOPEL KAHANA, THE THEORY OF MARRIAGE IN JEWISH LAW 26–28 (1966); ISAIAH GAFNI, THE JEWS OF BABYLONIA IN THE TALMUDIC ERA 266–73 (1990) (Heb.); MICHAEL L. SATLOW, JEWISH MARRIAGE IN ANTIQUITY (2001); ADIEL SCHREMER, MALE AND FEMALE HE CREATED THEM: JEWISH MARRIAGE IN THE LATE SECOND TEMPLE, MISHNAH AND TALMUD PERIODS 299–320 (2003) (Heb.); Bernard S. Jackson, *How Jewish Is Jewish Family Law?*, LV/2 J. JEWISH STUD. 201 (2004).

[64] The author of Zafnat Pa'aneah of Dvinsk (Yosef Razin, 1858–1936) inquired into the same matter; *see* YOSEF RAZIN, RESP. ZAFNAT PA'ANEAH vol. 1 ch. 21 p. 9 (1999).

[65] The Palestinian Talmud's unique and more egalitarian approach of equating the bride's ability to unilaterally demand a divorce with the groom's ability to do so, as reflected in the various stipulations documented in ancient Palestinian *ketobut*, has already been noted by MORDECHAI A. FRIEDMAN, JEWISH MARRIAGE IN PALESTINE vol. 1, 63 (1980); ibid, JEWISH POLYGYNY IN THE MIDDLE AGES 52–53 (1986) (Heb.). For a scholarly assertion that even according to the Babylonian Talmud, a woman can initiate her own the divorce, see Westreich, *supra* note 3.

[66] *See* more extensively in Chapter 2 of this book. It should be emphasized that the Babylonian Talmud does not allow such wide freedom of contract, certainly not concerning nonmonetary aspects. It should be noted that even Friedman, in his comprehensive research on Palestinian

4 THE WIFE'S RENOUNCING OF HER *ONAH* RIGHTS

4.1 *General*

The renouncing of a legal right is an important issue in every jurisdiction, both ancient and modern, including in Jewish law, where it has produced lively halakhic discussions. This issue has been extensively addressed in various branches of Jewish law and particularly in private law, including family law.[67] Nonetheless, in my opinion, this detailed and complicated issue has not received the attention it deserves in the scholarly literature, with the exception of one PhD dissertation written recently on the subject of relinquishment in Jewish law.[68] In my discussion in this section, I present the basic outline of the limits of freedom of contract in placing conditions on the *onah* obligation. An examination of the various Talmudic discussions and especially the literature of the *rishonim* reveals a strong connection between the freedom of contract with regard to a given legal right and the ability to renounce that right, despite the fact that, *prima facie*, this connection is not an inevitable one.[69] I begin the discussion with an exploration of the connection between these two legal institutions in the Amoraic literature. I then explore this connection in greater detail in the literature of the *rishonim*, who have addressed at length the essence of the connection between the husband's ability to make conditions regarding his wife's *onah* right and her ability to renounce them.

4.2 *The Amoraic Literature*

The strong connection between a debtor's ability to make conditions regarding his or her legal obligation and the beneficiary's ability to renounce his or her rights can be deduced from several Talmudic discussions. The anonymous *tanna* in the Mishnah in *Bava Batra* 8:5, which holds that there is no valid way of making a condition that is contrary to the Torah law that a firstborn is entitled to receive a

ketubot, concluded that there was far broader freedom of contract in Palestine than in Babylonia. In stark contrast to the Palestinian *ketubot*, the Babylonian documents have become rigid and follow a fixed pattern and fixed text that does not allow for any private and particular stipulations and conditions.

67 *See, e.g.*, Mordechai Ilan, *A Woman Relinquishing Her Right for Maintenance*, 3 TECHUMIN 123 (1982) (Heb.).

68 *See* BARUCH KAHANE, RELINQUISHMENT IN JEWISH LAW (Doctoral dissertation, 2006) (Heb.). It is worth noting that even MENACHEM ELON, JEWISH LAW CASES AND MATERIALS (1999) brings only a few sources under the entry "concession" (*vitur*), and there is no entry for the word "renouncing" (*mehila*). For scholarly articles in which the issue of renouncing is discussed only incidentally, see the following Hebrew sources: ITAMAR WARHAFTIG, UNDERTAKING IN JEWISH LAW – ITS VALIDITY, CHARACTER AND TYPES 3–8 (2001); BARUCH KAHANE, GUARANTEE LAW in the index, s.v. "Renouncing" (Nahum Rakover ed., 1991); AVRAHAM SHEINFELD, TORTS in the index, s.v. "Renouncing" (Nahum Rakover ed., 1991).

69 *See* SHALOM ALBECK, PRINCIPLES OF TALMUDIC PRIVATE LAW 347 and in the index, s.v. "Renouncing" (1994) (Heb.).

double portion of the inheritance from his parents, is identified in the Babylonian Talmud, *Bava Batra* 126b, as R. Meir. This is because he is the *tanna* who maintains that one may not stipulate about what is written in the Torah. A *priori*, this anonymous *tanna* cannot be identified as R. Judah, because R. Judah maintains that one may make conditions regarding monetary matters, even if they are contrary to what is written in the Torah. The Talmud then rejects this assumption and maintains that even R. Judah would agree with what is written in the Mishnah – that the right of the firstborn is not subject to stipulation, as the firstborn would not agree to renounce his full right to receive a double portion of the inheritance. In other words, by the same token that one may not renounce a halakhic right, one may also may not stipulate in its regard. The essence of the discussion is as follows:

> [Must] it be said [that] our Mishnah is not in accordance with R. Judah? For, if [it be suggested that it is in accordance with] R. Judah, surely he said, [it may be asked] [that] in money matters one's stipulation is valid. For it was taught ... [Our Mishnah] may be said [to be in agreement] even [with the view of] R. Judah; [only] there, she knew [his conditions] and renounced her privilege [but] here, [the son] did not renounce [his privileges].

A similar conclusion may be reached based on another discussion in the Babylonian Talmud, *Bava Metzia* 51a, where the Talmud attempts to reconcile the opinion of Samuel, who contends that it is possible to make a mutual condition to annul the principal of deception (*ona'ah*) in monetary matters, with the opinion of R. Judah, who generally maintains that one may make conditions in monetary matters. Finally, the Talmud rejects this problematic reconciling and concludes that even the opinion of Rab can be reconciled with R. Judah's opinion because when a bride agrees to renounce her clothing and sustenance rights, she is fully aware of her rights and can therefore renounce them. But, in the case of *ona'ah*, the buyer cannot anticipate that he or she will be defrauded and therefore can neither stipulate with regard to his or her legal right nor renounce it. The discussion in *Bava Metzia* 51a is as follows:

> It has been stated: If one says to his neighbor, "I agree to this sale on condition that you have no claim of overreaching against (defrauding) me" — Rab said: He [nevertheless] has a claim of overreaching against him. Whereas Samuel said: He has no claim of overreaching against him. Shall we say that Rab ruled in accordance with R. Meir, and Samuel in accordance with R. Judah? For it has been taught... Rab can answer you: My ruling agrees even with R. Judah. R. Judah states his view there only in that case, because she knew [of her rights], and renounced them; but here, did he know [that he was defrauded], that he should make renunciation! ... Raba said: There is no difficulty; one refers to a general [condition]; the other to a particular [stipulation]. As it has been taught.

Thus, the Talmud assumes at the outset of the discussion that only the opinion of Samuel, who regards *ona'ah* as a dispositive element, can be reconciled with the opinion of R. Judah, who contends more broadly that all monetary matters are dispositive ones and therefore subject to stipulation. But one of the other possible Talmudic explanations suggests that even the opinion of Rab is consistent with R. Judah's opinion, since in the case of *ona'ah* the buyer is not aware that he or she will be defrauded and therefore cannot renounce his or her right to *ona'ah*. In view of the strong connection that I am trying to establish between the ability to make a condition regarding a legal obligation and the ability to renounce this obligation, there is no way that buyers can make a condition to abolish the *ona'ah* just as there is no way that they can renounce the *ona'ah* since they are unaware of its existence. But, even according to Rab, it is highly likely that in any other case where it is possible to renounce a legal obligation, it is also possible to make stipulations in its regard.

4.3 *The Literature of the* Rishonim *and the* Halakhah

4.3.1 The Literature of the *Rishonim*

The strong connection between the beneficiary's option to renounce a right and the debtor's option to waive one of his or her obligations was explored by Rabbeinu Gershom in his commentary to the passage in *Bava Batra* 126b mentioned earlier. According to him, a bride might renounce her groom's monetary obligation to provide her clothing and sustenance because she is happy and enthusiastic about marrying him. But her *onah* right is not a monetary right and therefore is not subject to stipulation and may not be canceled, even according to R. Judah, just as it also may not be renounced by the bride. This connection between the inability to renounce a particular right and the inability to subject it to stipulation applies in the scenario of annulling the son's right to inherit from his parents, where the son is unaware that his right is being annulled. Since he is unaware that his right has been annulled, obviously he cannot renounce it and therefore it cannot be subject to stipulation. A similar connection is found in the commentary of Rashbam (Shmuel ben Meir) to this passage.[70] In other words, even if the heir is silent, his silence cannot be interpreted as his agreeing to the annulment of his right, which is how the

[70] *See* Rashbam's commentary to BT *Bava Batra* 126b, s.v. "*bedavar shel mamon*'" and "*hatam ka machla.*" Similarly, Meiri, Beit Ha-Behirah, in his commentary ad hoc, s.v. "*hamekadesh,*" holds that if the heir is aware of his inheritance rights, he may renounce his right and the right may be subject to stipulation. This is also the view of Ritba in his novellae on BT *Bava Batra* 126b, s.v. "*hacha lo ka machil.*" Viewing *onah* as bodily discomfort that cannot be subject to stipulation as any other monetary right was already determined by Rashi in his commentary to the following: BT *Bava Metzia* 51a, s.v. "*Rabbi Yehudah*"; ibid, 94a, s.v. "*bedavar shel mamon*"; BT *Kiddushin* 19b, s.v. "*bedavar shel mamon.*" Many other *rishonim* have ruled in this vein, such as the Tosafists in BT *Ketobut* 56b, s.v. "*veshaminan*" and Ran (Rabbeinu Nissim) in his commentary to BT *Kiddushin* (25b in Isaac Alfasi (Rif), s.v. "*garsinan*").

Talmuds generally interpret such silence.[71] This is because the son does not fully agree to relinquish his right but is remaining silent in order not to upset his father that he does not fully agree to totally give up his inheritance rights while his father is still alive.

Nahmanides, in his commentary to the discussion in BT *Bava Batra* 126b, alludes to a very important innovation that would later be used by other *rishonim*.[72] The Tannaitic dispute regarding the possibility of imposing a condition in the marriage contract that nullifies the bride's right to clothing, sustenance, and *onah* depends upon a correct understanding of the condition imposed by the husband. According to R. Meir's understanding of it, such a condition contradicts a biblical obligation and is therefore invalid by virtue of "one who stipulates about what is written in the Torah." But in R. Judah's opinion, it is not the husband's intention to explicitly abolish any of his biblical spousal obligations but only to convince his wife to renounce her *onah* right, and therefore this stipulation is valid. In view of this innovative interpretation, Nahmanides explains that even an explicit condition on the part of the bride to renounce her *onah*, clothing, and sustenance rights is invalid because these rights are not optional for either the bride or the groom but are a biblical obligation imposed on the husband. Therefore, any attempt to waive or renounce them is invalid. But later on in his discussion, Nahmanides makes another fundamental innovation, and for the first time we encounter a distinction between making a condition regarding a right and renouncing the right.

After an extensive discussion of the different aspects of the principle of "one who stipulates about what is written in the Torah," Nahmanides' concludes that whereas there is no validity to a unilateral stipulation on the part of the husband, an explicit renouncement by the wife is valid.[73] This innovative conclusion is consistent with my explantation of the rationale behind this basic halakhic ruling – that a direct condition that uproots the biblical *onah* obligation explicitly contradicts what is written in the Torah, but a condition that the bride renounce her rights is not invalid, since that does not constitute an explicit and direct contradiction of what is written in the Torah. My second explanation regarding the principle of "one who stipulates about what is written in the Torah" is that there is no validity to an attempt to subject a biblical obligation to stipulation because of the absence of intention (*gemirut da'at*) on the part of the stipulator, as it is not his intention to contradict what is written in the Torah.[74] Similarly, we can explain that any stipulation that the bride renounce her

[71] For a discussion of the possible interpretations of a person remaining silent, see, e.g., BT *Sanhedrin* 29b and the parallels. It should be noted that this silence is not always an indication of agreement to what is being said.

[72] *See* the various commentaries to BT *Ketubot* 56a and the parallels in the Babylonian Talmud. For an example of one of the *aharonim* with a similar interpretation, see Mishneh la-Melekh (*Ishut* 6:10; 15:1).

[73] *See* Nahmanides' commentary on BT *Bava Batra* 126b, s.v. "*harei zo mekudeshet*."

[74] *See* Margalit, Public Regulation, *supra* note 8, at 85–89.

rights does not create a problem of intention (*gemirut da'at*), as it is not the husband's intention to explicitly and directly uproot any of his biblical obligations.

In addition, Ritba in his commentary to BT *Bava Batra* 126b[75] rejects the accepted approach of the *rishonim* that defines the *onah* obligation as a binding and unchangeable element. Unlike the accepted approach of the *rishonim*, and following the Palestinian Talmud's unique view, Ritba determines that *onah*, like clothing and sustenance, is only a dispositive element. He finds two justifications to support his opinion. One is the general attitude of the Palestinian Talmud, which has been discussed extensively in this chapter. But, even according to the approach of the Babylonian Talmud in the discussion in BT *Bava Kama* 93a – which maintains that one may renounce bodily discomfort,[76] as bodily discomfort and pain can be translated into financial terms – since we are dealing with the wife's bodily discomfort and pain that she may renounce, she may also subject it to stipulation and even totally nullify it.

As mentioned earlier, this opinion is cited by the Mordekhai on BT *Bava Metzia*, by Yosef Kolon (Maharik) root (*shoresh*) 10, and by other early halakhic authorities.[77] Likewise, Yosef Haviva (Nimukei Yosef) in his commentary to BT *Bava Metzia* (31a in Isaac Alfasi [Rif], s.v. "*bempharesh*") differentiates between a transaction that stipulates explicitly that it does not include the principle of *ona'ah* and a transaction in which there was only an implied stipulation. According to him, only in the case of an explicit stipulation (releasing the vendor from *ona'ah*) may the buyer renounce it, as the buyer is fully aware of the *ona'ah*. But, if this stipulation is only implied, then the buyer cannot renounce it, as he or she is not aware of it, and by the same token it cannot be subject to stipulation. Similarly, only a bride who is fully aware of her various spousal rights may renounce them.

4.3.2 The *Halakhah*

Maimonides does not deal explicitly with the question of whether a wife has the halakhic capacity to relinquish her *onah* right. There is only one related source in the Mishneh Torah that deals with the special permission a wife may give her husband to refrain from fulfilling his obligation of engaging in conjugal relations with her. As I elaborate shortly, the basis for this ruling is perhaps rooted in the wife's

75 *See* Novellae of Ha-Ritba, BT *Bava Batra* 126b, s.v. "*ve-R. Judah*" and his commentaries to the Talmudic discussions in BT *Bava Metzia* 51a, s.v. "*R. Judah*"; BT *Kiddushin* 19b, s.v. "*R. Judah.*"

76 A more in-depth discussion of the capacity to make stipulations to exempt the person causing injury from paying the injured party for bodily discomfort and pain is beyond the scope of this book. *See* Sheinfeld, *supra* note 68, at 13–14, 17–18 and the references listed by the editor of Novellae of Ha-Ritba, Tractate Bava Metzia 141 *(S. Refael ed., 1993)*.

77 *See* our discussion in *supra* notes 55–56 and accompanying text. *See also* the commentary Mishneh la-Melekh on Maimonides, *Ishut* 6:10; Darkei Moshe haKatzar, *Even ha-Ezer* 38:8; and the commentary Beit Shmuel on *Shulhan Arukh, Even ha-Ezer* 69:5.

general ability to renounce her *onah* right.[78] Since Maimonides writes in his ruling that the wife gave this permission to the husband just after they were married, one wonders whether this ruling applies only in such circumstances – that is, after the *kiddushin* and *nissuin*. Thus, if the permission is given before these two ceremonies have taken place, the permission is invalid because the wife's right to conjugal relations with the husband is relevant only after the wedding, and obviously she cannot renounce a right before she is eligible for it. Or alternatively, perhaps a wife can renounce her *onah* right both before and after the *kiddushin* and *nissuin* ceremonies, and it might even be preferable from a halakhic perspective if she were to renounce her upcoming right before she becomes entitled to it.

A *priori*, the latter alternative is more problematic because it is uncertain whether she truly desires to renounce her conjugal right before she gets married but is simply pretending to do so because of her strong wish to be married. Moreover, an early renouncement can be complicated, as she is renouncing a legal right that does not exist until she is married. As was explained extensively elsewhere,[79] halakhically, the contract beneficiary can waive a right, and the buyer and the seller may buy and sell a right, only if it exists. Therefore, any obligatory contractual right that does not yet exist, such as the husband's *onah* obligation before he is married, cannot be subject to stipulation and/or cannot be renounced.

Halakhically, a betrothed couple has no conjugal rights before marriage, only sexual prohibitions, at least according to the Oral Law.[80] One may ponder whether a wife can later on retract her earlier renouncement of her *onah* right and whether she may do so even if her husband has already made an acquisition (*ma'aseh kinyan* or *derekh kinyan*) based on her not retracting her earlier renouncement, which would make it more difficult for her to retract her permission, as was explained extensively elesewhere. Clearly, if any sort of acquisition was made, many *poskim* hold that this permission is irreversible.[81] However, many other halakhic authorities contend that if the renouncement is given only for a short period of time, and is not permanent, it is valid.[82]

78 Maimonides, *Ishut* 15:1.

79 *See* Yehezkel Margalit, *Marriage According to the Law of Moses and Israel – Between Family Law and Contract Law* (forthcoming, 2018).

80 *See* the commentaries Mishneh la-Melekh and Lehem Mishneh on Maimonides, *Ishut* 15:1. A compromise opinion can be found in Mishneh la-Melekh, which generally maintains that there is no point in renouncing a spousal right before the wedding but only after it. *See* Tur, *Hoshen Mishpat* 29:12 and Rama's remarks to *Shulhan Arukh*, ibid, 8.

81 *See* Yosef ben Moshe Mitrani in his novellae to Tractate *Kiddushin* 19b, s.v. "*bedavar shebemamon*," who concluded that a woman may retract her initial agreement. This conclusion is held by many other *aharonim*, as this renouncing is definitely not irreversible, as the woman may retract it at any time later on. *See also* Yehoshua ben Moshe Y. Seigel, Resp. Oznei Yehoshua, vol. 1 ch. 22 p. 109d (1914); Ovadia Hadaya, Resp. Yaskil Avdi, *Yoreh Deah* vol. 5 ch. 27 letter *gimel* (1931); Yitzhak Elhanan Spektor, Resp. Ein Yitzhak, *Even ha-Ezer* vol. 1 ch. 4 (2004).

82 *See* Aiibishitz, *supra* note 53, at *Ishut* 14:6; Eliyahu Tufik, Resp. Kol Eliyahu vol. 2 ch. 11 (1966); Rahamim Y. Franco, Resp. Shaare Rahamim, *Even ha-Ezer* vol. 1 ch. 16 p. 27c (2009); Moshe ben Avraham Yisrael, Resp. Masat Moshe vol. 1 ch. 7 p. 121a (1998).

5 THE WIFE'S PERMISSION TO VIOLATE HER *ONAH* RIGHT

5.1 *The* Rishonim

Another aspect of the dispositive elements of the *onah* obligation can be deduced from a Talmudic discussion that was cited at the beginning of this chapter regarding the amount of time a husband may leave home to study Torah without his wife's permission. The point of departure for the continuation of our discussion is the basic assumption common to the two Talmuds, with the exception of some minor, unimportant differences in nuance between the conclusions of the Babylonian[83] and Palestinian[84] traditions, according to which if the husband receives his wife's permission to leave home for a longer period of time than that prescribed in the Mishnah in Ketubot 5:6 for performing his conjugal duty, he may do so despite the fact that this will harm his wife's *onah* right. The plain meaning of this text involves the restrictions on the amount of time that laborers and different professionals may leave home without their wives' permission. In relating to this Mishnah, the *rishonim* disagree as to whether this source also regulates the amount of time that rabbinical scholars may be away from home.[85] Those who argue that the source does indeed limit the time of rabbinical scholars away from home have difficulty explaining how these rabbinical scholars leave home for longer periods of time than allowed in the text despite the fact that their wives have given them permission to do so.

In the context of our discussion, I wish to note the interpretation of the Tosafists in their commentary ad hoc,[86] that indeed the Mishnah is also limiting the amount of time that rabbinical scholars may leave home. However, since their wives eagerly supported their husbands' desire to leave home to study Torah, even for very long periods of time, their husbands did not have to convince or persuade them to agree. The Tosafists infer from the discussion in the Mishnah that if a wife fully agrees and gives explicit permission to her husband to leave home in order to learn Torah, he may do so, even for very long periods of time. Avraham ben David of Posquieres (Raavad) arrived at the same conclusion, and this is also the *halakhah* as determined in the *Tur*.[87] This innovative opinion of the Tosafists and Raavad was later cited by many *rishonim*.[88]

[83] BT *Ketubot* 62a. The Talmudic discussion relates to the Mishnah in *Ketubot* 5:6, which was previously cited *supra* note 33 and the accompanying text.

[84] PT *Ketubot* 5:5 (30a).

[85] For a summary of the various opinions in this regard, see *Tur*, *Even ha-Ezer* 76.

[86] Tosafot BT *Ketubot* 62a, s.v. "*ela orcha*."

[87] *Tur*, *Even ha-Ezer* 76.

[88] This is a very common conclusion among many *rishonim*. *See*, *e.g.*, Rabbeinu Asher (Rosh) in his commentary to BT *Ketubot* 5:29; Novellae of Ha-Rashba, ibid, s.v. "*orcha*" who suggests in one of his explanations that as long as the husband manages to convince his wife, he may leave home; Ritba in his novellae wrote that if the wife renounced her *onah* right, there is nothing wrong with leaving home.

However, reservations regarding this general conclusion may be found in the novellae of Aharon Halevi (Raha).[89] In his opinion, the Talmudic discussion relates only to the case of a woman who gave her husband vague permission to leave home but did not indicate for how long. Apart from this unique circumstance, it cannot be inferred from this source that the husband has general and unlimited permission to leave home for very long periods of time, even when his wife grants him such permission. This restricted approach toward leaving the wife for very long periods of time was adopted by some of the *rishonim*, such as Yeshayah Aharon of Trani (Riaz).[90] To summarize, halakhically it is difficult to find explicit permission to violate the wife's *onah* right. One can only find permission to leave home for learning Torah, and even this permission is only temporary.

5.2 *The* Halakhah

As mentioned in the previous section, Maimonides ruled that a wife may give her husband permission to refrain from his duty to have conjugal relations with her.[91] The author of Lehem Mishneh, in his commentary to this ruling, asks how a wife may grant such permission to her husband, since we have already learned that any such conditions imposed on the marriage contract are invalid. Lehem Mishneh's second explanation to this ruling of Maimonides differentiates between making conditions regarding spousal rights and renouncing those rights. In his opinion, a general condition to permanently eliminate the wife's *onah* right is invalid, whereas temporary permission for the husband to refrain from fulfilling her right is permissible. The inevitable additional conclusion to be drawn from this view is that in the case of temporary permission, the wife may at any time retract her initial permission to refrain from her conjugal rights and insist on receiving her full right to conjugal relations.[92] The precise meaning of granting such and the question of whether the wife can later retract it have been discussed extensively in the literature of the *aharonim*. A *priori*, one may speculate whether, after receiving the wife's permission, the husband's obligation to have conjugal relations with his wife is totally abolished and this is an irreversible act, since the husband's obligation can be annulled even if

[89] Novellae of Aharon haLevi (Raha), Tractate *Ketubot* 61b, s.v. "*hatalmidim*." This exception is bought in the name of Raha by Ritba in the name of others (*veacherim pirsho*).

[90] Piskei Riaz 5:4 letter *yud*. Similarly, SHLOMO BEN SIMEON DORAN, RESP. RASHBASH ch. 383(a) (1968) placed restrictions on leaving one's wife for a very long period of time based on Raavad's opinion.

[91] Maimonides, *Ishut* 15:1; Maimonides, *Issurei Biah* 21:11, as was determined also in *Shulhan Arukh Even ha-Ezer* 76:6.

[92] Many *aharonim* have concluded that a woman's agreement that her husband may refrain from her *onah* is reversible and she can retract it at any time; *see, e.g.*, OVADIA YOSEF, RESP. YABIA OMER *Hoshen Mishpat* vol. 3 ch. 2 para. 3 (1954).

his wife agreed to it orally, or whether, since we are dealing with the woman's discomfort and pleasure, even if she gave explicit permission, she can still retract it.

In this section, I focus only on those commentaries and *poskim* who argue that this permission is not a mere renouncing but is a unique and explicit permission that the wife is allowed to give the husband to refrain from having conjugal relations with her.[93] The opinion that the wife cannot retract her initial permission may be found in a responsum of Yaakov ben Yehuda Weil[94] regarding the case of a man whose wife entreated him not to have conjugal relations with her for a very long period of time. When she realized that he would not do as she asked, she became angry and insisted that he swear to do so. However, when he placed his hands on the Bible to swear to it, she abruptly changed her mind and asked him not to swear to do so. At the end of the responsum, Weil concludes that the husband is no longer obligated to his wife's *onah* because, as in our general discussion regarding the wife being permitted to violate her *onah* right, when the wife permits her husband not to fulfill his *onah* obligation, she loses this right, as concluded in the Talmud. This is thus the inevitable conclusion in the above responsum.

By contrast, an opinion that allows the wife to retract her initial permission may be found in the commentary Mishneh la-Melekh on Maimonides' above ruling. According to Mishneh la-Melekh, such permission is not an ordinary renouncing, but it is an independent mechanism that may be retracted at any time.[95] As mentioned in the previous section, there is a dispute based on Maimonides' ruling with regard to a bride who grants the groom permission after they are married to refrain from fulfilling her *onah* right. The dispute is whether this permission is valid if she granted him the permission after the betrothal ceremony but before the marriage ceremony. Prisha supports the position that this initial permission is valid and writes that Maimonides' ruling is an innovative one. Despite the fact that the wife married without any special condition or stipulation, later on in their spousal life, she may nevertheless grant her husband permission to refrain from fulfilling her *onah* right. It can be deduced from his interpretation that it is preferable for a bride to grant permission to her intended husband before they are married, as this condition may be explicitly written into their marriage contract.[96]

Among the *poskim* who reject the validity of any such permission given by the wife before the wedding is the author of Mishneh la-Melekh in his alternative commentary on Maimonides' above ruling. After reaching the conclusion that this

[93] Such discussion can be found in ELIYAHU BEN AVRAHAM MIZRACHI, RESP. MAIM AMUKIM vol. 2 ch. 44 (1970).

[94] YAAKOV BEN YEHUDA WEIL, RESP. MAHARIV ch. 1 (2001).

[95] Mishneh la-Melekh, *Ishut* 6:10, s.v. "*od*." Many *aharonim* hold a similar opinion, such as MOSHE BEN YITZHAK, RESP. MAHARAM MINTZ ch. 19 p. 41c (1991).

[96] Prisha, *Even ha-Ezer* 76:17. Prisha's opinion was cited by several *aharonim*, such as Akiva Eiger in his commentary to *Shulhan Arukh*, ibid, 1; JOSEPH S. Nathanson, RESP. SHOEL U'MASHIV vol. 3 ch. 108 (4th ed., 1973); Haim Benbenishti, in his commentary Knesset haGedolah on *Tur, Even ha-Ezer* 69:6.

permission is not a renouncement but is an independent mechanism, it may be granted only in the relevant time period – namely, after they are married. This is because before this point in time, there is no conjugal obligation, and therefore any permission that is given to refrain from it is useless and invalid.[97] Further on, Mishneh la-Melekh rejects Prisha's opinion because it makes no sense that Maimonides validates any permission that is given before the wedding, since according to Maimonides there is no valid option of making a condition with regard to the *onah* obligation. This holds true even if there is an explicit stipulation in the marriage contract because "there is no conditional marriage," as is explored in Chapter 3 of this book.[98]

6 EPILOGUE

As was extensively discussed in section 1, the halakhic perception of conjugal relations is totally different from that in civil law. *Halakhah* typically endeavors to regulate in detail even this intimate and private relationship. Thus, according to the accepted halakhic practice today, conjugal relations are a binding element of Jewish marriage. There are even sanctions against a spouse who is reluctant to fulfill his or her share in this obligation, and in extreme circumstances such refusal is even a valid justification for coercing divorce on the insubordinate spouse. Nonetheless, this chapter calls for a reconsideration of this accepted traditional thesis and for a dispositive rereading of the Tannaitic and Amoraic foundations of this obligation to thus shed light on other possible interpretations of these ancient halakhic sources. In other words, we are not dealing with a totally binding halakhic obligation but with one that has some dispositive aspects that make it subject to stipulation, to varying degrees. I have traced the different views of the two Talmuds. Whereas the Babylonian Talmud – and following it, the accepted *halakhah* – treat this obligation as a binding one, the Palestinian Talmud regards it as a dispositive obligation.

Furthermore, the post-Talmudic literature, including the responsa literature and the novellae, clearly demonstrate that there are prominent *rishonim* and *aharonim* who have accepted the Palestinian rather than the Babylonian tradition. Thus, they allow for much "freedom of contract," both to impose an explicit stipulation in the marriage contract and to allow the wife to renounce or give permission to her husband to refrain from fulfilling the *onah* obligation, whether temporarily or permanently. I have attempted to explore the initial outlines of the limits of the "freedom of contract" that is available to spouses who marry according to the law

97 Mishneh la-Melekh, *Ishut* 15:1. This opinion was cited in the commentary Pithei Teshuva on *Shulhan Arukh, Even ha-Ezer* 76:5.

98 *See also* Ishmael ben Avraham Yizhak, Resp. Zera' Emet vol. 2 ch. 105 p. 116b, s.v. "*aharkakh*" (1786); Parashat ha-Melekh on Maimonides, *Ishut* 6:10; Hadaya, *supra* note 36, at para. 13.

of Moses and Israel (*kedat Mosheh veYisrael*) – in other words, whether and what exactly is the extent to which private ordering can regulate the various aspects of the conjugal relationship, and perhaps even waive it entirely. This is in contrast to the accepted halakhic perception of the conjugal obligation as a prototype of the prohibition against making conditions regarding any biblical obligation, since it comes under the category of "one who stipulates about what is written in the Torah."

2

"Freedom of Contract" in Jewish Family Law – The Differences between the Babylonian and Palestinian Talmuds

INTRODUCTION

In Chapter 1, I began a discussion of the legality, feasibility, and scope of a possible halakhic "freedom of contract" in the spousal sexual relationship. This discussion produced the interesting conclusion that the Palestinian Talmud is far more flexible than the Babylonian Talmud is in this regard. In this chapter, I go a step further in the attempt to explore whether this difference in flexibility is sporadic and random or whether it is a reliable prototype of the broader perspectives of those two canons. If the latter conclusion is correct, we have a very important, unique, and ancient precedent for the halakhic possibility of much greater flexibility and room for private ordering, which has become far more common in the modern era for several reasons. It should be emphasized that even though in the case of a disagreement between the two Talmuds, *halakhah* is determined in the vast majority of cases according to the Babylonian Talmud and not the Palestinian Talmud, there are some *poskim* (halakhic decisors) who maintain that the *halakhah* should be based on the Palestinian Talmud, which should be regarded as the dominant Talmud. Moreover, it is widely accepted that if there is no explicit disagreement between the views of the Babylonian and Palestinian Talmuds, the latter view should be regarded as the more reliable one. But to begin the discussion, I first explore the urgent modern need and acceptance of privately regulating the various aspects of the spousal relationship.

Recently we have been witness to a growing interest in nuptial agreements, both in Jewish law and in civil law. In civil law, it is customary to trace the "meta-story" of the development of civil family law from sacrament to status and from status to contract.[1] Indeed, over the last fifty years, we have seen the development of nuptial

[1] For an exhaustive discussion, see JOHN J. WITTE, FROM SACRAMENT TO CONTRACT: MARRIAGE, RELIGION, AND LAW IN WESTERN CULTURE (1997), and more briefly, SHAHAR LIFSHITZ, CONTRACTUAL REGULATION OF SPOUSAL RELATIONSHIP IN CIVIL LAW 263–68, 280 (PhD thesis, Bar-Ilan University, 2002) (Heb.). *See also* the references listed in Chapter 4 of this book, at nn.3–5.

agreements to regulate different aspects of marriage in civil law, both in Israel and around the world.[2] Over the last twenty-five years, there has also been an increasing interest in the halakhic perspectives of "freedom of contract" for couples who wish to marry according to Jewish law, with regard to stipulations that regulate their economic relationship, either during their marriage or in the event of the breakdown of the marriage as a result of divorce or the death of one of the spouses. These halakhic agreements are generally referred to as prenuptial agreements. They are primarily intended to reduce the number of cases of a husband who refuses to give his wife a *get* (religious divorce) by imposing monetary fines on a recalcitrant husband (or wife) to prevent the partner opposing the divorce from hindering the other partner from going through with the divorce.[3]

Because of certain halakhic problems, contemporary halakhic authorities disagree over the validity and enforceability of such prenuptial agreements. Proponents of prenuptial agreements contend that these contracts can resolve or at least reduce the problem of the chained woman – the *agunah* – a problem discussed in depth in Chapter 3. The opponents, however, argue that if prenuptial agreements are used on a regular basis, they will lead to dramatic and far-reaching negative ramifications for the Jewish family structure. Recently, in a very convincing article, Amihai Radzyner (Faculty of Law, Bar-Ilan University) noted that the Israeli state rabbinical courts bitterly oppose such prenuptial agreements, whereas their American counterpart, the Rabbinical Council of America, strongly supports the validity of these agreements.[4] This clearly demonstrates that the discourse in this regard is more a political issue than a purely halakhic issue.[5] Put differently, the prenuptial agreement is a

2 *See* MARTHA M. ERTMAN, LOVE'S PROMISES: HOW FORMAL & INFORMAL CONTRACTS SHAPE ALL KINDS OF FAMILIES (2015); Jeffrey A. Parness, *Parentage Prenups and Midnups*, 31 GA. ST. U. L. REV. 343 (2015); Unif. Premarital Agreement Act 9c U.L.A. 39 (1983); Unif. Premarital and Marital Agreements Act 9c U.L.A. 13 (Supp. 2014) (stating that in 2012, the Uniform Premarital Agreement Act had been adopted in some form by twenty-six jurisdictions); Lifshitz, ibid, at 141–45, 191–92; Brian Bix, *Bargaining in the Shadow of Love: The Enforcement of Premarital Agreements and How We Think about Marriage*, 40 WM. & MARY L. REV. 145 (1998); Marjorie Maguire Shultz, *Contractual Ordering of Marriage: A New Model for State Policy*, 70 CAL. L. REV. 204, 250, 273 (1982).

3 There are numerous halakhic articles that deal with these agreements. *See* the various references listed in Chapter 3 of this book, at n.10. In addition, in Israel there has been a lively halakhic discussion of this matter in Hebrew in 21–22 TECHUMIN (2001–02); 20 TZOHAR (2005), and additional articles about this issue continue to appear in these journals. *See also* MONIQUE S. GOLDBERG & DIANA VILLA, ZA'AKAT DALOT: HALAKHIC SOLUTIONS TO THE AGUNOT OF OUR TIME 3–100 (2006) (Heb.).

4 For a general discussion of the standard version of the Rabbinical Council of America's prenuptial agreement, see www.theprenup.org/prenupforms.html; www.theprenup.org/whatdoes.html. For a list of prominent *poskim* who support this prenuptial agreement, see www.theprenup.org/rabbinic.html.

5 *See* Amihai Radzyner, *Gittin – Mitzvot That Depend on Eretz Israel? Prenuptial Agreement for Avoiding Get Refusal: Between America and Israel* (to be published). For a similar discussion, see Avishalom Westreich, *Right to Divorce in Jewish Law: Between Politics and Ideology*, 1 INT'L J. JURISPRUDENCE FAM. 177 (2010).

good example of the urgent need for implementation of freedom of contract in modern Jewish family law. Outside of Israel, where the rabbinical courts have no halakhic monopoly, the agreement works quite well, both theoretically and practically. In Israel, unfortunately, political and ideological concerns prevent the practical application of this important contractual device for the modern Jewish family.

In this chapter, I reexamine the scope of the Talmudic freedom of contract as reflected in post-Talmudic rabbinic law, including in the authoritative halakhic codices – Maimonides' Mishneh Torah and *Shulhan Arukh*. I focus primarily on issues that are nonmonetary in nature (regarding which there is no room for negotiation) but rather that derive from marital status. I am referring to those issues that, from a purely halakhic perspective, are neither monetary (*mamona*) matters nor matters of ritual (*issura*).[6] These include a woman's ability to unilaterally initiate divorce proceedings against her husband, even without resorting to the claim of *me'is 'alay*[7] – that is, that she no longer wishes to live with him – and the ability to waive spousal rights and obligations, such as the husband's obligation to have a conjugal relationship with his wife, the husband's obligation to pay the basic *ketubah* sum (*ikkar ketubah*),[8] and the husband's right to inherit his wife.

This chapter does not deal with the freedom of contract that exists regarding spousal monetary matters, as this has been discussed extensively elsewhere.[9] In the monetary context, there is much room for private ordering, whether it is regarded as freedom of contract per se or as the right of the beneficiary to renounce his or her rights vis-à-vis his or her spouse. Similarly, we will not be discussing freedom of contract regarding marital *issura* matters, as such freedom of contract, if it exists at all, is much more limited, as explained in the following paragraph.

6 For the distinction between monetary matters and *issura*, see MENAHEM ELON, JEWISH LAW: HISTORY, SOURCES, PRINCIPLES vol. 1, 109–25 (3d enlarged ed., 1988) (Heb.). For the legal implications of the distinction between Torah law and rabbinical decrees, see Elon, ibid, 189–98; TALMUDIC ENCYCLOPEDIA vol. 2, 74–77 (Shlomo Zevin et al. eds., 1978). For the possible implication of this distinction in the context of family law, see Bernard S. Jackson, *Mishpat Ivri, Halakhah and Legal Philosophy: Agunah and the Theory of "Legal Sources,"* 1 JEWISH STUDIES, AN INTERNET JOURNAL 69 (2002) passim; ibid, *Agunah and the Problem of Authority: Directions for Future Research* 1 MELILAH 1 (2004) passim.

7 For a discussion of this claim, see Moshe Schapiro, *Divorce on Grounds of Revulsion*, 2 DINE ISRAEL 117 (1971) (Heb.); Razon Arussi, *The Ethnic Factor in Rabbinical Decision-Making – Enforcement of Divorce on Grounds of Revulsion in the Yemenite Community*, 10–11 DINE ISRAEL 125 (1981–83) (Heb.); ELIMELECH WESTREICH, TRANSITIONS IN THE LEGAL STATUS OF THE WIFE IN JEWISH LAW: A JOURNEY AMONG TRADITIONS, in the index, s.v. "*Tnai Monogamia*"" (2002) (Heb.); BERNARD S. JACKSON ET AL., AGUNAH: THE MANCHESTER ANALYSIS passim (2011), http://static1.1.sqspcdn.com/static/f/784513/11612882/1302166384333/BSJ+ARU+Final+v2.pdf?token=RSyrg%2F9cedI5z83pXkaDqfKWoZQ%3D.

8 The term "*ketubah*" can refer either to the nuptial agreement, as explained later, or to the payment to the (former) wife in the case of divorce or her husband's death. Generally, the meaning of this term is clear from the context, but where it is not, I have occasionally used the expression "*ketubah* payment" to indicate the latter meaning.

9 *See* Yehezkel Margalit, *Marriage According to the Law of Moses and Israel - Between Family Law and Contract Law* (forthcoming, 2018).

It should be noted, as was extensively explored elsewhere, that halakhically, the status of an obligatory contract (a contractual obligation regarding something that does not yet exist) is very problematic, and it is not at all clear whether such a contract is valid if it is not accompanied by an act of acquisition (*ma'aseh kinyan* or *derekh kinyan*).[10] Nonetheless, we must distinguish between the halakhic validity of the modern obligatory contract and the ancient and traditional freedom of contract that exists with regard to certain spousal rights and obligations. If the halakhic validity of freedom of contract with regard to monetary spousal matters is problematic, then freedom of contract regarding marital *issura* matters is far more problematic, since the latter issues are regarded as mandatory biblical rights and obligations and therefore cannot be waived or changed, and certainly not totally abolished.[11] Nevertheless, I believe that a reexamination of the relevant Tannaitic and Amoraic sources may provide us with a picture that differs from the traditional one. More specifically, I wish to suggest that some rabbinic views recognize the possibility of creating a "personalized" marital structure that differs from that of the accepted halakhic structure.[12]

In the first section of this chapter, I explore the Talmudic roots and limitations of spousal freedom of contract. The second section focuses on a reexamination of the Palestinian Amoraic sources regarding this possible freedom of contract[13] and the way they are reflected in the post-Talmudic rabbinic literature. In my opinion, these sources demonstrate the differences between the perspectives of the Palestinian Talmud and the Babylonian Talmud concerning the legitimacy of waiving one of the husband's two most basic obligations and one of his main rights – the conjugal

10 *See* Ron S. Kleinman & Amal Jabareen, *Transfer of Ownership in E-Commerce Transactions from the Perspective of Jewish Law: In Light of Israeli and American Law*, in THE OXFORD HANDBOOK OF JUDAISM AND ECONOMICS 499, 507 (Aaron Levine ed., 2010) ("In order for the transfer of ownership and the creation of an obligation to have legal validity according to Jewish law, they generally require – in addition to intention (*gemirut da'at*) on the part of the parties – a physical act, referred to as the *mode of acquisition* (*ma'aseh kinyan* or *derekh kinyan*)"; Ron S. Kleinman, *Contemporary Halakhic Decisors, Commercial Practices, and Civil Law*, 19 REV. RABBINIC JUDAISM 78, 80, 84–85 (2016). *See also* the following sources in Hebrew. ITAMAR WARHAFTIG, UNDERTAKING IN JEWISH LAW – ITS VALIDITY, CHARACTER AND TYPES 3–8 (2001); BERACHYAHU LIFSHITZ, PROMISE: OBLIGATION AND ACQUISITION IN JEWISH LAW 383–93 (1998); David Bass, *Contracts According to Din Torah*, 1 KETER 17 (1996).

11 *See, e.g.*, NAFTALI Z. BERLIN, RESP. MESHIV DAVAR vol. 4 ch. 49, s.v., *"a"d maamr"* (1894); ELIEZER BERKOVITS, TENAI BENISSU'IN UVEGET in the preface to the book of Yehiel Y. Weinberg (1967) (Heb.); BEN-ZION M. UZIEL, RESP. MISHPATEI UZIEL *Even ha-Ezer* vol. 5 ch. 46 p. 135 (1964).

12 *See, e.g.*, Michael J. Broyde's proposal to "shape" the modern halakhic marital relationship according to one of four alternative models. That is the only way to allow a couple real freedom to choose at the outset the marriage model most appropriate for their needs and avoid the "one size fits all" monolithic halakhic structure. *See* MICHAEL J. BROYDE, MARRIAGE, DIVORCE, AND THE ABANDONED WIFE IN JEWISH LAW: A CONCEPTUAL UNDERSTANDING OF THE AGUNAH PROBLEMS IN AMERICA 15–28 (2001).

13 In Chapter 4 of this book, I discuss the Babylonian Talmud's approach to determining the exact duration of the marriage at its outset (the temporary marriage).

obligation, paying the *ikkar ketubah*, and inheriting his wife. Whereas in the Palestinian literature there is much room for private ordering, in the Babylonian sources it is more narrow and limited or even nonexistent. Furthermore, I claim that even just normatively speaking, the Palestinian Talmud's unique approach enables a woman to unilaterally initiate divorce in accordance with an explicit stipulation that was agreed upon to this effect in the marriage contract, even if her husband strongly opposes the divorce.

1 THE DIFFERENCE BETWEEN BINDING AND DISPOSITIVE ELEMENTS OF JEWISH FAMILY LAW

One of the basic questions in Jewish law is whether a legal obligation is to be classified as a ritual matter or as a monetary obligation? This classification is even more problematic in family law than in other areas, where ritual and monetary matters are intertwined. For example, are the husband's obligations to his wife as set down in the *ketubah*[14] and his right to inherit his wife[15] considered monetary matters, or do they also entail *issura*, nonmonetary aspects? The implications of this classification question are well-known and relevant to every branch of Jewish law. One of the classical instances of this problem is discussed in the Babylonian Talmud:

> If one says to a woman, "Behold, thou art betrothed unto me on condition that thou hast upon me no claims of sustenance (food), raiment (clothing) and conjugal rights," she is betrothed, but the condition is null; this is R. Meir's view. R. Judah said: In respect of money matters, his condition is valid.[16]

According to R. Meir, the obligations under discussion here cannot be waived, as they are based on Torah law.[17] But according to R. Judah, even though these are Torah obligations, they nevertheless are subject to negotiation and may be waived because of their monetary nature. The issue at stake here is whether these are considered binding obligations, which are not subject to stipulation, or dispositive obligations, which are subject to negotiation between the two parties. There is much discussion in the halakhic literature as to whether particular obligations should be

[14] *See* an extensive discussion of this point in Section 2.2. For a summary of the views regarding the husband's obligation to pay the *ikkar ketubah*, see BENZION SCHERESCHEWSKY, FAMILY LAW IN ISRAEL 101 (4th ed., 1993) (Heb.).

[15] For a summary of the different views, see the following references in Hebrew: TALMUDIC ENCYCLOPEDIA vol. 25, 451–62 (Shlomo Zevin et al. eds., 2002); YEDIDYA COHEN, ENACTMENTS OF THE SAGES REGARDING MATRIMONIAL PROPERTY vol. 1, 1–34 (1997); Israel Schepansky, THE TAKKANOT OF ISRAEL vol. 2, 227–29 (1992).

[16] BT *Ketubot* 56a and the parallels.

[17] It should be emphasized that R. Meir's stringent approach is supported by R. Yohanan ben Baroka and perhaps even by the son of the latter, R. Ishmael, who maintains that "if someone makes a condition which contradicts Torah law, the condition is null and void," even with regard to monetary matters. *See* Mishnah *Baba Batra* 8:5; BT *Baba Batra* 130a; JACOB N. EPSTEIN, INTRODUCTION TO THE TEXT OF THE MISHNAH vol. 1, 618 (2000) (Heb.).

construed as binding or dispositive. This dispute, which dates back to Tannaitic times, reflects the dilemma of the proper and legitimate halakhic limitations of a couple's freedom to privately regulate their various spousal rights and obligations – and even perhaps totally abolish them. The basis for this disagreement is the question of whether a given legal obligation is classified as binding, and therefore nonnegotiable, or as dispositive, and therefore subject to change. Considerable discussion of this sort has focused on the boundaries and justification of the halakhic principle that "if someone makes a condition which contradicts Torah law, the condition is null and void."[18]

First, however, let me cite one example of the considerable freedom of contract regarding conditions of a monetary nature that is available to a couple about to be married:

> A man may marry a woman on condition that he does not have to provide her with food[19] or support. Moreover, he may make an agreement with her that she maintain him and teach him Torah. Joshua the son of R. Akiba[20] married a woman and made an agreement with her that she maintain him and support him and teach him Torah. There were years of famine, and [the husband and the wife] went and divided their property. She began to complain against him to the Sages. When he came to court he said to them, "She is more credible to me than any man." She said to them, "Indeed, he made such an arrangement with me." The Sages said to her, "There is nothing after agreement" (i.e., the agreement is binding).[21]

[18] *See* Nahum Rakover, *Coercive Marital Relations between a Man and His Wife*, 6–7 SHNATON HA-MISHPAT HA-IVRI 295, 299 (1979–80) (Heb.). For a general review of stipulations that contradict Torah law, see LIFSHITZ, *supra* note 10, at 176–85.

[19] A careful reading of the Palestinian Talmud easily demonstrates that the practice of marrying a woman and stipulating that the husband is exempt from his basic obligation to provide her sustenance was so common that the discussion in Tractate *Nedarim* officially regulates this situation. *See* PT *Nedarim* 10:4. For a discussion of the levirate wife who obligated herself to sustain her levirate husband, see PT *Yevamot* 4:12 (6b) and the parallel YALKUT SHIMONI, Samuel 2, *perek* 6, *remez* 143.

[20] A *midrash* relates that this son of R. Akiva did not cease his Torah learning even on his wedding night; *see* MIDRASH TEHILLIM 59:3 and YALKUT SHIMONI, Prov., § 958. For a further discussion of the identity of Joshua, the son of R. Akiva, see SEDER TANNAIM VE-AMORAIM vol. 2 letter 2 (1998) and the sources cited by Chaim Y. D. Azulai (Hida) on Tannaim ve-Amoraim, ibid, *letter gimel*. *See also* Shamma Friedman, A *Good Story Deserves Retelling – The Unfolding of the Akiva Legend*, 3 JEWISH STUDIES, AN INTERNET JOURNAL 55, 85 (2004), https://www.biu.ac.il/js/JSIJ/3-2004/Friedman.pdf.

[21] Tosefta *Ketubot* 4:7. The reading *ahar ha-kitzah* ("after agreement") is confirmed by other texts (with the exception of the parallel in PT *Ketubot* 5:2 (29d), "after acquisition there is no further action"). For this use of *kitzah* as "agreement," see also Tosefta *Baba Metziah* 3:21: "But if he agreed on a salary ... there is nothing [no further discussion] after the agreement" (*ahar ha-kitzah*); Tosefta *Baba Metziah* 11:23: "They may enforce their agreement" (*kitzatan*), and cf. the parallel in BT *Baba Batra* 8b. These passages indicate that *kitzah* is used in the sense of "conditions" or "agreement." *See* the following sources in Hebrew: SAUL LIEBERMAN, TOSEFTA KI-FSHUTAH: A COMPREHENSIVE COMMENTARY ON THE TOSEFTA TRACTATE KETUBOT vol. 6, 244–45 (1967); LIFSHITZ, *supra* note 10, at 337–38; YITZHAK D. GILAT, STUDIES IN THE DEVELOPMENT OF THE HALAKHA 240–43 (1992).

This is a prime example of the independence granted to the parties to define their monetary relationship. Room for negotiation is so great that in the above source, the standard situation is reversed: not only was the husband released from his obligation to support his wife, but also the wife undertook to support her husband and supply all of his needs while he studied Torah. It is noteworthy that this source deals only with monetary aspects of spousal private ordering, wherein there is much halakhic room for such freedom of contract. But regarding the conjugal relationship (*ishut*), which is the focus of the discussion in this section, such agreements are very limited and their scope is much narrower, and *a priori* a couple cannot make changes in this regard. This halakhic framework is in stark contrast to other ancient near-eastern legal systems, such as the Code of Hammurabi or those reflected in ancient non-Jewish Babylonian marriage contracts in which it appears that a couple is allowed to reach an agreement as to what would be the fate of an adulteress who betrayed her husband.[22]

Over the last century, documents discovered in the Cairo *genizah* have revealed that in Palestine, the *ketubah*, the earliest prenuptial agreement known to us, was a living, dynamic document. This is in contrast to Babylonia, where the text of the *ketubah* was rigid and conservative, as noted by scholars of the Cairo *genizah*.[23] Zvi M. Rabinovitz (1908–91, Department of Talmud, Tel Aviv University) suggests that the different approaches to the *ketubah* in Palestine and Babylonia derive from the different approaches of the Talmuds compiled in these two centers of Jewish learning.[24] The question that arises is whether these differences in outlook are limited to monetary matters or whether they extend to nonmonetary issues as well. I will now proceed to explore the relevant sources in the Palestinian Talmud, from which one can deduce the freedom of contract that existed in its unique view of family law.

2 DISPOSITIVE ELEMENTS OF THE MARRIAGE CONTRACT, AS REFLECTED IN THE PALESTINIAN TALMUD

2.1 *Conjugal Duty*

As I noted previously and extensively in Chapter 1,[25] the interpretation of two *halakhot* in Tosefta *Kiddushin* 3:7–8 suggests that according to R. Judah,

22 *See* CHAIM TCHERNOWITZ, HISTORY OF HEBREW LAW 225–28 (1943) (Heb.).

23 For a discussion of the array of unique stipulations documented in Palestinian *ketubot*, see MORDECHAI A. FRIEDMAN, JEWISH MARRIAGE IN PALESTINE: A CAIRO GENIZA STUDY 391–418 (1980); ibid, *Ketubot from Eretz Israel from the Geonic Period* 1 TE'UDAH 58 (1980) (Heb.); ibid, JEWISH POLYGYNY IN THE MIDDLE AGES 52–53 (1986) (Heb.) (hereinafter FRIEDMAN, POLYGYNY).

24 Zvi M. Rabinovitz, *M. A. Friedman, Jewish Marriage in Palestine – A Cairo Geniza Study, I-II, Tel Aviv and New York* 1980–1, 55 TARBIZ 456 (1986) (Heb.).

25 At subsection 3.1. *See also* YEHEZKEL MARGALIT, PUBLIC REGULATION AND PRIVATE AGREEMENT ABOUT SPOUSAL CONJUGAL PRIVILEGES IN JEWISH LAW 66 (LLM thesis, Bar-Ilan University, 2006) (Heb.).

the husband's duty to have a conjugal relationship with his wife is a dispositive one and therefore open to negotiation in the same way as are monetary matters (e.g., the duty to clothe his wife). This approach is adopted without reservation by the Palestinian *amoraim*.[26] Indeed, an examination of the Palestinian Talmud's treatment of this subject reveals that in one case it apparently quotes the text of the Tosefta and accepts it, and in two other cases it regards this approach as normative. From these sources, we can infer the Palestinian Talmud's unique approach, which makes it possible to waive the husband's basic obligation to supply his wife with all her needs, including his conjugal obligation, or alternatively to waive the wife's obligation to fulfill her household duties.[27]

This broad freedom of contract also includes obligations that are clearly not monetary matters per se and that cannot be traded or assigned to a third party but that the Palestinian Talmud nonetheless defines as *mamona* and allows to be waived. Discussed extensively elsewhere are the various possible explanations for the difference between the two Talmuds on such issues as whether the conjugal duty is a monetary matter, whether the source of the conjugal obligation derives from the Torah or was extrapolated by Talmudic sages, whether the conjugal obligation is the essence of marriage or derives from it, and whether the conjugal obligation is a monetary obligation or a personal obligation.[28] To summarize the above basic Amoraic disagreement,[29] the approach of the Palestinian tradition is totally different from that of the Babylonian Talmud and from the accepted *halakhah*.[30] According to the accepted view, any stipulation imposed in the marriage contract that waives the husband's obligation of a conjugal relationship with his wife is void because it contradicts an injunction laid down in the Torah. However, according to the unique attitude of the Palestinian Talmud, not only is such a condition not regarded as a one that contradicts an injunction laid down in the Torah, but also the Palestinian Talmud states explicitly that this stipulation neither contradicts nor is included in this basic halakhic principle.

[26] Obviously, caution is necessary when attempting to determine the Palestinian Talmud's approach based on citations of Tannaitic sources.

[27] This fundamental approach in the Palestinian Talmud should be compared with the discussion in PT *Kiddushin* 1:2 (59c), which appears to contradict or at least restrict the ability to waive the conjugal obligation. For a discussion of possible ways of reconciling these discussions, see MARGALIT, *supra* note 25, at 70–72.

[28] *See* Yehezkel Margalit, *On the Dispositive Foundations of the Obligation of Spousal Conjugal Relations in Jewish Law*, 18 JEWISH L. ASS'N STUD 164 (2008).

[29] As one can infer from the following Babylonian discussion (*Gittin* 84b) – "R. Adda the son of R. Ika replied: When we say that where a stipulation is made to break an injunction laid down in the Torah the condition is void, we refer for instance to a stipulation to withhold the food, raiment and marriage duty [of a married woman], where it is the man who nullifies the injunction."

[30] As was determined in the authoritative halakhic codices, see Maimonides *Ishut* 6:9–10; *Shulhan Arukh, Even ha-Ezer* 38:5.

2.2 *Ikkar Ketubah*

As mentioned at the beginning of this chapter, a husband's obligation to pay his wife's *ikkar ketubah* is one of his most basic spousal undertakings because, according to *halakhah*, it is what forms the basis of the entire spousal relationship (*zikat ishut*), yet it is one of the most difficult spousal obligations to define. Firstly, the two Talmuds have different views regarding the obscure roots of this obligation. According to one view, its source is from the Torah and it derives directly from the biblical *mohar*,[31] while a different view posits that it is only a rabbinical enactment,[32] and each of these views dictates different limitations on the freedom to negotiate in its regard. The two Talmuds contain very detailed discussions about the Amoraic dispute referred to in the previous section. The general assumption of the Babylonian Talmud[33] is that the *ketubah* is of rabbinic origin, whereas most of the relevant passages in the Palestinian Talmud assume that the *ketubah* is required by Torah law.[34] The origin of the entire discussion on the limitations of a couple's freedom to totally waive or, at the least, to reduce the amount of the *ikkar ketubah* is based on the Mishnah in *Ketubot* 1:2.

This Tannaitic source states, "A maiden – her *kethubah* is two hundred [*zuz*], and a widow – a *maneh*."[35] The freedom of contract that is available to a couple in this regard is discussed in the Mishnah in *Ketubot* 5:1 as follows: "Although [the sages] have enacted that a virgin collects two hundred *zuz* and a widow one *maneh*, if he [the husband] wishes to add, even a hundred *maneh*, he may do so." For the purposes of our discussion, we focus on the last part of this Mishnah, which deals with the possibility that a couple may mutually agree to reduce the *ikkar ketubah*:

[31] The debate revolves around the following references, *inter alia*: PT *Ketubot* 3:5 (27d); Tosefta *Ketubot* 12:1 (Lieberman edition) p. 95; PT *Ketubot* 8:11 (32b); and BT *Ketubot* 82b. *See* BIBLICAL ENCYCLOPEDIA vol. 4, 702–06 (Moshe D. Cassuto et al. eds., 1954) (Heb.). But, as summarized in ADIEL SCHREMER, MALE AND FEMALE HE CREATED THEM 302–04 (2003) (Heb.), all these traditions agree that we must distinguish between the ancient biblical *mohar* payment and the rabbinical wedding payment – the *ketubah*.

[32] *See* Robert Brody, *Is the Ketubba of Biblical or of Rabbinic Origin*, NETI'OT LEDAVID: JUBILEE VOLUME FOR DAVID WEISS HALIVNI 37, 39 (Yaakov Elman et al. eds., 2004) (Heb.).

[33] *See* BT *Yevamot* 89a and the parallel BT *Ketubot* 39b, and cf. e.g., BT *Ketubot* 54a, 110b, and BT *Gittin* 49b; Shlomo Goren, *The Ketubah in the Babylonian Talmud and in the Palestinian Talmud*, 3 TORAH SHE-BE'AL PEH 119 (1961) (Heb.).

[34] *See* PT *Yevamot* 13:11 (36b); PT *Ketubot* 1:1 (25a); BT *Ketubot* 29b; PT *Ketubot* 3:5 (27d); PT *Yevamot* 15:3 (14d); and the parallel PT *Ketubot* 4:8 (29a).

[35] One may speculate whether this is a Tannaitic decree that halakhically anchors the commonly accepted practice to pay a virgin 200 *zuz* and 100 *zuz* if she is a widow or divorcee, or whether this is an attempt to determine the minimum payments for a woman's *ketubah*. SCHREMER, *supra* note 31, at 241–43 supports the first alternative. In any event, if the husband wishes to add to his wife's basic payment, he is free to do so, since this is his voluntary addition. As this is a monetary matter, there is full freedom of contract to add to the minimum amounts that the sages determined.

> R. Judah ruled: if [a husband] wishes he may write out for a virgin a deed for two hundred *zuz* and she writes [a quittance], "I have received from you a *maneh*," and for a widow [he may write out a deed for] a *maneh* and she writes [a quittance] "I have received from you fifty *zuz*." R. Meir ruled: [the intercourse of] any man who undertakes to give a virgin less than two hundred *zuz* or a widow less than a *maneh* is an act of prostitution.[36]

According to R. Meir, who maintains that it is prohibited to live even a single moment with one's wife if she does not have a *ketubah*,[37] any attempt to reduce the basic payment of the *ketubah* is rejected out of hand, and if anyone imposes such a stipulation with his wife, the marriage is invalid and his conjugal relationship with her is no less than prostitution. Thus, we are not dealing with a monetary obligation per se, which may be waived, but with a unique spousal undertaking, and any attempt to subject it to stipulation is halakhically prohibited and may even invalidate the entire marriage. It should be noted that R. Meir, whose view was accepted as *halakhah*, contends that not only is it generally prohibited to impose stipulations on or to nullify various spousal monetary obligations, but also in the specific case of attempting to reduce the *ikkar ketubah*, such a stipulation is invalid. This is so because, despite the fact that we are dealing with a monetary obligation, as was extensively explored above, the classification of the obligation under discussion is unclear. It is not strictly a monetary matter but in effect falls somewhere between a monetary and a ritual (*issura*) obligation. If the husband does not obligate himself to pay the full *ketubah*, the betrothal ceremony does not establish their spousal relationship (*zikat ishut*), and instead of creating a halakhically valid marriage (*kedat Mosheh veYisrael*),[38] their sexual relationship is regarded as a casual sexual relationship.

A wife who is not entitled to the full basic sum of her *ketubah* might worry throughout her conjugal life that she is not regarded as halakhically married, as are Jewish brides who are entitled to their full *ikkar ketubah*. Any groom who reduces his bride's *ikkar ketubah* is actually casting aside the deep halakhic meaning of the conjugal relationship with his wife, thus transforming their intimate act from one that is imbued with holiness to a meaningless act that may even be regarded as prostitution.[39] According to R. Judah, who agrees fundamentally with R. Meir that

[36] This basic disagreement is documented also in the parallels BT *Ketubot* 51a; 54b.

[37] Such as BT *Ketubot* 57a; BT *Baba Kama* 89a–b. Many of the *Geonim* accepted R. Meir's position to determine the *halakhah*. *See, e.g.*, Teshuvot HaGeonim ch. 112 p. 60 (Harkavi edition); Teshuvot HaGeonim ch. 46 p. 5 (Coronel edition). It should be noted that scholars of *halakhah* maintain that R. Meir generally adopted an extremely stringent approach, in line with other extreme halakhic opinions, such as those of Beit Shammai and the Essenes sect. In any event, the *halakhah* in this case is according to R. Meir's position. *See* Maimonides *Ishut* 10:7; *Shulhan Arukh, Even ha-Ezer* 66:9.

[38] For a discussion of the words "*kedat Mosheh veYisrael*," see Chapter 3 of this book, at n.85.

[39] For more about this explanation, see Schereschewsky, *supra* note 14, at 101 nn.39–41 and the various references listed there; Benjamin Lipkin, *Ius Dispositivum in Jewish Law*, 35 Sinai 111, 116 (1954) (Heb.).

there is no halakhic validity to directly waiving the husband's obligation of the *ikkar ketubah*, it is possible to arrive at the same result of reducing this amount by writing a fictional deed affirming that the bride has already received part of the sum of her *ketubah*.

In addition, there is an opinion cited in the Babylonian Talmud, Tractate *Ketubot* 56b, that one may explicitly reduce the sum of the *ikkar ketubah*, but this opinion is attributed only to R. Yose. Thus, R. Meir strongly and totally rejects any attempt to stipulate to reduce the *ikkar ketubah*. In his opinion, it makes no difference whether the stipulation was written into the marriage contract before or after the wedding ceremony, as he states explicitly, "If any man assigns . . . a sum less than" (*kol hapohet*).[40] However, according to R. Yose, there is freedom of contract even concerning this central obligation, as it too is a monetary undertaking per se.[41] The following is the text in the Babylonian Talmud:

> R. Meir ruled, if any man assigns to a virgin a sum less than two hundred *zuz* or to a widow less than a *maneh* his marriage is regarded as an act of prostitution. R. Yose ruled: One is permitted [to contract such a marriage]. R. Judah ruled: If the man wished he may write out for a virgin a bond for two hundred *zuz* while she writes for him, "I have received from you a *maneh*"; and [he may write a bond] for a widow for a *maneh* while she writes for him, "I have received from you fifty *zuz*."

In the Babylonian Talmud, R. Yose is the only *Tanna* who maintains that the husband may reduce the sum of the *ikkar ketubbah*.[42] However, in the parallel discussion in the Palestinian Talmud, we find an opinion similar to that of R. Yose, according to which the husband's obligation to pay the *ikkar ketubbah* may be waived completely. There this opinion is attributed to the sages.[43] Thus we read in the Palestinian Talmud, *Ketubot* 5:2 (29d):

> What is a wife and what is a concubine? R. Meir says, a wife has a *ketubah*, and a concubine has no *ketubah*. R. Judah says, both have a *ketubah*. A wife has a *ketubah* and the *ketubah* stipulations; a concubine has a *ketubah* but no *ketubah* stipulations. R. Judah in the name of Rav: these are the opinions of R. Meir and R. Judah.

40 *See* the Tosafot, *Ketubot* 56a, s.v. "*kol hapohet*" in their commentary ad hoc.

41 The precise point of the disagreement between R. Meir and R. Judah and the essence of R. Yose's innovation are not clear and deserve a separate examination. To summarize this point, according to R. Judah and R. Yose, the *ikkar ketubah* may be reduced. The only difference between them is that according to R. Yose, it can be accomplished also orally, whereas in R. Judah's opinion, it requires a written bond affirming that the wife has already received part of her *ketubah* payment. The reason for this is that any oral agreement is void, because sometimes, as in this case, the sages' enactment is even more stringent than the Torah law.

42 *See also* BT *Ketubot* 57a. In any case, in the Palestinian Talmud, this unique opinion is brought by the redactor in the name of the sages, whereas in the Babylonian Talmud, it is mentioned only as the opinion of a single *amora*.

43 *See* the conclusion of Saul Lieberman, Hilkhot Ha-Yerushalmi of Rabbi Moses Ben Maimon 54 at the end of n.*shin* (1947) (Heb.).

> But the words of the sages: "A man may marry a wife and stipulate with her not to feed her and not to provide for her."

According to the Geonim, cited in Hilkhot Ha-Yerushalmi of Rabbi Moses Ben Maimon in the edition of Saul Lieberman (1898–1983, Professor of Talmud, The Jewish Theological Seminary of America),[44] the sages' view refers to the disagreement between R. Meir and R. Judah in the above Tannaitic dispute concerning the rights of a concubine. Whereas according to R. Meir, the difference between a wife and a concubine is their eligibility to receive any *ketubah* payment – the former is eligible while the latter is not – according to R. Judah, both are eligible and the difference between them is their eligibility to all the other *ketubah* stipulations. By contrast, according to the sages, not only can the husband not obligate himself to the *ketubah* payment, but also he may even nullify the various other *ketubah* obligations, such as food and support.

However, in my opinion, this explanation appears highly problematic, and it is very difficult to reconcile it with the plain sense of the text for several reasons. First, if the sages are addressing the issue of the difference between a wife and a concubine, they should use the same terminology of *ketubah* and *ketubah* stipulations, rather than using general language that does not appear to fit the context of the passage. Second, if according to the sages, there is a valid option of marrying a woman without her receiving any monetary rights, what is the difference between a wife and a concubine as regards their monetary rights?[45] Third, generally speaking, the sages' words are very vague. The general language that they use can fit both the context of the Tannaitic dispute regarding the difference between a wife and a concubine as well as any other discussion concerning a monetary stipulation, such as the one that appears in the Mishnah regarding the wife's right to receive her *ketubah* payment.

This problematic interpretation of the above Tannaitic dispute in the Palestinian Talmud was rejected by other commentators on the Palestinian Talmud, who maintain that the sages' view refers to the dispute between R. Meir and R. Judah

[44] *See* LIEBERMAN, ibid, at 56 and cf. idem, LIEBERMAN, *supra* note 21, at 244. Thus, according to these *Geonim*, we are dealing with a stipulation to waive the husband's other *ketubah* stipulations and not the *ikkar ketubah* itself. Thus, if the bride explicitly waives her *ketubah* rights, her stipulation is valid, since in monetary issues one can stipulate even against what is written in the Torah. *See* H. Hirschfeld, *In the Book of Megilat Starim*, in FESTSCHRIFT ZUM SIEBZIGSTEN GEBURTSTAGE A. BERLINER'S: GEWIDMET VON FREUNDEN UND SCHULERN, the Hebrew section 46 (1903) (Heb.); the response of Rav Hai Gaon in BENJAMIN M. LEWIN, OTZAR HA-GEONIM, *Rosh Hashana*, the commentaries section 89 n.*gimel* (1928).

[45] It should be emphasized that from the ritual (*issura*) perspective, obviously there is a great difference between a wife and a concubine: whereas a wife is officially married via *kiddushin* and *nissuin*, and therefore must be given a *get*, a concubine does not need to be given a *get*. This is the consensus with the exception of Rabbeinu Asher (Rosh), who holds in his responsa that even a concubine must receive a bill of divorce and may therefore be entitled to certain spousal rights.

in the Mishnah about *ikkar ketubbah*. According to this opinion, then, the husband may renegotiate or even nullify his obligations to pay the *ikkar ketubah*. Commentators on the Palestinian Talmud found several possible explanations for this innovative approach. The author of Korban ha-Edah (David ben Naphtali Frankel, 1704–62, German rabbi) ad loc. (s.v "*almenat shelo*") states as follows:

> Even though [the husband] is obligated according to Torah law, as it is written, "He shall not withhold clothing, sustenance," the sages hold that if someone makes a condition contradicting Torah law, the condition is valid, and also, that food and the *ketubah* are rabbinic decrees, and are therefore open to negotiation between the couple.

According to the first interpretation, despite the fact that, according to Torah law, the husband is obligated to his wife's *ikkar ketubah* right, the sages argue that if the husband makes a condition contradicting Torah law, the condition is still valid. But, according to the second explanation,[46] the sages claim that since both the wife's *ketubah* and her maintenance are only rabbinic decrees, the two are actually dispositive obligations and can be waived. The author of Sdeh Yehoshua (Yehoshua R. Benbenishti, 1590–1665, Turkish rabbi) tends toward the Korban Ha-Edah's first interpretation and writes as follows: "The sages say that a man may marry and make conditions, and this is not considered a violation of Torah law, since monetary conditions are binding."

According to these latter commentators, the appropriate order of the various discussions in the Palestinian Talmud is as follows: after dealing with the Mishnah and the beginning of the Amoraic discussion that focuses on the ability of a bride to waive her *ikkar ketubah*, the Palestinian Talmud discusses this issue again, but not before presenting the dispute between R. Meir and R. Judah regarding the difference between a wife and a concubine. Although it is the style of the Palestinian Talmud to jump from one subject to another, as some scholars have already noted,[47] the discussion at hand exhibits a unique textual phenomenon in which the continuity of the discussion is interrupted in order to present the Tannaitic dispute over the scope of a concubine's rights.[48] We also see elsewhere in the Palestinian Talmud that the wife's rights to her *ikkar kettubah* can be renegotiated or nullified. For example, we read in the Palestinian Talmud, *Ketubot* 1:2 (25b):

> There came a case before R. Hanina of a woman whose *ketubah* was less than 200 *zuz*, and he said she should take what he had written for her. … They said in the

[46] This holds true also regarding an obligation that involves ritual aspects (*issura*), as explained above in the text at note 39. To the best of my knowledge, this dissident opinion does not appear elsewhere.

[47] *See* the following references in Hebrew: Elyakim G. Ellinson, *The Concubine in the Talmudic Literature*, 73 SINAI 127, 130 (1973); ZECHARIAH FRANKEL, INTRODUCTION TO THE PALESTINIAN TALMUD 39 (1967).

[48] A phenomenon that some scholars have attempted to interpret, such as Ellinson, ibid.

> name of R. Huna, in a place where one does not write a *ketubah*. But in a place where one writes a *ketubah*, what she presents she collects.[49]

R. Hanina, a first-generation Palestinian *amora*, was dealing with the case of a woman whose *ketubah* amounted to less than 200 *zuz*, contrary to the common halakhic practice of paying more than this minimal amount and contrary to the fundamental prohibition of reducing this amount. R. Hanina ruled that despite the reduction of her *ketubah* payment, she must take what he had written for her. R. Hanina's ruling is based on the basic assumption that the option of reducing the *ikkar ketubah* referred to in the above Mishnah in *Ketubot* 5:1 is relevant only where it is not the practice to write a *ketubah*. But, in every place where it is customary to write a *ketubah*, there is complete freedom to change the amount of the *ketubah* and even reduce it below the accepted minimum.[50] Thus, according to the Palestinian tradition, wherever it is the common practice to write a *ketubah*, the couple is free to mutually add to or reduce the *ikkar ketubah* that the sages determined. From this discussion in the Palestinian Talmud, it appears that even R. Yohanan, who is mentioned later on, essentially agrees with R. Huna's position and even supports it with an additional Tannaitic source.[51]

Another discussion in a slightly different context in the Palestinian Talmud that supports this innovative interpretation and repeats R. Huna's position almost word for word is presented in the name of the *amora* Rav in *Ketubot* 9:9 (33c): "Rav said, at a place where one does not write a *ketubah*. But at a place where one writes a *ketubah*, what she produces she collects."[52] It is obvious from the context of Rav's statement that the default price set for the *ketubah* applies only where it is not the common practice to write a *ketubah*, but wherever it was common practice to write a *ketubah*, whatever amount is written in the *ketubah* is what she collects.

[49] *See* the parallel PT *Ketubot* 9:9 (33c). For interpreting this mystifying discussion, see SAUL LIEBERMAN, ON THE YERUSHALMI 30 (1929) (Heb.); LIEBERMAN, *supra* note 21, at 390; DANIEL SPERBER, ROMAN PALESTINE, 200–400: MONEY AND PRICES 398–401 (1991).

[50] It is noteworthy that from a historical perspective, writing a *ketubah* was apparently common practice until the mid-Tannaitic period, although there are several documented cases from this period in which no *ketubah* was written and even certain places where the official custom was to not write one at all. But, later on, writing a *ketubah* became a binding legal requirement, although as yet there were no sanctions against a couple who did not write one. For documentation of the places where it was not the practice to write a *ketbuah*, see Mishnah *Ketubot* 4:7; BT *Ketubot* 16b; 89a; BT *Baba Metziah* 17b–18a; BT *Sotah* 7b.

[51] This is the interpretation of the author of Pnei Moshe in his commentary ad hoc to the discussion in the Palestinian Talmud. However, the author of Korban Ha-Edah explains it differently. As we have seen earlier, SCHREMER, *supra* note 31, at 244 n.52 rejects the latter problematic explanation, maintaining that it is totally unclear how R. Yohanan's statement fits into this context.

[52] In the scholarly literature, one can find a comparison of the discussions in the Palestinian Talmud and the parallel discussions in the Babylonian Talmud. For such a comparison with BT *Ketobut* 89a–b, see Israel Francus, *Birorim and Biorim in Masechet Ketubot*, 73 SINAI 24, 36 (1973) (Heb.), and with the parallel BT *Baba Metziah* 17a, see Israel Francus, *Tnai Beit Din and Maase Beit Din*, 115 SINAI 148, 149 (1995) (Heb.).

This means that the amount may differ from the set price in either direction – very often it is higher, but sometimes it is lower.[53] It should be noted that the acceptance of this opinion as the normative opinion, and certainly its documentation as halakhic practice, is totally rejected in the Babylonian Talmud. As mentioned earlier, in the Babylonian Talmud, an opinion of this kind is brought in the name of R. Yose as an unaccepted minority opinion, it is mentioned only once in the framework of the fundamental dispute between R. Meir and R. Judah, and it receives no further mention in any other sources.[54]

But even the all-embracing halakhic approach, based on the Babylonian Talmud, which rejects out of hand any possibility of reducing the *ikkar ketubah,* should be qualified in light of a difference of opinion by Nahmanides. This eminent Talmudic commentator and *posek* distinguishes between the case of a husband who wishes to continue to live with his wife after reducing her *ikkar ketubah,* in which event his stipulation is void, and a case in which he is about to divorce his wife, in which event the stipulation is valid. In the latter scenario, his condition is valid, even if the reduction of his wife's *ikkar ketubah* was mutually agreed upon already at the outset of their marriage, since if a bride renounces her *ketubah* rights, the renouncement is valid and it is no longer a matter of a ritual (*issura*) prohibition but a purely monetary obligation. It is worth noting that there are some *rishonim* who adopted this distinction in practice.[55]

2.3 *A Husband's Right to Inherit His Wife*

Besides the husband's obligation of conjugal relations with his wife as part of a Jewish marriage according to the law of Moses and Israel (*kedat Mosheh veYisrael*), the husband has nine additional spousal obligations. In return, he receives four rights to which his wife is obligated, *inter alia,* the right to inherit her upon her death.[56] These obligations are not in any way dependent on the couple's wishes or consent but *a priori* are nonnegotiable and binding. This means that these spousal obligations fall under the category of a halakhic obligation *ex lege,* even if the

[53] This is Adiel Schremer's interpretation of these discussions in the Palestinian Talmud; *see* SCHREMER, *supra* note 31, at 244–45.

[54] It should be note that the *halakhah* in practice nowadays, based on the Babylonian Talmud's perspective, defines the *ikkar ketubah* as a binding obligation, and thus any attempt to privately waive it is invalid. *See* Maimonides *Ishut* 12:6 and *Shulhan Arukh* 69:6. *See also* SCHERESCHEWSKY, *supra* note 14, at 99, who writes that although there is freedom of contract with regard to various *ketubah* stipulations, one can make no stipulations regarding the *ikkar ketubah*, similar to the husband's obligation to a conjugal relationship and his right to inherit his wife.

[55] *See* the commentary of Rabbeinu Asher (Rosh) to BT *Ketubot* 56a; the commentary of the author of Maggid Mishneh to Maimonides *Ishut* 12:6; *Beit Yosef, Even ha-Ezer* 69:1–7.

[56] Maimonides *Ishut* 12:1–2 and extensively in the commentary in Mishneh la-Melekh ad hoc; *Shulhan Arukh, Even ha-Ezer* 69:1.

husband did not obligate himself in their regard, either in writing or orally.[57] There are three basic questions concerning the limitations of a couple's freedom to waive the husband's right to inherit his wife. First, what is the source and the scope of this right – is it a biblical one and therefore any attempt to circumvent it contractually is restricted, or is it only a rabbinic enactment, regarding which there is greater latitude to waive it as long as there is no explicit rabbinic prohibition to do so? Second, is this a purely monetary obligation or is some ritual (*issura*) element involved, which would restrict the freedom of contract?

Third, if normatively this right of the husband's is indeed open to stipulation, how is it put into practice? Does the groom renounce his right? Does the bride unilaterally waive it by means of an explicit stipulation in her marriage contract that she is marrying him only on condition that he does not inherit her? Or perhaps both parties mutually agree to waive it? Regarding the first question, the matter of whether we are referring to a biblical right or a rabbinical decree has been discussed extensively in the two Talmuds. In any event, all agree that the practice of a husband inheriting his wife is a very ancient one and has been part of Jewish tradition as well as that of all other ancient nations.[58] The dispute among the sages revolves entirely around the question of whether the source of this ancient custom is the Torah or whether it derives only from a rabbinical decree.[59] As to the second and third questions, numerous and nuanced halakhic details in their regard are found in the two Talmuds and in the literature of the *rishonim*.[60] Since our purpose here is to explore possible different views of the two Talmuds regarding the extent of the freedom of contract that exists in this regard, the discussion in this section focuses entirely on a unique stipulation documented in the Palestinian Talmud but that receives no mention whatsoever in the Babylonian Talmud.

Some argue that the husband's right to inherit his wife is one of several monetary enactments promulgated by the sages to preserve the family cell, to strengthen the couple's common economic interests, and to prevent hostility between them. However, in some cases this right was considered harsh and unjust.[61] It seems

57 *See* SCHERESCHEWSKY, *supra* note 14, ibid.

58 For a comparison of the husband's right to inherit his wife in Torah law and in ancient near eastern law, see LOUIS M. EPSTEIN, THE JEWISH MARRIAGE CONTRACT 83–85 (1954) (Heb.); Josef Fleishman, *The Inheritance of a Mother's Dowry in Ancient Near East Law and in Ancient Jewish Law*, 23 DINE ISRAEL 95 (2005) (Heb.).

59 For a summary of the various opinions regarding this issue, see the references listed in *supra* note 15. For a brief summary of this issue, see Yedidya Cohen, *The Inheritance of a Wife of Her Husband in the Communal Enactments*, 6–7 SHENATON HA-MISHPAT HA-IVRI 133, 135 n.4 (1979–80) (Heb.).

60 *See* the following sources in Hebrew: TALMUDIC ENCYCLOPEDIA vol. 25, 506–628 (Shlomo Zevin et al. eds., 2002); Israel Francus, *Mahloket Kadmonim Be-Din Vittur Ha-Ba'al Lareshet Et Ishto*, 106 SINAI 97 (1990); COHEN, *supra* note 15, at 152–77; YOSEF RIVLIN, INHERITANCE AND WILLS IN JEWISH LAW 87–102 (1999).

61 Simcha Assaf, *Different Decrees and Customs Relating to the Husband's Right of Inheritance*, 1 MADDA'EI HA-YAHUDUT 80 n.1 (1926) (Heb.). Indeed, already in the Tannaitic literature there

particularly harsh when the wife dies childless and the husband inherits her property, and it is even more problematic when the wife dies shortly after her marriage.[62] Documentary evidence exists of a unique condition that was common in Palestine during the Talmudic period, and possibly even earlier, whereby the husband is prevented from inheriting his wife if she dies without children. An examination of the relevant passages in the Palestinian Talmud suggests that this condition was widely known and well established: "R. Yose said: Those who write 'if she should die childless, her property should return to her father's family' write a monetary condition which is a valid condition."[63] In the parallel source, this statement appears in the name of another sage, R. Isaac: "R. Isaac said: About those who write, if she should die without children, all that was hers shall revert to her father. This is a stipulation about money; the stipulation is valid."[64]

At the wedding ceremony, the groom would declare that he will not inherit his future wife should she predecease him. Thus, the couple had the power to reach an agreement regarding the husband's (non)inheritance of his wife's property.[65] It seems that this position contradicts that of R. Shimon ben Gamliel and other *tannaim* who maintained that the husband had no right to make an agreement

were halakhic tools designed to restrict these harsh and unjust consequences, such as the *ketubat benin dichrin*, whose aim was to ensure that even if the husband inherited his wife's dowry, upon his death it would be inherited only by her heirs and not by any heirs of her husband's other wives. It should be noted that this ancient enactment became a binding *ketubah* stipulation in the Tannaitic literature, even if it was not explicitly stated in the *ketubah*. *See* Mishnah *Ketubot* 4:1; BT *Ketubot* 52b–53a; EPSTEIN, *supra* note 58, at 79–92.

62 Assaf, ibid, wished to prove the extent to which the practice of the husband inheriting his wife was common in Jewish history based on a condition to the contrary in a Karaite *ketubah* that stated explicitly that the husband would not inherit his wife, as is the practice in rabbinic Judaism. For a discussion of the Karaite objection to the husband's right to inherit his wife, see AARON B. ELIJAH OF NICOMEDIA, SEFER MITZVOT GADOL GAN EDEN 153, 1 *(1972). Friedman assumes that there was actually a major influence of rabbinic* ketubot *on Karaite* ketubot, *but the unresolved question is whether the Karaite* ketubot *were influenced more by the Babylonian or by the Palestinian* ketubot. *See* Mordecai A. Friedman, *On the Relationship of the Karaite and the Palestinian Rabbanite Marriage Contracts from the Geniza*, 15 TEU'DAH 145, 151 (1956) (Heb.). Friedman points out, *inter alia*, the documented evidence of the influence of the Palestinian *ketubah* on the Karaite *ketubah* regarding the condition of returning the wife's dowry to her inheritors from her father's family, should she die childless, see, ibid, at 151. For an opinion opposing that of Friedman regarding this possible influence, see JUDITH OLSZOWY-SCHLANGER, KARAITE MARRIAGE DOCUMENTS FROM THE CAIRO GENIZA 263–71 (1998).

63 PT *Ketubot* 9:1 (32d). For a discussion of the accurate version of R. Yose's statement, see COHEN, *supra* note 15, at 156 nn.278–86.

64 PT *Baba Batra* 8:5 in SAUL LIEBERMAN & ELIEZER S. ROSENTAL, YERUSHALMI NEZIQIN 102 (2008) (Heb.).

65 Numerous medieval authorities considered such conditions valid. The first of these was Isaac Alfasi (Rif), who cited the Palestinian Talmud's text in a slightly different form: "Those who write for their wives," presumably to make fully clear that the husband had made this condition with his wife. This ruling was accepted by *Beit Yosef Even ha-Ezer* 69. Other halakhic authorities who held this opinion include Nahmanides, Novellae on *ketubot* 83b; YIZHAK BAR SHESHET PARPERET, RESP. RIBASH ch. 64 (1546); YOSEF IBN LEV, RESP. MAHARI BEN LEV vol. 2 ch. 30 (1959).

with his wife that he will not inherit her property, since such a condition contradicts Torah law and is therefore null and void.[66] It is noteworthy that this stipulation was well known to the *rishonim*, and variations of this condition may even be found in their commentaries and novellae.[67] A careful analysis of R. Yose's condition is of great importance, since the ability to nullify a husband's right to inherit his wife's property is one of the most widely discussed issues in the history of *halakhah*. In later periods, we find numerous enactments that sought to completely or partially nullify the husband's right to inherit his wife. The Talmudic basis for these enactments was usually R. Yose's aforementioned condition.[68] Indeed, this unusual condition from the Palestinian Talmud is already cited in various Geonic works,[69] and various Palestinian *ketubot* include such a clause. The application of this condition spread from Palestine to Babylonia, Egypt, Italy, and southern France.[70]

In the opinion of Mordechai A. Friedman (Department of Talmud, Tel Aviv University), Jews of Palestinian origin immigrated to Egypt and introduced this condition into their *ketubot*, and this custom then spread elsewhere.[71] Interestingly,

[66] This was also the position of Rid; *see* ISAIAH THE ELDER OF TERANI (RID) RESP. HA-RID ch. 65 (1967); Francus, *supra* note 60, at 114 suggests that just as we have found an Amoraic disagreement in the Palestinian Talmud as to whether the *halakhah* in this regard should be determined according to R. Shimon Ben Gamliel, there is perhaps a similar discussion among the Amoraic sages Rav and R. Kahana in the Babylonian Talmud.

[67] For documentation of this version or very similar versions, see Novellae of RASHBA on Tractate *Gittin* 13b; ha-Rid, ibid; SHLOMO BEN AVRAHAM BEN ADERET (RASHBA), RESP. RASHBA vol. 6 ch. 254 (1958); DAVID BEN SHLOMO IBN AVI ZIMRA (RADBAZ), RESP. HA-RADBAZ vol. 3 ch. 497 (1950); SAMUEL BEN MOSHE DE MEDINA, RESP. MAHARASHDAM *Even ha-Ezer* ch. 128 (1959). This condition was established as *halakhah* also in *Beit Yosef, Even ha-Ezer* 118.

[68] For a review of enactments annulling a husband's right to inherit his wife, see Assaf, *supra* note 61. For a discussion of a husband's right to refrain from inheriting his wife, see, e.g., the following references in Hebrew: EPSTEIN, *supra* note 58, at 89 n.30; ELIEZER WOLFF, YERUSHAT BENEI HA-ZUG BA-MISHPAT HA-IVRI VE-HA-YISRAELI 114 ff. (JurD thesis, Hebrew University, 1971); COHEN, *supra* note 15, at 319–49. For a discussion of what is referred to as the "Toledo enactment" regarding such matters, see, e.g., Shraga Abramson, *On the Takkanah of Tuletula (Toledo) Regarding the Husband's Inheritance of His Wife's Estate*, 60(2) ZION 201 (1995) (Heb.); Aharon Choueka, *The Controversy Concerning the Takkanah of Tuletula Regarding the Husband's Inheritance of His Wife's Estate*, 68(1) TARBIZ 87 (1999) (Heb.).

[69] *See, e.g.*, Jacob N. Epstein, *Sefer Ha-Ma'asim Li-Vnei Eretz Yisrael*, 1 TARBIZ 40 (1930) (Heb.); TESHUVOT HA-GEONIM ch. 111 p. 120 line 15 (Simcha Assaf ed., 1942); and the fragments of a Geonic commentary attributed to Rabbenu Hananel. *See* BENJAMIN M. LEWIN, OTZAR HA-GEONIM, KETUBOT, *likkutei perush rabbenu hananel* 94–96 (1928).

[70] *See* AVISHALOM WESTREICH, TALMUD-BASED SOLUTIONS TO THE PROBLEM OF THE AGUNAH 29, 32 (2012) ("The Palestinian custom of *ketubbah* stipulations, and in particular the Palestinian divorce clause, continued (maybe even expanded) in the post-Talmudic era, as reflected in Palestinian *ketubbot*.").

[71] *See* YESHAYAH AHARON OF TRANI (RIAZ), SEFER HA-MAKHRIA, ch. 47 (1779); ISAAC B. ABBA MARI, SEFER HA-ITTUR, *Ketubot*, 30b; SEFER HA-SHETAROT LE-RAV HAI GAON 57 (Simcha Assaf ed., 1930). *See also* the following sources in Hebrew: Friedman, *supra* note 62, at 153 n.17; FRIEDMAN, *supra* note 23, at 40; Jacob N. Epstein, *Notes to the Jewish-Aramaic Papyri of Aswan*, in STUDIES IN TALMUDIC LITERATURE AND SEMITIC LANGUAGES vol. 1, 320, 327–28 (Ezra Z. Melamed ed., 1984) (Heb.). *See also* JACOB MANN, THE JEWS IN EGYPT AND IN

this Palestinian tradition reached the Babylonian *Geonim* at a time of Babylonian Talmudic supremacy. This condition is cited also in the works of many medieval halakhists.[72] Some scholars claim that it may be possible to infer a more comprehensive conclusion from this stipulation – that according to early *halakhah*, a couple could impose additional *ketubah* stipulations before they married, even with regard to their conjugal relationship.

In the opinion of these scholars, this freedom of contract enabled a couple to privately regulate even their intimate relationship and not only their spousal monetary day-to-day life. This leads us to the inevitable conclusion that at that time, the principle that "if someone makes a condition which contradicts Torah law, the condition is null and void" had not yet been established. In this pre-halakhic framework, even ritual matters (*issura*) were regarded as monetary matters, and therefore stipulations concerning a couple's conjugal relationship were valid.[73] Whether this contention is correct or not, in my opinion there is no doubt that the scope of freedom of contract reflected in the Palestinian Talmud regarding the groom's ability to waive his inheritance right is much broader than that which is reflected in the Babylonian Talmud.

2.4 *A Woman's Right to Initiate Divorce*

I now consider another stipulation mentioned in the Palestinian Talmud that does not appear in the Babylonian Talmud. This stipulation apparently applies to the case of a woman who demands a divorce because of her hatred for her husband:

> R. Yose said: For those who write [a stipulation in the marriage contract]: "if he grows to hate her or she grows to hate him," it is considered a condition of monetary payment, and their condition is valid.[74]

Palestine under the Fatimid Caliphs 381 (1920); Asher Gulak, Otzar Ha-Shetarot 33 (1926).

[72] *See* Benjamin M. Lewin, Ginze Qedem vol. 2, 30–31 (1922); Lewin, *supra* note 69, at 61–62, and the sources mentioned there. *See also* Francus, *supra* note 60, at 112–14. For a summary of the views of Lewin, Assaf, and Epstein about ascribing this source to Rabbenu Hananel, see Cohen, *supra* note 60, at 156 n.291.

[73] *See* Tchernowitz, *supra* note 22, at 269–70. For defining what is a biblical obligation as opposed to a rabbinic enactment, and the different implications that derive from this distinction – with regard to the appropriate limits of freedom of contract – see Benjamin De Vries, Toldot Hahalacha Hatalmudit 69–80 (1966) (Heb.); Gilat, *supra* note 21, at 239–48.

[74] PT *Ketubot* 5:8 (30b). It is noteworthy that even though this stipulation was not anchored in the authoritative halakhic codices of Maimonides and *Shulhan Arukh*, it was cited as *halakhah* in the work Hilkhot Ha-Yerushalmi, which is ascribed to Maimonides. *See* Lieberman, *supra* note 43, at 56 n.*zayin*, who wrote that apparently Maimonides eventually deleted it from his codex. For the parallel, slightly different version of R. Yose's statement in the Palestinian Talmud, see PT *Baba Batra* 8:8 (16c); Lieberman & Rosental, *supra* note 64, at 105. For a discussion of this unique source, see Avishalom Westreich, *The Wife's Right to Divorce in Jewish Law: History, Dogmatics and Hermeneutics*, 62 J. Jewish Stud. 340, 354–55 (2011); Shlomo Riskin, Women and Jewish Divorce: The Rebellious Wife, the Agunah and

The meaning of this stipulation is unclear. Its vagueness is due to the fact that the passage contains only the protasis (the clause expressing the condition) "if he grows to hate her or she grows to hate him" and the apodosis (the clause expressing the consequence) is missing.[75] Thus, it is difficult to definitively deduce that the wife may impose a condition in her marriage contract stating that if she comes to hate her husband, she may unilaterally initiate a divorce. According to one interpretation, this stipulation deals with the monetary aspects of a divorce; thus, R. Yose maintains that conditions regulating the *ketubah* payment to a divorcee are valid, since they are considered monetary conditions. In other words, this innovative condition gives a couple freedom to stipulate and change only the rabbinical enactment of paying the wife her *ketubah* if she initiates the divorce.[76] Alternatively, R. Yose might mean that a woman may demand a divorce if she hates her husband, just as a husband may divorce a wife he hates. It is noteworthy that accepting the wife's claim that her husband is *me'is 'alai* and she no longer wishes to live with him was a common halakhic practice even later until Rabbeinu Tam annulled it in the twelfth century.[77]

This interpretation can be supported by the fact that the Palestinian Talmud is citing an abbreviated form of this stipulation, without the apodosis, which may indicate that this was a common stipulation and everyone knew the exact meaning of this abridged condition, since it was well known and a common practice in Palestine at that time.[78] It is similar to other common, well-known stipulations cited

The Right of Women to Initiate Divorce in Jewish Law, A Halakhic Solution 31–32 (1989); Epstein, *supra* note 58, at 198 n.19.

75 *See* Westreich, *supra* note 70, at 28 ("Accordingly, the reason why the *Amoraim* do not discuss the right to demand divorce is that it was already known and accepted, rather than this being the 'point of the innovation' of the condition. The same conclusion applies to the missing apodosis of R. Yose's condition.").

76 This is the interpretation of Epstein, *supra* note 58, at 127. He finds support for his assumption in the heavy financial penalty that was attached to the "hate condition" appearing in papyrus G, which would be imposed on the husband should he divorce his wife in a humiliating manner. According to Epstein, the only reasonable explanation for this ambiguous condition is that it deals with a husband who unilaterally divorces his wife without following the law and its regulations and therefore should pay a very large fine. For the interpretation of this ancient *ketubah*, see Yaron, *infra* note 101, at 67–81; Porten, *infra* note 101, at 22 lines 22–26. But Adiel Schremer rejects any attempt to deduce from this papyrus any definite conclusion regarding a woman's ability to demand a divorce; *see* Adiel Schremer, *Papyrus Se'elim 13 and the Question of Divorce Initiated by Women in Ancient Jewish Halakhah*, 63 Zion 377, 378 n.4 (1998) (Heb.). *See also* David I. Brewer, *Jewish Women Divorcing Their Husbands in Early Judaism: The Background to Papyrus Se'elim 13*, 92(3) Harvard Theological Rev. 349, 353f., 356 (1999); Robert Brody, *Evidence for Divorce by Jewish Women?*, 50 J. Jewish Stud. 230 (1999); Bernard S. Jackson, *Some Reflections on Family Law in the Papyri*, XIV Jewish L. Ass'n Stud. 141 (Hillel Gamoran ed., 2002).

77 For a discussion of this ruling by Rabbeinu Tam, see Jackson et al., *supra* note 7, passim. For his alternative solution for solving the problem of the Jewish chained woman, see R. Chaim Jachter & Ezra Frazer, Gray Matter: Discourses in Contemporary Halachah 17f. (2000).

78 This is a parenthetical conclusion of Jacob N. Epstein. He is even trying to reconstruct the full wording of the stipulation according to the text in papyrus G; *see* Epstein, *supra* note 71.

in the Palestinian Talmud for which the phrase "For those who write" (*eilin dekatvin*) is used.[79] Dogmatically speaking, I find it difficult to accept the first interpretation, since there is nothing innovative about it. Even though we are dealing with a derivative of the divorce process that is regarded as ritual (*issura*) in nature, in effect we are dealing only with the monetary aspects of this process, with regard to which there is generally complete freedom of contract.

Therefore, in view of this problem and in light of the unique approach found in the Palestinian Talmud discussed earlier in this chapter, according to which there is considerable liberty to negotiate conditions that potentially violate Torah prohibitions (e.g., conditions regarding *ikkar ketubah*, marital relations, and the husband's right to inherit his wife), I prefer the second interpretation. Thus, the Palestinian Talmud regards the wife's demand for a divorce as a monetary matter, and this demand may therefore be stipulated in an agreement between the couple.[80] A similar stipulation is found in the Palestinian Talmud regarding monetary settlements in the case of a couple who divorced because the wife grew to hate her husband. The Talmud states:

> they saw a man putting his mouth on her mouth. The case came before R. Yose, who said that she should leave without *ketubah*. ... They brought the *ketubah* and found written in it: if this X marries this Y as her husband and should no longer desire (hates)[81] his company,[82] she shall take half the *ketubah* sum.[83] R. Abun said,

[79] For additional appearances of this phrase, see PT *Ketubot* 9:10 (32d); PT *Baba Batra* 8:5; PT *Ketubot* 5:8 (30b); PT *Baba Batra* 8:8 (16c). Another possible source is PT *Shevuot* 6:6 (37b) in the discussion concerning a stipulation that enabled the lender to seize the properties of the debtor even after his death. This is also the conclusion of LIFSHITZ, *supra* note 10, at 182.

[80] For an interpretation of the Palestinian Talmud's justification for according validity to the stipulation that enables either spouse to unilaterally initiate a divorce because it regards it as a monetary matter, not in the plain halakhic sense, but in order to define it as being subject to stipulation as if it were a monetary matter and therefore a valid condition and not something that contradicts what is written in the Torah, see Friedman's two explanations, *supra* note 23, at 319–21 – "'monetary stipulations' include agreements to forfeit a right or benefit assured one by law."

[81] *See* LIEBERMAN, *supra* note 43, at 61; FRIEDMAN, *supra* note 23, at 329; RISKIN, *supra* note 74, at 31 n.16. *See also* JACKSON ET AL., *supra* note 7, at 63 and more generally, WESTREICH, *supra* note 70 (for a discussion of the Palestinian *ketubah* stipulations, the Geonic *moredet*, and the rebellious wife in the Palestinian Talmud).

[82] The version in Ms. Leiden, and following it the *editio princeps* (printed editions) of the Palestinian Talmud, mistakenly reads בשור פוטי instead of בשותפותיה. For a clarification of the reading of this text, see Jacob N. Epstein, *Li-Seridei Ha-Yerushalmi*, 3 TARBIZ 15, 25 n.18 (1932) (Heb.); BOAZ COHEN, JEWISH AND ROMAN LAW vol. 1, 295 n.72 (1966). The correct reading (בשותפותיה) is found in Simon Hopkins, *A New Autograph Fragment of Maimonides' Hilkhot Ha-Yerushalmi*, 28 J. SEMITIC STUD. 273, 288–89 (1983); LIEBERMAN, *supra* note 43. *See also* FRIEDMAN, *supra* note 23, at 329 ("*Shutafut* 'partnership' here clearly denotes 'marriage', as in Syriac. This felicitous term is particularly befitting in a stipulation which describes man and wife as equal partners in the business of marriage, each of whom can withdraw from the partnership at will.").

[83] PT *Ketubot* 7:6 (31c). For the precise version of this condition and an interpretation of it, see Epstein, *supra* note 71. LIEBERMAN, *supra* note 43, at 61 n.*resh-shin* wrote that R. Yose himself

> since she agreed that he should put his mouth on her mouth it is as if she hated him; she has only half the *ketubah*.

This passage deals with a wife who stipulated with her husband in the marriage contract that should she grow to hate him, she would be permitted to demand a divorce but would be eligible to collect only half of the sum of her *ketubah*. In the end, she was found kissing a man who was not her husband. Following this inappropriate behavior and according to what was written in her own *ketubah*, R. Abun ruled that she should be divorced but that she retain the right to receive half of her *ketubah* payment. It is difficult to determine definitively whether this source deals with a woman's right to unilaterally initiate a divorce based on an explicit stipulation in her *ketubah* or whether it is only regulating her monetary rights following her request to divorce her husband. However, it seems that we may understand from R. Abun's words that he deduced from the woman's conduct that she hated her husband, and that was the only grounds for her divorce. In other words, we are indeed dealing with a woman's ability to initiate a divorce,[84] as was concluded recently in the scholarly literature:

> Unilateral divorce is not explicitly mentioned in the Palestinian Talmud either in the *sugya* of the kiss story or in R. Yose's condition. The *Amoraim* discuss mainly the financial aspects of the condition. ... However, these aspects were probably accompanied by divorce, and this presumes that it includes unilateral divorce on the part of the wife ... which means that the wife has the right to demand and obtain a unilateral divorce. One possible interpretation is that the wife's entitlement to a coerced divorce is achieved by the quoted condition.[85]

did not need to examine the actual *ketubah* of the woman under discussion, since this stipulation was so common that R. Yose could deal with it as a general accepted *ketubah* stipulation, even though it was never actually written in the document that was brought to him. *See also* Westreich, *supra* note 70, at 31 ("We may conclude from this fact that the content of the divorce stipulation was known and common and there was no substantial need for it to be written. This might be also the reason why R. Yose in the Palestinian Talmud does not give any details of the divorce clause, but only rules that it is legitimate."). For reference to this condition in modern Israeli rabbinical courts, see Rabbinical Court 1064/1954, 1501/1954, Anonymous v. Anonymous, 1 PDR 257, 265 (11.01.55).

[84] This is the opinion of Epstein, *supra* note 58, at 131 n.39. Similarly, he concludes that in this case the woman is fined and loses half her *ketubah* payment. *See also* Friedman, *supra* note 23, at, 319–20.

[85] *See* Westreich, *supra* note 70, at 27. Jackson et al., *supra* note 7, has doubts as to the meaning of the hate condition. On the one hand, he writes at 64 ("Yet the 'kiss case' illustrates the utility of the clause also for determining entitlement to divorce."), yet, on the other hand, he writes at 66 ("Without more information, an entire spectrum of possibilities is theoretically open for consideration, each with some historical (if not rabbinic) precedent."). For the opposing view, which maintains that the clause regulates only the financial aspects of the divorce process, see Jackson et al., *supra* note 7, at 62–63 ("However, there is also academic support for the dominant (but not exclusive: see § 3.20, below) rabbinic view, that the condition related only to (special) financial terms of (a voluntary) divorce."). For a prominent proponent of this opinion, see Naphtali Lewis, Ranon Katzoff & Jonas C. Greenfield, *Papyrus Yadin 18*, 37

In any case, the hate clause is also mentioned in the writings of such medieval halakhists as Nahmanides, Ritba, and Maharam of Rothenburg.[86] Meiri, in his work Beit Ha-Behirah on the Babylonian Talmud, refers to the Palestinian Talmud's condition about spousal hatred in an interesting way. In his commentary on Tractate *Ketubot* 63a, he writes in the name of his teachers' teachers that such a condition is valid in a case where a woman hates her husband and wants to force him to divorce her. These rabbis maintained that the Geonic decree regarding a woman who claims that her husband is revolting to her is based on this condition, which has become so widespread that it may be considered a concomitant condition of the *ketubbah* (*tenai ketubah*), which is binding even if was not actually included in the *ketubah*. Meiri writes,

> And my teachers testified that their teachers explained that the Geonic innovation about this matter is based on what is written in the Palestinian Talmud: "[Regarding] those who write that if he hates her or if she hates him this is a monetary condition, which is valid." In other words, if they stipulate that if he hates her he must divorce her, with both her regular and additional *ketubah* payments, and similarly if she hates him, he must divorce her, whether with complete or partial payment of the *ketubah*, everything is valid, as per what they have stipulated. . . . They wrote about this that the *Geonim* innovated as they did because they were accustomed to write in their *ketubot* that if she hates him, she should receive her *ketubah* and leave him. . . . And since the custom became widespread, they made this practice binding, even if it was not written, just as if it were written, like other *tenai ketubah*.[87]

This statement by Meiri clearly indicates that this condition of spousal hatred enables a woman to demand a divorce, and that this was a common and well-known practice. As was concluded recently by Avishalom Westreich:

> Accordingly, the link between the two traditions does not relate to the coerced divorce but rather to the financial aspects of the rebellious wife. Nevertheless, taking the words of Me'iri's teachers' teachers (as cited in Me'iri's commentary) out of their context in Me'iri's text reveals a different intention: it appears that Me'iri's teachers' teachers tried to legitimate the coerced divorce itself and not

Israel Exploration Journal 229, Chapter II – *Legal Commentary* by Ranon Katzoff 236–47 (1987).

[86] *See* Novellae of Rashba on Tractate *Ketubot* 64a (by Nahmanides, but mistakenly attributed to Rashba); Novellae of Ritba, ibid, s.v. "*u-le-inyan moredet*" (whose comments imply that the condition applies to the monetary arrangements between husband and wife where the wife rebels against her husband); Rabbi Meir b. Baruch of Rothenburg (Maharam), Sha'arei Teshuvot 19 (1891). The condition is also cited by Asher Gulak, Otzar Ha-Shetarot 33 (1926) (Heb.).

[87] Meiri, Bet Ha-Behirah on BT *Ketubot* 63b, s.v. "*amar ha-Meiri*" 269–70 (1977). For a discussion of this testimony, see Friedman, *supra* note 23, at vol. II 42f; Riskin, *supra* note 74, at 82; Jackson et al., *supra* note 7, at 67–71; Westreich, *supra* note 70, at 33–38.

> (only) the financial aspects. ... The divorce clause accordingly gives the wife the right to initiate unilateral divorce.[88]

Additional support for Meiri's claim[89] that the Geonic decree is based on the spousal hatred condition appearing in the Palestinian Talmud is found in a responsum by Rashba, which states,

> This is the law of the rebellious wife and of the wife who finds her husband revolting. But Rabbi Alfasi wrote in his Laws. ... Perhaps the *Geonim* only made these decrees for their own generation as a temporary measure, but now we may not be lenient about the matter, and Nahmanides ... and Rabbi Zerahiah ha-Levi ... wrote similarly. [The] Palestinian Talmud [states]: R. Yose said those who write, If he hates or she hates, this is a monetary condition, and the condition is binding.[90]

Why is the Palestinian Talmud cited at the end of this passage? Was Rashba attempting to intimate that the Palestinian Talmud was the source of the Geonic tradition, as Meiri maintains? Moreover, perhaps this passage too alludes to the possibility that the Palestinian Talmud's "hate clause" is not merely a monetary stipulation but a condition that seeks to enable the wife to demand a divorce if she so desires. If my assumption is correct that the Palestinian Talmud offers spouses greater freedom of contract, it is safe to assume that a wife is indeed eligible to unilaterally initiate a divorce. This is based on the fact that all these intertwined issues involving both ritual and monetary aspects are defined in the Palestinian tradition as monetary matters, and therefore there are no restrictions on privately and mutually regulating them. I believe that my assumption can find support in the Geonic literature, such as in a Geonic response that Mordecai A. Friedman ascribes to Rav Hai or Shrira Gaon, which he published in the mid-1970s.[91]

88 Westreich, *supra* note 70, at 34.

89 Leib Moscovitz notes that while Meiri attributes this interpretation to his teachers' teachers, their view might well have been based on conjecture rather than tradition.

90 *See* Shlomo ben Avraham ben Aderet (Rashba), Resp. Teshuvot HaRashba HaHadashot ch. 176, pp. 124–25 (2005), cited in Teshuvot Hakhmei Provence ch. 73 (Avraham Sofer ed., 1967); *see also* the editor's notes ad loc., p. 277.

91 *See* Mordechai A. Friedman, *Polygamy – New Information from the Genizah*, 43 Tarbitz 166, 168–70 (1974) (Heb.); Friedman, Polygyny, *supra* note 23, at 29–32 in his discussion of to whom this responsum should be attributed. *See also* Jackson et al., *supra* note 7, at 67–68 ("Rav Hai Gaon and some Rishonim – Ramban and others – explain the divorce clause of the Yerushalmi as a clause which was required for the financial agreements. But each had their particular motivations."); Westreich, *supra* note 70, at 36 ("Rav Hai Gaon, who legitimates some kinds of financial arrangements in cases of the rebellious wife on the basis of: 'since it is a condition of monetary payment, and it is valid'. This is almost word for word the Palestinian justification of the *ketubah* clause and it is cited here as a support for monetary aspects rather than for coercion."). Friedman ponders the key question of whether the stipulation is valid only as regards the monetary aspects of the divorce process or whether its deeper meaning is that it enables a woman to demand a divorce. For a discussion of the reasoning behind the above ruling, see Warhaftig, *supra* note 10, at 381–82.

The essence of the responsum was to definitively validate a monogamy clause, since it is in effect a monetary condition and therefore, as with all monetary conditions, should be halakhically valid. This holds true even though the monogamy clause prohibits the husband from taking a second wife and should he wish to take a second wife, he must divorce his first wife, and thus, the clause goes beyond regulating the monetary compensation for which the first wife is eligible. Nonetheless, this stipulation is still defined as a monetary one even though on the surface it could easily be defined as a ritual matter, which is not open to private ordering. From the clear-cut answer in this responsum and especially the reasoning on which it is based, we can infer that the monogamy clause is a monetary condition in all respects and is therefore a valid stipulation.[92] To put it differently, the common denominator of the Palestinian Talmud's "hate clause" and the monogamy clause is that they both regulate ritual aspects by defining them as monetary conditions, and they are therefore halakhically valid. Similarly, Rabbi Shimon ben Tzemach Duran argues in one of his responsa that the monogamy clause is a purely monetary one and the condition is therefore valid.[93]

In addition to the Palestinian Talmud's broad and unique approach to extensive spousal freedom of contract, I wish to suggest another possible dogmatic interpretation for this general flexible attitude and more specifically for the existence of the Palestinian Talmud's "hate clause." The Palestinian Talmud's conceptualization of the Jewish marriage is more egalitarian than that of the more conservative Babylonian Talmud and that of its main successor – *halakhah*. This egalitarian perspective affords a couple far greater freedom of contract, which somewhat reduces gender disparities.[94] A fine example of this can be found in the unique style of numerous Palestinian *ketubot*, which clearly reflect this egalitarian attitude with the incorporation of a couple's mutual obligations to honor and respect each other. This is in distinct contrast to their counterpart, the Babylonian *ketubah*,

[92] This conclusion should be regarded with reservation in light of the Geonic enactment of *me'is'alay*, discussed above in the accompanying text at *supra* note 7. According to this approach, it is sufficient for the wife to make this claim in order to initiate a divorce, and in the opinions of Rav Hai and Rav Shrira Gaon, she is also entitled to her *ketubah* payment, or at least the *ikkar ketubah*. In any event, there is no reason to nullify at the outset any private agreement, which, in practical terms, enables the woman to unilaterally demand a divorce, even though the ramifications of this agreement may be that she is entitled to receive only her *ikkar ketubah*.

[93] *See* Shimon ben Tzemach Duran, Resp. Tashbetz vol. 1 ch. 94 (1998). For a further discussion of this point, see Boaz Cohen, *Conditions in Jewish and Roman Law*, *in* Wolfson Jubilee Volume English Section 203, 222 n.79 (Saul Lieberman ed., 1965). For additional documentation of the monogamy clause in medieval times, see Jose L. Lacave, Medieval Ketubot from Sefarad 134–36 (2002). For a more extensive discussion of the monogamy clause, see Westreich, *supra* note 7.

[94] For another matter in which the Palestinian Talmud's tradition appears to have been more favorable to woman and for a discussion of the ancient egalitarian environment that served as the backdrop to the writing of the Palestinian Talmud's, in some cases going so far as to suggest that a woman could deliver the *get* to the man, see Jackson et al., *supra* note 7, at 65 n.419.

where such mutual stipulations are totally absent.[95] By the same token, the typical Palestinian *ketubah* emphasizes the couple's mutual agreement that they are marrying of their own free will and informed consent, without coercion or duress, as compared to the rigid Babylonian text, where the dominant or perhaps sole contractor is the husband.[96]

It can perhaps be assumed that in light of the Palestinian Talmud's egalitarian point of view, the Palestinian tradition is not content simply with a couple's mutual honor and respect but is actively attempting to mitigate the bitter traditional discrimination against the wife with regard to her inability to initiate the divorce process. In other words, we are not dealing only with a unique theoretical Palestinian tradition that defines marriage as a spousal partnership, but also with the important, practical, and far-reaching ramification of equating the husband's and the wife's right to unilaterally demand a divorce should either of them grow to hate his or her spouse. The dogmatic far-reaching ramifications of this egalitarian Palestinian perspective are obvious, as suggested here:

> The results are (dogmatically, rather than historically) far reaching: a preliminary agreement between the spouses can be a basis for marriage annulment, and the fact that it was done in Erets Israel in the past gives it its legitimization.[97]

Even if one disagrees with the essence of my dogmatic innovation, I still claim that the numerous Cairo *genizah* findings, and Mordecai A. Friedman's compelling proof in his monumental research on Jewish marriage in Palestine,[98] strongly support my basic theme. Friedman's extensive research, cited in this chapter, and the different *ketubot* he deciphered in his book[99] expose us to a rich variety of Palestinian marriage contracts[100] from which we can infer that we are indeed

[95] As has been pointed out by several scholars, such as Friedman, *supra* note 62, at 148; FRIEDMAN, *supra* note 23, at 189–91; Ze'ev W. Falk, *Mutual Obligations in the Ketubah*, 8 JOURNAL OF JEWISH STUDIES 215 (1957).

[96] For a discussion of this point, see what Mordechai A. Friedman's writes in his research on the relationship between the Palestinian and Karaite *ketubot*. *See* Friedman, *supra* note 62, at 148; Rabinovitz, *supra* note 24, at 458–59; FRIEDMAN, POLYGYNY, *supra* note 23, at 52–3; FRIEDMAN, *supra* note 23, at 63. For an overview of the *ketubah* stipulations that were added to the Palestinian *ketubot*, which were already found in the Palestinian Talmud, see Rabinovitz, *supra* note 24, at 460.

[97] *See* WESTREICH, *supra* note 70, at 38. *See also* Avishalom Westreich, *Divorce on Demand: The History, Dogmatics, and Hermeneutics of the Wife's Right to Divorce in Jewish Law*, 62 J. JEWISH STUD. 340, 360–63 (2011). *See also* JACKSON ET AL., *supra* note 7, at 64 ("In short, even if the clause was used primarily to determine financial consequences, its partnership terminology could certainly fortify the woman's position"), and compare to his discussion of the usage of partnership terminology in post-Talmudic *ketubot*, see JACKSON ET AL., *supra* note 7, at 70.

[98] *See* FRIEDMAN, *supra* note 23, at 312–46; ibid, *Divorce upon the Wife's Demand as Reflected in Manuscripts from the Cairo Geniza*, 4 JEWISH L. ANNUAL 103 (1981).

[99] *See* a list of research by FRIEDMAN in *supra* note 23.

[100] *See also* WESTREICH, *supra* note 70, at 30–31 ("It appears therefore that the divorce clause in the Palestinian *ketubbot* was written as part of a general custom in the Land of Israel, according to which court stipulations were frequently written, even though they were not strictly required.

dealing with the important and innovative ability of a woman to demand a divorce, even if it is "only" because she has grown to hate her husband, without her providing any objective reasons for the divorce.[101]

CONCLUSION

In this chapter I attempted to shed light on the dispositive aspects of Talmudic Jewish family law, aspects that have never been established as *halakhah* in the authoritative halakhic codices. The essence of the discussion focused on the broad scope of aspects in family law that may be subject to stipulation according to the unique attitude of the Palestinian Talmud. I tried to provide convincing evidence that we are dealing with a coherent and systematic Palestinian approach to the freedom of contract at a couple's disposal and not with random discussions regarding one particular element or another of the spousal obligations of a Jewish marriage. In my opinion, the discussion demonstrates the essential difference between the Babylonian and Palestinian Talmuds on this issue: in the former, freedom of contract, if it exists at all, is highly restricted, whereas in the latter, it is broader and far more flexible. Whatever the dogmatic explanations for this difference, ancient Jewish history has shown us that a variety of stipulations were indeed incorporated into the Palestinian marriage contracts. In stark contrast to them, the wording of the Babylonian *ketubot* quickly became rigid, fixed, and unchangeable, rejecting any private and nonstandard additions and stipulations.

To conclude this chapter, I wish to quote the most recent, comprehensive, and thorough scholarly conclusion on this issue:

> This accords the Yerushalmi an enormous dogmatic weight: it confirms in this very context that customs and norms lacking a normative basis in the Babylonian Talmud can be justified on the basis of the Yerushalmi. And if such traditions were still relevant for the *Rishonim*, even centuries after their actual use, the posqim of our time too may consider what dogmatic weight should be given to such solutions.[102]

Perhaps the increasing civil interest in prenuptial agreements will kindle a corresponding interest in the dispositive elements of halakhic family law and revive the

This assumption is supported by the fact that some Palestinian *ketubbot* mention only the existence of the divorce stipulation without its details").

[101] A similar stipulation is documented in the *ketubah* found in Sefer Ha-Shetarot Le-Rav Hai Gaon, *supra* note 71, at 56. The eligibility of a woman to unilaterally initiate a divorce has been discussed extensively in the research literature, see the various articles listed in Chapter 4 of this book, n.8. *See also* Katzoff & Greenfield, *supra* note 85; Friedman, *supra* note 23, at 318–416; ibid, *Termination of Marriage upon the Wife's Request*: *A Palestinian Ketubba Stipulation*, 37 PAAJAR 29 (1969); Reuven Yaron, The Law of the Elephantine Documents 67–81 (1968) (Heb.); Bezalel Porten, Archives from Elephantine 260–62 (1968).

[102] *See* Jackson et al., *supra* note 7, at 69; Westreich, *supra* note 70, at 37.

freedom of contract between couples that once existed in Palestine, as described in this chapter. And even if this discussion cannot influence actual halakhic praxis, I hope that this chapter is of theoretical value, as a contribution to the study of Jewish law. When, if ever, a halakhic discourse will emerge on the appropriate broader freedom of contract to be given to couples who marry according to Jewish law, I hope that the conclusions arrived at in this chapter will form the initial outlines of this urgently needed discussion. But, in the meantime, even though my conclusions are not practical, they should at least serve as a theoretical possible alternative.

3

Is There Really No Conditional Marriage?

INTRODUCTION

In Chapter 2, I explore the greater flexibility regarding different aspects of the Jewish marriage contract (*ketubah*) that existed during the ancient Talmudic era and even for several centuries afterward than was adopted in the authoritative halakhic codices of Maimoniodes and *Shulhan Arukh*. I focused on specific aspects of Jewish spousal life, such as the husband's conjugal obligation to his wife, the amount of the *ketubah* payment, the husband's right to inherit his wife, and the wife's right to initiate divorce. In Chapter 4, I discuss the specific and unique scenario of the temporary marriage for an agreed period of time, which is actually a specific condition stipulated in the marriage contract. In the present chapter, I address the far broader, and thus far more problematic issue of finding a reliable solution to the heart-wrenching situation of the *agunah* (Jewish chained woman) by utilizing the mechanism of a conditional marriage. For those readers who are unfamiliar with this serious problem and the proposed solution, I first briefly discuss the ancient "evidence-based" *agunah* and the modern "halakhic" *agunah*.

The distress of the traditional evidence-based *agunah*, who remained chained to her marriage after her husband's death because halakhically there was insufficient proof, was regarded as a major issue by halakhists. As is extensively explained in Chapter 4, *poskim* (halakhic decisors) have always made every possible effort to alleviate the *agunah*'s plight in view of the grave prohibition against engaging in a sexual relationship with a married woman (*eshet ish*), as well as the acutely problematic possible by-product of *mamzerut*. The never-ending halakhic effort to seek a solution, regarding which the Talmud explicitly states, "[T]he Sages work diligently to solve the problem of the Jewish [chained – Y. M.] women," has been termed "*takanat agunot*."[1] The sages regarded this humane and halakhic problem as

[1] For a discussion of "*takanat agunot*," see BT *Ketubot* 2a; 3b; 5a; 7a. For an explanation of this notion, see Aryeh Cohben, *Giddul's Wife and the Power of the Court: On Talmudic Law*,

seriously as they regarded cases involving capital punishment, and freeing an *agunah* is regarded as equivalent to rebuilding one of the ruins of supernal Jerusalem.[2] The original problem of the evidence-based *agunah* is totally different from the problem of the modern-day halakhic *agunah*. The situation of the latter is far worse, due to the fact that the recalcitrant husband appears before a *beit din* (rabbinical court) that, by law, has the exclusive power to order him to give his wife a *get* but does not have the ability to force him to do so.

The *beit din*'s only recourse is to attempt to convince the husband to obey its verdict. At least in Israel, a *beit din* may impose various civil sanctions on the husband, including imprisonment, but in the final analysis, if the recalcitrant husband still insists on chaining his wife, nothing can really be done about it. For various reasons, the *beit din* hesitates to impose even those sanctions that may cause the husband to change his mind and release his wife.[3] It should be emphasized that the chained woman is not only a local Israeli problem, but also a worldwide, universal Jewish challenge. It is ironic that the root of the problem in Israel is the absence of separation of church and state, while outside of Israel the problem is actually due to the separation of church and state.[4]

In the last few decades, countries throughout the world, including the United States, England, Wales, and Canada, have rendered verdicts[5] and enacted

Gender, Divorce and Exile, 9 S. Cal. Rev. L. & Women's Stud. 197, 216 n.73 (1999–2000); Mark Baker, *The Voice of the Deserted Jewish Woman, 1867–1870*, 2(1) Jewish Social Studies 98, 99 (1995). For a description of this original "evidence-based" *agunah* and the devices for dealing with it, see the following references in Hebrew: Otzer HaPoskim vol. 3–7 ch. 17 (1967); Menachem Elon, The Status of Women: Law and Judgment, Tradition and Transition: The Values of a Jewish and Democratic State 297–313, 340–72 (2005); Yitschak Z. Kahane, Sefer HaAgunot: Osef Mekorot Im Perushim Berruim Veherot (1954); ibid, Methods to Allow an Agunah to Marry (1947).

2 This phrase was apparently first mentioned by Joel Sirkes, Resp. Bayit Chadash HaChadashot ch. 64 (1988), and it is attributed to the *kabbalist* Aryeh Hayon; *see* Yael Levin, *Freeing One Agunah Is Like Rebuilding One of the Ruins of Supernal Jerusalem*, 23 Dine Israel 163 (2005) (Heb.).

3 For a discussion of the capacity of a *beit din* to assist a foreign *agunah* to issue a stay of exit order against her husband while he is visiting Israel, see Moshe Drori, *International Jurisdiction of the Rabbinical Courts in Israel*, 24 Justice 30 (2006).

4 For a review of the roots of the problem in and outside Israel, see Susan Aranoff & Rivka Haut, The Wed-Locked Agunot: Orthodox Jewish Women Chained to Dead Marriages (2015); Susan M. Weiss & Netty C. Gross-Horowitz, Marriage and Divorce in the Jewish State: Israel's Civil War (2013); Irving A. Breitowitz, Between Civil and Religious Law: The Plight of the Agunah in American Society (1993); Michael J. Broyde, Marriage, Divorce, and the Abandoned Wife in Jewish Law: A Conceptual Understanding of the Agunah Problems in America (2001); and more briefly Aviad Hacohen, The Tears of the Oppressed: An Examination of the Agunah Problem: Background and Halakhic Sources 20–22 (2004). For a collection of various sources dealing with this problem, see the website of the International Coalition for *Agunah* Rights at http://icar.org.il.

5 For a survey of these judicial solutions, see the various articles in the English section of 10–11 Dine Israel 7–129 (1981–83).

laws[6] addressing this problem, and other forms of legislation in this regard have been suggested and discussed in Scotland, South Africa, and elsewhere.[7] I am confident that as soon as the rabbinical courts internalize the fact that there is a real and serious halakhic problem that must be resolved, a halakhic solution will be found to this acute humane, civic, and halakhic predicament.[8] Among the halakhic solutions that have been suggested down through the ages[9] are several contractual solutions – most importantly, prenuptial agreements[10] – as

[6] *See*, respectively, N.Y Dom. Rel. Law § 236b, 253 (McKinney 1986); Divorce (Religious Marriages) Act 2002 Chapter 27, www.opsi.gov.uk/acts/acts2002/ukpga_20020027_en_1; (Canadian) Divorce Act 1985 § 21.1; and (Ontario) Family Law Act 1986 §§ 2(4)–(7), 56(5)–(7). Of course, the New York legislation, which is nicknamed "the *get* law," has been hotly debated both in academic and rabbinical circles, such as Lawrence M. Warmflash, *The New York Approach to Enforcing Religious Marriage Contracts: From Avitzur to the Get Statute*, 50 Brook. L. Rev. 229 (1983–84); Tanina Rostain, *Permissible Accommodations of Religion: Reconsidering the New York Get Statute*, 96(5) Yale L.J. 1147 (1987); Gedalia D. Schwartz, *Comments on the New York State "Get Law" – Jewish Law?: Examining Halacha, Jewish Issues and Secular Law* (1994), www.jlaw.com/Articles/get_law1.html; Michael J. Broyde, *Some Thoughts on New York State Regulation of Jewish Marriage: Covenant, Contract or Statute?*, 5 Fam. L. 55 (2011) passim and more extensively ibid; and Chaim Z. Malinowitz, *The 1992 New York Get Law: An Exchange*, 31(3) Tradition 23 (1997).

[7] *See* the proposal in Scotland dated March 16, 2005, regarding "Improving Family Law" § 12 (1999), to adopt the British legislation that enables the court to block any civil divorce in the case where religious divorce did not take place as required. *See also* the South African bill dated November 22, 1996, to add § 5A to the Divorce Act, 1979 (Act No. 70 of 1979).

[8] *See* the insightful remarks by David M. Manish Babad, Resp. Havatzelet Hasharon *Even ha-Ezer* ch. 28 (1931), which were quoted in Mordechai Y. Breisch, Resp. Chelkat Yaakov *Even ha-Ezer* ch. 56 (1951). This responsum was cited also in Pinhas Shifman, *The New Agunah: Religious Divorce in Israel*, 6 Alei Mishpat 27, 28 (2007) (Heb.).

[9] For a survey of the various solutions, see Monique S. Goldberg & Diana Villa, Za'akat Dalot: Halakhic Solutions to the Agunot of Our Time (2006) (Heb.); Bernard S. Jackson et al., Agunah: The Manchester Analysis (2011), http://static1.1.sqspcdn.com/static/f/784513/11612882/1302166384333/BSJ+ARU+Final+v2.pdf?token=RSyrg%2F9cedI5z83pXkaDqfKWoZQ%3D; Avishalom Westreich, Talmud-Based Solutions to the Problem of the Agunah 82 (2012); Melanie Landau, Tradition and Equality in Jewish Marriage: Beyond the Sanctification of Subordination (2012). For an evaluation and critique of the latter, see Gail Labovitz, *Review of Melanie Landau*, Tradition and Equality: Beyond the Sanctification of Subordination, 4(1) Religion & Gender 70 (2014), www.religionandgender.org/articles/abstract/10.18352/rg.9491/; Avishalom Westreich, Tradition and Equality in Jewish Marriage: Beyond the Sanctification of Subordination *by Melanie Landau (review)*, 28 Nashim: A J. Jewish Women's Stud. & Gender Issues 147 (2015), https://muse.jhu.edu/login?auth=0&type=summary&url=/journals/nashim/v028/28.westreich.html, besides the solution of annulment of marriage (*hafka'at kiddushin*), which is discussed *infra* note 57.

[10] *See, e.g.*, Susan M. Weiss, *Sign at Your Own Risk: The RCA Prenuptial May Prejudice the Fairness of Your Future Divorce Settlement*, 6 Cardozo Women's L.J. 49 (1999); The Prenuptial Agreement: Halakhic and Pastoral Considerations (Basil Herring & Kenneth Auman eds., 1996); Irving Breitowitz, *The Plight of the Agunah: A Study in Halacha, Contract, and the First Amendment*, 51 Md. L. Rev. 312 (1992); Michelle Greenberg-Kobrin, *Civil Enforceability of Religious Prenuptial Agreements*, 32 Columbia J.L. & Social Problems 359 (1991); Rachel Levmore, *The Prenuptial Agreement for the Prevention of GET-Refusal*, https://iyim.org.il/wp-content/.../07/Article-The-Prenuptial-Agreement.doc; ibid, *Rabbinic Responses in Favor of Prenuptial Agreements*, 42(1) Tradition 29 (2009); David J. Bleich,

well as partial contractual solutions, such as a mistaken marriage (*kiddushei taut*)[11] and conditional marriage.[12] In the past half decade, there have been halakhic and academic discussions regarding the difference between the latter two solutions[13] as well as the suggestion to combine at least two of the above-mentioned solutions.[14]

A Suggested Antenuptial Agreement: A Proposal in Wake of Avitzur, 7 J. HALACHA & CONTEMPORARY SOC'Y 25 (1984).

11 For a rabbinic discussion, see OTZER HAPOSKIM vol. 13 ch. 39 subpara. 5 (1972). For a scholarly discussion, see HACOHEN, *supra* note 4; Michael J. Broyde, *Error in the Creation of Marriages in Modern Times under Jewish Law*, 22 DINE ISRAEL 39 (English Section) (2003)(BROYDE, *supra* note 4, at appendix B); J. David Bleich, *Survey of Recent Halakhic Periodical Literature: Kiddushei Taut: Annulment as a Solution to the Agunah Problem*, 33 TRADITION 90 (1998); Susan Aranoff, *Two Views of Marriage – Two Views of Women: Reconsidering Tav Lemeitav Tan Du mi-Lemeitav Armelu*, 3 NASHIM 199 (2000); YEHUDAH ABEL, CONFRONTING "IGGUN": A COMBINATION OF THREE POSSIBLE SOLUTIONS TO THE PROBLEM OF THE CHAINED WIFE IN JEWISH LAW 3–33 (2011), http://static1.1.sqspcdn.com/static/f/784513/11612871/1302166030207/Yehudah+Abel+Confronting+%27Iggun+2009.pdf?token=VXB5sjDSEIg7rFUyitCwbQ%2FSYlo%3D. For a review of Hacohen's book, see Michael J. Broyde, *Review Essay: An Unsuccessful Defense of the Bet Din of Rabbi Emanuel Rackman:* The Tears of the Oppressed *by Aviad Hacohen*, THE EDAH JOURNAL 4:2 (2004), www.edah.org/backend/journalarticle/4_2_broyde.pdf; Bernard S. Jackson & Avishalom Westreich, *Book review of Aviad Hacohen, The Tears of the Oppressed, An Examination of the Agunah Problem: Background and Halachic Sources*, 17 JEWISH L. ANNUAL 303 (2007).

12 For rabbinic discussions of conditional marriage in Hebrew, see THE CONSTANTINOPLE BET DIN, KIDDUSHIN AL TENAI (1924); YEHUDAH LUBETSKY, EYN TENAI BENISSUIN (1930); and the series of articles by Zevi Gertner & Bezalel Karlinski, *Eyn Tenai beNissuin*, 8 YESHURUN 678 (2001); ibid, 9 YESHURUN 569 (2001); ibid, 10 YESHURUN 711 (2002). For a critique and evaluation of the approach in this series, see Yehudah Abel, *Comments on "'En Tenai BeNissu'in" by R. Zevi Gertner and R. Bezalel Karlinski* (Working Papers of the Agunah Research Unit, http://static1.1.sqspcdn.com/static/f/784513/11612816/1302165409993/Yehudah+Abel+Comments+by+R.+Zavi+Gertner+2008.pdf?token=KWWAVKlqn5e7bj6MB5UrhV2slUM%3D (ABEL, *supra* note 11, at appendix III, 92–93). For scholarly writing, see ELIEZER BERKOVITS, CONDITIONALITY IN MARRIAGE AND DIVORCE (1967) (Heb.); AVRAHAM C. FREIMAN, SEDER KIDDUSHIN VENISUIN AHAREI HATIMAT HATALMUD 366–94 (1944) (Heb.); MOSHE MEISELMAN, JEWISH WOMAN IN JEWISH LAW 103–09 (1987). For a discussion of the relationship between conditional marriage, coercing the *get*, and annulling the *kiddushin*, see Yehudah Abel, *Hafqa'ah, Kefiyyah, Tena'im* (Working Papers of the Agunah Research Unit, June 2008, http://static1.1.sqspcdn.com/static/f/784513/11612810/1302165339947/Yehudah+Abel+Hafqa%27ah+Kefiyyah+Tena%27im+2008.pdf?token=c6U9xvBnSlpgv6gKGLrXyvv7sao%3D.

13 For a discussion of the halakhic attempt to combine those two solutions, see Tosafot *Bava Kama* 110b, s.v. "*ada'ata*"; Tosafot HaRosh *Ketubot* 47b, s.v. "*shelo*"; and MOSHE FEINSTEIN, RESP. IGGROT MOSHE *Even ha-Ezer* vol. 1 ch. 79–80 (1959); vol. 4 ch. 121. For a discussion of the precise difference between a conditional marriage and mistaken marriage, see Avishalom Westreich, *Umdena as a Ground for Marriage Annulment: Between Mistaken Transaction (Kiddushei Ta'ut) and Terminative Condition*, 20 JEWISH L. ASS'N. STUD. 330 (2010) (Westreich, *supra* note 9, at 78–105).

14 For the most recent rabbinical-academic suggestions for combining the three possible solutions – conditional marriage + annulment + preparing the *get* at the betrothal or alternatively by a delayed *get* – see BERKOVITS, *supra* note 12, as suggested in Yehudah Abel, *The Plight of the Agunah and Conditional Marriage*, 1 MELILAH 31 (2005/1), http://static1.1.sqspcdn.com/static/f/784513/11612748/1302164478633/Yehudah+Abel+Plight+of+the+Agunah+and+Conditional+Mar

In Section 1, I explore the halakhic and meta-halakhic challenges that every conditional marriage must address. In Section 2, I review possible refutations to the claims of *poskim* throughout the generations that there is no conditional marriage, which they base on the Talmudic dictum that any condition imposed on the marriage is contrary to the Written Law and therefore invalid. I also provide support for my claim that in the unique context of conditional marriage, this argument is based more on rhetoric and emotion than on substance and *halakhah*.[15] Such support may be found in the writings of many *rishonim* (early halakhic authorities) and *aharonim* (later halakhic authorities) regarding a condition imposed in the marriage contract exempting the wife from the obligation of a levirate marriage (*halitzah*) should her husband die childless and his brother have leprosy (*mukkeh shehin*). This condition is halakhically valid and is not regarded as contrary to the Written Law. In Section 3, I review the original force and scope of the Talmudic dictum that there is no conditional marriage in order to attempt to prove – as has already been argued by some *rishonim* – that on the contrary, any Jewish marriage actually is a conditional marriage.

Following this, I explore the innovation of the author of *Trumat Hadeshen* and other *aharonim* that now that the *kiddushin* (betrothal) and *nissuin* (marriage) ceremonies have merged into one wedding ceremony, any agreed-upon stipulation imposed in the *kiddushin* contract (*kiddushin ketubah*) is actually a conditional marriage and is regarded as if it were imposed in the *nissuin* contract (*ketubah*). In Section 4, I provide examples from the Tannaitic and Amoraic literature of conditions that are imposed in the betrothal contract, some of which actually constitute a conditional marriage. Thus, we have reliable ancient historical and halakhic precedents that can serve as the backdrop and basis for the proposed contemporary halakhic conditional marriage, as a solution to the *agunah* problem. In Section 5, I conclude with the argument that theoretically, a conditional marriage is halakhically feasible, but in practice (*halakhah lemaaseh*), for various halakhic reasons, today's *poskim* are reluctant to adopt this important potential solution.

riage+2008.pdf?token=lJWm300NvHYcu700bTyw07mN668%3D (hereinafter Abel, *The Plight*); Michael J. Broyde, A *Proposed Tripartite Prenuptial Agreement to Solve the Agunah Problem: A Solution without Any Innovation*, 20 Jewish L. Ass'n Stud. 1 (2010). For an evaluation of Broyde's proposal, see Yehudah Abel, *Comments on R. Broyde's Tripartite Agreement* (Working Papers of the Agunah Research Unit, July 2009), http://static1.1.sqspcdn.com/static/f/784513/11612873/1302166102187/Yehudah+Abel+Comment+on+Dayan+Broyde%27s+Tripartite+Agreement+2009.pdf?token=KQ9J2S4rDIS%2FomB8Q2HZAygf2xs%3D; Jackson et al., *supra* note 9, passim. For the proposed Manchester combined solution, see Jackson et al., *supra* note 9, at 195–211 (conditional marriage + annulment + *kefiyat get*); Avishalom Westreich, No-Fault Divorce in Jewish Tradition 94–95 (2014) (Heb.) (*kefiyat get* + annulment), http://www.idi.org.il/media/4563/the_right_to_divorce.pdf.

15 For a discussion of a similar claim that the arguments against conditional marriage are emotional in nature, see Westreich, *supra* note 9, at 78.

1 THE HALAKHIC PROBLEMS OF A CONDITIONAL MARRIAGE

1.1 *Problems That Are Purely Halakhic*

In Judaism, unlike the other monotheistic religions, divorce is not a constitutive judicial decree adjudicated by a judge or a religious authority that ends a marriage. According to Torah law, a divorce depends entirely on the willingness of the husband to give his wife a *get*. All that remains for the rabbinical court is to oversee the husband handing the bill of divorce to his wife.[16] If the husband does not hand the *get* to his wife of his own free will and with his informed consent, there is no judicial decree that can effect the couple's divorce. This basic, traditional framework originates in the account of the biblical act of divorce described in Deuteronomy 24:1, with the husband the active party and the wife passive: "A man takes a wife and possesses her. She fails to please him because he finds something obnoxious about her, and he writes her a bill of divorcement, hands it to her, and sends her away from his house."[17]

This framework is also deeply rooted in Tannaitic sources, which require a *get* from the husband as one of two sole means by which a woman is released from her marriage. The conclusion of a halakhic *midrash* on Deuteronomy 24:1 states, "to teach that he [the husband – Y. M.] divorces her only of his own free will, but the woman is divorced with her consent or against her will."[18] This is the exact meaning of the Mishnah in *Kiddushin* 1:1, which plainly posits that "A woman ... acquires her freedom in two [ways – Y. M.] ... she acquires her freedom by divorce or by her husband's death."[19] It is also reflected in some of the Talmudic discussions (*sugyot*). For example, there is a rhetorical question in the Babylonian Talmud, "Be thou my wife today but tomorrow thou are no longer my wife, can she get out without a *get*?" In addition, the Palestinian Talmud states explicitly,

> R. Abbahu in the name of R. Johanan: "This shall be an elevation sacrifice for thirty days," it is elevation sacrifice for thirty days; after thirty days it automatically becomes profane ... "You are preliminarily married to me for thirty days," she is preliminarily married. What is the difference between dedication and a woman? We find that a dedication can be eliminated without redemption but we do not find that a woman could leave without a divorce document.[20]

In other words, even according to Amoraic views – such as that of R. Johanan in the above passage and of Abaye and Ulla in the parallel Talmudic discussions – intrinsic sanctity, such as that of sacred property (*hekdesh*), may terminate automatically,

[16] *See* Benzion Schereschewsky, Family Law in Israel 279–81 (4th ed., 1993) (Heb.).
[17] The New JPS Translation ad loc (2d ed., 1999).
[18] *See also* Mishnah *Yevamot* 14:1; Maimonides, Laws of Divorce, 1:1–2.
[19] *See*, respectively, BT *Kiddushin* 13a; PT *Kiddushin* 1:1 (58a).
[20] *See*, respectively, BT *Yevamot* 88b; PT *Kiddushin* 3:1 (32a).

without the need for any halakhic act. However, the annulment of the spousal relationship (*zikat ishut*) of a Jewish married woman is possible in only two ways – by receiving a bill of divorce from her husband or upon his death. In view of these Talmudic rulings, the *halakhah* unequivocally determines that a *get* is needed to dissolve a marriage.

Therefore, it appears that there is no other way to dissolve this relationship, including by means of an explicit stipulation in the marriage contract that terminates the marriage, without necessitating a bill of divorce. If there is no halakhic possibility of ending the spousal relationship (*zikat ishut*) by means of a condition imposed in the *kiddushin* ceremony, there is even less of a possibility to do so when the couple is already married once the *nissuin* ceremony has been conducted. In the *kiddushin* ceremony, the woman halakhically acquires the status of a married woman as regards the prohibitions involved and is prohibited from having a sexual relationship with all other men. Yet, it is only in the *nissuin* ceremony that she officially becomes a wife for all intents and purposes, including all the rights that it entails.

For the purposes of our discussion, it should be noted that when a couple marry and engage in a conjugal relationship and a financial and emotional partnership, applying a stipulation that was imposed in the *kiddushin* and *nissuin* ceremonies becomes far more problematic. This is because of the halakhic maxim that "*Eyn adam oseh beilato beilat zenut*" ("no one wishes to make his intercourse with a woman one of prostitution"). Thus, even if an explicit condition is attached to both the *kiddushin* and the *nissuin* contracts that the marriage will be annulled following fulfillment of that condition, thus terminating the marriage without a divorce document, there is still substantive halakhic concern that prevents us from relying on it and releasing the wife without a *get*.

This is due to the fondness regarding the sexual act, which causes the husband to abandon his terminative condition with the intention of leading a full spousal and conjugal life with his wife, rather than having a conditional and unstable marriage that may render their sexual act one of prostitution (*zenut*).[21] That is why there are a variety of explicit statements in the Babylonian Talmud that, *prima facie*, reject from the outset any attempt to impose an explicit condition, either in the *kiddushin* or in the *nissuin* contracts, that will annul the marriage. Such statements include "there is no conditional marriage" and "there is no condition in the [wedding] canopy" (no stipulation is attachable to marriage).[22] These principles apply not only to a unilateral condition by one of the parties, but also to a condition mutually agreed upon by the couple.

[21] For a summary of the halakhic aspects of this axiom, see Talmudic Encyclopedia vol. 1, 653–61 (Shlomo Zevin et al. eds., 1978). This is one of the central pitfalls of any conditional marriage, as is explained in depth in the text at *infra* note 142.

[22] Such as BT *Yevamot* 107a. This principle came up indirectly also in the discussion in BT *Yevamot* 94b. The extent to which this principle was regarded as axiomatic and immutable may be seen in some of the responsa of the *aharonim*, such as Lubetsky, *supra* note 12, at 14.

The bitterest opponents of any type of conditional marriage were Yehoshua Boaz (c. 1518–57, Talmudist, Sabbioneta-Savigliano, Italy), author of Shiltey HaGibborim – a commentary on the compendium of *halakhot* by Yizhak Ben Yaakov Alfasi (Rif) of various tractates of the Babylonian Talmud – and his teacher, Yeshayah Aharon of Trani (Riaz) (died c. 1280, Italian Talmudist).[23] Both maintained that even when the groom explicitly stipulates that he is marrying the bride in accordance with his terminative stipulation, the condition is void and the marriage is valid since "*Eyn adam oseh beilato beilat zenut.*"[24] This stringent approach was taken for granted by some prominent *poskim*, such as Samuel ben Uri Shraga Phoebus (died 1706, Polish rabbi and Talmudist, Woydyslaw, Poland), author of the commentary *Beit Shmuel* on *Shulhan Arukh, Even ha-Ezer.*[25] According to the stringent opinions, even if the groom firmly insists on maintaining the initial condition imposed in the marriage contract, it is presumed that this is not his true intention and that in practice he renounces it in the course of his spousal and conjugal life, in view of the basic nonnegotiable halakhic principle that "no one wishes to make his intercourse with a woman one of prostitution."

1.2 *Problems That Are Meta-Halakhic*

Beyond the halakhic necessity for a *get* in order to annul the marriage, a conditional marriage may encounter halakhic obstacles that are not purely halakhic, but that, in my opinion, are of a more meta-halakhic nature.[26] From discussions of *poskim* concerning the meaning of the Talmudic maxim that there is no conditional marriage, it can be inferred that the Jewish marriage is intended to be permanent and not temporary, and therefore not subject to stipulation and certainly not annulled without the need for a *get*. Thus, it is not surprising that in the heat of the halakhic debate against conditional marriage, the discussions and reasons turned to considerations that were non-halakhic, in the guise of *halakhah*.

The emphasis was on the general concern that, given the challenges of modern times, imposing any condition in the marriage contract could undermine the sanctity of this unique Jewish institution. Many rabbis and scholars have already concluded that the vast majority of the arguments against the possible halakhic

[23] For a discussion of his stringent approach and for Berkovits's refutation of it, see *supra* note 12; Abel, *supra* note 11, at 20–24, 91. *See also* Jackson et al., *supra* note 9, at 24, 48, 61, 84, 176.

[24] *See* Jackson et al., *supra* note 9, at 23–26, 84, 177–78, 202; Abel, *supra* note 11, at 22–23.

[25] The source of this stringent attitude is in the commentary Shiltey HaGibborim on Rif, *Ketubot* 74a. *See also* Danishevsky's harsh words to the French rabbis in Lubetsky, *supra* note 12, at 18.

[26] The issue of meta-*halakhah* has been discussed extensively in recent years. For the specific way it is used in the subject under discussion, see Westreich, *supra* note 9, at 78 ("The use of terminative conditions as a possible solution to the *agunah* problem is no less discussed and no less accompanied by halakhic and meta-halakhic debate"); Abel, *supra* note 11, at appendix IV, 104 ("It is their consideration of the halakhic and meta-halakhic issues that we need and without it nothing can be done."); and more broadly in the *agunah* context, see Jackson et al., *supra* note 9, at 7, 49, 147, 167–74, 196, 205–06.

solution of a conditional marriage involve meta-halakhic concerns and not purely halakhic pitfalls. Nevertheless, according to Yosef Glicksberg (1933–, Chief Rabbi of Givatayim, Israel), there are indeed two major problems that are purely halakhic – that there is no conditional marriage and that "whoever makes a stipulation that is contrary to what is written in the Torah, his stipulation is null and void."[27]

But in my opinion, even the first and most ancient opposition to conditional marriage – that it is contrary to Torah law – is more of a meta-halakhic issue than a purely halakhic one. A pronounced attempt to turn a meta-halakhic concern into a purely halakhic argument can be found in the writings of several *poskim* who use the general claim that any stipulation imposed in the marriage contract is void because it is contrary to Torah law. This is based on the oft-repeated Talmudic statement that "whoever makes a stipulation that is contrary to what is written in the Torah, his stipulation is null and void." Thus, for example, in his commentary Beit Meir on *Shulhan Arukh*,[28] Meir Posner (1725–1807, rabbi, Danzig) brings an argument that revolves around an innovation of Shlomo ben Avraham ben Aderet (Rashba – 1235–1310, medieval halakhist and Talmudist, rabbi of the main synagogue of Barcelona) in his novellae to the Talmud: if a bride and groom explicitly stipulate during the marriage ceremony that the marriage will be a temporary one, they have an equal right to end the marriage.

Thus, the sweeping statement in the Talmud that a wife can never initiate divorce appears to be incorrect.[29] To summarize Rashba's unique approach, it is possible to impose an explicit stipulation both in the *kiddushin* and in the *nissuin* contracts. This is not regarded as contrary to what is written in the Torah, and thus, the condition is valid. Moreover, if the terminative condition is not used, both the *kiddushin* and the *nissuin* remain intact; otherwise, both are annulled. However, the

[27] *See*, respectively, Yosef Glicksberg, *Conditional Marriage*, 12 TORAH SHE-BE'ALPE 134, 134 (1970) (Heb.); Ariel Picard, *The Proposal of Rabbi Uzziel for Resolving the Agunah Problem*, in RABBI UZZIEL AND HIS PEERS: STUDIES IN THE RELIGIOUS THOUGHT OF ORIENTAL RABBIS TWENTIETH-CENTURY ISRAEL 230 (Zvi Zohar ed., 2009) (Heb.). For a summary of the ethical and policy-driven arguments, such as undermining the sanctity of Jewish marriage, "wife-swapping," thinking of divorce at the time of marriage, and the halakhic arguments as well as the practical considerations of the conditional marriage, see ABEL, *supra* note 11, at 6–38.

[28] Meir Posner, Beit Meir, *Even ha-Ezer* 38 subpara. 1 (2007). Similarly, Lubetsky and Danishevsky presented this argument several times in their letters; *see* LUBETSKY, *supra* note 12, at 8, 36. For a discussion of additional rabbinic opinions that agree with the argument in this pamphlet and for an attempt to refute it, see JACKSON ET AL., *supra* note 9, at 65, and more extensively Abel, *The Plight*, *supra* note 14, at 23–25 (ABEL, *supra* note 11, at 29–32). The argument that such condition is contrary to what is written in the Torah was presented in the Rabbinical Court 1064/1954, 1501/1954, Anonymous v. Anonymous, 1 PDR 257, 259 (11.01.55) by a husband who claimed that before the wedding his wife had promised him that their marriage would be a temporary one and she would accept a bill of divorce from him even if it were only a few months after the wedding took place.

[29] SHLOMO BEN AVRAHAM BEN ADERET, NOVELLAE TO GITTIN TRACTATE 84a, s.v. "*ato bedidah*" (1981). *See also* ABEL, *supra* note 11, at 30–31, 55, 61, 66, 73. For a broader discussion of a woman's right to initiate a divorce, see the various references listed in Chapter 4 of this book, n.8.

author of Beit Meir regards the incorporation of such a stipulation in the wedding ceremony as a purely halakhic problem, as it is contrary to what is written in the Torah. This is because it is an axiomatic principle of the Written Law that the only device for releasing a married woman from the marital bond during her husband's lifetime is by the husband giving her a *get*, only should he so desire, and therefore any stipulation in this regard is rejected from the outset.[30]

2 NOT EVERY CONDITIONAL MARRIAGE IS CONTRARY TO WHAT IS WRITTEN IN THE TORAH

Contemporary scholars such as Eliezer Berkovits (1908–92, rabbi, theologian, and educator, Nagyvárad, Austria-Hungary–Jerusalem) and Yehudah Abel (rabbi, PhD, research fellow – Agunah Research Unit, University of Manchester, U.K.) have remarked, correctly in my opinion, that the author of Beit Meir was presenting a possible rather than a definitive opinion. He was not defiantly rejecting Rashba's approach. Nevertheless, opponents of a conditional marriage have repeatedly cited the opinion of the author of Beit Meir as if it were a categorical statement and a practical halakhic ruling (*halakhah lemaaseh*), despite the fact that his view is contrary to Rashba's explicit ruling. Moreover, in doing so, the opponents of a conditional marriage also had to force the straightforward meaning of Rashba's words in order for it to be consistent with the opinion in Beit Meir.

As Abel writes, "Nevertheless, some rabbis quoted in ETB (*Eyn Tnai BeNissu'in* [*There is No Conditional Marriage*]) took up the suggestion of the Bet Meir and tried to explain the words of Rashba in such a way that they should not contradict the suggestion of the Bet Meir."[31] In my opinion, there is no halakhic basis to the claim in Beit Meir, since the principle that "whoever makes a stipulation that is contrary to what is written in the Torah" applies only when the condition will definitely uproot what is written in the Torah. But, in the issue under discussion, there is no certainty at the time of the wedding ceremony that the terminative condition will be used and that there will be any need to annul the marriage, and thus, nothing here is contrary to what is written in the Torah.[32] Support for my claim may be found in the Babylonian Talmud, *Gittin* 84b:

[30] For an explanation of the acute need for receiving a bill of divorce from the husband because it is a biblical obligation, see the COMMENTARY OF AVRAHAM MIN HAHAR ON TRACTATE NEDARIM 29*a*, s.v. "alma pakaa" (1962).

[31] *See*, respectively, BERKOVITS, *supra* note 12, at 87–88; Abel, *The Plight*, *supra* note 14, at 24 (ABEL, *supra* note 11, at 31). *See also* LUBETSKY, *supra* note 12, at 30.

[32] For a discussion of this central halakhic principle, see JACKSON ET AL., *supra* note 9, at 73–74, and more broadly in the following sources in Hebrew: Nahum Rakover, *Coercive Marital Relations between a Man and His Wife*, 6–7 SHNATON HA-MISHPAT HA-IVRI 295 (1979–80); BERACHYAHU LIFSHITZ, PROMISE: OBLIGATION AND ACQUISITION IN JEWISH LAW 176–85 (1998); YEHEZKEL MARGALIT, PUBLIC REGULATION AND PRIVATE AGREEMENT OF SPOUSAL CONJUGAL PRIVILEGES IN JEWISH LAW 81–89 (LLM thesis Bar-Ilan University, Faculty of Law, 2006) and more briefly in the previous chapters of this book.

> Rav Adda the son of Rav Ika replied: When we say that where a stipulation is made to break an injunction laid down in the Torah the condition is void, we refer for instance to a stipulation to withhold the food, raiment and marriage duty [of a married woman], where it is the man who nullifies the injunction ... where he is unquestionably nullifying [the injunction].

This Talmudic discussion was adopted as a practical principle by Rabbeinu Asher (Rosh – 1250/1259–1327, rabbi and Talmudist, Cologne, the Holy Roman Empire Toledo). According to him, if at the time of the wedding it is not certain that the condition will be used, then the condition is not regarded as contrary to what is written in the Torah.[33] Moreover, even as regards the essence of the argument, various *aharonim* have rejected the opinion in Beit Meir that in these circumstances a terminative condition is contrary to what is written in the Torah.[34]

According to these *poskim*, when a groom intentionally and of his own free will imposes a terminative condition both in the *kiddushin* and in the *nissuin* that his wife will be released from the marriage following a mutually agreed-upon condition, this condition is valid and their marriage can be dissolved. This is so even if he is reluctant at the time of the divorce ceremony to fulfill his initial agreement, as his present reluctance does not contradict what is written in the Torah. The reason is that this man intentionally and willingly restricted and obligated himself by agreeing to divorce his wife under certain agreed-upon circumstances. Therefore, even if at the moment of the divorce he wishes to withdraw from his initial obligation, he is nevertheless regarded as someone who is acting according to his initial free will and is divorcing his wife of his own volition.[35]

2.1 *Conditional Marriage – Annulment of the Marriage in the Case of Subjection to a Levirate Marriage*

From the end of the era of the *rishonim* – approximately the fifteenth to sixteenth centuries – there were numerous *poskim* who have maintained that it is possible to

[33] *See* Rabbeinu Asher, Resp. Rosh rule 33 ch. 1 (1954). This basic ruling was applied later on by numerous *poskim*, such as Yosef Hazan, Resp. Hikrey Lev *Even ha-Ezer* vol. 7 ch. 58, pp. 438, 440 (1998); Chaim Ben Izhak Or Zarua, Resp. Maharah Or Zarua ch. 41 (1960); Eliyahu Ben Avraham Mizrahi, Resp. Mayim Amukim vol. 2 ch. 59, s.v. "*omnam*" (1970); ibid, ch. 71, s.v. "*tshuva*"; Aaron ben Yosef Sasson, Resp. Torat Emet ch. 64, s.v. "*beinyan*" (2006).

[34] *See*, respectively, Aryeh Heller, Avnei Miluim *Hilkhot Ishut* ch. 38 subpara. 24 (1995); Avraham Y. Karelitz, Hazon Ish Nashim Hilkhot Kiddushin ch. 56 subpara. 20 (1968). *See also* more extensively Menashe Ben Eliezer Klein, Resp. Mishne Halakhot vol. 4 ch. 191 (1970). For a discussion of a similar argument, see Abel, *The Plight*, *supra* note 14, at 24–25 (Abel, *supra* note 11, at 31).

[35] A similar conclusion was arrived at by the following *aharonim*: David Friedman of Karlin, Piskei Halakhot *Hilkhot Ishut* vol. 2 letter 28 n.198 (1971); Judah L. Graubart, Resp. Havalim Baneimim vol. 2 ch. 79 (1975); Mordechai Z. Etinger, Resp. Maamar Mordechai ch. 24 (1968).

impose an explicit terminative condition in both the *kiddushin* and the *nissuin* contracts in order to prevent a woman from becoming subject to a levirate marriage. This terminative condition would retroactively annul her marriage to her late husband, so that she is no longer regarded as his legal widow, and thus there is no need for the levirate ceremony. This is actually the essence of the innovation of Mahari Bruna, which is explained in depth in the next chapter.[36]

According to Mahari Bruna's ruling, this terminative condition is not contrary to what is written in the Torah – despite the fact that, on the surface, it makes it possible also to impose a stipulation in the marriage contract that will release the wife from her recalcitrant husband – and the widow may be released without any need to fulfill what is explicitly written in the Torah, the obligation of either *halizah* or *yibbum*.[37] *Rishonim* as well as *aharonim* have invested enormous effort to explain why this sort of terminative condition is not a stipulation that is contrary to what is written in the Torah. Their explanation is that stipulating against what is written in the Torah is problematic only when the stipulation will, for unrighteous reasons, uproot an obligation that is explicitly articulated in the Torah, but when the stipulation is made for righteous reasons, the condition is valid.[38]

Since Mahari Bruna's condition is imposed in the wedding ceremony in order to prevent an apostate brother from convincing the widow to convert, this stipulation is not contrary to what is written in the Torah.[39] Any stipulation that stipulates against what is written in the Torah is void, since we assume that it was not someone's real intention to break a Torah law; however, in the situation of the levir, the stipulation was imposed explicitly for the sake of the bride and not the groom and therefore should not be nullified. According to Yonathan Aiibishitz (1690–1764, Polish rabbi and Talmudist, Prague), such a stipulation is not contrary to the Torah by virtue of the fact that when the condition is imposed, there is no certainty that it will be applied, as the wife might have offspring or the husband might divorce her before she becomes subject to *halizah*.[40] Other *aharonim* have raised other reasons why this condition might not be fulfilled, such as the possibility that the apostate brother dies before she or her husband

[36] *See* JACKSON ET AL., *supra* note 9, at 60, 71–73, 82, 85, 89–91, 176, 179, 194; ABEL, *supra* note 11, at 4, 12–20, 24–25, 29–34, 98; Westreich, *supra* note 13, at 339–41 (Westreich, *supra* note 9, at 90–92).

[37] For this halakhic determination, see YEHIEL M. EPSTEIN, ARUKH HASHULHAN *Even ha-Ezer* 157:14 (2007). For a summary of this point, see BERKOVITS, *supra* note 12, at 46–49, 68–71.

[38] YONATHAN AIIBISHITZ, BNEI AHUVA *Hilkhot Yibbum* ch. 1 (1965); HAZAN, *supra* note 33, at ch. 58.

[39] *See* ARYEH L. BEN ISAAC HOROWITZ, RESP. HAREI BESAMIM vol. 2 ch. 233 (1984). For a complete review of these responsa, see Nisan Zaksh, *Conditional Marriage*, 1 NOAM 52, 54–55 (1958) (Heb.).

[40] *See* the responsum at the end of the book by AIIBISHITZ, *supra* note 38. Danishevsky wrote similarly to the French rabbis; *see* LUBETSKY, *supra* note 12, at 18.

dies, in which case she would be exempt from marrying him and therefore a conditional marriage of this type should be permitted.[41]

It should be noted that various halakhic authorities have stated explicitly that Mahari Bruna's stipulation is a unique exception to the general halakhic principle that there is no conditional marriage, an exception that has even been codified as *halakhah* in the authoritative halakhic codices.[42] According to them, the all-inclusive Talmudic maxim that there is no conditional marriage applies only to the case of releasing a wife from the bonds of marriage during the husband's lifetime based on the condition imposed in the marriage contract. But this basic principle does not apply to a stipulation that upon the husband's death, the wife is released without being subject to *halizah* or *yibbum*.[43] I now present a more general discussion of the Talmudic dictum that there is no conditional marriage, its limitations as interpreted by different *rishonim*, and the claim that, ironically, all Jewish marriage ceremonies are actually conditional.

3 THERE IS CONDITIONAL MARRIAGE(!)

3.1 *The Straightforward Meaning of "There Is No Conditional Marriage"*

Opponents of imposing a terminative stipulation in the marriage contract as a possible solution to the *agunah* problem have made determined broad use of the halakhic principle that "there is no conditional marriage" and "there is no condition in the [wedding] canopy." This is clearly reflected in the title of the famous pamphlet *Eyn Tenai BeNissuin* that was published in 1930 to block the attempt of the Constantinople rabbinical court to put into practice the device of a terminative stipulation.[44] However, there are numerous *rishonim* who maintain that this is not an absolute and unchangeable halakhic principle but only an optional one. The Tosafists were the first to hold this view.

[41] *See* Zaksh, *supra* note 39, at 56 in the names of the author of Noda Beyhudah and Ben-Zion M. Uziel. For a refutation of this claim, see Zvi Makovsky, Resp. Yehave Daat ch. 17 (1935), who rejected the possibility of applying to this unique stipulation the principle "whoever makes a stipulation which is contrary to what is written in the Torah, his stipulation is null and void." *See also* Rahamim Y. Franko, Resp. Shaarei Shamayim *Even ha-Ezer* vol. 2 ch. 37 (1881), who dealt at length with the question of whether this stipulation is contrary to what is written in the Torah and concluded that it is not.

[42] Moshe Isserlish (Rema), *Shulhan Arukh, Even ha-Ezer* 157:4. This stipulation was brought earlier by Isserlish in his commentary to *Tur, Darkei Moshe, Even ha-Ezer* 157:5. Ehrenberg claims that the majority of prominent later halakhic authorities (*gedoley hador*) agree that there is indeed conditional marriage but only when the marriage is annulled upon the husband's death, see Yehoshua Ehrenberg, *Conditional Marriage*, 1 Noam 75, 103 (1958) (Heb.).

[43] For a discussion of the difference between these two stipulations, see, e.g., Moshe Ben Shmuel Sofer, Resp. Hatam Sofer (*Even ha-Ezer* 2) vol. 4 ch. 68 (1970); Berkovits, *supra* note 12, at 13–15.

[44] For the application of this claim, which was argued repeatedly in the pamphlet, see the letters of Lubetsky, Rabinowitz, and Epstein. *See*, respectively, Lubetsky, *supra* note 12, at 8, 24. *See also* the discussion of it by Abel, *supra* note 11, at 32–33.

In several places in the Babylonian Talmud, the Tosafists explain that the principle does not mean that attaching a condition in the marriage contract is absolutely invalid, but rather, that it was not the common practice to do so, as people tended to forego it in order to avoid the possibility of engaging in illicit intercourse. Thus, this principle is not a normative halakhic axiom but simply reflects changing social norms.[45] Similarly, based on the Tosafists' explanation, some *aharonim* maintain that this Talmudic dictum applies only *a priori* (*lehatkhila*) when there is no agreed-upon explicit stipulation in the marriage contract. But, if it is known that the groom imposed an explicit condition, then the condition is valid, since there is indeed conditional marriage.[46]

Moreover, Yehezkel ben Yehudah Landau (1713–93, rabbi and Talmudist, Opatów, Poland-Prague) even castigated a student of his who asked him how he could support imposing a condition in the marriage contract, since there is no conditional marriage.[47] Likewise, Yehiel M. Epstein (1829–1908, rabbi and *posek*, Babruysk, Russian Empire-Navahrudak) adopted this lenient approach in his halakhic code, *Arukh Hashulhan*, as a practical halakhic device and explained at length how it could be implemented (*halakhah lemaaseh*).[48] On the basis of his opinion, one may deduce that this principle, which, *prima facie*, prohibits any attempt to impose an explicit condition in the marriage contract, is a relative rather than an absolute principle. In other words, if the couple agrees in the wedding ceremony that their marriage is a conditional one, then it is indeed a conditional marriage, the stipulation is valid, and the marriage status is annulled upon the fulfillment of the condition. It should be emphasized that this halakhic innovation has even been put into practice by some *poskim*.

3.2 *Today, Any Condition in the Kiddushin Contract Applies Also to the Nissuin Contract*

Several *poskim* have presented a nuanced but very important argument that in the modern era, with the combining of the *kiddushin* and *nissuin* ceremonies under the wedding canopy, any condition imposed in the *kiddushin* contract is actually imposed also in the *nissuin* contract. In the Mishnaic and Talmudic periods, these two ceremonies were separated, and in the case of a virgin, there was even a one-year interval between the ceremonies in order to give the bride sufficient time to prepare

[45] *Yevamot* 107a, s.v. "*Bet Shammai*" and compare with *Ketubot* 73a, s.v. "*lo tema*." It was cited and discussed by many *aharonim*, such as Danishevsky in Lubetsky, *supra* note 12, at 34. For a discussion of this important innovation, see Jackson et al., *supra* note 9, at 60; Abel, *supra* note 11, at 36; Westreich, *supra* note 13, at 334 n.15 (Westreich, *supra* note 9, at 90–92).

[46] *See*, *inter alia*, David Ben Haim, Resp. Radakh ch. 9 (2008). This *aharonim's* unique approach is cited and discussed by Chaim Benbenishti, Knesset ha-Gedolah *Tur Even ha-Ezer*, ch. 157 gloss Beit Yosef letter 18 (1961); Ovadia Hadaya, Resp. Yaskil Avdi *Even ha-Ezer* vol. 3 ch. 6 (1931).

[47] *See* Yehezkel ben Yehuda Landau, Resp. Noda Beyhudah 1st ed. *Even ha-Ezer*, ch. 56 (1880).

[48] Yehiel M. Epstein, Arukh Hashulhan *Even ha-Ezer* 157:14 (2007). Other *poskim* have followed this lenient approach; *see* Berkovits, *supra* note 12, at 40–45.

herself for her marriage. If the bride was a widow or a divorcee, this period was much shorter – only one month.[49]

In the post-Talmudic era, the time interval between the two ceremonies led to some serious problems[50] because after the *kiddushin* ceremony, the bride's status was (almost) that of a married woman, but only as regards her obligations and not her rights. Moreover, she did not enter the groom's house until after the wedding ceremony, and if the couple wished to end the relationship before the wedding ceremony took place, the bride had to receive a bill of divorce, as in the case of a married woman. Therefore, at the beginning of the twelfth century, various enactments combined those two ceremonies into a single ceremony under the wedding canopy. By the sixteenth century, this had become the accepted norm among most Jewish ethnic groups, with the exception of several Oriental sects that still separate them even today.[51]

Thus, since the common practice today is a single combined ceremony that incorporates both the *kiddushin* and the *nissuin* ceremonies under the wedding canopy,[52] the author of *Trumat Hadeshen* and other prominent *poskim* maintain that today any condition imposed in the *kiddushin* contract is actually imposed also in the *nissuin* contract.[53] It should be noted that this halakhic innovation was accepted by numerous other *aharonim*.[54] Thus, Yosef Hazan (1741–1822, *posek*, Izmir, Turkey-Israel) relied on this innovation and even claimed that had Yosef Karo seen Rabbeinu Asher (Rosh)'s above argument, he probably would have agreed with Mahari Bruna and not rejected his opinion regarding the imposing of a condition to exempt a widow from the obligation of *yibbum* with an apostate levir brother-in-law.[55] A similar understanding can be found among other *aharonim* who argue that in the combined ceremony under the wedding canopy, the *nissuin* ceremony completes the *kiddushin* ceremony, and therefore, any condition imposed in the *kiddushin* is thus also imposed in the *nissuin* and we actually have a valid conditional marriage.[56]

49 *See* Mishnah *Ketubot* 5:2; BT *Ketubot* 57a. At that time, the unification of those two ceremonies was very rare; *see* Adolf Büchler, *Das judische Verlobins und die Stellung der verlobeten eines Priesters im ersten unt zweiten Jahrhundert*, in FESTSCHRIFT ZU ISRAEL LEWY'S SIEBZIGSTEM GEBURTSTAG 110, 121–22 (M. Brann und J. Elbogen eds., 1911).

50 For a review of those problems and for a discussion of the attempts to deal with them, see FREIMAN, *supra* note 12, at 17–18, 28–29, 31–32, 43, 60–62, 83, 151–53, 180, 268, 270, 295.

51 For a summary of this issue, see SCHERESCHEWSKY, *supra* note 16, at 34.

52 Moshe Isserlish (Rema), *Shulhan Arukh, Even ha-Ezer* 55:1. This is mentioned by him also ibid, 61:1.

53 This is mentioned in Yosef Karo, Beit Yosef, *Even ha-Ezer* 157:4–5, s.v. "*uma shekatav*" and is rejected by him, as mentioned earlier, because he maintains that it is contrary to what is written in the Torah.

54 *See, e.g.*, HAIM BEN ITZHAK OF VOLOZHIN, RESP. HUT HA-MESHULASH vol. 3 ch. 3 (1882); YOSEF S. NATANSON, RESP. SHOEL UMESHIV 1st ed. vol. 1 ch. 197 (1973); SOFER, *supra* note 43, at vol. 2 ch. 68; LANDAU, *supra* note 47, at ch. 56; AVRAHAM Y. KOOK, RESP. EZRAT COHEN (*Even ha-Ezer*) ch. 42 (1985); YAAKOV WEINBERG, RESP. SRIDEI ESH vol. 1 ch. 90. p. 250 (1961).

55 HAZAN, *supra* note 33.

56 *See* Aryeh L. Ben Asher Gunzberg, Shaagat ARYEH ch. 93 (1735) as cited in MEIR SIMCHA OF DVINSK, OR SAMEACH, *Ishut* 10:1 (1910).

3.3 *Every Jewish Marriage Is Actually a Conditional One*

Earlier in this chapter, I attempted to establish that the Talmudic dictum "there is no conditional marriage" is an optional rather than an absolute principle, and that there are several exceptions that decrease its rigid all-inclusiveness. In this section I take this a step further and argue that, according to a number of *rishonim*, *aharonim*, and scholars of *halakhah*, every Jewish marriage is in essence a conditional marriage, rendering the decisive argument that there is no room in *halakhah* for conditional marriage even more problematic. The main discussion in this regard involves another possible halakhic solution to the problem of the *agunah* – the annulment of the marriage (*hafqa'ah/ hafka'at kiddushin*).[57]

This unique mechanism is based on the premise that the sages have the power to annul the *kiddushin* and thus also the *nissuin* based on the fact that the *kiddushin* is a conditional act that is valid only if the sages affirm it. This is the straightforward but deeper meaning of the Talmudic maxim "*kol ha mekadesh adata derabbanan mekadesh*" (When a man betroths a woman, he does so under the conditions laid down by the rabbis). The critical importance of utilizing the above mechanism that in every Jewish wedding there is a terminative condition that can retroactively annul the marriage ("When a man betroths a woman, he does so under the conditions laid down by the Rabbis") was noted by Eliezer Berkovits as the basis for a possible reliable solution to the *agunah* problem.[58]

Similarly, Samuel Atlas (professor of philosophy and Talmud, Hebrew Union College-Jewish Institute of Religion, 1900–77) attests to the centrality of this halakhic framework that, in certain circumstances, can invalidate and even render a marriage totally void retroactively, thus preventing the need for a *get*, as the couple is not regarded as married.[59] Indeed, there are several *rishonim* who have concluded that any Jewish marriage is a conditional one, based on the well-known words recited under the wedding canopy, "I hereby betroth you *kedat Mosheh veYisrael*" (according to the laws of Moses and Israel).[60]

57 *See* David Novak, Halakhah in a Theological Dimension 29–44 (1985); Shlomo Riskin, Women and Jewish Divorce: The Rebellious Wife, the Agunah and the Right of Women to Initiate Divorce in Jewish Law. A Halakhic Solution (1989); ibid, *Hafka'at Kiddushin: Towards Solving the Aguna Problem in Our Time*, 36(4) Tradition 1 (2002); Jeremy Wieder & Shlomo Riskin, *Hafka'at Kiddushin: A Rebuttal*, 36(4) Tradition 37 (2002); Abel, *supra* note 11, at 46–64; Jackson et al., *supra* note 9, at 141–66; Westreich, *supra* note 9, at 41–59; Avishalom Westreich, *Hafka'at Kiddushin (Annulment of Marriage): Reexamination of an Old Debate*, 27–28 Sidra 111 (2013) (Heb.) (ibid, *Annulment of Marriage (Hafka'at Kiddushin): Re-examination of an Old Debate*, http://static1.1.sqspcdn.com/static/f/784513/11612805/1302165216787/Avishalom+Westreich+Annulment+of+Marriage+2008.pdf?token=76V70xZQdDv2JQcFEdSwZdowP24%3D).

58 Berkovits, *supra* note 12, at 157.

59 Samuel Atlas, When a man betroths a woman, he does so under the conditions laid down by the Rabbis, 75 Sinai 119, 119 (1974) (Heb.).

60 *See* Rashi's comentary to BT *Yevamot* 9b, s.v. "*adata derabbanan*" and Tosafot *Ketubot* 3a, s.v. "*adata derabbanan mekadesh.*"

According to these *rishonim*, this statement is an explicit terminative condition, similar to the Tannaitic stipulation that are explored in the next section: "(If a man said to a woman,) 'I hereby betroth you on the condition that my father will consent.' . . . If his father consented she is betrothed but if his father did not consent she is not betrothed."[61] Moreover, since it is halakhically permissible to impose a stipulation in the marriage contract that a third party – in this case, the sages – approve a given marriage, if the condition is not fulfilled, this marriage is void, since it lacks the final required consent of the sages.[62] Several prominent *aharonim* also held this view and even implemented it in practice that annulling the *kiddushin* is possible in light of this understanding that every Jewish marriage is a conditional one, and without the consent of the sages, it may be annulled.[63]

There is a debate in the scholarly literature regarding the precise way in which the annulling mechanism works. It is commonly agreed that it is based on an explicit terminative condition, but the debate revolves around whether there is the additional need for a *get*, even an "invalid" *get*, in order to effect the annulment, or whether, since we are dealing with a terminative condition, there is no additional requirement in order to invalidate the marriage.[64] The first and less revolutionary option is supported by some scholars of the Talmud, such as Avraham Weiss (1895–1970, professor of Talmud, Yeshiva University, New York), who claims that according to the view of some *rishonim*, the annulment mechanism requires a *get*, even an "invalid" one, in order to effect the annulment.[65] But, a much more innovative approach may be found in the writings of other scholars, such as Samuel Atlas, who argues that there is no need for any sort of *get*, since the conditional marriage is an independent mechanism and the *kiddushin* will be automatically annulled.[66]

Similarly, Arye Edrei (professor of law, Faculty of Law, Tel Aviv University) is of the opinion that according to these *rishonim*, there is no need for a *get* in order to

61 BT *Ketubot* 73b.

62 *See* the novellae of Ritva and Raha in Shita Mekubetzet to *Ketubot* ad loc. This principle is cited also in the names of Rashi and Rabbeinu Karashkas. Ritva was cited and discussed in BEN-ZION M. UZIEL, RESP. MISHPATEI UZIEL *Even ha-Ezer* vol. 2 ch. 46 (1964); *Responsum on Eyn Tenai BeNissuin*, 8 YESHURUN 715 (2001) (Heb.). For a summary of the opinons of the *rishonim* in this regard, see BERKOVITS, *supra* note 12, at 158–95 and more briefly at 195–98; TALMUDIC ENCYCLOPEDIA vol. 2, 137–38 (Shlomo Zevin et al. eds., 1978).

63 These *aharonim* include PINHAS HALEVI HOROWITZ, HAHAFLAA *(1860) and* AKIVA EIGER, NOVELLAE TO TRACTATE *Ketubot* 3a (1990); WEINBERG, *supra* note 54; SOFER, *supra* note 43, at *Even ha-Ezer* vol. 3 ch. 108. For a discussion of the latter reference, see BERKOVITS, *supra* note 12, at 160–62.

64 *See, e.g.*, DAVID HALIVNI, SOURCES AND TRADITIONS: A SOURCE CRITICAL COMMENTARY ON SEDER NASHIM 530 (1968) (Heb.); ISAAC HALEVY, DOROT HARISHONIM vol. 2, 509 (1967) (Heb.); HANINA BEN-MENAHEM, JUDICIAL DEVIATION IN TALMUDIC LAW: GOVERNED BY MEN, NOT BY RULES 41–50 (1991); Westreich, *supra* note 57.

65 AVRAHAM WEISS, THE TALMUD IN ITS DEVELOPMENT 390 (1954) (Heb.).

66 *See* Atlas, *supra* note 59, at 120–1. *See also* Samuel Atlas, Addition to When a man betroths a woman, he does so under the conditions laid down by the Rabbis, 79 SINAI 102, 105 (1976) (Heb.), and compare with Israel Francus, And Again, When a man betroths a woman, he does so under the conditions laid down by the Rabbis, 77 SINAI 91, 92–93 (1975) (Heb.).

annul a marriage, since in any event, the entire marriage is a conditional one.[67] The essence of his innovation is the premise that the mechanism of conditional marriage is a reliable basis for annulling a marriage, despite the fact that the husband is still alive and has not given his wife a bill of divorce; however, this option has been neglected throughout the ages. To summarize this issue, both in the literature of the *rishonim* and in the scholarly literature, there are important opinions that regard every Jewish marriage as a conditional one, and thus there is no need for any form of *get* in order to release a woman from a dead-end marriage.

4 HALAKHIC EXAMPLES OF CONDITIONS IN THE *KIDDUSHIN* AND *NISSUIN* CONTRACTS

4.1 *The Tannaitic Literature*

4.1.1 General

The Tannaitic literature presents numerous discussions of terminative conditions that were imposed primarily in the *kiddushin* contract but also in the *nissuin* contract. The profusion of these discussions clearly reflects the extent to which imposing conditions in the marriage contract, or at least in the *kiddushin*, was a common, accepted practice. There are two main categories of spousal conditions – one that looks out for the woman's welfare and the other that benefits the husband.[68] Since the groom is the active and dominant player in the wedding ceremony, by nature, the vast majority of the conditions are on his behalf. Thus, the burden of proof falls on the bride that she has fulfilled the condition and/or performed the deeds that were agreed upon in the agreement. On the other hand, conditions that are on the bride's behalf are far rarer, since the bride is a

[67] *See* Arye Edrei, *The Beit Din's Prerogatives in Marital Law*, 21 SHNATON HA-MISHPAT HA-IVRI 1, 32 (1998–2000) (Heb.).

[68] Numerous *aharonim* have noted the nature and uniqueness of a condition that is on the woman's behalf, and which the groom cannot cancel unilaterally. *See, e.g.*, YONAH LANDSOFER, RESP. ME'IL TZEDAKAH ch. 1 (1968); LANDAU, *supra* note 47; and see a discussion of it in BERKOVITS, *supra* note 12, at 55–60; Abel, *The Plight*, *supra* note 14, at 26–29 (ABEL, *supra* note 11, at 14); JACKSON ET AL., *supra* note 9, passim; Westreich, *supra* note 9, passim. Other *aharonim* have explained that the principle "there is no conditional marriage" is valid only in a case where the condition was imposed by the groom, since "no one wishes to make his intercourse with a woman one of prostitution." But, when the condition imposed in the marriage contract is on behalf of the bride, this halakhic principle does not apply; *see* ISRAEL LIFSHITZ, RESP. OR ISRAEL ch. 44 (1770); HAZAN, *supra* note 33. In addition, there is a further qualification to the principle that there is no conditional marriage, that even if the bride later on rescinds her initial stipulation, she may do so only with regard to monetary matters. But in the issue under discussion – the endeavor to prevent her from becoming an *agunah*, the terminative condition marriage is valid and she cannot withdraw her initial stipulation. *See* UZIEL, *supra* note 62, at *Even ha-Ezer* vol. 5 ch. 46 (2002). It is worth noting that this distinction has been accepted as *halakhah*, for example in Yechiel M. Epstein, Arukh Hashulhan *Even ha-Ezer*, 157:14 (2007).

more passive player than the groom is. It is worth noting that the terminative condition under discussion, which is intended to prevent the *agunah* problem, is even more uncommon.

Conditions on the woman's behalf that are mentioned in the Tannaitic literature include an act that the husband is obligated to perform, such as working for his wife as a laborer or giving her a sum of money.[69] In addition, there are conditions that make the validity of the marriage dependent on matters relating to the groom, such as his ownership of land, his having a particular personal status, and so on.[70] Conditions that are on behalf of the groom include stipulations that make the validity of the marriage dependent on the bride, such as her personal status or that she has not taken on vows nor has blemishes. There is even a discussion of a terminative condition that makes the validity of the marriage dependent upon the agreement of a third party. The latter two stipulations are crucial to the subject under discussion, and I will now proceed to explore them more thoroughly.

4.1.2 Conditions That the Bride Has Not Taken on Vows nor Has Blemishes – A Practical Example of a Condition in the *Nissuin* Contract?

The Mishnah in *Ketubot* 7:7 states as follows:

> If a man betrothed a woman on condition that she was not subject to any vows and she was found to be under a vow, her betrothal is invalid. If he married her without making any conditions and she was found to be under a vow, she may be divorced without receiving her *kethubah*. [(I)f a woman was betrothed] on condition that she has no bodily defects, and she was found to have such defects, her betrothal is invalid. If he married her without making any conditions and she was found to have bodily defects, she may be divorced without a *kethubah*. [71]

The first part of this Tannaitic source deals with what is perhaps the best-known and simplest example of a stipulation in the *kiddushin* that has the power to invalidate the marriage – whether the woman has taken on vows or has blemishes. If, during the period of time between the *kiddushin* and the *nissuin*, the woman is found to have either of the above, the *kiddushin* is annulled retroactively.[72] But, the end of this Mishnah is ambiguous. Is it a continuation of the first part of the Mishnah, and

[69] *See*, respectively, Mishnah *Kiddushin* 3:6 and the parallel passage in Tosefta (Liberman edition) *Kiddushin* 3:3; Mishnah *Kiddushin* 3:2.

[70] *See*, respectively, Mishnah *Kiddushin* 3:3 and in the parallel passage in Tosefta (Liberman edition) *Kiddushin* 3:4; Mishnah *Kiddushin* 2:2 and in the parallel Tosefta (Liberman edition) *Kiddushin* 2:5; Mishnah *Kiddushin* 2:3.

[71] Mishnah *Ketubot* 7:7 and in the parallel passage in Mishnah *Kiddushin* 2:5; Tosefta (Liberman edition) *Ketubot* 7:8. For parallel sources of this Tosefta, see PT *Ketubot* 7:7 (31c); PT *Kiddushin* 2:4 (62c); BT *Ketubot* 74b. For a discussion of the relationship between the Mishnah and the Tosefta of Tractate *Ketubot*, see Jacob N. Epstein, Introduction to the Text of the Mishnah vol. 1, 296–97 (1948) (Heb.).

[72] For a discussion of this unique stipulation, see Berkovits, *supra* note 12, at 13.

thus we are dealing with a groom who had betrothed his bride with this explicit condition and was silent in its regard during the *nissuin* ceremony? Or is it a separate and independent scenario dealing with a groom who did not impose any explicit or even implied stipulation, either in the *kiddushin* or in the *nissuin*? The first interpretation – that in the *nissuin* ceremony the groom did not reaffirm the condition he attached to the *kiddushin* contract – is the important one for the present discussion. It is a good example of an explicit halakhic mechanism that enables the bride to be released from the marriage without the need for a bill of divorce despite the fact that she is married to him. This Tannaitic precedent supports the view that conditions may be imposed in the *nissuin* ceremony.

4.1.3 A Condition That a Third Party Will Affirm the Validity of the *Kiddushin*

Another Mishnah, in *Kiddushin* 3:6, states as follows:

> [If he says,] "On condition that [my] father consents," if his father consents, she is betrothed; if not, she is not betrothed. If his father dies, she is betrothed; if the son dies, the father is instructed to say that he does not consent.

This stipulation deals with a condition that is on the man's behalf. It states that the *kiddushin* is valid only if the groom's father, or some other third party, consents to it.[73] The first part of the Mishnah completely sanctions this condition. Thus, the *kiddushin* is valid only after the condition has been fulfilled – that is, after the father of the betrothing groom gives his consent. If the father does not consent, the *kiddushin* is retroactively annulled. The more complicated case is the second part of this source, which states that if the father died and did not state his opinion one way or the other, the woman is still betrothed. A possible explanation for this ruling is that we assess the groom's intention, which is to receive his father's approval of his wish to marry this specific bride, and thus avoid disappointing him with an undesirable daughter-in-law.

However, since the father died and can no longer be disappointed, the initial stipulation does not apply and there is no need to receive the father's agreement. But, in my opinion, it appears that the estimation of the groom's intention can be interpreted in one of two mutually exclusive ways – that the *kiddushin* is valid if the father explicitly states his positive affirmation or if he does not explicitly reject his son's choice, which is the equivalent of a positive affirmation. Therefore, if the father dies without disagreeing with his son's choice, that is equivalent to his positive agreement. Possible support for my explanation may be found in the Tosefta, which appears to contradict the Mishnah and reads as follows:

[73] *See, e.g.*, Tosefta (Lieberman) *Kiddushin* 3:5: "I hereby betroth you on the condition that a third party will consent."

> [If he says,] "On condition that [my] father consents," however, if his father has not consented,[74] she is betrothed, since perhaps he will consent later on. If his father dies, she is betrothed; if the son dies, there was such a case and the father was instructed to say that he does not consent. ... [If he says,] "On condition that [my] father consents," if his father consents, she is betrothed; if not, she is not betrothed. [75]

The Tosefta appears to contradict the Mishnah, since according to the wording in the above version, the father did not express his explicit agreement, and according to the Ms. Erfurt version of the Tosefta, he even explicitly expresses his disagreement with his son's choice, but the *kiddushin* is nevertheless valid. Perhaps the groom's genuine intention was that as long as his father did not positively disagree in a way that is irreversible, the bride is betrothed, since, as the Tosefta explains, perhaps he will change his mind later on, if only for a second.[76] If my interpretation is correct, these two Tannaitic sources need not be regarded as contradicting one another but rather as two separate statements.[77] The possibility that these two sources do not contradict each other, but that one source interprets the other, may also be inferred from Amoraic discussions in this regard in both the Palestinian Talmud and the Babylonian Talmud. The discussion in the Palestinian Talmud is as follows:

> "On condition that my father agree; if the father agreed, she is preliminarily married; if the father does not agree, she is not preliminarily married;" silently he does not agree. "If the father died, she is preliminarily married;" silently he agreed. "If the son died, one instructs the father to say that he does not agree;" silently he agreed. ... R. Yannai returned and explained the Mishnah: "On condition that my father agree; if the father agreed, she is preliminarily married; otherwise she is not preliminarily married," he said on condition that [the father] express his opinion but he did not. "If the father died, she is preliminarily married;" as if he had given his opinion. "If the son died, one instructs the father to say that he does not agree," as if he had given his opinion. R. Zeira said [before R. Yasa]: can R. Yannai explain the Mishnah as he wishes? He answered him, so says R. Simeon Ben Laqish.[78]

In his first interpretation, R. Yannai, like the redactor of the Talmud, explains that the two incidents discussed in the Mishnah are not precisely the same. But, after changing his mind, R. Yannai explains that in the first case the stipulation requires

74 The version in Ms. Erfurt reads, "On condition that [my] father will not consent"; *see* Saul Lieberman, Tosefta Ki-fshutah: A Comprehensive Commentary on the Tosefta *Kiddushin* 944–46 (1973) (Heb.).

75 *See* Tosefta (Lieberman) *Kiddushin* 3:6–7. For an interpretation, see Lieberman's commentery ibid.

76 In the first printed edition of the Tosefta, the version is "after an hour" (*leachar shaah*) whereas in the Erfurt version it is "for another hour" (*leshaah acheret*). In any event, the two versions have the same meaning – that perhaps in the future, the father will withdraw his implied or his explicit initial objection.

77 For a disussion of the precise relationship between these two Tannaitic sources, see Epstein, *supra* note 71, at 598–606; Hanoch Albeck, Introduction to the Mishna 92 (1959) (Heb.).

78 PT *Kiddushin* 3:5 (64b).

the positive agreement of the father to his son's *kiddushin*, whereas in the second and third cases, there is no need for such explicit consent, as long as the father does not explicitly disagree, since we assume that his intention is to agree to it, even if he does not state so explicitly.[79] But, in the Babylonian Talmud, both R. Joseph Bar Ammi and the redactor of the Talmud[80] hold that the meaning of the stipulation is that the father does not give a negative and irreversible immediate disagreement, as in the first opinion, or in the course of the next 30 days, as in the second opinion. The following is the discussion in the Babylonian Talmud:

> What is meant by "on condition that [my] father consents?" Shall we say, providing that my father [explicitly] says "yes"? Then consider the middle clause: If his father dies, she is betrothed. Surely he did not say "yes!" hence [it must mean] that he does not consent: yet why, seeing that he was silent? Hence [it must mean that] he said to her, "on condition that my father does not [explicitly] object."[81] ... R. Joseph b. Ammi said: "After all, it has one connotation, and what is meant by 'on condition that [my] father consents'"? On condition that he does not protest within thirty days from now.[82]

In the parallel passage to the above discussion, in the continuation of Tosefta *Kiddushin* 3:7 cited earlier, there is another important condition that does not involve only the *kiddushin* ceremony, but that may also ultimately nullify the validity of the entire marriage retroactively, since it is a condition imposed also in the sexual relationship that was part of the *nissuin* ceremony. This is another reliable precedent for validating a conditional marriage, which depends entirely on the

[79] This is the interpretaion of Hanoch Albeck, Mehkarim ba-beraita u-va-tosefta ve-yaḥasan la-talmud 158–59 (1970) (Heb.). This explanation is supported by the version of the Palestinian Talmud documented in the Cairo Genizah, see Louis Ginzberg, Yeruhalmi Fragments from the Genizah 230 (1909) (Heb.).

[80] For an analysis of this discussion in the Babylonian Talmud, see Avraham Weiss, Studies in the Literature of the Amoraim 414 (1962) (Heb.).

[81] There is a deliberation in the Babylonian Talmud over whether this is a suspensive condition (*condicio suspensiva*) that postpones the validation of the *kiddushin* until the condition is fulfilled, or a terminative one (*condicio resolutiva*) that determines that the *kiddushin* is valid as long as any agreed-upon event does not take place. The condition "that [my] father consents" is a suspensive condition, whereas the condition "that [my] father does not object" is a terminative condition. For a possible halakhic distinction between these two conditions, see the following sources in Hebrew: Zeev W. Falk, The Law of Marriage 158–63 (1983); Berachyahu Lifshitz, *The Theoretical Basis of the Condition in Jewish Law*, 4 Mishpatim 636, 644–47 (1973) (Heb.). For a discussion of the distinction between various halakhic conditions, see Shillem Warhaftig, The Jewish Law of Contract 153–64 (1974) (Heb.). Based on this legal distinction, it is possible to distinguish between Hillel's condition and the Palestinian *simphon*, both will be discussed later on in this chapter. Whereas the first is a suspensive condition and the *kiddushin* will become valid upon the fullfilment of an agreed-upon event, the latter is a *condicio resolutiva* and the *kiddushin* is valid as long as an agreed-upon event does not take place, namely that the groom does not marry his bride during the agreed-upon time, see Freiman, *supra* note 12, at 11–12.

[82] BT *Kiddushin* 63a. In a comparison of the Talmudic discussions on this issue, Weiss contends that the Palestinian Talmud is the original source, while the Babylonian Talmud is a much later one, see Weiss, *supra* note 80, at 46–47.

agreement of a third party – the father of the groom in this case. The continuation of this Tosefta reads as follows:

> [If a man said to a woman,] "I will have intercourse with you on the condition that my father will consent," she is betrothed to him even if his father did not consent. R. Simeon b. Judah, however, stated in the name of R. Simeon, if his father consented she is betrothed but if his father did not consent she is not betrothed, since the intercourse derives from the initial *kiddushin*.

Some *aharonim* have pointed out that these Tannaitic sources are, as also understood in the Amoraic literature, halakhic exceptions to the basic principle that there is no conditional marriage.[83]

4.1.4 A Condition That Postpones the Validity of the *Kiddushin* until the *Nissuin* Ceremony

The few conditions found in the Tannaitic literature that are on the woman's behalf include an ancient condition ascribed to Hillel the Elder, dating back to the last third of the first century BCE. Scholars are of the opinion that it is the first documented encounter with the various problems arising throughout the ages with regard to the Jewish wedding ceremony.[84] The text reads as follows:

> When the people of Alexandria betrothed women, and then someone came from the market and stole her [and married her], and the matter came before the Sages, they considered declaring the children bastards (*mamzerim*). Hillel the Elder said to them: "Bring me the *Ketubah* of your mothers." They showed them to him, and it was written, "When you enter my house you will be my wife according to the custom of Moses and Israel"[85] [and they did not declare the children bastards].[86]

83 *See, e.g.*, ELAZAR BEN ISRAEL LANDAU, COMMENTARY YAD HA-MELEKH ON MAIMONIDES *Ishut* 6:17, s.v. "*nistapakti.*"

84 For more on this understanding, see BERKOVITS, *supra* note 12, at 11.

85 In the parallel Palestinian sources, such as PT *Yevamot* 15:3 (14d); PT *Ketubot* 4:8 (28d), the version is "*kedat Mosheh veYehodae.*" For the history of the rejection of this version and the acceptance of the version that is prevalent today – "*kedat Mosheh veYisrael*" – see TALMUDIC ENCYCLOPEDIA vol. 8, 25 n.20 (Shlomo Zevin et al. eds., 1978) (Heb.); David Flusser & Shmuel Safrai, *In the Image of the Form of His Likeness*, in ISAAC LEO SEELIGMANN VOLUME, ESSAYS ON THE BIBLE AND THE ANCIENT WORLD vol. 2 (Hebrew section), 453 (Alexander Rofe & Yair Zakovitch eds.,1983) (Heb.); Menachem Kister, *Kedat Moshe veYehudai: On the History of a Legal-Religious Term*, in ATARA L'HAIM: STUDIES IN THE TALMUD & MEDIEVAL RABBINIC LITERATURE IN HONOR OF PROF. HAIM ZALMAN DIMITROVSKY 202, 207 (Daniel Boyarin et al. eds., 2000) (Heb.); and in the various references listed in ASHER GULAK, LEGAL DOCUMENTS IN THE TALMUD IN LIGHT OF GREEK PAPYRI AND GREEK AND ROMAN LAW 59 n.36 (edited and supplemented by Ranon Katzoff, 1994) (Heb.).

86 Tosefta (Lieberman edition) *Kiddushin* 4:9. The text in brackets was added based on the text in the parallel passage in BT *Baba Metzia* 104a. It should be noted that the Alexandrian provenance of this betrothal practice is confirmed and criticized by PHILO OF ALEXANDRIA, DE SPECIALIBUS LEGIBUS vol. III, 72 (1975). *See also* ZEEV W. FALK, INTRODUCTION TO JEWISH LAW OF THE SECOND COMMONWEALTH vol. II, 286 (1978), as cited in JACKSON ET AL., *supra* note 9, at 64 n.418; Perets Segal, *Jewish Law during the Tannaitic Period*, in AN INTRODUCTION

The words in brackets at the end appear only in the parallel source in the Babylonian Talmud and in all the manuscripts and printed editions of this Babylonian Talmudic source, but they do not appear in any of the parallel Palestinian sources. This addition demonstrates better than anything else the original aim of Hillel's innovative and courageous reading of the *ketubah*, which led him to conclude that according to the straightforward sense of the text, the *kiddushin* becomes valid only when the bride stands under the wedding canopy. Since in the case under consideration, the bride did not reach this irreversible point, she was not regarded as married to the groom and not even betrothed to him. The man who kidnapped her from under her wedding canopy did not kidnap a married woman, and her children from him are not *mamzerim*.

Scholars disagree as to the sociological and legal background that led to these kidnappings. Asher Gulak (1881–1940, Faculty of Law, The Hebrew University of Jerusalem, Latvia-Israel) suggests that the kidnappings reflect the disrespect of Alexandrian Jews, who were probably greatly influenced by the gentile jurisdictions under whose shadow they lived, and therefore belittled the betrothal and did not prevent the kidnapper from taking the betrothed woman for a wife.[87] Thus, it was necessary to add this unique stipulation, which postponed the serious halakhic ramifications of a woman being regarded as married from the time of the *kiddushin* to the later time of the *nissuin* ceremony.[88]

According to Yizhak Heinemann (1876–1957, The Hebrew University of Jerusalem, Germany-Israel), the kidnappings took place against the backdrop of the inevitable clash between the patriarchal approach and the father's domination over his daughter's marriage on the one hand, and the daughter's desire to choose her husband on her own and of her own free will on the other. Thus, on more than one occasion, the father would betroth his daughter and even compel her to marry against her will, causing the daughter to arrange that her lover "kidnap" her and force her to marry him.[89]

to the History and Sources of Jewish Law 137 (Neil S. Hecht et al. eds., 1996); Breitowitz, *supra* note 4, at 59.

[87] *See* Gulak, *infra* note 119, at 366. Büchler has already pointed out the possible Egyptian influence, see Büchler, *supra* note 49, at 123 n.12 (Adolf Büchler, Studies in Jewish History 139 n.1 [1956]). For a scholarly overview of the possible influence of Greco-Egyptian law and Roman law, see the references listed in Gulak, *supra* note 85, at 52–55 nn.22–26. For the more general influence of foreign jurisdictions on *halakhah*, see Bernard S. Jackson, *How Jewish Is Jewish Family Law?*, LV/2 J. Jewish Stud. 201 (2004).

[88] *See* Isaac Halevy, Dorot Harishonim vol. 1, 103, 355–56 (1967) (Heb.).

[89] *See* Yizhak Heinemann, Philons griechische und judische Bildung: Kulturvergleichende Untersuchungen zu Philons Darstellung der judischen Gesetze 301 n.1 (1932). For an anthropological study that deals with the sociological significance of kidnapping women for marriage, see Judith Evans-Grubbs, *Abduction Marriage in Antiquity: A Law of Constantine (CTh IX.24.1) and Its Social Context*, 79 J. Roman Stud. 59 (1989). For a general overview of kidnapping women for marriage in the ancient near-east, see Josef Fleishman, *Socio-Legal Aspects of Genesis 34*, 13 Shenaton: An Annual for Biblical and Ancient near Eastern Studies 141 (2002) (Heb.).

Samuel Belkin (1911–76, second president of Yeshiva University, New York) argued that due to the religious prohibition against sexual relations during the period between the *kiddushin* and the *nissuin* ceremonies, the Jewish community in Alexandria began to belittle the *kiddushin*, which resulted in an urgent need to postpone the validity of the *kiddushin* until the *nissuin* ceremony.[90] Boaz Cohen (1899–1968, professor of Talmud at the Jewish Theological Seminary of America, New York) maintains that the delayed validation of the *kiddushin* until the *nissuin* ceremony was intended to enable those Jews who wished to rescind their initial intention and agreement to marry to do so without incurring any far-reaching halakhic problems.[91] Thus, as we are dealing with the case of a betrothed woman for whom the prohibition of a married woman (*eshet ish*) who is not permitted to another man applies, and thus the problem of *mamzerut*, Hillel convinced the sages that it was preferable to interpret the *ketubah*'s text in his innovative way.

This was instead of annulling the second *kiddushin*, of the kidnapping husband, despite the fact that he had acted improperly (*shelo kadin*) and that there was reliable halakhic justification for treating this case in the same way as in the annulment of the marriage in the famous Naresh kidnapping case. In that case, a minor orphan girl was (only rabbinically) married to a man who sought to marry her (biblically) once she became an adult, but someone kidnapped her and married her before her husband remarried her. According to R. Ashi's innovative explanation, no *get* was needed from the kidnapper because even though the second man had taken her and betrothed her before her husband had remarried her, his betrothal, though valid according to Torah law, was annulled by the rabbinic authorities (*[A]fqeinho Rabbanan lekiddushin mineh*) on the grounds that "He acted improperly; they, therefore, treated him also improperly, and deprived him of the right of valid betrothal" (BT *Yevamot* 110a). We can assume that had there been no children from the second marriage in the Alexandrian case, the Talmudic sages would indeed have annulled that marriage and validated the first *kiddushin* of the original husband, as in the Naresh case, where the kidnapping husband had had a sexual relationship with the girl before she was officially married to either of them.

Commentators and scholars have pointed to the various aspects to Hillel's innovative act. First, although we are dealing with the prohibition of a married woman (*eshet ish*), who is forbidden to other men, and the consequential problem of

[90] *See* SAMUEL BELKIN, PHILO AND THE ORAL LAW: THE PHILONIC INTERPRETATION OF BIBLICAL LAW IN RELATION TO THE PALESTINIAN HALAKAH 243, 246–47 (1940). A similar halakhic situation existed in Galilee and Judea in this era; *see* Tosefta (Lieberman Tosefta) *Ketubot* 1:4; PT *Ketubot* 1:4 (25c).

[91] *See* Boaz Cohen, *On the Theme of Betrothal in Jewish and Roman Law*, 18 PROCEEDINGS OF THE AMERICAN ACADEMY FOR JEWISH RESEARCH 67, 92–93 (1948) (ibid, JEWISH AND ROMAN LAW 304–06 [1966]). Cohen suggests that Roman law, in which betrothal agreements could be canceled easily and even unilaterally, and Egyptian law, in which this practice was common, served as fertile soil for the development of this type of halakhic practice.

mamzerut, Hillel relied on the simple meaning of the *ketubah* text, and despite being the minority opinion, he enabled the woman to marry the kidnapper, thus resolving the problem of *mamzerut*.[92]

Second, on the surface it appears that we are not referring to an explicit halakhic stipulation but only a layperson's phrase that was written into the *ketubah* simply to describe the point in time at which a betrothed woman becomes a married woman – when she enters his house. Moreover, we are dealing with a very marginal detail of the *ketubah* text, and thus it is extremely difficult to attribute such importance to the phrase that it has the power to postpone the entire validity of the *kiddushin* until the *nissuin* ceremony. This is in stark contrast to other precedents of relying on the simple meaning of the text that are mentioned in the same Tannaitic source, which clearly deal with explicit valid legal stipulations.[93] However, one may still argue that it is the very redundancy of this marginal phrase that demonstrates its integral part in the *ketubah* text. Thus, its deep meaning is that the validation of the entire *kiddushin* is postponed until the bride stands beneath the wedding canopy.[94]

Third, we are dealing here only with interpreting a layperson's language, not with the interpretation of the official language of an enactment of the sages or a halakhic document.[95] There is a debate among scholars as to where exactly lay the innovation in Hillel's interpreting the layperson's language. Boaz Cohen maintains that this unofficial language had become the formal, accepted halakhic text, not a single word of which was allowed to be changed. This best explains the disagreement of the sages, who refused to demonstrate any flexibility, even at the expense of *mamzerut*, whereas Hillel exhibited a more lenient attitude and a more liberal and flexible interpretation of the *ketubah* text.

However, Ranon Katzoff (1938–, professor of classical studies and general history, Bar Ilan University) rejects this explanation for several reasons: The Tosefta introduces the *a priori* opinion of the sages just before Hillel reads the text of the Alexandrian *ketubah*, after which there is no clear indication that there was still a dispute between the sages and Hillel. Furthermore, the phrase "interpreted the layperson's language" in the broader literary context of this Tannaitic source does not signify flexibility in formulating legal documents. Instead, Katzoff suggests that Hillel's innovation lies in his brilliance and

92 *See* Yaakov ben Moshe Berab, Resp. Mahari Berab ch. 9 (1988); Yosef Karo, Resp. Avkat Rokhel ch. 108 (1960).

93 For other examples of interpreting layperson's language, see PT *Ketubot* 4:8 (29a) and the parallel PT *Yevamot* 15:3 (14d).

94 Possible support for this understanding can be found in the writings of several *rishonim*, such as Nahmanides *Baba Metzia* 104a, s.v. "*veefshar lomar*."

95 Ibid, s.v. "*veharav Yehudah*" and see the parallel passage in the commentary of Rav Hai Gaon, cited and discussed by Shmuel Grinberg, *Interpreting Layman's Language*, 12 Sinai 346 (1947) (Heb.).

resourcefulness in resolving halakhic problems by requesting important relevant information from an unexpected source.[96]

Fourth, commentators and scholars disagree as to whose *ketubah* text Hillel had interpreted. If it was the *ketubah* of the kidnapped bride, then this stipulation did indeed appear in the relevant *ketubah*. That is the straightforward meaning of the source, namely that after the sages wished to declare the children *mamzerim*, the text states that "Hillel the Elder said to them: 'Bring me the *Ketubah* of your mothers.' They showed them to him, and it was written." Thus, the *ketubah* text that Hillel was referring to was the one most relevant for him – the *ketubah* of the kidnapped bride. A more innovative explanation is that the text was not that of the kidnapped bride's from the *kiddushin ketubah* but a different one – whether the *ketubah* that the kidnapper gave her[97] or the kidnapped bride's *nissuin ketubah*.[98]

In all these scenarios, there is still legal justification to assess the initial intention, whether that of the kidnapper or that of the first husband of the kidnapped bride in either the *kiddushin* or the *nissuin ketubah* that she received from him; therefore there is enough halakhic room to deduce that we are dealing with a valid terminative or at least suspensive condition that can retroactively annul the marriage.[99] Moreover, several commentators[100] and scholars[101] even maintain that the *ketubah* text interpreted by Hillel was not associated with the *ketubah* related to the

96 Similar to the question regarding bringing a knife for slaughtering the Passover sacrifice in BT *Pesahim* 66a. For scholarly views, see, Cohen, *supra* note 91; and GULAK, *supra* note 85, at 55 n.26.

97 *See* Gulak, *infra* note 119. For a summary of the opinions of these *rishonim*, see SAUL LIEBERMAN, TOSEFTA KI-FSHUTAH: A COMPREHENSIVE COMMENTARY ON THE TOSEFTA *Ketubot* 246–47 (1955) (Heb.).

98 *See* the interpretations of Nahmanides, Rabbi Nissim ben Reuven Girondi (Ran) and Nimukei Yosef on BT *Baba Metzia*, ibid.

99 Close to this Tannaitic source and its parallels, there are many discussions about interpreting layperson's language with regard to assessing the intention of the contracting party at the time that he or she imposed an explicit condition in the marriage contract; *see* Tosefta (Lieberman edition) *Ketubot* 4:10–13; Mishnah *Ketubot* 4:6; PT *Ketubot* 4:8 (28d); PT *Yevamot* 15:3 (13d); BT *Baba Metzia* 104a. For assessing the intention of the contracting party, see ALBECK, *supra* note 79, at 140–41.

100 This option is mentioned in the novellae of Shlomo ben Avraham ben Aderet (Rashba), as cited in Shita Mekubetzet, *Baba Metzia* 104.

101 For a summary of these approaches, see LIEBERMAN, *supra* note 97, in his short interpretation to the above-mentioned Tosefta, at 68. It is worth noting that there is a similar dispute among scholars regarding interpreting layperson's language in Mishnah *Ketubot* 4:6: "R. Eleazar b. Azariah gave the following exposition in the presence of the Sages in the Vineyard of Jabneh: '[Since it was provided that] the sons shall be heirs [to their mother's kethubah], and the daughters shall be maintained [out of their father's estate, the two cases are to be compared]: As the sons cannot be heirs except after the death of their father, so the daughters cannot claim maintenance except after the death of their father." Albeck contends that we are dealing with an interpretion of the wording of an explicit condition imposed in the *ketubah*, while Epstein maintains that it is only an implied condition that was not explicitly written in the *ketubah*; *see*, respectively, ALBECK, *supra* note 79, at 140; and EPSTEIN, *supra* note 71, at 728 n.3.

kidnapping case. Rather, Hillel was referring to the general wording of the betrothal *ketubah* that was customary among Alexandrian Jewry.

This is exactly the explanation appearing in a responsum by Rashba as to why the sages wished to declare the children *mamzerim*: had the condition been written explicitly in the kidnapped bride's *ketubah*, the sages would never have dared to even suggest it.[102] One way or another, the essence of Hillel's innovation according to Rashba is that he relied on the text of someone else's *ketubah* to conclude that it was the general custom to use this wording in a *ketubah*. Thus, even though Hillel based his ruling only on an "implied condition,"[103] it is regarded as a valid and accepted halakhic stipulation for all intents and purposes. In several responses, Rashba maintains that the interpreted *ketubah* text was not that of the kidnapped woman.[104] Rashba also argues in other responsa that Hillel's innovation was based on an "implied condition" that was not explicitly imposed in the wedding contract of the relevant individuals but that nonetheless has halakhic validity and the capacity to annul the marital status, as if the annulment had been determined by a *beit din*.[105]

4.2 *The Amoraic Literature*

4.2.1 General

As in the Tannaitic literature, the Amoraic literature contains many discussions of different conditions that were imposed in both the *kiddushin* and *nissuin* contracts. The conditions on the woman's behalf include a condition from which the woman profits, such as the husband working for her as a laborer[106] or giving her a certain amount of money;[107] or conditions that validate the marriage only if the groom owns land,[108] if he is wealthy,[109] or if he has a certain personal status and so on.[110] One may deduce from the mention of all of these stipulations that imposing various conditions in the *kiddushin* that could ultimately postpone and even retroactively

[102] *See* Shlomo ben Avraham ben Aderet (Rashba), Resp. HaRashba vol. 5 ch. 76 (1958). A similar conclusion may be found in Yizhak Bar Sheshet Parperet, Resp. HaRibash ch. 399 (1992); Moshe Ben Yizhak Alshakar, Resp. Maharam Alshakar ch. 48 (1959). Both concluded that this is the interpretation of Rashba.

[103] For a discussion of the difference between an explicit stipulation and an implied stipulation in the *ketubah*, see Elimelech Westreich, Transitions in the Legal Status of the Wife in Jewish Law: A Journey among Traditions (2002) (Heb.). For a more general dicsussion of an implied stipulation in *halakhah*, see Itamar Warhaftig, Undertaking in Jewish Law – Its Validity, Character and Types 130, 244 (2001) (Heb.).

[104] *See* Shlomo ben Avraham ben Aderet (Rashba), Resp. HaRashba vol. 3 ch. 17, s.v. "*tshuva*" (1958); ibid, vol. 4 ch. 186 (1958).

[105] *See* ibid, vol. 5 ch. 76, s.v. "*veod ani*" (1958).

[106] BT *Kiddushin* 63a; PT *Kiddushin* 3:6 (64b).

[107] BT *Kiddushin* 64a; PT *Kiddushin* 3:2 (63d).

[108] PT *Kiddushin* 3:3 (64b) and BT *Kiddushin* 60b on Mishnah *Kiddushin* 3:3.

[109] PT *Kiddushin* 2:2 (62c) and BT *Kiddushin* 48b on Mishnah *Kiddushin* 2:2.

[110] Such as in PT *Kiddushin* 2:3 (62c) and BT *Kiddushin* 49b on Mishnah *Kiddushin* 2:3.

annul it continued to be prevalent even during the Amoraic period. This conclusion finds support in the Talmudic phrase, "I hereby betroth you on the condition that," which appears repeatedly in both Tannaitic and Amoraic literature. Time after time, the Talmudic sages regarded these stipulations seriously and scrutinized every aspect of them. If they reached the conclusion that the condition had definitely not been fulfilled, the *kiddushin* and even the *nissuin* could be annulled.

4.2.2 A Condition in the *Nissuin*! – A Condition That the Bride Is Not Subject to Any Vows nor Has Blemishes

The possibility of imposing an explicit condition in the *nissuin* contract, as reflected in the Tannaitic literature,[111] was also discussed by Amoraic sages. Since these discussions are long, detailed, and complicated, and since they deal with other issues that relate to the maxim "*Eyn adam oseh beilato beilat zenut*"[112] and that are beyond the scope of this chapter, I present only the relevant parts of these discussions. The Babylonian Talmud presents the following dispute regarding the Mishnah in *Ketubot* 7:7:

> It was stated: If a man betrothed a woman on condition [that she was under no vow] and married her without attaching any conditions, it is necessary, Rab ruled, that she shall obtain from him a letter of divorce; and Samuel ruled: It is not necessary for her to obtain a letter of divorce from him.[113]

The context of this Amoraic discussion is a dispute regarding the case of a couple who had stipulated in their *kiddushin* that the bride is not subject to any vows, and perhaps that she also does not have any blemishes,[114] but the stipulation was not repeated in the *nissuin* ceremony. In Samuel's opinion, there can be a conditional marriage, since according to him the bride does not need a *get*, which means that her *kiddushin* and *nissuin* are annulled. The reason for the annulment is based on an evaluation of the groom's intention, which is that he wished to marry the bride only on the basis of their initial stipulation. Thus, if she did not fulfill her obligation, she is not betrothed and therefore also does not need to receive a bill of divorce from the husband in order to be released from the marriage. However, according to the plain meaning of the passage, Rab too might agree with Samuel's innovative opinion in a scenario where the husband repeats the stipulation both in the *nissuin* and before the consequent sexual relationship. This possibility appears in the

[111] *See supra* note 71 and the accompanying text.

[112] *See* Abel, *supra* note 11, at 22–23; Jackson et al., *supra* note 9, at 23–24, 84, 177–78, 202.

[113] BT *Ketubot* 72b and the parallel passage in BT *Kiddushin* 50a; PT *Kiddushin* 2:5 (62c) and the parallel passage in PT *Ketubot* 7:9 (31c). For a discussion of these Amoraic texts and for a more general discussion of the phenomenon of "contradictory passages" (*sugyot muhlafot*), see Leib Moscovitz, *Sugyot Muhlafot in the Talmud Yerushalmi*, 60 Tarbiz 19 (1991) (Heb.); Jacob N. Epstein, Introduction to Amoraitic Literature: Babylonian Talmud and Yerushalmi 276–79 (1962) (Heb.); Saul Lieberman, The Talmud of Caesarea 20 (1931) (Heb.).

[114] *See* Rashi's commentary ibid, s.v. "*kidsha al tnai*"; *Melechet Shlomo* on Mishnah *Ketubot* 7:7, s. v. "*sheein ba mumin.*"

continuation of the above Talmudic discussion, in Rabbah's explanation of the dispute between Samuel and Rab, and is supported with another Amoraic opinion:

> Rabbah stated: They differ only in the case of an error [affecting] two women, but where an error [affects] one woman all agree that she requires no divorce from him. . . . [So] it was also stated: R. Aha b. Jacob stated in the name of R. Johanan. If a man betrothed a woman on a certain condition and then had intercourse with her, she, it is the opinion of all, requires no letter of divorce from him.[115]

In both the literature of the *rishonim* and the authoritative halakhic codices, there are also opinions that maintain that the Talmud was discussing only the case of a groom who did not repeat the condition in the *nissuin*. However, if he explicitly confirmed their initial stipulation under the wedding canopy and/or before entering into a conjugal relationship, the condition is valid and the entire marriage may be annulled retroactively if the condition was not met. Based on these Talmudic discussions, some *rishonim* and *aharonim* concluded that there are prominent *amoraim*, such as Samuel,[116] who claim that there can be a conditional marriage, and it is even possible that Rab concurs on this point.[117] Eliezer Berkovits and other scholars have tried to prove that there are numerous *rishonim* who support the opinion found in Hagahot Oshri commenting on Rosh that indeed the entire marriage may be annulled retroactively. This lenient approach is contrary to the opinion found in Shiltey HaGibborim, discussed above in Section 1.1, and it is conceivable that even the opinion in Shiltey HaGibborim concurs with the opinion in Hagahot Oshri.[118]

4.2.3 The Palestinian *Simphon*

In the Palestinian Talmud, there is an extensive discussion of a unique condition that is clearly on the woman's behalf that states that if the groom went away after the *kiddushin* and did not return by the stipulated date, or alternatively did not fulfill his agreed-upon undertaking, the *kiddushin* will be retroactively annulled and he may even be subject to a financial penalty. This is different from Hillel's interpretation of the Alexandrian

[115] BT *Ketubot* 73b–74a. For a summary of the opinions of the *rishonim* on this issue, see Berkovits, *supra* note 12, at 15–38 and more briefly at 38–40.

[116] For these claims, see Tosafot *Yevamot*, 107a, s.v. "*Beit Shamai*" and in the parallel Tosafot *Ketubot* 73a, s.v. "*lo teima*"; the novellae of Shlomo ben Avraham ben Aderet (Rashba) and the commentary Bet ha-Behirah, ibid; Avraham Ben Shimon Sofer, Resp. Chachmei Provence ch. 29 (1967).

[117] Shmuel Eidels, Maharsha Hiddushei Halakhot, *Yevamot* 107a.

[118] *See* Berkovits, *supra* note 12, at 45. For a comprehensive summary of this issue, see Berkovits, *supra* note 12, at 40–45. In addition to the *poskim* mentioned in *supra* note 48 who maintain that, in practice, there is conditional marriage, one may add the following *poskim*: Eliyahu ben Shlomo Zalman (Gra), Biur Hagra *Even ha-Ezer* 177:13; Aibishitz, *supra* note 38, at *Hilkhot Yibbum* ch. 1; Teshuvot Maimoniot, *Hilkhot Ishut* letter 29. For the counterclaim that the opinion in Shiltey HaGibborim is definitely not a lone opinion but is supported in several *rishonim* such as Rashi, Yizhak Ben Yaakov Alfasi, Rabenu Yeruham, Rama, see Ehrenberg, *supra* note 42. For a summary of his article, see ibid, at 95–96.

ketubah, discussed above in Section 4.1.4, where both spouses benefited equally from the cancelation of the *kiddushin*.[119] The discussion states as follows:

> R. Abbahu in the name of R. Johanan: The following is the contract text: "I, X son of Y, contract a preliminary marriage with you, Z, daughter of U, on condition that I give you property A and definitively marry you by day B. If that day should pass without me having taken you in, I shall have no claim on you."[120]

Talmudic scholars have pointed out that the term "*simphon*" [121] in Amoraic literature may be understood in two ways – a unique contractual stipulation and a receipt (*shovar*).[122] In other words, it is a clause in the *kiddushin* contract, which could even be a separate contract, that cancels the *kiddushin* in the event of a breach of the initial agreement or in case the condition was not fulfilled. The *simphon* in the *kiddushin* differs from a business *simphon* in the timing of its writing. Whereas in the business context it is normally written after the writing of the sales contract, at the time of the *kiddushin* it must already exist, because if it were written later on, it would not have the power to retroactively annul the *kiddushin*.[123] In any event, the *kiddushin simphon* has the power to entirely invalidate the *kiddushin* or at least the contractual obligations.[124] The Palestinian *simphon* is clearly a specific case of a conditional *kiddushin* that consists of two stipulations – the first obligates the groom to give his bride an agreed-upon sum of money or any other item, and the second determines the agreed-upon time of their *nissuin*. Consequently, if the groom does not marry the bride on the agreed-upon date, the *kiddushin* is retroactively nullified.

Scholars are of the opinion that the main goal of the *simphon* was to weaken the validity of the *kiddushin*, similar to the Alexandrian custom of postponing the *kiddushin* until the time of the *nissuin* during the Tannaitic period. With the *simphon*, however, this ultimate goal was far more obvious. On the one hand, it

[119] *See* Gulak, *supra* note 85, at 56. For the general legal nature of the *simphon* in the *kiddushin*, see Asher Gulak, *Deed of Betrothal and Oral Stipulation in Talmudic Law*, 3 Tarbitz 361, 366 (1932) (Heb.).

[120] PT *Kiddushin* 3:2 (63d). This passage was cited and discussed in Nahmanides' novellae on *Kiddushin* 60b; Shlomo Luria's commentary Yam Shel Shlomo, *Kiddushin* ch. 3; Levi Ben Yaakov Haviv, Resp. Maharlbah ch. 134 (1865).

[121] *See* Daniel Sperber, A Dictionary of Greek and Latin Legal Terms in Rabbinical Literature 119 (1984) ("postscript to document, codicil, special stipulation within a written contract").

[122] *See* Saul Lieberman & Eliezer S. Rosental, Yerushalmi Neziqin 132–33 (2008) (Heb.). For the various scholars' interpretations of this word, see Marcus Jastrow, A Dictionary of the Targumim, the Talmud Babli and Yerushalmi, and the Midrashic Literature 982 (1950); Gulak, *supra* note 119, at 119; Michael Sokoloff, A Dictionary of Jewish Palestinian Aramaic of the Byzantine Period 375 (1990). For a discussion of a possible Greek influence on the Palestinian *simphon*, see Gulak, *supra* note 85, at 56.

[123] For this argument, see Gulak, *supra* note 85, at 56.

[124] *See* Rashi's commentary to BT *Kiddushin* 10b, s.v. "*simphon*" and his comentary to the parallel passage in BT *Baba Metzia* 20b, s.v. "*simphon*." It is also the interpretation of Tosafot Yom Tov on Mishnah *Baba Metzia* 1:8, s.v. "*simphonot*" and the commentary of Korban ha-Edah to the discussion in the Palestinian Talmud, ad loc.

had the power to completely annul the *kiddushin*, while on the other hand, its purpose was to apply pressure on the groom to fulfill his initial undertaking and to marry the bride at the agreed-upon time. This was reinforced with a financial incentive, because if the groom did not do so, he would lose the sum of money he had already given the bride, even if the *kiddushin* were to be annulled.

From the detailed and comprehensive discussion in the Palestinian Talmud, we may infer that this was the common practice throughout almost the entire five Amoraic generations (220–400 CE), as it was debated both by the second-generation *amora* R. Yohanan and by the fifth-generation R. Mana. The use of the *simphon* may have had even earlier roots, based on the word "*simphona*" that appears in an ancient Hebrew papyrus found in Elephantine in Egypt, dating back to the third–fourth centuries BCE or at least to the generation of the destruction of the Temple (70 CE).[125] Indeed, the Palestinian Talmud contains many discussions with regard to this stipulation, which clearly reflects the frequency with which the *simphon* was used in Palestine.[126]

The Amoraic disputes that concern the *simphon* include discussions of the way to deal with the following: the case of a groom who had intended to fulfill his contractual obligation but was coerced into not doing so; the difference between coercion in the *kiddushin* and coercion in the *get* and how to word the *simphon* in order to prevent such claims of coercion; a bride's claim that the groom did not fulfill his contractual obligation; a groom who married his bride without fulfilling his contractual obligation; and two witnesses who testify to the *simphon* in the *kiddushin* and various incidents that occur during the *simphon* period – such as the groom repeating the *kiddushin* ceremony but this time without imposing any condition, or the groom divorcing the bride during this period, or the groom's death. The extent to which the *simphon* was regarded as a valid legal condition in the betrothal ceremony can be deduced from two other discussions in the Palestinian Talmud. The first deals with the validity of a *simphon* that was signed by two witnesses and the groom instead of by the requisite three witnesses, who are meant to serve as a *beit din*. The discussion is as follows:

> If there was one witness for the groom, one witness for the bride, and the groom signed personally: R. Abbahu said, it is a *simphon*, R. Abba said, it is preliminary marriage, for I am saying that he did not really intend a *simphon* but thought that it would permit her sister to him.[127]

[125] *See* BT *Kiddushin* 10b. For a general overview of the Jewish community in Elephantine and its various legal documents, see REUVEN YARON, THE LAW OF THE ELEPHANTINE DOCUMENTS (1968) (Heb.); BEZALEL PORTEN, JEWS OF ELEPHANTINE AND ARAMEANS OF SYENE FIFTH CENTURY BCE (1974) (Heb.).

[126] The *simphon* is discussed in the context of *kiddushin* in the following references: PT *Eruvin* 3:5 (21b); PT *Gittin* 7:6 (49a); PT *Kiddushin* 3:2 (63d). For a discussion of the *simphon* in a broader commercial context, see PT *Baba Metzia* 1:8 (7d–8a). For mention of the *simphon* without a discussion of it, see PT *Megillah* 1:9 (71c); PT *Baba Batra* 10:1 (17c).

[127] PT *Kiddushin* 3:2 (63d).

Before presenting this dispute, the Palestinian Talmud describes the choosing of the three witnesses to serve as a *beit din* and validate the *simphon*. These witnesses adjudicate the case and accept or reject the claim that the agreement was not fulfilled should one of the parties to the contract later on try to rescind the agreement. The passage in the Palestinian Talmud is as follows: "The following is the way of contracting: One witness for the groom and one witness for the bride; those two together select a third in order to have two witnesses for each side." In the case under discussion, the three witnesses were not chosen in the usual manner, namely, that each party chooses his or her own witness and the third witness is chosen jointly by the first two witnesses. Instead, the groom himself signed as a witness instead of an agreed-upon third witness. Since the *simphon* is a valid condition imposed in the *kiddushin* contract, there is actually no difference between it and a conditional *kiddushin*. Therefore, all concur that *a priori* a *simphon* is valid.

The dispute between the Amoraic sages, R. Abbahu and R. Abba, concerns whether the above-mentioned scenario is a valid conditional *kiddushin*. Thus, according to R. Abba, if the condition is not fulfilled, the *kiddushin* is annulled and the bride must return to the groom whatever she received from him. But according to R. Abbahu, we are dealing with a *kiddushin simphon* and therefore, even though the *kiddushin* ceremony is void, the groom must fulfill his undertaking and give the bride exactly what was contractually promised to her. In addition, from the continuation of the above Talmudic source as well, one can conclude that the *simphon* is a valid *kiddushin* stipulation for all intents and purposes. The source below deals with a quarrel between a couple as to whether their *kiddushin* is a conditional one because of the *simphon* or whether they have a valid *kiddushin*. The text states:

> If it was *simphon* in his opinion and preliminary marriage in her opinion, R. Hanina said, it is *simphon*, R. Haggi in the name of R. Zeira said, it is preliminary marriage. R. Hanina was taking up arms against R. Haggai, when R. Hila said to him, accept Haggai, for Haggai is a thinking man; this is what R. Zeira said. In the first Adar, R. Hila died. In the second Adar, a case came before R. Hananiah, the colleague of the rabbis, and he wanted to rule following R. Haggai. R. Samuel bar Immi told him R. Hila was wrong when he told you, accept Haggai, for Haggai is a thinking man. R. Haggai said, a Mishnah supports him: "You married me preliminarily" and he says, "I did not marry you preliminarily." He is permitted her relatives but she is forbidden his relatives.

As in the text of the first discussion, which presents a dispute between the bride and the groom as to whether their *kiddushin* was conditional since it included a *simphon*, there is an Amoraic dispute regarding the groom's obligation to give his bride what was initially contractually promised to her. According to R. Hanina, it is a *simphon*, and the groom must fulfill his initial obligation, but according to R. Zeira, since it is only a conditional *kiddushin*, he is exempt from his contractual undertaking. However, for the purposes of our discussion, I wish to suggest that the *simphon* has the power to invalidate not only the *kiddushin* but also the *nissuin*. The Talmud states as follows: "That is,[128] if not both of them agree. But if both of them agree, both may invalidate the preliminary marriage."

The simplest interpretation of this text is that it is actually a continuation of the previous discussion, which deals with either the need for witnesses or perhaps even the earlier case where the groom married his betrothed during the time period stipulated in the *simphon*. But these interpretations are difficult and seem forced. A more innovative explanation is that the *simphon* has the power to retroactively annul the marriage status due to the nonfulfillment of the initial stipulation imposed in the *kiddushin* even though the bride and the groom are already halakhically married. In other words, when the groom marries the bride during the time period stipulated in the *simphon*, he is forced (by the *beit din*) to fulfill his initial contractual undertaking to give his wife whatever he had promised. However, if a quarrel develops later on as to whether the groom did indeed fulfill his obligation toward the bride, his testimony is not regarded as reliable without evidence as proof. In other words, the innovation in the above text is that when the parties mutually agree that the husband has not fulfilled his initial contractual obligation, the marriage is annulled. Support for this explanation is found in David Frankel's commentary on the Palestinian Talmud ad loc (Korban ha-Edah, s.v. "*hada deat amar*").

A similar innovative understanding of the couple's mutual ability to annul both the *kiddushin* and the *nissuin* can be found in a discussion in the Palestinian Talmud dealing with a levirate marriage. When the levir and the woman both claim that they have not had conjugal relations, we believe them. But, when there is a dispute between them in this regard, and the levir claims that they have had a sexual relationship, he is not trusted, even if later on he insists that they never had a sexual relationship. The text reads as follows:

> [If, after thirty days,] (*kahada*)[129] he says, "I had sexual relations with her," and she says, "I have not had sexual relations with him," even though he retracted and claimed, "I did not have sexual relations with her," he has not got the power to make such a claim, for in the first place he claimed, "I did have sexual relations with her." But if at the outset he said, "I did not have sexual relations with her," both of them have the power to uproot the prevailing assumption [by reason of their agreement].[130]

[128] For an interpretation of the phrase "*hada deat amar*" (that is), see the following scholarly references: Zecharias Fraenkel, Introduction to the Jerusalem Talmud 10:2 (1967) (Heb.); Epstein, *supra* note 113, at 464 n.16; Moscovitz, *supra* note 113.

[129] For the meaning of this phrase, see the following scholarly sources: Epstein, *supra* note 113, at 326; Israel Levy, Jahresbericht des judisch-theologischen Seminars 181 (1895–1914) (Heb.).

[130] PT *Yevamot* 13:14 (14a). It should be noted that the phrase "*lo hakol mimenu*" (he has not got the power) is used on several occasions in the Palestinian Talmud, such as in PT *Gittin* 1:1 (43b); PT *Kiddushin* 1:3 (60a); PT *Kiddushin* 3:7 (64b).

Thus, if indeed the couple can agree that the initial contractual undertaking was not fulfilled, and therefore the marriage is annulled, this constitutes yet another Amoraic source from which we can infer that it is halakhically feasible to impose a condition in both the *kiddushin* and the *nissuin* ceremonies. Despite the fundamental, accepted principle that a conditional marriage is invalid, scholars disagree as to whether the *simphon* was a common practice also in Babylonia or whether it was specifically a Palestinian practice. According to Avraham C. Freiman (1889–1948, Jewish law scholar, Austria-Israel), this practice was not common in Babylonia and any discussion of it in the Babylonian Talmud is only incidental and intended to clarify a Tannaitic dispute.[131] Yet, one may argue that the *simphon* was commonly used also in Babylonia. Theoretically, the usage of the *simphon* in the *kiddushin* was accepted by the Babylonian *amoraim*, and it would be reasonable to assume that even in that era the principle was put into practice. But, in my opinion, it is very difficult to transpose a Palestinian Tannaitic practice to the context of the later Amoraic era in Babylonia. Thus, theoretical knowledge of this practice does not necessarily mean that it was adopted in practice, and therefore no definitive conclusions can be inferred from it.

In addition, in my opinion there is good reason to assume that this practice was necessary in Palestine, where it was common for Torah scholars to abandon their families in order to study Torah or, alternatively, to engage in trade overseas.[132] Thus, the danger of becoming an *agunah* was far greater among women in Palestine than among their Babylonian counterparts. In the post-Talmudic literature as well, we find remnants of this practice dating back to the end of the tenth century CE in Egypt and to the beginning of the eleventh century CE in Tyre, based on documents found in the Cairo Geniza.

These documents include *kiddushin ketubot* from the Babylonian community in Damascus, which date back to approximately 933 CE;[133] *kiddushin ketubot* from

[131] *See* Freiman, *supra* note 12, at 12. It is worth noting that the *simphon* is mentioned in the Babylonian Talmud only in BT *Kiddushin* 10b–11a; BT *Ketubot*. 57b–58b. It is not at all clear that the context of these references is a *kiddushin* and a stipulation imposed in the *kiddushin* contract, but perhaps a mistaken marriage after finding a blemish in the woman. In a broader context, the *simphon* can be found in the following Babylonian Talmud sources: BT *Baba Metzia* 20b–21a; BT *Sanhedrin* 31b.

[132] This is the conclusion of Avraham C. Freiman; *see* Freiman, *supra* note 12, at 12. For the phenomenon of the husband abandoning the home and family in order to study Torah in the Talmudic era, see Margalit, *supra* note 32, at 32–33. The extent to which this practice was common during this period may be inferred from the collection of *aggadic* stories in BT *Ketubot* 62b–63a. It should be emphasized that later on in Babylonia, this practice became very extreme, as illustrated in the instructions appearing in BT *Eruvin* 22a that a person who is eager to grow in Torah learning should leave his family without money, like "him who can bring himself to be cruel to his children and household like a raven." For sharp criticism of this practice of abandoning ones home for a long period in order to study Torah, see BT *Gittin* 6b: "Jews who come from there [Babylon] to here [Eretz Israel] fulfill in their own persons the words of the Scripture: They have given a boy for a harlot and sold a girl for wine and have drunk."

[133] For a description of the former *ketubot*, see Mordechai A. Friedman, Jewish Marriage in Palestine vol. I, 209–10 (1980) and his analysis ibid, vol. II, 396. For the latter *ketubah*, see Friedman, ibid, vol. I, 196, and his analysis ibid, vol. II, 383.

Tyre, dating back to approximately 1011–37 CE; a fragment (TS AR 54.78) of a *kiddushin ketubah* dating back to the end of the tenth century/beginning of the eleventh century CE.[134] In other words, there is sufficient evidence to assume that the practice of incorporating the *simphon* into the *kiddushin ketubah* survived until the end of the Geonic era and the beginning of the *rishonim* period – that is, throughout the entire era in which the *kiddushin* ceremony was separate from the *nissuin* ceremony, as was extensively discussed above. Moreover, there are additional remnants of this Palestinian practice, to varying degrees, even in the responsa literature.

This practice is discussed, *inter alia*, in sources that clearly indicate its survival even into the late post-Talmudic era, such as in a responsum by Yizhak Ben Yaakov Alfasi (Rif) concerning a conditional *kiddushin* enactment that was in practice in one of the communities in Spain.[135] This stipulation, on behalf of the woman, dictated that if the groom did not return home by an agreed-upon date after his betrothal to the bride, the *kiddushin* would be annulled. It was imposed by the bride in the *kiddushin ketubah* probably after the groom recited the *kiddushin* formula and just before she received the *kiddushin ketubah* from him.[136] The possibility of mutually agreeing to extend the agreed-upon period of time for fulfilling the initial contractual obligations is found later on in a responsum by Rabbeinu Asher (Rosh).[137] Even during the era of the Alhambra Decree, when the Jews were expelled from Spain, there is documentation of a conditional *kiddushin* ceremony similar to the Palestinian *simphon*. The father of the bride claimed that his daughter's betrothal was a conditional one. Since the groom did not return home as was initially agreed upon, having died overseas, the *kiddushin* was retroactively annulled and the bride was exempt from the *halizah* obligation.[138]

In another case, dating back to c. 1525, there is a document of testimony for a conditional *kiddushin* drawn up by two Syrian sages using the same wording as that of Levi Ben Haviv (1480–1541, prominent Jerusalem *posek* and leader, Zamora Spain-Israel). This document was most carefully worded, based on the Palestinian

[134] The latter document was described by Shelomo D. Goitein as a deed of betrothal; *see* Shelomo D. Goitein, A Mediterranean Society: The Jewish Communities of the Arab World as Portrayed in the Documents of the Cairo Geniza vol. III, 86 n.60 (1967).

[135] Yizhak Ben Yaakov Alfasi, Resp. Rif ch. 118 (1969). That this responsum was the first rabbinic enactment in a Western country that was similar to the Palestinian *simphon*; *see* Freiman, *supra* note 12, at 34.

[136] Freiman, ibid, supports the conclusion that we have remnants of the *simphon* practice in light of the halakhic practice that may be inferred from Yosef ben Meir ibn Migash, Resp. HaRi Migash ch. 53 (1959), that, at least in Spain, the bride would reply to the groom that she agrees to marry him. This practice was mentioned and discussed also in Shmuel ben Moshe de Medina, Resp. Maharashdam *Even ha-Ezer* ch. 27 (1959). Freiman explores the circumstances that created the need for this halakhic device, namely that in this period most Jewish communities were located near sea ports and there was the grave concern that the groom would set sail and disappear, thus leaving his wife an *agunah*, and therefore there was a great need for finding a reliable solution for this problem.

[137] Rabbeinu Asher, Resp. Rosh rule 35, ch. 9 (1954).

[138] Yaakov ben Moshe, Resp. Mahari Birav ch. 43 (1988).

simphon, and is therefore effective even in the case of a groom who claims that he was coerced from fulfilling his contractual obligations, and the bride may be released from the betrothal ceremony without the need for a *get*.[139]

5 EPILOGUE – CONDITIONAL MARRIAGE EXISTS IN THEORY BUT NOT IN PRACTICE

In the modern era, many variations of conditional marriage have been proposed as a possible solution to the *agunah* problem. The past century has been witness to much debate, generated by a variety of halakhic problems and approaches to halakhic policy,[140] over whether conditional marriage should be applied in practice (*halakhah lemaaseh*).[141] In a pamphlet titled *Eyn Tnai BeNissu'in*, Tzvi Gertner and Bezalel Karlinski (two contemporary rabbis and *poskim*) listed the different arguments of the various *poskim* who bitterly oppose this halakhic device, dividing them into five main categories: (1) the problem of making a stipulation that is contrary to what is written in the Torah; (2) there is no conditional marriage; (3) practical concerns; (4) ethical concerns – such as undermining the sanctity of the Jewish marriage ceremony; and (5) concern that women may easily release themselves from their marriage.[142] In this chapter, I tried to prove that the arguments used in the first two (main?) categories – the halakhic arguments against conditional marriage – are not very convincing and can be refuted. Moreover, there are several *rishonim* who hold that, in practice, all Jewish marriage ceremonies are actually conditional ones. Therefore, this particular claim that there is no halakhic room for imposing conditions in the marriage contract is definitely problematic.

In the second part of this chapter, I tried to shed light upon the large number of Tannaitic and Amoraic discussions of conditional *kiddushin* and even conditional *nissuin*. My claim that conditional marriage really exists is much more persuasive in light of the various *rishonim* and *aharonim* who maintain that in the modern era, with the combining of the *kiddushin* and *nissuin* ceremonies, any condition that is

[139] Levi Ben Yaakov Haviv, Resp. Maharlbah ch. 134 (1865). Freiman, *supra* note 12, at 119–20 assumes that remnants of this practice may be found also in Haviv, ibid, at ch. 120; Moshe ben Yitzhack Elshakar, Resp. Maharam Elshakar ch. 32 (1959).

[140] For a discussion of conditional marriage as a window to different approaches to Jewish law, interpretation, and moral agency, see Landau, *supra* note 9, at 110–25.

[141] For a review of the various proposals that have been suggested, see Freiman, *supra* note 12. For an overview and analysis of the rabbinic discussions regarding the proposals of Uzziel and Berkovits, see, respectively, Abel, *supra* note 12; Abel, *supra* note 11. For a discussion of further possible rabbinic support for Berkovits's proposal, see Marc B. Shapiro, Between the Yeshivah World and Modern Orthodoxy: The Life and Works of Rabbi Jehiel Jacob Weinberg 1884–1966 190–91 (1999) and compare with Gertner & Karlinski, *supra* note 12, at 747 n.117; Jackson et al., *supra* note 9, at 58–59.

[142] *See* Gertner & Karlinski, *supra* note 12, in the first part of their article, which deals with the main arguments against the proposal of the French rabbis. For categorizing those claims, see Abel, *The Plight*, *supra* note 14, at 28–30; Abel, *supra* note 11, at 6–38. Zaksh, *supra* note 39, at 62–67 counts forty(!) halakhic objections, but in my opinion, the vast majority of them overlap.

imposed in the *kiddushin* contract is actually also imposed in the *nissuin* contract, for all intents and purposes. Thus, we can confidently and safely argue that, halakhically, there is conditional marriage.[143] In my opinion, even the so-called purely halakhic arguments are based mainly on meta-halakhic concerns of undermining the sanctity of the Jewish marriage.[144] The traditional rabbinic opposition to conditional marriage has muted the call for its practical implementation, as Yehudah Abel writes:

> The debate over conditional marriage as a possible solution to the problem of 'iggun receives relatively little attention from contemporary halakhic authorities. The issue is assumed to have been "put to sleep" by the opposition to the French and Turkish proposals of the early 20th century.[145]

The following is the most recent comprehensive and thoroughly researched conclusion concerning the feasibility of this halakhic device as a reliable solution to the *agunah* problem:

> We may conclude that conditional marriage (conditions attached to both qiddushin and nissu'in) would be effective according to the vast majority of posqim. . . . This is the position of the major codes of Jewish Law: *Yad*, *Shulhan Arukh* and *Levush* and seems to have been recognised even within 'Eyn Tnai BeNissu'in itself. The commentators on both the *Yad* and the *Shulhan 'Arukh* are silent on this point, which means they all agree. . . . This is also apparent from the number of *posqim* who have proposed global conditional marriage in practice.[146]

Our sages (Mishnah *Avot* 2:16) taught us that "He [i.e., R. Tarfon] used to say: it is not [incumbent] upon thee to finish the work, but neither art thou a free man so as to [be entitled to] refrain therefrom." Let us hope that the recent intensive academic discourse on this unique and important halakhic device for, *inter alia*, resolving the problem of the *agunah* will convince the *poskim* who advise and guide the rabbinical courts on how to solve the various *iggun* problems to use it in practice (*halakhah lemaaseh*). As to the contention that the first two (main?) objections to using conditional marriage are more of a meta-halakhic concern than a purely halakhic concern, I wish to quote R. Akiva who concluded elsewhere, "If this is an authentic tradition we shall accept it; but if it is only a logical deduction, there is a rebuttal."[147]

[143] For a similar conclusion, see Abel, *The Plight*, *supra* note 14, at ("However, it is accepted by most authorities that the Talmud does not mean that a condition in *nissu'in* is *impossible*"); ABEL, *supra* note 11, at appendix II, 79–91 ("*Posqim* who Accepted the Practical Possibility of Conditional Marriage as a Solution for the Tragedy of 'Iggun"); Westreich, *supra* note 9, at 82 ("However, the conceptual basis of conditional marriage was generally accepted as viable, at least in principle.").

[144] *See* David Z. Hoffmann in *Lubetsky*, *supra* note 12, at 18; Pinhas Halevi Horowitz, in *Lubetsky*, *supra* note 12, at 14; Meir Simcha of Dvinsk, in *Lubetsky*, *supra* note 12, at 32.

[145] *See* Abel, *The Plight*, *supra* note 14, in the abstract.

[146] JACKSON ET AL., *supra* note 9, at 61–62. *See also* ibid, at §§ 3.33, 6.40.

[147] *See* Mishnah *Yevamot* 8:3; Mishnah *Keritot* 3:9; PT *Yevamot* 8:3 (9c) etc.

4

Temporary Marriage – A Possible Solution to the Problem of the *Agunah*?

INTRODUCTION

At the outset of the last chapter, Chapter 3, I explored the use of contractual devices, such as conditional marriage and prenuptial agreements, to deal with, or at least lessen, the dismal plight of the *agunah*. Throughout that chapter, I also tried to overcome the main halakhic obstacle to using contractual mechanisms – the well-known Talmudic dictum "there is no conditional marriage." With this background in mind, in this chapter I take the issue one step further and explore a unique contractual stipulation, which may be perceived as a form of conditional marriage – the temporary marriage. I discuss the temporary marriage in general and more specifically as a possible solution for the heart-wrenching case of the *agunah*.[1]

I begin the discussion by making the important distinction between a conditional marriage in general and a temporary one – as will be explained at length later on. A conditional marriage is a sort of terminative condition in which the marriage is annulled in certain agreed-upon circumstances, such as in the case of an *agunah*. As is discussed more extensively in Section 3, temporary marriage is actually much more than merely a specific terminative condition with a purely prospective effect. The *kiddushin* declaration itself dictates that the marriage's duration and even its very existence will expire on an agreed-upon date, and no *get* is required to terminate that marriage. For example, the groom may declare under the wedding canopy, "Today you are my wife, but after such and such a time, you are no longer my wife," and if the bride accepts this stipulation, their marriage simply ends on the said date.[2]

[1] For the claim that there is nothing in Jewish law to prevent a temporary marriage, either for a period of days or months, or with a view to dissolving it at an unspecified future date, see HAIM COHN, JEWISH LAW IN ISRAELI JURISPRUDENCE 16 (1968); Bernard Meislin, *Jewish Law of Marriage in American Courts*, 11 J. FAM. L. 271, 275 n.13 (1971–72).

[2] *See also* BERNARD S. JACKSON ET AL., AGUNAH: THE MANCHESTER ANALYSIS 84 n.351, 131–32 (2011), http://static1.1.sqspcdn.com/static/f/784513/11612882/1302166384333/BSJ+ARU+Final+v2.pdf?token=RSyrg%2F9cedI5z83pXkaDqfKWoZQ%3D.

The Jewish marriage has always been a shining example of a strong and stable family cell. It differs from the Catholic Christian marriage, which is an institution surrounded by the halo of a holy sacrament that cannot be nullified, even with the agreement of the two partners – "Therefore what God has joined together, let no man put asunder."[3] It also differs from the Islamic marriage, which is closer to a legal agreement than to a sacrament,[4] wherein the husband alone may annul the marriage, either unilaterally or by mutual consent.[5] This is especially true of the Shi'ite marriage – the *muta*[6] – which may annul itself without any divorce proceedings at a predetermined date. Between these two extremes is the Jewish marriage, which may be annulled under specific circumstances or by the agreement of both partners.[7]

3 Mark 10:9. *See also* PHILLIPS RODERICK, PUTTING ASUNDER: A HISTORY OF DIVORCE IN WESTERN SOCIETY 15–30, 34–39 (1988); JOHN WITTE, FROM SACRAMENT TO CONTRACT: MARRIAGE, RELIGION, AND LAW IN THE WESTERN TRADITION (1997); ZEEV FALK, MARRIAGE AND DIVORCE: REFORMS IN THE FAMILY LIFE OF GERMAN-FRENCH JEWRY 11ff, 55ff (1961) (Heb.).

4 Compare the conclusions of the following articles and books in Hebrew: SHLOMO D. GOITEIN & AHARON BEN SHEMESH, ISLAMIC LAW IN THE STATE OF ISRAEL 218 (1957) ("the marital bond is a civil contract between two parties"); YAAKOV MERON, MOSLEM LAW IN COMPARATIVE PERSPECTIVE 177 (2001) ("Marriage in Islam is a contractual agreement.)"; GUY BEHOR, BETWEEN VISION AND REALITY: LAW IN THE ARAB WORLD 270 (2002) ("Under Islamic law, the marriage contract is a commercial contract, which is entered into by an offer and the acceptance of the offer and any disputes are settled under contractual law (*majles*), i.e., place and time, between the woman's guardian and her future husband"). This statement is quoted also by the president of the Shari'a appeals court in Israel, his honor the Quadi Sheikh Tavik al-Aslia in T.P. (B.S.) 140/83 The State of Israel v. Amar ben Mehusan id al-Tsaria, P.M. 1986(2) 336, 346 (1985). This approach is reflected in legislation – specifically in paragraph 35 of Ottoman family law – which states, "Marriage is initiated by a proposal and the acceptance of the proposal either by the sides or by their representatives." Similarly, paragraph 2 of the Jordanian law governing personal status defines marriage as "a legal contract between a man and a woman with the aim of establishing a family and bearing children." For a comprehensive discussion of the Islamic conception of marriage, see ABD AL ATI, *infra* note 56, at 50–64 n.95. For a discussion as to whether the Islamic marriage is a contract or a sacrament, along with a comparison of the Jewish and Christian approaches to marriage, see ABD AL ATI, *infra* note 56, at 56–59.

5 For a comparison of the Islamic approach with the different Christian approaches – Catholicism emphasizes the sacramental nature of the marriage while Protestantism is less rigid and far more flexible – see THEODOR VON KIPP & MARTIN WOLFF, DAS FAMILIENRECHT 114 (1923). For a more detailed account, see Dagmar Coester-Waltjen & Michael Coester, *Formation of Marriage in Persons and Family*, in INTERNATIONAL ENCYCLOPEDIA OF COMPARATIVE LAW vol. 4, 6 (Mary A. Glendon ed., 1997).

6 For a discussion of the husband's ability to annul a marriage at any time without his wife's agreement, even if the marriage has been consummated, see ZIBA MIR-HOSSEINI, MARRIAGE ON TRIAL: A STUDY OF ISLAMIC FAMILY LAW: IRAN AND MOROCCO COMPARED 165 (1993). For this unique type of marriage, which is problematic because it is closer to institutionalized prostitution than to institutionalized marriage, see Willi Heffening, *Mut'a* in ENCYCLOPAEDIA OF ISLAM vol. 7, 757–59 (C. E. Bosworth et al. eds., 1960), and more extensively the discussion in Section 5.

7 *See* BENZION SCHERESCHEWSKY, FAMILY LAW IN ISRAEL 279 (4th ed., 1993) (Heb.); TALMUDIC ENCYCLOPEDIA vol. 6, 354 (Shlomo Zevin et al. eds., 1954) (Heb.). For a legal disagreement over whether halakhic marriage is a normal contract, which is the opinion of judge Haim Cohen, or

The marriage depicted in the Written Law is similar to the Muslim marriage. The husband alone has the right to dissolve the marriage, and the wife can neither initiate nor demand a divorce.[8] However, the decrees of Rabbenu Gershom Meor ha-Golah (c. 1000 CE) equated the wife's position with that of her husband, and the husband could no longer divorce his wife against her will, but both sides had to agree to the divorce. In other words, just as a marriage requires that both parties agree to it of their own free will, from that time onward, the dissolution of a marriage also required the consent of both parties.[9] I would point out that this is not substantive equality but rather formal equality; as experts in different aspects of Jewish family law point out, the definitions of unfaithfulness that are a sufficient basis for the dissolution of a marriage, the justifications for divorce, and the methods of compelling divorce are not symmetrical, with the husband's position far stronger than that of his wife.[10]

Moreover, a woman's status in a Jewish marriage is much worse when her husband obstinately refuses to grant her a divorce or her brother-in-law refuses to carry out *halitzah* in order to release her from a levirate marriage. As was explored at length in Chapter 3, there has been considerable discussion regarding the source of the problem of the woman's status and possible solutions for this unique situation of

a special contract, in accordance with Judge Moshe Zilberg's ruling, see Israeli High Court 337/62 Rizenfeld v. Jacobson, 17 PD 1009, 1026–27 (1963). For a historical sketch, from the development of Jewish marital laws to Christian sacramental marriage laws, see Michael L. Satlow, *Slipping toward Sacrament: Jews, Christians and Marriage*, in JEWISH CULTURE AND SOCIETY UNDER THE CHRISTIAN ROMAN EMPIRE 65 (Richard Kalmin & Seth Schwartz eds, 2003).

8 For a discussion of a woman's right to initiate her divorce, see the various articles in 4 DINE ISRAEL (1973) (Heb.); Avishalom Westreich, *The Wife's Right to Divorce in Jewish Law: History, Dogmatics and Hermeneutics*, 62(2) J. JEWISH STUD. 340 (2011); Lena Salaymeh, *Every Law Tells a Story: Orthodox Divorce in Jewish and Islamic Legal Histories*, 4(1) UC IRVINE L. REV. 19 (2014). For the possibility of finding sources, at least in the Palestinian Talmud and in Palestinian tradition, that a woman may, in principle, introduce a condition at the time of the marriage that if she should hate her husband, he would be forced to divorce her, just as he could divorce her if he hated her, see the discussion in Chapter 2 of this book.

9 *See* RABBEINU ASHER, RESP. HA-ROSH ch. 42, s.v. "*dayo*" (1954). For confirmation of the effectiveness of this decree and its wide acceptance in different communities, see, e.g., RABBI NISSIM BEN REUVEN GIRONDI (THE RAN) RESP. HA-RAN ch. 38 (1950). For a summary of the different opinions regarding this decree, see TALMUDIC ENCYCLOPEDIA vol. 17, 378 (Shlomo Zevin et al. eds., 1990) (Heb.); SCHERESCHEWSKY, *supra* note 7, at 280–81.

10 For criticism of the religious marital structure in general, and the Jewish structure in particular, see Zvi H. Triger, *The Gendered Racial Formation: Foreign Men, "Our" Women, and the Law*, 30 WOMEN'S RTS. L. REP. 479 (2008–09); ibid, *Freedom from Religion in Israel: Civil Marriages and Cohabitation of Jews Enter the Rabbinical Courts*, 27(2) ISRAEL STUD. REV. 1 (2012); ibid, *"A Jewish and Democratic State": Reflections on the Fragility of Israeli Secularism*, 41 PEPP. L. REV. 1091 (2014); Ruth Halperin-Kaddari & Yaacov Yadgar, *Between Universal Feminism and Particular Nationalism: Politics, Religion and Gender (In)Equality in Israel*, 31(6) THIRD WORLD Q. 905 (2010); and more extensively RUTH HALPERIN-KADDARI, WOMEN IN ISRAEL: A STATE OF THEIR OWN (2004). For a discussion of the different halakhic aspects of the refusal to grant a *get*, see, e.g., Rachel Levmor, *Pre-Nuptial Agreements with the Aim of Preventing the Husband's Refusal to Give a Get*, 23 SHNATON HA-MISHPAT HA-IVRI 127, 144–45 (2005) (Heb.) and all the other references discussed in Chapter 3 of this book.

levirate marriage and of the husband's refusal to grant a divorce, which in the opinion of many halakhic authorities is the most problematic and difficult halakhic issue in general and in family law in particular. However, in my opinion, temporary marriage (*kiddushin lezman*) may provide a halakhic solution to this problem, a solution that unfortunately has been neglected by both rabbinical authorities and scholars. This solution of temporary marriage has been rejected and not allowed to be put into practice. Nonetheless, in this chapter I illustrate its Talmudic sources and trace its influence on halakhic rulings, on the responsa literature, and on the rulings of the rabbinical courts, and I call for a reassessment of this approach.

In Section 1, I examine an obstacle to temporary marriage that is based on a Talmudic teaching and the application of this obstacle in *halakhah*. The major difference between a regular marriage and a temporary one is that in the latter, there is no necessity for a *get* in order to end the marriage. The position of the authorities who rule that there is no necessity for a *get* in the case of temporary marriage is discussed in Section 2. Section 3 focuses on the nature of a conditional marriage and a temporary marriage, their common features and differences, including their relative advantages and disadvantages. In Section 4, I analyze the Talmudic sources regarding the subject of "Who would be mine for a day?" which, in the eyes of many commentators and scholars, is a classic Talmudic application of a temporary marriage. Section 5 is devoted to an elaboration of the Shi'ite temporary marriage for pleasure, its historical sources, its modern applications, and its influence on Jewish and Karaite responsa. Section 6 explores the common roots of the Talmudic temporary marriage and the Shi'ite marriage for pleasure in ancient Persian law. I conclude this chapter with a search for practical applications of temporary marriage to solve the problem of the *agunah*.

1 OBSTACLE TO TEMPORARY MARRIAGE BASED ON A TALMUDIC TEACHING

Our exploration of the roots of a temporary marriage in Talmudic sources begins with a related discussion that occurs in two different places in the Babylonian Talmud warning a man not to continue living with his wife once he has decided to divorce her. Clearly, this would apply in a case where, at the time of the wedding ceremony, the husband sets specific limits to the length of the marriage. This would appear to be the ultimate conclusion in the case of the Talmudic discussion of "Who will be mine for a day?" (BT *Yevamot* 37b), which is discussed in greater detail in section 4. The two sources in the Babylonian Talmud are as follows:

> A Tanna taught: R. Eliezer b. Yaakov said: A man must not marry a woman if it is his intention to divorce her, for it is written, Devise not evil against thy neighbour, seeing he dwelleth securely by thee.
>
> (*Yevamot* 37b)

> R. Mesharsheya said to Rava: If a man has made up his mind to divorce his wife, but she still lives with him and waits on him, what are we to do with him? [He replied:] We apply to him the verse, Devise not evil against thy neighbour, seeing he dwelleth securely by thee.
>
> (*Gittin* 90a)

Different commentators[11] have already wondered why the *amora* R. Mesharsheya needed to establish what had already been established much earlier by the *tanna*, R. Eliezer ben Yaakov. What new contribution did he make? However, why did the compiler of the Talmud not use R. Eliezer ben Yaakov's *beraita* to support R. Mesharsheya's position? Various explanations have been offered. Zerach Warhaftig[12] provides a straightforward answer – that the only thing to be learned from the *beraita* in Tractate *Yevamot* is that it is forbidden to deceive one's wife by entering into the marriage with the intention of divorcing her. R. Mesharsheya, however, is dealing with the case of a man who married in the standard manner but whose attitude toward his wife changed later on. In this case, it is forbidden to plan to divorce her while continuing to live with her as her husband. The husband must refrain from marital intimacy and start divorce proceedings immediately. Maimonides (Laws of Divorce, 10:21) states that the husband should not continue living with his wife after deciding to divorce her – "A person should not marry with intention of divorcing and she should not remain with him if his intention is to divorce her."

Various rabbinic authorities have suggested that Maimonides' statement is a halakhic prohibition and not just advice as to the correct way to behave.[13] Other commentators on Maimonides write that the prohibition also applies in the case of a standard marriage that was conducted according to all halakhic requirements, where the husband's decision to divorce his wife was made after the wedding and even where the marriage was not yet consummated.[14] Similarly, the author of Prisha (*Tur, Even ha-Ezer*, chapter 25, letter 31), Joshua ben Alexander haCohen Falk (1555–1614), rules that the husband is not permitted to wait until after the wedding ceremony to tell his wife that he intends to divorce her, even if he tells her before having conjugal relations with her. However, other authorities point out that if he did marry her for a stated period, he need not divorce her.[15] Similarly, Maimonides ruled that it is prohibited to continue marital relations with "a woman whom he intends to divorce" after he has reached his decision (Forbidden Relations, 21:12) – "And he should not have marital relations with her after he has

[11] *See* Isaiah Pick Berlin's query in his commentary *Hidushe ha-Shas le-Masekhet Gittin*, 9 with regard to his commentary on this Talmudic discussion.

[12] *See* Zerach Warhaftig, Zrichat Hashani on Tractate Nashim 88 (2000) (Heb.).

[13] Moshe ben Haviv, Get Pashut ch. 119, para. 6, s.v. "*Ve-Ra'iti*" (1980).

[14] *See* Pri Hadash, aleph. For a similar halakhic conclusion based on Talmudic sources, see Warhaftig, *supra* note 12.

[15] Yosef S. Nathanson, Resp. Sho'el u-Meshiv, early edition, vol. 2 ch. 6, s.v. "*ve-Hine*" (1993).

decided to divorce her, and if he does so, some of his sons will not be righteous but rather insolent and some will be rebellious and criminal."[16]

However, in the same chapter (*halakhah* 28), Maimonides distinguishes between two situations. In the first, the husband decided to divorce his wife and has not yet informed her. In this case, he must divorce her immediately. In the second, both parties have agreed to a temporary marriage. In this case, Maimonides rules, "It is forbidden for a person to marry with the intention of divorcing his wife, as it is written, you should not devise harm against your fellow who lives trustfully with you, but if he announced that it is a temporary marriage, it is permitted."

Many authorities disagree with Maimonides and prohibit a temporary marriage, even with prior agreement,[17] whereas others posit that with prior notification, it is permissible but the husband is not permitted to wait until after the marriage to inform his wife. However,[18] a number of rabbinic authorities accepted Maimonides' distinction, including Moshe ben Yaakov of Coucy (thirteenth century), in his book *Sefer Mitzvot Gadol* on the 613 commandments, and Menachem ben Shlomo Meiri (1249–1315), who expressed a similar opinion in his work *Bet ha-Behirah* in the section relating to this Talmudic passage. In his halakhic codex, the *Shulhan Arukh* (*Even ha-Ezer*, 119:1; ibid, 2:10), Yosef Caro, follows Maimonides' ruling in two separate instances; in each of which, he states, "A person should not marry a woman with the intention of divorcing her. If he gave prior notice that the marriage is for a limited period, it is permissible."[19]

2 HALAKHIC OPINIONS THAT A TEMPORARY MARRIAGE MAY BE DISSOLVED WITHOUT A *GET*

Based on a discussion in the Babylonian Talmud (*Nedarim* 29b), a number of early halakhic authorities arrived at a tentative conclusion that according to Abbaye, a temporary marriage is valid and may be dissolved without a *get*, however, in actuality, they did not rule in this way.[20] This unprecedented statement regarding the validity of a temporary marriage and its dissolution without a *get* is discussed by Haim Benbenishti (1603–73) in his work *Knesset ha-Gedolah*:

> The compiler said, If a man marries a woman and tells her, 'I am marrying you for thirty days and after thirty days you are free to remarry', it is not clear whether the

[16] *See also* Yosef Caro in *Shulhan Arukh, Even ha-Ezer* 25:8.

[17] For this opinion, see Yechiel M. Epstein, Arukh ha-Shulhan *Even ha-Ezer* 119:10 (2007) and Otzar ha-Poskim vol. 1 ch. 2, 11:47 (1966).

[18] *See, e.g.*, Reem haCohen, Bade Aharon 211 n.27 (1993) (Heb.). For a different opinion, see Moshe Shick (Maharam Shick) in his notes to *Shulhan Arukh Even ha-Ezer* 119:1.

[19] For a summary of the discussion, see Ben-Zion M. Uziel, Resp. Piskei Uziel be-She'elot ha-Zman ch. 54 (1977). For an incomplete summary, see Talmudic Encyclopedia, *supra* note 7, at 412–13.

[20] *See Hidushe ha-Rashba veha-Ran le-Nedarim* 29b.

> marriage is valid and whether after the thirty days the woman may be released without a *get*. In my opinion, the marriage is valid, and if somebody else marries her within the thirty-day period, the second marriage is invalid, and after thirty days she is released without a *get*.[21]

The author of *Knesset ha-Gedolah* goes even further, arguing that the condition that the wife is married for only thirty days is regarded as valid by those rabbinic authorities who do not accept Mahari Bruna's condition with regard to levirate marriage, discussed extensively in the previous chapter. The basis of his argument is that Mahari Bruna's condition contradicts the Written Law, whereas the condition that the wife is married for only thirty days does not. Furthermore, in both cases, retroactive annulment of the marriage does not transform the marital relations into prostitution, since the woman was consecrated to one particular man, and at worst should be regarded as a *pilegesh* (concubine, a relationship with a lesser status than that of a wife). He writes:

> Even Bet Yosef, which disagrees with Terumat ha-Deshen, ibid, chapter 157 regarding the case of levirate marriage, agrees that in our case, where a condition was made that the wife is married for only thirty days, there is no necessity for a *get*. In the former case (Terumat ha-Deshen's condition, which is a variation of Mahari Bruna's condition), the condition was invalid because it contradicted the Written Law and a condition which contradicts the Written Law is automatically invalid, whereas the latter case does not contradict the Written Law, and the condition is therefore valid.

Benbenishti raises one question: if the husband dies without issue before the end of the period allotted to the marriage, is the wife subject to the obligation of a levirate marriage? On the one hand, the husband is allowed to set a condition to the marriage, but he cannot override the obligation of a levirate marriage. On the other hand, it is possible that when the marriage condition expires, the obligation of a levirate marriage may disappear, since the obligation applies only in a valid marriage. Benbenishti's ruling is that the wife is not subject to the obligation of a levirate marriage in such circumstances.

One of the rabbinic authorities who rejected the position presented in *Knesset ha-Gedolah*[22] is Isaac Nuñez Belmonte, the author of *Sha'ar ha-Melekh*, who distinguished between two situations: if the husband died childless and the widow is subject to levirate marriage, stipulating that her marriage may be annulled is valid, since the marriage was based on the assumption that it would be annulled should a

[21] His commentary to *Tur Even ha-Ezer* vol. 1, Laws of Marriage, 38 (1961).

[22] For a partial list, see Be'er Heitev, 38:1; Akiva Eiger, Resp. Teshuvot Hadashot *Even ha-Ezer* ch. 15 (2002); Ben-Zion M. Uziel, Resp. Mishpatei Uziel *Even ha-Ezer* vol. 2 ch. 44–45 (1964); Yehoshua Ovadia, Resp. Yismah Levav *Even ha-Ezer* ch. 11 (1998); Isaac Nuñez Belmonte, Sha'ar ha-Melekh *le-Gerushin* 8:9 (2006); Ovadia Hadaya, Resp. Yaskil Avdi *Even ha-Ezer* vol. 3 ch. 6 (1931).

levirate marriage be required. However, in a temporary marriage, the marriage itself, although intended for a limited period, is a valid marriage and cannot be annulled without a *get* and certainly not on the basis of an oral contract. Petah ha-Sha'ar (Yitzhak ben Moshe Sandrosi), in his commentary to *Sha'ar ha-Melekh*, rejected this distinction, and wrote that in *Kenesset ha-Gedolah*, the two cases were regarded as similar: In the case of a levirate marriage, the financial arrangement made for the bride at the betrothal is valid until a specific condition is met (i.e., the need for a levirate marriage) and then is converted into a gift for the woman, thus retroactively nullifying the entire *kiddushin* and *nissuin*. Likewise, at the end of the term of a temporary marriage, the money that was originally part of the marriage contract is converted into a gift to the wife. Thus, she is not married and therefore not subject to levirate marriage.[23]

There are modern halakhic authorities who seem to accept the novel approach of *Knesset ha-Gedolah* that a temporary marriage is valid and is dissolved without a divorce procedure. See, for example, the responsa of Joseph S. Nathanson,[24] Eliyahu Hazan,[25] and Ovadia Hadaya,[26] although the latter requires a *get* in order to cover all possible problems. As regards the scholarly discourse in this regard, I would mention Zeev Falk who, some forty years ago, suggested, *inter alia*, that the problem of a husband's refusal to grant a divorce could be resolved by a prenuptial agreement that the bond between the couple is severed upon the husband's death or his unjustified refusal to agree to a divorce. This idea was raised as a solution to the problem of the *agunah*. After discussing sources that support his approach, he writes:

> If this assumption is correct, it would be possible to make a marriage which would be valid until one of two conditions is fulfilled – either the death of the husband or a divorce decision handed down by a recognized rabbinical court. In the first case, the marriage will be annulled by death and the widow will not be liable to levirate marriage. In the second case, the court's decision would be sufficient to annul the marriage. I would hope that rather than using this means, the husband would understand his position and give the divorce of his own volition.[27]

Incidentally, I would point out that there are no halakhic problems and no abrogation of the Written Law in the views of the halakhic authorities cited above

[23] *See* Isaac Nuñez Belmonte, Hidushe Sha'ar ha-Melekh on Tractate Kiddushin 58b and n.1 (2000).

[24] *See* Joseph S. Nathanson, Resp. Shoel u'Meshiv ch. 35 21b (2d ed., 1964). Falk, *supra* note 3, at 95 adds a reference to Yad Shaul, an additional work by Joseph S. Nathanson on the laws of vows, ch. 221, para. 19 (1991); Moshe ben Habib in his commentary to Tractate *Sukkah* 41b, s.v. "*kitvu*" (1998) suggests that the notion of temporary sacred property (*hekdesh*) may be valid.

[25] Elijah B. Hazan, Resp. Taalumot Lev vol. 3 ch. 41 (1903).

[26] *See* Hadaya, *supra* note 22, at *Even ha-Ezer* ch. 6.

[27] *See* Falk, *supra* note 3, at 97. For a critical discussion of his suggestion, see Elisha Schoenbaum, *[on] Z. W. Falk, The Divorce Action by the Wife in Jewish Law*, 6 Dine Israel 303 (1975) (Heb.).

and in Falk's approach since in their opinion there is no halakhic necessity for a *get*.[28] The need for a *get* and the problem of conditions that contradict Written Law apply to marriages regulated by Jewish law. However, these concerns do not apply to a marriage condition that completely annuls the marriage retroactively or a condition that sets the duration of a given act, such as a marriage entered into for a fixed period of time. In the latter two cases, the marriage is entered into for a specific time by mutual agreement and the marriage is valid during the agreed-upon period. I explain the two types of conditions and the relationship between them, along with their advantages and disadvantages, in the next section.

3 THE DIFFERENCES BETWEEN A CONDITIONAL MARRIAGE AND A TEMPORARY MARRIAGE

Elsewhere, I discussed the existence of two types of conditions – a narrative that defines an act and a narrative that supports or annuls an act.[29] The first condition defines the extent of the act to which the condition is applied; in other words, the condition does not apply to the act but only to its legal consequences. The second type of condition is capable of annulling or supporting the act to which it applies. In our case, the condition of Mahari Bruna is a narrative that confirms or annuls the act of the marriage itself. It is capable of retroactively annulling the marriage in a case where a woman becomes subject to the obligation of levirate marriage.

This revolutionary condition gave rise to complex halakhic debates and much controversy over the possibility of entering into a conditional marriage. The subject of the controversy was the validity of setting forth conditions at the time of the marriage ceremony that could lead to a retroactive annulment of the marriage, especially in the case of a husband who adamantly refuses to divorce his wife.[30] Adding preconditions to the marriage ceremony may solve not only the problem of levirate marriage, as I briefly pointed out above, but also the problem of the *agunah*. The solution of introducing preconditions may annul the marriage retroactively and render a *get* superfluous for ending the marriage.

However, various halakhic authorities claim that a condition that annuls a marriage is valid only after the husband's death or in the case of a refusal by the husband's brother to perform *halitzah* in order to circumvent a levirate marriage. But, in the case of a husband who adamantly refuses to divorce his wife, the condition is not strong enough to annul the marriage and release the wife without

[28] *See* the discussion in Chapter 3 of this book.

[29] *See* the discussion in Yehezkel Margalit, *Marriage According to the Law of Moses and Israel – between Family Law and Contract Law* n. 101 (forthcoming, 2018).

[30] For a discussion of the different types of conditional marriage that have been suggested to solve the problem of the *agunah*, see the discussion in this book, Chapter 3.

a *get* that is written in accordance with all the halakhic requirements. As discussed extensively in the previous chapter, this approach is partially based upon the Talmudic dictum "*En tnai be-Nisuin*" (there is no conditional marriage);[31] in other words there are no valid conditions, even those that annul a marriage retroactively, that do not require the granting of a *get*. Even if such a condition were to be effective in annulling a marriage, this solution could be too detrimental to the sanctity of the Jewish family and could undermine the foundations of both problematic and nonproblematic Jewish marriages. This sort of criticism is found in the writings of both halakhic authorities[32] and scholars[33] who view this as an attempt to undermine Jewish marriage, which, in their opinion, should reflect solidity and eternity.

On the other hand, marriage for a predetermined period of time is considered a limiting condition, and thus a less radical solution, since it does not annul the marriage retroactively but only from a particular moment onward. It may thus be more acceptable from a halakhic point of view since there is less concern of undermining the stability of the marriage. However, there are those who claim that from a halakhic perspective, annulment of a marriage might be easier than ending a marriage at a given point in time, as may be seen in the halakhic discourse regarding marriage annulment.[34] Furthermore, since the condition of a predetermined period is mutually agreed upon by both partners, it may not be applicable to every case of a husband refusing to grant a divorce. Another problem is the recommended length of the marriage. If the period is too long, what are the advantages of a fixed-length marriage? If the period is too short, it might discourage couples from marrying, since extending the marriage by mutual agreement gives rise to other halakhic problems.

[31] This general rule appears in only one discussion in BT *Yevamot* 107a and developed into a general rule in the period of the early rabbinic authorities. *See, e.g.*, ISAAC BEN MOSHE (OR ZARUA), SEFER OR ZARUA vol. 1 – Laws of Levirate Marriage and Marriage, ch. 617 (1958). Among the later rabbinic authorities, see, e.g., Lechem Mishneh, Laws of Divorce, 10:6; ARYEH HELLER, AVNEI MILUIM ch. 39 (2000); DAVID BEN HAIM, RESP. HA-RADAKH ch. 9 (2008); HAIM BEN ITZHAK OF VOLOZHIN, RESP. HUT HA-MESHULASH vol. 3 ch. 3 (1882); HAIM YEHEZKEL BEN YEHUDA LANDAU, RESP. SHIVAT ZIYYON ch. 71 (1881); CHAIM OZER GRODZENSKI, RESP. AHIEZER *Even ha-Ezer* vol. 1 ch. 9 (1960); HADAYA, *supra* note 22.

[32] *See, e.g.*, UZIEL, *supra* note 22. For further discussion, see the many different rabbinic authorities mentioned above in *supra* notes 21–24 and accompanying text, who rejected *Knesset ha-Gedolah*'s suggestion to annul a marriage that was entered into for a predetermined period without requiring a *get*.

[33] *See* AVRAHAM C. FREIMAN, SEDER KIDDUSHIN VENISUIN AHAREI HATIMAT HATALMUD 296–397 (1944) (Heb.).

[34] In the discussions on the annulment of a marriage, many of the early halakhic authorities were uncertain as to whether it is effective retroactively or from the moment of the annulment. *See, e.g.*, Rashi's commentary, BT *Ketubot*, 3a, s.v. "*Tinah* and *Kidesh be-Biah Mae*" and compare this with the novellae of Ritba, cited in Shita Mekubetset, Tractate *Ketubot*, ibid, s.v. "*ve-Katav ha-Ritba*."

4 "*MAN HAVYA LE-YOMA*" (WHO WILL BE MINE FOR A DAY?)

In exploring Talmudic sources that are relevant to our discussion, we come across a puzzling and astonishing issue in the Babylonian Talmud. There are two parallel sources that may serve as evidence for the validity of a temporary marriage that is agreed upon at the time of the marriage ceremony itself. Such marriages are dissolved by a *get*, and according to some of the authorities discussed above, a *get* itself may not be necessary for dissolving the marriage. I am referring to the discussion of "*kiddushin lezman*" (temporary marriage) evoked by the appeal of Rav and R. Nahman, two of the most important Babylonian *amoraim*, "Who will be mine for a day?"[35] Below is the text (BT *Yoma* 18b, with the parallel in BT *Yevamot* 37b):

> Whenever Rav came to Darshis, he would announce: Who would be mine for a day? Whenever R. Nahman[36] would come to Shekunziv he would have it announced: Who will be mine for a day?[37] But has it not been taught: No man should marry a woman in one country and then go and marry a woman in another country lest they [their children] marry one another, with the result that a brother would marry his sister or a father his daughter, and one would fill all the world with bastardy to which the scriptural passage refers: And the land became full of lewdness? – I will tell you: [The affairs of] the Rabbis are well-known. But did not Rava say: If one has proposed marriage to a woman and she has consented then she must await seven clean days? – The Rabbis informed them before by sending their messenger earlier. Or, if you like, say: They only arranged for private meetings with them, because "You cannot compare one who has bread in his basket with one who has no bread in his basket."

The Talmud is amazed that the sages allowed themselves such behavior, as their conduct violates a ruling in a *beraita* (external *mishnah*), which forbids marrying a woman in one place and then leaving her to reside in another place. As R. Eliezer ben Yaakov points out, this is because of the danger that a brother will not know about his half-sister from the same father, and they will inadvertently marry and produce *mamzerim*. This text is extremely difficult to comprehend. The rabbis have reason to fear their evil inclination (*yetzer hara*), but they must also fear their Creator. On the one hand, if we are talking about cohabitation that is not fully

[35] BT *Yoma* 18b; BT *Yevamot* 37b. For a clarification of the exact wording of the text, which is relevant to the issue of "Who will be mine for a day," see, e.g., EPHRAIM E. AUERBACH, HAZAL PIRKEI EMUNOT VE-DEOT 422 n.28 (Heb.) and the variants quoted by AVRAHAM LEES (compiler) DIKDUKEI SOFRIM HA-SHALEM ON TRACTATE YEVAMOT vol. 2, 33–34 (1983) with the wealth of authorities quoted in the latter work.

[36] In the Munich manuscript, we find his full name "R. Nahman bar Yitzhak" even though this addition is not found in the manuscript editions of *Yevamot*. For an attempt to identify the sage, see Elman, *infra* note 95, at 153 n.29.

[37] In the version in Tractate *Yevamot*, Rivan and other early authorities, as well as the manuscripts, prefer "יומי," as do Rashash and Rashi.

halakhically valid, as in the case of an additional wife to the first wife who is legally married to the sage (and is living in a different place), how do we justify these sages' inappropriate deeds?[38] Perhaps the text is an Amoraic documentation of the halakhic approach to temporary marriages of a predetermined length and their annulment at the end of that period (apparently with a *get*, although opinions are not unanimous). On the other hand, if the text is indeed referring to a temporary marriage, how do we explain this immoral behavior of sages who were already legally married yet took an extra wife for a predetermined period[39] and made the specific condition of a temporary marriage before the marriage?[40]

Rashi, in his commentary to the texts in *Yoma* and *Yevamot*, explains that the words "Who will be mine for a day?" refer to a search for a woman who would agree to be married for one or several days while the sage is in town, after which they would separate. It would seem that the text is referring to a full marriage requiring a divorce procedure to end it. On the other hand, the Talmud suggests – and such suggestions sometimes have the status of a halakhic ruling – that the woman is not fully married but has simply been designated for him. Indeed, many of the early rabbinic authorities followed the opinion of the tosafist RI- (Rabbi Yitzhak ben Shmuel the Elder) who asserts that the text is not referring to a proper marriage, but a woman is allocated to the sage de jure but not de facto. The purpose was to ensure that the sages would be able to satisfy their sexual needs,[41] but the marriage was not a full marriage that requires a *get*.[42] Similarly Yitzhak bar Sheshet (Rivash, ch. 398) writes:

> But it would seem that this is only a designation; in other words a woman is selected and makes preparations to marry the rabbis if the rabbis should wish to do so. The rabbis would not marry them; but would make a condition to marry them should they [the rabbis] so desire. This would calm their sexual urges, as a woman was available in the town and was prepared to marry them should they so wish.

[38] *See, e.g.*, ADIEL SCHREMER, Male and Female He Created Them: Jewish Marriage in the Late Second Temple, Mishnah and Talmud Periods 206 (2003) (Heb.), who assumed that the text is not discussing fully legal marriages because these marriages do not involve normal, day-to-day family life, but "he is renting an escort service for the night." For a similar criticism of the sages' behavior, see A. S. Hershberg, *Yofya ve-Hityafuta shel ha-Isha bi-Zman ha-Talmud*, 4 HE-ATID 1 (1923) (Heb.), who wrote, "Even our sages in the Talmud had different notions of modesty and immorality according to the time and the place." For a comparison of modesty in the Jewish society of Palestine and the lack of modesty in Babylonian Jewish society, see idem, at 4–10.

[39] Moshe D. Her, *Ha-Nisuin mi-Behina Socio-Economit Lefi ha-Halakha*, in MISHPAHOT BEIT YISRAEL 37, 40 (1976) (Heb.) together with the sources he cites in n.16.

[40] For a discussion of the extent to which the early rabbinic authorities took the text literally to mean a full marriage, including marital relations that could end in pregnancy, see Tosafot in B. T. *Yevamot*, s.v. "*Yihudi.*" For a rejection of this view, see, e.g., Hagahot Maharam and YISSACHAR EILENBERG, RESP. BEER SHEVA ch. 26 (2004). For further discussion, see UZIEL, *supra* note 22, at ch. 45 pp. 132–34.

[41] *See, e.g.*, the unequivocal statement by ASHTORI HAPARCHI, KAFTOR VA PERACH ch. 44 (1994).

[42] For further discussion of the difference between Rashi's explanation and that of the Tosafists, see Maharsha, s.v. "*Yihudi be-Alma.*" For a summary of the first six opinions presented, see SHLOMO GANZFRIED, LEHEM VE-SIMLA on the *Shulhan Arukh, Yore De'ah* 192:10 (1997).

Isaiah the Elder of Terani (Rid) holds a similar view. He writes that this is not a full marriage with the right to have intercourse but only permission to be with the woman. "One may claim that they were not alone together in one bed, but were together in the same house; he remained with the men and his wife remained with the women." One group of early rabbinic authorities is of the opinion that the marriage was a fully legal marriage but without sexual intercourse. Therefore, the sage would set down a condition at the time of the marriage that the marriage is valid only while he is in town, and when he leaves town, the woman will agree to a divorce. According to Rabbenu Hananel, this is a fully legal marriage that requires a *get* to dissolve it before the sage leaves town. He writes, "So, who will be mine for a day *and when I leave the place I will divorce her*. ... How can you say that they had intercourse with her. They did not [have intercourse] but only enjoyed her company."[43] (my emphasis – Y. M.) Meiri, in his work *Bet ha-Behirah*, explained the Talmudic text as follows:

> This describes how one of our sages would marry a woman temporarily in every town in which he stayed, even where his stay was as short as one day, in order to control his sexual urges, and he would make a condition that he was marrying her for a short period *in order that she should agree to a divorce afterwards*, and no sexual relations took place. They would merely occupy the same house, so that he should not feel the lack of a wife and could more easily resist his urges. (my emphasis – Y. M.)

Some rabbinic authorities tried to dismiss the problem of the Talmudic text by claiming it to be pure slander that was not originally part of the Babylonian Talmud but was inserted by a student of one of the sages who had erred in his ways or wished to mock.[44] According to Chaim Bloch, the text was inserted by residents of Shekunzib who were known for their sense of humor. The sages made no such declaration, but rather, it was simply a joke by a resident of Shekunzib, in which he incorporated the name of a prominent person.[45] Other commentators attempted to mitigate the problem of taking a wife in a temporary marriage for a predetermined period rather than conducting an official marriage ceremony with a *hupah* and *kiddushin* by defining this deed as *pilagshut*, whose only purpose was to save these sages from their evil inclinations. Shmuel Shtrason (Rashash), in his commentary to this text in *Yoma*, explains, "We would explain that he did not marry by means of *kiddushin* and *hupah* but retained them for intercourse as a *pilegesh* (concubine) according to the rulings by Ra'avad and Nahmanides that a *pilegesh* is permitted to commoners. ... A regular marriage requires counting seven days of purity, but this form does not."

43 Rabbenu Hananel's commentary to Tractate Yoma *18* (1993).

44 *See* Yosef Z. Diner (Ritzad), Novellae to Tractate Zebahim vol. 4, 88 (1999).

45 *See* Chaim Bloch, Veda ma-sheTashiv 26–30 (1962) (Heb.). In his introduction, he rejects the two suggestions of Moshe Leiter, Zuto shel Yam (1932) (Heb.), that the sages' announcement was intented to eradicate the practice of marrying a woman without following the proper halakhic procedure and to save a man from sinning by instituting preventive measures. He bases himself on a responsum by Yitzhak Ettinger, Resp. Mahariya ha-Levi ch. 16 (1970), who also found the announcement unclear and puzzling.

Yaakov ben Zvi Hirsch Ashkenazi Emden (1698–1776) used this precedent for his famous ruling permitting a man to take a *pilegesh* based on these two sages who took women without a *hupah* and *kiddushin*. He writes,

> It is said in the first chapter of *Yoma* that when Rav reached *Darshish*, he announced, "Who will be mine for a day?" People were amazed and asked if he had intercourse with her. I wrote that this proves that a commoner is allowed to take a *pilegesh*, because it is obvious that a commoner would not write a *ketubah* for one day, but would take her as a *pilegesh* and he does not have to write *ketubah* for her, therefore there is no problem that he is not allowed to remain with her without a *ketubah*. The intention is that a man should not hold his wife in contempt and be able to divorce her easily, and this permanence refers only to taking a wife who requires a *ketubah*. Since this permanence was explicitly agreed between them, he cannot change the conditions without her agreement. However, in the case of a *pilegesh*, she has agreed to his conditions. This is obviously the case for those rabbis who were interested in a temporary arrangement for one day and would be leaving the following day.[46]

Other authorities were of the opinion that this was not a legal marriage in which sexual intercourse is permitted but rather a marriage for a fixed time that did not include sexual relations but simply serving the husband, such as housekeeping and the like. As explained in a Geonic commentary, "There was no sexual intercourse but the woman would serve in the house during the day."[47] Some early rabbinic authorities were of the opinion that the marriage was legal, and there was no need for divorce when the sage left town because the women were available every time the sage returned.[48] Other authorities ruled that the marriage was valid and a *get* was required in order to abrogate it. According to Avraham min ha-Har (1315) in his commentary to *Yevamot*, s.v. "*le-Yome*," we can understand that the text is referring to a valid marriage that must be dissolved by providing a *get*: "Who will be mine for a

[46] *See* Yaakov B. Emden, Resp. She'elat Ya'abez vol. 2 ch. 15 (2004). For a similar scholarly perspective, which concludes that this is a case of *pilagshut*, see Elman, *infra* note 95, at 155. For a discussion of the *pilegesh* in the Bible, see the following reference in Hebrew: Yaakov Ariel, *Ha-Pilegesh u-Ma'amadah ha-Hilkhati be-Miqra*, 8 Megadim 57 (1989). Taking a *pilegesh* was a common practice in Maimonides' day, and he refers to it in various responsa, see Shimon Shtober, *Al Shte She'elot she-Hufnu el Rabenu Avraham ben ha-Rambam (referring to a slave-Pilegesh)*, 6–7 Shnaton Ha-Mishpat Haivri 399 (1979–80). For a modern attempt to revive the institution of *pilagshut* using these precedents, see, e.g., Zvi Zohar, *Halakhic Positions Permitting Nonmarital Sexual Intimacy*, 17 Akdamot 11 (2006). Needless to say, this suggestion was strongly criticized, *inter alia*, by Yehuda H. Henkin, *Aharita mi Yeshurena*, 17 Akdamot 33 (2006); Shmuel Ariel, *Pilagshut ena "Haverut,"* 17 Akdamot 41 (2006); Michal Tikachinski & Rachel Sperber-Frankel, *Tazhiram min ha-Pilegesh*, 17 Akdamot 67 (2006) and Zvi Zohar's response to the objections, in *Teshuva le-Magivim*, 17 Akdamot 77 (2006).

[47] Quoted in Otzar ha-Geonim on BT *Yoma*.

[48] These opinions were summarized by Uziel in his responsa, see Uziel, *supra* note 19, at ch. 54. For a similar approach, see, e.g., Moshe Feinstein, Dibrot Moshe on BT *Yevamot* 82 n.68 (1979), who reached the conclusion that there was no issue of divorce, since the woman would be called for every time the sage returned to the city, which occurred frequently.

day while I am staying here *and I will divorce her*. They would do so in every place they visited, even though they already had wives and children. This is the first explanation." (my emphasis – Y. M.)

Other academic scholars offered some strange explanations in their struggle to understand this puzzling text. Yet all were an apologetic attempt to avoid the obvious meaning.[49] In their opinion, it cannot be deduced from the text that the reference may indeed be to a temporary marriage. Their explanations included the following: Rav wished to do away with the negative custom of a wedding that was conducted without prior matchmaking and therefore asked his fellow citizens to arrange a marriage for him; the act was to counter the evil inclination and to prevent a possible test of a sexual nature, and the sage therefore wished to marry in order to neutralize his evil inclination;[50] due to the halakhic prohibitions of being alone with the wife of the innkeeper and questions of *kashrut* regarding the food, together with problematic relationships with the sages' wives, the sages preferred to take an extra wife, if "she [the extra wife – Y. M.] agreed";[51] the Persians used to offer a woman to important guests who arrived without their wives, and therefore the sages made the fictitious announcement that they were looking for wives in order to prevent the Persians from sending them a Persian woman.

Further explanations include the following: The announcement "Who will be mine for a day?" is not a search for a woman with whom to conduct marital relations but a search for a place to stay while in the town. This is neither a public declaration nor a search for a wife but a halakhic statement or popular saying briefly alluding to the issue of sexual intercourse on the Day of Atonement. These statements are a result of problems between the sages and their wives, hinting that they could take additional wives, or perhaps the wives' behavior may have been the result of these declarations.[52]

Before presenting a novel explanation of the Talmudic text, and what I consider an interesting approach, which I discuss in some detail, I will discuss an ancient and unique Muslim form of marriage that does not appear to be relevant to our discussion and is most certainly antithetical to the spirit of Judaism. It may, however,

49 *See* Simeon Lowy, *The Extent of Jewish Polygamy in Talmudic Times*, 9 J. Jewish Stud. 115, 123 (1958); Isaiah Gafni, The Jews of Babylonia in the Talmudic Era 272 (1990) (Heb.).

50 *See*, respectively, the following sources in Hebrew: Ben-Zion M. Uziel, *Man Havya le-Yom*, 99–100 Ha-Posek 1979 (1948); Bloch, *supra* note 45, at 26. For a rejection of this explanation, see Margaliot, *infra* note 52. It is interesting to note that Chaim Berlin, Resp. Nishmat Hayyim ch. 142 (2008) raised this possibility but ultimately rejected it.

51 *See* comment by editor of Ha-Posek to Uziel's article, ibid, at 1542.

52 For a review of the last four explanations, and several rejections of these explanations, see the following research in Hebrew: Explanations: Reuven Margaliot, *Man Havya le-Yoma*, 21 Sinai 176 (1947). Rejections: Uziel, *supra* note 50; Shmuel Kraus, *Man Havya le-Yoma*, 22 Sinai 299 (1948); Ben-Zion M. Uziel, *Man Havya le-Yoma*, 101–02 Ha-Posek 1554 (1949); Noah Aminah, *Man Havya le-Yoma*, 81 Sinai 169 (1977). For further discussion, see Yaakov Neusner, A History of the Jews in Babylonia vol. 2, 130 (1966).

shed light on the ancient Persian-Babylonian roots of temporary marriage, which are reflected in the Babylonian Talmud.

5 THE SHI'ITE TEMPORARY MARRIAGE FOR PLEASURE (زواج متعة – *MUTA*)

5.1 *General*

The Shi'ite temporary marriage – *muta* – is a temporary marriage whose main purpose is pleasure. When the marriage contract expires, the woman is available again for marriage to anyone, without this entailing any formal divorce procedure. This form of marriage has been discussed in some detail in the scholarly literature[53] and has even been the subject of a film that examines this unique type of marriage.[54] Traditionally, the *muta* marriage has been one of the points of contention between Sunni and Shi'ite Islam; it was permitted by the latter but categorically forbidden by the former.[55] It seems that today, the situation is reversed, and those who previously forbade the marriage tend to permit it, while those who used to permit the marriage now raise objections to it in order to limit its prevalence.[56] There are those who claim that Shi'ite Islam tended to permit it because the Shi'ites were a persecuted minority, fleeing from place to place, and it was necessary to develop a form of marriage that was suitable to this way of life.[57] Other scholars claim that this was the reason Shi'ite ideologists clothed the institution in holiness,[58] to the extent that some Imams have ruled that a person who has not tried this form of marriage has not completely fulfilled the precepts of Islamic marriage.[59]

One of the interesting religious justifications for this Shi'ite approach is the Sunni opposition. Any Shi'ite who enters into such a marriage gains spiritually, especially if he marries one of Muhammad's descendants. It would seem that ignoring the prohibition to the *muta* marriage laid down by Caliph Omar in the seventh century

[53] *See* SHAHLA HAERI, LAW OF DESIRE: TEMPORARY MARRIAGE IN SHI'I ISLAM (1989); ABU'L-QASIM GOURJI, TEMPORARY MARRIAGE (MUT'A) IN ISLAMIC LAW (1987); ARTHUR GRIBETZ, STRANGE BEDFELLOWS: MUTAT AL-NISA AND MUTAT AL-HAJJ: A STUDY BASED ON SUNNI AND SHII SOURCES OF TAFSIR, HADITH AND FIQH (1994).

[54] The film is called *Zu'aj al-Mat'a* (*The Mistaken Marriage*), which, according to Behor, contributed to the cessation of such marriages that were far too common in Egypt in the 1970s; *see* BEHOR, *supra* note 4, at 275 n.41.

[55] This conclusion is based on IGNAC GOLDZIHER, INTRODUCTION TO ISLAMIC THEOLOGY AND LAW 209 (Andras & Ruth Hamori trans., 1981). For an exhaustive discussion of the differences between the Sunni and Shi'ites, see HUSAIN M. JAFRI, THE ORIGINS AND EARLY DEVELOPMENT OF SHI'A ISLAM (1979).

[56] *See* HAMMUDAH ABD AL ATI, THE FAMILY STRUCTURE IN ISLAM 108–09 (1977).

[57] For a discussion of this claim, see ABD AL ATI, ibid, at 106.

[58] *See* GOITEIN & BEN SHEMESH, *supra* note 4, at 129.

[59] "The believer is only perfect when he has experienced a muta." The source for this claim is al-Ḥurr al-'Āmilī, *Wasā'il al-Shī'a* 69, 2 (1288); ABD AL ATI, *supra* note 56, at 103.

CE would probably give God pleasure according to the Shi'ite approach, particularly in view of Sunni opposition to it.[60] This form of marriage is built on mutual agreement (*lāzim*), established by the marriage proposal and its acceptance (*ḳabūl&īdjāb*), and requires specifying the time span for the marriage (*adjal*), which may vary from one day to several years but no more than ninety-nine years. It is not clear what happens to an agreement that has no clearly defined time span. Does it become a standard marriage, or is the marriage contract null and void?[61] The contract must also include the exact payment to be made to the woman who agrees to these conditions (*adjr/mahr*), otherwise the contract is null and void.[62]

The *muta* marriage was customary for traveling men, but not exclusively, and it permitted them to take additional wives over and above their four legal wives. The *muta* marriage expires at the agreed-upon time; however, the groom can terminate the agreement at any time, whereas the bride cannot terminate it at all. Thus, in these temporary marriages, women are treated like the object of a lease – the man can discard them at any time, thus breaking the contract and thus giving the male a lot of freedom.[63] However, a *muta* marriage cannot be extended, even by mutual agreement. Instead, a new marriage ceremony and bridal contract is required prior to the expiry of the original contract. This marriage does not place any obligations on the husband with regard to his wife, not even food and lodging, and there are no rights of inheritance on either side. However, according to some opinions, if the marriage contract contains a specific stipulation, it must be legally validated.[64]

5.2 *The Ancient Roots of the Shi'ite Temporary Marriage*

The *muta* form of marriage was common among Arabs as early as the fourth century CE.[65] It appears that *muta* marriages were known in the Jahiliyya period (the time

[60] *See* Haeri, *supra* note 53, at 167; Kristen Cherry, *Marriage and Divorce Law in Pakistan and Iran: The Problem of Recognition* 9 Tulsa J. Comp. & Int'l L. 319, 339 (2001).

[61] *See* Jane Khatib-Chahidi, *Sexual Prohibitions, Shared Space and Fictive Marriages in Shi'ite Iran, in* Women and Space: Ground Rules and Social Maps 112, 126 (Shirley Ardener ed., 1981); Amal J. Nasir, The Islamic Law of Personal Status 59 (1990); Tamilla F. Ghodsi, *Tying a Slipknot: Temporary Marriages in Iran*, 15 Mich. J. Int'l L. 645, 667–68 (1994).

[62] *See* Haeri, *supra* note 53, at 51–53. For a review of contract law from both the practical and procedural aspects, which affect family law, and where this form of marriage differs from the standard marriage, see Il'ia P. Petrushevsky, Islam in Iran 144, 231 (Hubert Evans trans., 1985); Cherry, *supra* note 60, at 336–40. For a review of the relevant practical and procedural Muslim requirements regarding the validity of this contract and the attempt to merge the two types of marriage, see Al Ati, *supra* note 56, at 108–09.

[63] *See* Edna Boyle-Lewicki, *Need World's Collide: The Hudad Crimes of Islamic Law and International Human Rights*, 13 N.Y. Int'l L. Rev. 43, 68 n.116 (2000).

[64] For a more exhaustive discussion, see Heffening, *supra* note 6.

[65] *See, e.g.*, Ammianus Marcellinus, xiv. 4, 4. Although, I should point out that it is difficult to connect the phenomenon that he discusses with the Islamic *muta* because in those days the woman would bring a tent and spear to the man she was interested in, and after a certain time she was allowed to leave him. For a review of the roots of the institution of marriage in early

period before Muhammad received his first revelation of the Qur'an) and were also very common in Eritrea.[66] Thus, the institution has a long history prior to its adoption by Islam.[67] It should be pointed out that in addition to the sources already mentioned, there are references to *muta* marriages in the fourth century, not only in the Arabian Peninsula, but also in Egypt[68] and among some of the peoples living in Canada and Mexico.[69] It is, however, most common nowadays in Iran (previously Persia), which was governed by Islamic law after the Arab conquest and the death of Muhammad in 632. It was relatively easy for different peoples to accept Islamic religious rule, as it offered equality and tolerance of the state that existed prior to the conquest.[70]

The term "*muta*" does not appear in the Qur'an. Some commentaries suggest that there is a verse in the Sura about women (سورة النساء 4:24) that contains a reference to this concept: فَمَا اسْتَمْتَعْتُم بِهِ مِنْهُنَّ فَآتُوهُنَّ أُجُورَهُنَّ فَرِيضَةً" (م.ت.ع)" ("Pay women who give you pleasure whatever you have promised"). It is generally accepted that Muhammad's warriors were allowed *muta* marriages when engaging in holy wars of *Jihad* away from home.[71] There are also a number of recorded cases of *muta* marriages at the beginning of Islam. In the *Hadith* Sahih Al-Bukhari collection, for example, there are four references to a *muta* marriage. In one case, permission for it was issued by Muhammad himself: "الا: كنا في جيش فأتانا رسولرسول الله صلعم فقال إنه قد أذِن لكم أن تستمتعوا، فاستمتِعوا"[72] ("We were in the army and a messenger arrived from Muhammad and said: Muhammad agreed that you should enjoy yourselves, so enjoy [*muta* marriages – Y. M.])." Another case that seems to indicate a *muta* marriage in this early period is mentioned in Altaramdi "Al-Jama al-Zhahah," which reads, "إنما كانت المتعة في أول الإسلام."[73] Indeed, for the price of a coat or a handful of dates, a man could marry an unmarried woman (*uyyām*) for a given period. This was especially the case when a man was in a foreign city, and he could marry a woman there who would provide for all his needs.

Later on, *muta* marriages were forbidden among Muslims. It is not clear when Muhammad forbade these marriages, but all Sunni authors of the *Hadith* agree that

Islam, see GERTRUDE H. STERN, MARRIAGE IN EARLY ISLAM 155 (1939); JOSEPH SCHACHT, THE ORIGINS OF MUHAMMADAN JURISPRUDENCE 266 (1950); ibid, AN INTRODUCTION TO ISLAMIC LAW 163 (1964).

66 *See* CONTI ROSSINI, PRINCIPI DI DIRITTO CONSUETUDINARIO DELL'ERITREA 189, 249 (1916).

67 For a discussion of this claim, see WILLIAM ROBERTSON SMITH, KINSHIP & MARRIAGE IN EARLY ARABIA 82 (1903).

68 *See* EDVARD A. WESTERMARCK, THE HISTORY OF HUMAN MARRIAGE 267–68 (1922); GEORGE A. WILKEN, DAS MATRIARCHAT (DAS MUTTERRECHT) BEI DEN ALTEN ARABERN 21–22 (1884); LUDWIG MITTEIS & GEORGE A. WILKEN, GRUNDZÜGE DER PAPYRUSKUNDE 203 (1912); EUGENIO GRIFFINI, CORPUS IURIS DI ZAYD IBN 'ALF 327 (1919).

69 Alzueg, vol. 1, 165.

70 *See* IRAN: A COUNTRY STUDY 11 (Helen Chapin Metz ed., 1989).

71 *See* DUR RAHMAN I. DOI, SHARI'AH: THE ISLAMIC LAW 155–56 (1984).

72 *See* MAHMOUD BE ISMAIL AL-BAHIRI, ZAHIH AL-BAHIRI: MISHKOL vol. 4, 16 (1950); LEONE CAETANI, ANNALI DEL'ISLAM 478 (1972).

73 ABU ISA M. TARMADI, AL-JAMA AL-ZAHIAH SNAN AL-TARAMADI vol. 3, 430 (1995).

muta marriages were forbidden. On the other hand, Shi'ite sages claim that everyone knows that these marriages were permitted, and in the absence of evidence to the contrary, the practice is still permitted. An example of the dispute over when the marriages were prohibited may be found in the book *Sunan Al-Darimi*, which suggests different dates for Muhammad's prohibition. The first source is "أخبرنا محمد بن يوسف، حدثنا ابن عيينة، عن الزهري، عن الربيع بن سبرة الجهني، عن ابيه، قال نهى رسول الله صلى الله عليه وسلم عن نكاح المتعة عام الفتح" – "he said: Muhammad forbade the *muta* marriage in 629."[74] The second source is "حدثنا محمد، حدثني ابن عيينة، عن الزهري، عن الحسن، وعبد الله، عن ابيهما، قال سمعت عليا، يقول لابن عباس إن رسول الله صلى الله عليه وسلم نهى عن المتعة متعة النساء وعن لحوم الحمر الأهلية عام خيبر"[75] – "Muhammad forbade the practice of *muta* marriages and marriages between blood relations in the *Hibar* year."[76] However, other scholars claim that *muta* marriages were still practiced in the eleventh to thirteenth centuries, at the time of the Caliph Abu Bakr.

5.3 *Contemporary Temporary Marriage*

There is comprehensive early eighteenth-century documentation of marriages for a limited time period that were brought for discussion to the Qadi in Sounan (Ṣan'ā'), in Southern Arabia.[77] In Mecca, both in modern and ancient times, the Sunnis conducted marriages for limited periods of time. These marriages were official and valid but incorporated the divorce formula (*ṭalāḳ*) for the time when the marriage would expire. This combination produced the same type of marriage as their Shi'ite brethren's *muta* marriage.[78] Documentation also exists about the practice of these marriages into the beginning of the twentieth century in Eastern Syria at Deir ez-Zor,[79] as well as for the practice of this type of marriage among the Falashas in Ethiopia today, where it is known as a "soldier's marriage." It is one of three types of Falasha marriages for a limited period of time that are mutually agreed upon by the couple.[80]

74 "The opening year" – the year when Mecca was opened to Muslims (629). In this year, Muslims were allowed to enter the Haram in Mecca for the first time.

75 Abdalla ben Abdalrahman al-Darami, Sanan Al-Daram vol. 2, 64 (1966).

76 For a list of sources, see Heffening, *supra* note 6.

77 *See, e.g.*, Alexander D. Hamilton, A New Account of the East-Indies 51 (1732), first mentioned by Wilken, *supra* note 68, at 19.

78 *See* documentation in C. Snouck Hurgronje, Mekka 156 (1888); C. Snouck Hurgronje, Verspreide geschriften vol. 6, 150 (1923).

79 *See* documentation in Victor Muller, En Syrie avec les Bedouins: les tribus du 231–32 (1931).

80 For a modern discussion of these marriages, see Hiba Basol-Taha, Temporary Marriage in Islam from the Perspectives of Shari'a, Civil Law and Social Norms (Arab.) (MA thesis, Bar-Ilan University, the Department of Arabic, 2008); Barbara Watson Andaya, *From Temporary Wife to Prostitute: Sexuality and Economic Change in Early Modern Southeast Asia*, 9(4) J. Women's History 11 (1998). For a website with a step-by-step explanation of how to perform the marriage, see www.mutah.com/how_do_i_do_mutah.htm.

There are recent claims that temporary marriage has been used to disguise prostitution in some Middle Eastern countries. Others argue that a temporary marriage is morally superior to the free "and decadent" male-female relationships in modern Western societies. Others maintain that such marriages are becoming newly popular among the majority Shi'ite population in Iraq, and they are becoming a convenient way of effectively legalizing prostitution and concubinage, with *muta* contracts for as short as an hour being upheld by Shi'ite clerics.[81]

In recent years, there have been a small number of civil-secular court rulings regarding *muta* marriages.[82] It is perfectly clear, even from this small number of examples, that these marriages are not recognized, even as putative marriages, as demonstrated in a ruling in the United States *In re Marriage of Vryonis*.[83] The case involved an Iranian woman in an unhappy *muta* marriage who sued for alimony. Her so-called husband denied the existence of any such marriage. In spite of the woman's honest and naive belief that she was married, the court ruled that the marriage was invalid. The reasons for the ruling were basically procedural, since the marriage was not compatible with California civil law. With regard to the marriage itself, there were no witnesses, no written proof, and no cohabitation. Therefore, there was absolutely no basis for the claim that there had been a marriage. A *muta* marriage was also addressed in Canadian law in the case of Y.J. v. N.J., where the court discussed the question of custody of a five-year-old Muslim girl born of a *muta* marriage, which was her father's second marriage. Again, the Canadian civil courts ruled that the marriage was invalid. The court did not relate to the religious aspects of such marriages, including the girl's legitimacy.[84]

81 *See* Olga Voinarevich, *A Fairy Tale Interrupted: The Long-Term Impacts of Child Marriage in Yemen and the Necessary Adjustments to Both Local and International Laws to Stop the Practice and to Protect Voiceless Child Brides*, 16 RUTGERS RACE & L. REV. 203, 213 n.65 (2015); John Witte & Joel A. Nichols, *Marriage, Religion, and the Role of the Civil State: More Than a Mere Contract: Marriage as Contract and Covenant in Law and Theology*, 5 U. ST. THOMAS L.J. 595, 601 n.27 (2008); Rodolphe J. A. De Seife, Muhammad Khalid Masud, Brinkley Messick and David S. Powers, eds., Islamic Legal Interpretation: Muftis and Their Fatwas, 42 AM. J. LEGAL HIST. 84, 86 (1998). *See also* Haider Ala Hamoudi, *Sex and the Shari'a: Defining Gender Norms and Sexual Deviancy in Shi'i Islam*, 39 FORDHAM INT'L L.J. 25, 41–45 (2015)

82 For a review of *muta* marriages in modern Islamic law, see, e.g., SACHIKO MURATA, TEMPORARY MARRIAGE IN ISLAMIC LAW (MA thesis, Divinity School, University of Tehran, 1974), www.al-islam.org/al-serat/muta; Brooke D. Rodgers-Miller, *Out of Jahiliyya: Historic and Modern Incarnations of Polygamy in the Islamic World*, 11 WM. & MARY J. WOMEN & L. 541 (2005); Dan E. Stigall, *Iraqi Civil Law: Its Sources, Substance, and Sundering*, 16 J. TRANSNAT'L L. & POL'Y 1, 52–53 (2006); Ala Hamoudi, ibid.

83 In re Marriage of Vryonis, 202 Cal. App. 3d 712 (Cal. App. 2 Dist.) For a discussion of the ruling see, e.g., Cherry, *supra* note 60, at 350–51. *See also* more generally, Marjorie M. Shultz, *Contractual Ordering of Marriage: A New Model for State Policy*, 70 CAL. L. REV. 204, 250, 273 (1982).

84 Y.J. v. N.J., (1994) O.J. No. 2359. *See also* In re Marriage of Dawley, 17 Cal. 3d 342 (1976), and more recently, In the Matter of the Marriage of Soleimani, 2012 WL 3729939 (Kan. Dist. Ct.). For a detailed discussion of the rulings in the American and Canadian courts, see Shahnaz Khan, *Race, Gender, and Orientalism: Muta and the Canadian Legal System*, 8 CAN.

5.4 *Shi'ite Temporary Marriage in Rabbinic and Karaite Halakhic Sources*

The negative opinion of the sages regarding *muta* marriages is already apparent in Geonic literature. The first to express an opinion in this regard was Saadia Gaon. In his commentary to the Pentateuch, he notes several times that the prohibition of the *kedeshah* refers to a *muta* marriage, and the *muta* marriage is therefore a biblical prohibition.[85] This opinion is found in the Cairo Genizah manuscript version of his commentary to Deuteronomy 23:18.[86] In his discussion of prostitution, Saadia Gaon places it in the first, most lenient category, as explained below (translated from the Arabic):

> The first category is a marriage for a limited period, for a woman who agrees to the marriage is called a *kedeshah*, as in the case of Tamar, the daughter-in-law of Yehudah. And it is written, "There shall be no harlot (*kedeshah*) of the daughters of Israel," a warning to both the husband and the wife. And why is it in the first category of forbidden marriages? Because it is a marriage with a *ketubah* and witnesses and *kiddushin*. The prohibition applies only because of the woman's situation after the termination of the marriage.

Similarly, in a fragment from the Kaufmann manuscript of Saadia Gaon's Sefer ha-Mitzvot, which was found in the Cairo Genizah, he writes (my translation from the Arabic), "It is prohibited for a man to marry a woman in a *muta* marriage, or for a woman to be married [in a *muta* marriage – Y. M.] for both of them are bound by 'There shall be no *kedeshah* of the daughters of Israel.'"[87]

J. Women & L. 249, 254 (1995); Pascale Fournier, *The Erasure of Islamic Difference in Canadian and American Family Law Adjudication*, 10 J.L. & Pol'y 51, 51–59 (2001). For a discussion of Western court rulings on Muta marriages, see Ann Laquer Estin, *Embracing Tradition: Pluralism in American Family Law*, 63 Md. L. Rev. 540, 565 n.153 (2004); Safiya Ghori, *The Application of Religious Law in North American Courts: A Case Study of Muta Marriages*, 10(1) J. Islamic L. & Culture 29, 37–40 (2008).

85 *See, e.g.*, his commentary on Genesis, 38:15, 21–22, where the term "*kedeshah*" appears in the story of Judah and Tamar, and he translates it using the root "*muta*." In his commentary to Deuteronomy 23:18, "There shall be no harlot (*kedeshah*) of the daughters of Israel, neither shall there be a sodomite of the sons of Israel," he uses a similar translation, and Zucker notes that the translation would thus read: "There shall be no temporary marriages among the daughters of Israel."

86 *See* Moshe Zucker, Al Tirgum Rasag la-Torah: Parshanut, Halakha u-Politika be-Tirgum ha-Torah shel Rabbi Sadya Gaon: Te'udot u-Mehkarim 477–78 (1959) (Heb.). *See also* Yosef Kapach, Perushe Rabbenu Sadya gaon al ha Torah 180 n.3 (1994).

87 Published by Alexander Scheiber & Yizhak Hahn, *(Manuscript) Leaves from Se'adya's Sefer Hamizwot*, 28 Tarbiz 48 (1959) (Heb.). For a detailed discussion of these sources, see Mordechai. A. Friedman, *Halakha as Evidence of Sexual Life among Jews in Muslim Countries in the Middle Ages*, 45 Peamim 89, 100–01 (1991) (Heb.). *See also* more generally, Daniel J. Lasker, *Saadya Gaon on Christianity and Islam*, in The Jews of Medieval Islam: Community, Society, and Identity 165 (Daniel Frank ed., 1995); David M. Freidenreich, *The Use of Islamic Sources in Saadiah Gaon's "Tafsīr" of the Torah*, 93(3/4) Jewish Q. Rev. 353 (2003);

Saadia Gaon's consistent approach raises two questions, one related to the content and the other technical. In both his commentary to the Pentateuch and his halakhic writings, Saadia Gaon wants to prove that the prohibition against a *muta* marriage has the status of a biblical prohibition. According to Moshe Zucker, this approach is not indisputable. According to Jewish halakhic sources, marriage for an agreed-upon period is legal and valid, and according to most authorities, it may be dissolved only by means of a *get*, as demonstrated in my detailed discussion of Babylonian and Palestinian Talmudic sources. Thus, if the status of this woman who has completed a marriage for a fixed period of time and remarries without a *get* from her first husband is the same as the status of an unmarried woman, the second marriage is permitted, as we have seen in the case of "Who will be mine for a day?" But if at the end of a temporary marriage without a *get*, this woman's status is the same as that of a married woman, in effect she is still married to her first husband and now faces the more serious problem of an adulteress and not a *kedeshah* (prostitute).[88]

In addition, Professor Eliezer Schlossberg (Department of Arabic, Bar-Ilan University) pointed out to me that this explanation of Saadia Gaon is extremely difficult to understand because he interprets the Bible's general and sweeping prohibition of a *kedeshah* as referring to a very particular type of marriage that, in his day, was practiced only among Shi'ites. A possible explanation for these two points, one relating to the content and the other technical, is offered by Haim Z. Hirschberg (Department of Jewish History, Bar-Ilan University):[89]

> Zucker concludes that Rabbi Saadia Gaon's ruling "requires careful analysis" from a halakhic point of view. It seems that one should look for a historical explanation in the customs of Muslim society that influenced certain phenomena in Jewish society. Marriages for an agreed period, which are called *muta* (pleasure) marriages are permitted in the Shi'a branch of Islam, which has been, and is still followed by the Muslim population of Persia, half the population of Iraq and a large proportion of Muslims in Syria and Lebanon. In Saadia Gaon's time, Isma'ili (extreme Shi'ite) influence increased in North Africa, and reached Egypt. It is conceivable that Jews in Persia, Iraq and Syria were influenced by Shi'ite Islam and demonstrated a more lenient approach to marriages for agreed periods, and left a woman without giving her a *get*. . . . Saadia Gaon's intention in translating Deuteronomy 23:18 in this way was to warn against those who wished to permit *muta* marriages.[90]

David H. Frankel, Studies in Saadiah Gaon's Arabic Translations 21 (MA thesis, The Ohio State University, 2012).

88 *See* Zucker, *supra* note 86, at 478.

89 Haim Z. Hirschberg, *Le-Heker Rav Sadya Gaon ve-Tequfato*, 31 Tarbiz 415, 421 (1962) (Heb.).

90 The Islamic influence on *halakhah* in the Geonic period has been discussed extensively. *See, e.g.*, J. Blumberg, *Munahim Mishpati'im Aravi'im mi-Dine ha-Kinyan be-Geonim uve-Rambam*, 14–15 Shnaton ha-Mishpat ha-Ivri 61 (1988–89) (Heb.). In addition to the vivid writing of Gideon Libson in Hebrew, see his seminal research, Gideon Libson, *Halakhah and Reality in the Gaonic Period: Taqqanah, Minhag, Tradition and Consensus: Some Observations*, in The Jews of Medieval Islam: Community, Society, and Identity 67 (Daniel Frank ed.,

Mordechai A. Friedman (Department of Talmud, Tel Aviv University)[91] adds another dimension by claiming that Saadia Gaon went even further and prohibited marriages for agreed periods even when the woman was given a *get* at the end of that period. He writes:

> It seems more likely that Saadia Gaon was referring to temporary marriages with a *get*, even though under Shi'ite Islamic law a woman is released from a *muta* marriage without a divorce. The fact that Jewish sages writing in Judeo-Arabic use a term borrowed from Islamic law does not necessarily mean that the Jewish institution is identical to the corresponding Islamic institution. They were referring to the closest equivalent to the halakhic institution. ... It would seem that the influence of the Islamic *muta* marriage led to the definition of *kadesh* and *kedeshah* in this way. The *muta* marriage was certainly regarded as abhorrent by Saadia Gaon and other sages, including Karaite sages. To them, this was not a marriage, but rather, legalized prostitution ... what is indubitable is that the Jewish leadership regarded temporary marriages as contrary to Jewish sexual ethics ... their abhorrence led them to take extreme measures: using creative hermeneutics, they created a new Torah prohibition.

Indeed, a similar approach to that of Saadia Gaon was adopted by Karaites such as Daniel Alkumsi[92] and David ben Avraham Alfasi,[93] who ruled that a *muta* marriage is forbidden and is nothing less than prostitution.

6 A COMMON PERSIAN ORIGIN – A COMPARISON OF THE BABYLONIAN TALMUDIC MARRIAGE AND SHI'ITE TEMPORARY MARRIAGE

Unlike the variety of problematic explanations of "Who will be mine for a day?" reviewed above, there are scholars who attribute this appeal by the sages to the Persian influence in Babylonia in the early centuries of the Common Era.[94]

1995) and more extensively, ibid, JEWISH AND ISLAMIC LAW: A COMPARATIVE STUDY OF CUSTOM DURING THE GEONIC PERIOD 1–15 (2003) (History of Comparative Research in Jewish and Islamic Law). *See also* M. Tirza Mitcham, *Sefer ha-Bagrut le-Rav Shmuel ben Hofni Gaon ve-Sefer ha-Shanim le-Rav Yehuda ha-Kohen* 68 (1999) (Heb.). For a general discussion of the influence of the surrounding culture on Jewish marriage, see GAFNI, *supra* note 49, at 266–73; Bernard. S. Jackson, *How Jewish Is Jewish Law?*, 55 JOURNAL OF JEWISH STUDIES 201 (2004); Isaiah. M. Gafni, *The Institution of Marriage in Rabbinic Times*, in THE JEWISH FAMILY: METAPHOR AND MEMORY 13 (David Kraemer ed., 1989).

91 Friedman, *supra* note 87.

92 *See* ABU YUSUF YA'KUB AL-KIRKISANI, YA'QUB AL-QIRQISANI ON JEWISH SECTS AND CHRISTIANITY: A TRANSLATION OF "KITAB AL-ANWAR" Book 1 (1984). For a similar translation, see Alanuar, at 728, quoted by ZUCKER, *supra* note 86, at 478 n.63.

93 *See* DAVID BEN AVRAHAM ALFASI, KITAB JAMA AL-ALFALATH vol. 2, 541 (1936–45). These two translations are to be found in Friedman, *supra* note 87, at 101–02.

94 Research on the influence of Persian law on the Jews living under its suzerainty has received attention in recent years. There is a periodical devoted to the subject, and several volumes have already been published. The periodical is edited by Shaul Shaked, and its name describes its

Marrying a woman for an agreed period, which is problematic according to the modern halakhic conception of marriage, was a well-known practice in the Persian era, at the time that the Babylonian Talmud was compiled. This practice derives from a more general practice of giving objects for a stated period, as "a gift to be returned." This fascinating approach appears in an article by Yaakov Elman (Department of Jewish History, Yeshiva University) in which he claims that the close contact of the Amoraic elite with Persian culture had a considerable influence on religious Jewish law, including the laws of marriage. He bases this conclusion on the fact that two of the most important *amoraim* in the Talmud openly admit to entering into what were apparently temporary marriages. He writes as follows:

> This is so even though two very prominent rabbis, the aforementioned R. Nahman and the first-generation *amora* Rav, entered into such marriages [temporary marriages – Y. M.]. . . . This is but one of many indications that the relationship of the Babylonian rabbinic elite to Sasanian culture was much closer than has been supposed. . . . The entire discussion presupposes that such marriages were contracted by prominent rabbis[95]

In his article, Elman paints a fascinating picture of the ancient Persian practice of giving articles for an agreed period, with the articles including women. It is therefore not surprising, in his opinion, that this practice was adopted by Babylonian Jews, including the sages. The need to fight the practice seems to prove the extent to which it had spread and become accepted, both socially and halakhically. He writes,

> The fact that these traditions continued to circulate with only technical objections raised, rather than objections that go to the heart of the institution, indicates that such temporary marriages had taken deep root within the Babylonian Jewish community . . . Though the second explanation by the redactors suggests that the marriage was not consummated then, this was only for technical reasons: no moral

content: IRANO-JUDAICA: STUDIES RELATING TO JEWISH CONTACTS WITH PERSIAN CULTURE THROUGHOUT THE AGES. Yaakov Elman has devoted a series of articles to the subject: Yaakov Elman, *"Up to the Ears" in Horses' Necks (BM 108a): On Sasanian Agricultural Policy and Private "Eminent Domain,"* 3 JEWISH STUDIES, AN INTERNET JOURNAL 95 (2004); *Marriage and Marital Property in Rabbinic and Sasanian Law*, in RABBINIC LAW IN ITS ROMAN AND NEAR EASTERN CONTEXT 227 (Catherine Hezser ed., 2003); *Middle Persian Culture and Babylonian Sages: Accommodation and Resistance in the Shaping of Rabbinic Legal Tradition*, THE CAMBRIDGE COMPANION TO THE TALMUD AND RABBINIC LITERATURE 165 (2007); *Acculturation to Elite Persian Norms and Modes of Thought in the Babylonian Jewish Community of Late Antiquity*, NETI'OT LEDAVID 31 (2004). In addition to the research by Adiel Schremer, there are a number of works that note the influence of the alien Persian environment on Jewish marriage in Persia: ELIYAHU AHDUT, MA'AMAD HA-ISHA HA-YEHUDIA BE-BAVEL BE-TEQUFAT HA-TALMUD 57 (PhD thesis, The Hebrew University of Jerusalem, 1999) (Heb.); MICHAEL. L. SATLOW, JEWISH MARRIAGE IN ANTIQUITY (2001).

95 *See* Yaakov Elman, *Returnable Gifts in Rabbinic and Sasanian Law*, VI IRANO-JUDAICA 139, 141 (2008). *See also* Zvi Septimus & Lena Selaymeh, *Temporalities of Marriage: Jewish and Islamic Legal Debates*, in TALMUDIC TRANSGRESSIONS: ESSAYS IN HONOR OF DANIEL BOYARIN 201 (Ishay Rosen-Zvi et al., 2017).

opprobrium was attached to such temporary arrangements. ... The nexus of the discussions is the potential violation of incest or the rules of impurity, not the impropriety of polygyny or temporary marriage.[96]

There are scholars who claim that this Persian practice is the basis for the Shi'ite *muta*, which slowly became an accepted social practice in the Persian-Shi'ite period prior to the emergence of Zoroastrianism.[97] Indeed, in a later period, the Persian book of rulings (the Sasanian law book) *Madayan i Hazar Dadestan*[98] contains a number of records of temporary marriages in which a woman is handed over by her legal husband or by her father – even though she may be married to another man – for a predefined period of time, or instructions for dealing with the case of a woman who admits that she gave herself to a man to serve as his wife for ten years, and so on.[99]

It seems highly likely that this Persian practice is the source of the Shi'ite *muta* marriage, and Babylonian Jews, most probably living in this environment, felt the impact of its influence on the structure of Jewish marriage in their community. Scholars such as Salo Baron point out that the institution of temporary marriage was almost certainly influenced by the polygamy that was prevalent in Babylonia[100] but was foreign to Palestine, where it was banned by the Roman authorities.[101] In all of the above writings, it appears that the Talmud is the only source not deterred by the possibility that the case of "Who will be mine for a day?" involved a temporary marriage for an agreed period, despite the fact that this case categorically contradicts the halakhic principle that it is forbidden to take more than one wife, especially when the wives are located in different towns.

It seems fairly obvious that these sages indeed sought wives for short periods of time when visiting towns far from home. The compilers of the two sources related

[96] Elman, ibid, at 151–54.

[97] *See, e.g.*, Bodil Hjerrild, *Islamic Law and Sasanian Law*, in LAW AND THE ISLAMIC WORLD: PAST AND PRESENT 49, 53 (Christopher Toll & Jakob Skovgaard-Petersen eds., 1995); Maria Macuch, *Die Zeitehe im Sasanidischen Recht – ein Vorlaufer der shi'itischen mut'a-Ehe in Iran?*, 18 ARCHAEOLOGISCHE MITTEILUNGEN AUS IRAN 187 (1985); Elman, *supra* note 95, at 154; ADIEL SCHREMER, JEWISH MARRIAGE IN TALMUDIC BABYLONIA 281 n.84 (PhD thesis, The Hebrew University of Jerusalem, 1996) (Heb.).

[98] For more on this ancient legal codex, see generally GEORGE W. CARTER, ZOROASTRIANISM AND JUDAISM (1970); WOMEN IN IRAN FROM THE RISE OF ISLAM TO 1800 (Guity Nashat & Lois Beck eds., 2003); JENNY ROSE, ZOROASTRIANISM: AN INTRODUCTION (2011).

[99] For early records, see Anahit Perikhanian, *Iranian Society and Law*, 3(2) CAMBRIDGE HISTORY OF IRAN 627, 649–50 (Ehsan Y. Sharter ed., 1983). Other sources are supplied by Elman, *supra* note 95, at 154 and the sources he cites in n.35.

[100] For information on the frequency of polygamy in Babylonia, see ALY-AHBAR MAHAREZI, LA FAMILLE IRANIENNE 133–34 (1938) together with the different sources cited by GAFNI, *supra* note 49, at 266–73; Elman, *supra* note 95, at 159–60.

[101] For a discussion of this matter, see SALO W. BARON, A SOCIAL AND RELIGIOUS HISTORY OF THE JEWS vol. 2, 226 (1952). With regard to the monogamous life of Jews under Roman suzerainty, see MORDECHAI A. FRIEDMAN, RIBUI NASHIM BE-YISRAEL 28–32 (1986) (Heb.); ELIMELECH WESTREICH, TRANSITIONS IN THE LEGAL STATUS OF THE WIFE IN JEWISH LAW: A JOURNEY AMONG TRADITIONS, in the index, s.v. "*Tnai Monogamia*" (2002) (Heb.); Adiel Schremer, *How Much Jewish Polygyny in Roman Palestine?*, 63 PROCEEDINGS OF THE AMERICAN ACADEMY FOR JEWISH RESEARCH 181 (2001).

only to the technical issues involved, without any implied condemnation of this practice. The other explanation, that temporary marriages are not real, valid marriages, is examined by the compilers only from a technical perspective, and there is no discussion of the substantive principles involved. The only question of principle discussed is the fear that these marriages may result in sibling marriages, thus resulting in incest. There is no condemnation of polygamy or of temporary marriages for a limited period.[102]

Thus, scholars such as Isaiah Gafni (Department of Jewish History, The Hebrew University of Jerusalem) concluded that the Jewish community was influenced by the Persian environment, where temporary marriages were common, and this was the background for the sages' attempt to enter into temporary marriages for an agreed period of time.[103] According to Zeev Falk,[104] Rashba may have reversed his earlier opinion – allowing a marriage for a predetermined period, after which the marriage would dissolve itself automatically without any divorce procedure – due to the negative effects of this practice on the structure of the Jewish family, where marriage would resemble the *muta* marriage: "Rashba was perhaps influenced by the disgust of Muslim judges for temporary marriage – *muta* – also known as renting, Ijara,[105] which they regarded to be closely related to prostitution."

It is of interest that contemporary scholars of Islamic family law in Israel have noted the Persian influence on the *muta* marriage,[106] and both Shlomo D. Goitein (The Hebrew University of Jerusalem) and Aharon Ben Shemesh (Tel Aviv University) have pointed out the possible connection between a *muta* marriage and the "one day" rabbinical marriage and the influence of Persian culture on the Jewish community in Babylonia.[107] Incidentally, even today, *muta* weddings are common in Persian culture, and it has even been proposed that the *muta* wedding be incorporated into Iranian law.[108] While the approach today is to make these marriage contracts for long

[102] This is the conclusion of several scholars, such as Her, *supra* note 39; Elman, *supra* note 95. *See also* the sharp criticism of NISSIM H. M. MIZRAHI, RESP. ADMAT KODESH *Even ha-Ezer* vol. 1 ch. 50 (1991).

[103] *See* GAFNI, *supra* note 49, at 272–73.

[104] *See* FALK, *supra* note 3.

[105] For an explanation of this term, see NOEL J. COULSON, A HISTORY OF ISLAMIC LAW 111 (1964). Lately, there has been extensive discussion of the modern use of this Islamic term, but from a financial perspective rather than the perspective of personal status. *See, e.g.*, Christopher F. Richardson, *Islamic Finance Opportunities in the Oil and Gas Sector: An Introduction to an Emerging Field*, 42 TEX. INT'L L.J. 119 (2006); Kimberly J. Tacy, *Islamic Finance: A Growing Industry in the United States*, 10 N.C. BANKING INST. 355 (2006); Michael J. T. McMillen, *Islamic Shari'ah-Compliant Project Finance: Collateral Security and Financing Structure Case Studies*, 24 FORDHAM INT'L L.J. 1184 (2001); Michael J. T. McMillen, *Islamic Business and Commercial Law: Contractual Enforceability Issues: Sukuk and Capital Markets Development*, 7 CHI. J. INT'L L. 427 (2007).

[106] *See* MERON, *supra* note 4, at 23.

[107] *See* GOITEIN & BEN SHEMESH, *supra* note 4, at 129.

[108] The *muta* marriage is still common in Iran; *see* RUHOLLAH KHOMEINI, A CLARIFICATION OF QUESTIONS: AN UNABRIDGED TRANSLATION OF RESALEH TOWZIH AL-MASAEL 311 (J. Borujerdi trans., 1984). There are a number of scholarly works on *muta* marriages in Iran. *See, e.g.*, works

periods, such as ninety-nine years, there are brokers who offer to conduct temporary marriages for traveling Persians, offering this service in any town for even the shortest periods of time. There is a Persian term for this service (*ezdevaje sigeh* or *ezdevaje movaghat*), which is translated as a sort of contract.[109]

7 A RELIABLE SOLUTION TO THE PROBLEM OF THE *AGUNAH*?

As I already pointed out in the previous chapters of this book, there are *a priori* more possibilities for flexibility in the different contractual aspects of the Jewish marriage ceremony than have actually been adopted. On specific matters, such as stipulations regarding the husband's sexual obligations to his wife, the minimum possible sum in the *ketubah*, the husband's right of inheritance, and the wife's right to a divorce, the Palestinian Talmud is more flexible than the Babylonian Talmud is. In this chapter, I have discussed temporary marriage for an agreed period of time with the intention of proving that the Babylonian Talmud offers more possible variations on Jewish marriage than does the Palestinian Talmud.

I have examined the Talmudic sources of a temporary marriage for an agreed period, as well as the opinions of rabbinic authorities who rule that this marriage can be dissolved without a *get* when the parties agree to the time period prior to the marriage. However, from a practical halakhic point of view, unlike the various monetary conditions that used to be attached to the marriage contract, temporary marriages for an agreed period, which were customary in the Persian-Babylonian

published in the 1930s: Dwight M. Donaldson, *Temporary Marriage in Iran*, 26(4) MOSLEM WORLD 358 (1936); U. M. Daudpota & Asaf A. A. Fyzee, *Notes on Mut'a or Temporary Marriage in Islam*, 8 JBBRAS 79 (1932). Examples of contemporary works include I. K. A. Howard, *Mut'a Marriage Reconsidered in the Context of the Formal Procedures for Islamic Marriage*, XX(1) J. SEMITIC STUD. 82 (1975); Shahla Haeri, *The Institution of Mut'a Marriage in Iran: A Formal and Historical Perspective*, in ISLAM CRITICAL CONCEPTS IN SOCIOLOGY vol. 3 Gender and the Family 154–72 (Bryan S. Turner ed., 2003); ibid, *Temporary Marriage and the State in Iran: An Islamic Discourse on Female Sexuality*, 59 SOC. RES. 201 (1992); ibid, *An Islamic Discourse on Female Sexuality: Temporary Marriage in Postrevolutionary Iran*, in IN THE EYE OF THE STORM: WOMEN IN POSTREVOLUTIONARY IRAN 98–114 (Mahnaz Afkhami & Erika Friedl eds., 1994); KHALID SINDAWI, TEMPORARY MARRIAGE IN SUNNI AND SHIITE ISLAM: A COMPARATIVE STUDY (2013). For a discussion of the legal aspect, see Ghodsi, *supra* note 61; Kristin J. Miller, *Human Rights of Women in Iran: The Universalist Approach and the Relativist Response*, 10 EMORY INT'L L. REV. 779 (1996); Alison E. Graves, *Women in Iran: Obstacles to Human Rights and Possible Solutions*, 5 AM. U. J. GENDER & L. 57 (1996); Susan W. Tiefenbrun, *The Semiotics of Women's Human Rights in Iran*, 23 CONN. J. INT'L L. 1, 61–62 (2007).

109 *See* EDWARD G. BROWNE, A YEAR AMONGST THE PERSIANS 505–06 (1927); JAKOB E. POLAK, PERSIEN: DAS LAND UND SEINE BEWOHNER: ETHNOGRAPHISCHE SCHILDERUNGEN vol. I, 207–08 (1865); JAMES J. MORIER, THE ADVENTURES OF HAJJI BABA OF ISPAHAN vol. 3 chs. 6–8 (1970); GEORGE N. CURZON, PERSIA AND THE PERSIAN QUESTION vol. 1, 164–65 (1996). For the practical aspects today of issuing Iranian visas to temporary wives, see 6 Immigration Law Service 2d PSD FAM Iran, Immigration Law Service, Second Edition, February 2016 Update, Reciprocity Schedules and Country Document Finder, http://travel.state.gov/content/visas/en/fees/reciprocity-by-country/IR.html.

period, cannot be adapted to contemporary conditions in the opinion of most rabbinical authorities and certainly not without a *get* from the husband.

The fact that there is very little discussion of temporary marriages in halakhic sources or in the cases brought before rabbinical courts shows the lack of interest in this approach. The discussions in the rulings of the rabbinical courts relate only to the issue of the wife's promise to agree to a divorce at a given time and whether the promise is binding.[110] There is no discourse regarding the husband's refusal to grant a divorce. According to Maimonides, it is possible to set conditions to a marriage prior to the wedding, but the dissolution of the marriage would still require the husband's agreement and a *get*. Other rabbinic authorities disagree with Maimonides and argue that it is improper to impose conditions on a marriage, but if such a marriage did in fact take place, its dissolution would still require a *get* despite a condition setting limits to the length of the marriage.

Practically speaking, Michael J. Broyde (School of Law, Emory University) suggests four possible "paradigms for marriage as grounds for divorce" in the post-Talmudic era, an important one being the "return to contractual rules."[111] Whether temporary marriage is a unique variation of a conditional marriage or an intact agreement that is actually permanent and is terminated by an agreed-upon date, there is no doubt that it falls under the category of a contractual marriage. There is a trend among some contemporary halakhic authorities[112] and academic

[110] *See*, among others, Rabbinical Court 1064/1954, 1501/1954, Anonymous v. Anonymous, 1 PDR 257, 259 (11.01.55); Rabbinical Court 189/1967 Anonymous v. Anonymous, 7 PDR 83, 101–02 (1 Adar Beit 1967); Rabbinical Court 980/1967 Anonymous v. Anonymous, 7 PDR 353, 367 (15 Tevet 1969); Supreme Rabbinical Court appeal 120/1969 Anonymous v. Anonymous, 8 PDR 3, 9 (12 Av 1969); David Malka, *Hithayyavut shel ha-Isha lifne ha-Nisuin le-Kabel Get*, 8 SHURAT HA-DIN 360 (2003) (Heb.). *See also* a recent case, file no. 056234263–21–1 Anonymous v. Anonymous, which was brought in 18 HA-DIN VEHA-DAYYAN 12–13 (24.06.07) (2008), www.yadlaisha.org.il/Image/uploaded/issue18(1).pdf.

[111] *See* MICHAEL J. BROYDE, MARRIAGE, DIVORCE, AND THE ABANDONED WIFE IN JEWISH LAW 15–28 (2001).

[112] For a combination of conditional marriage and annulling the kiddushin, see YAAKOV M. TOLEDANO, RESP. HA-YAM HA-GADOL ch. 71 (1931), discussed by FREIMAN, *supra* note 33, at 391; MENACHEM RIZIKOV, RESP. SHAAREI SHAMAYIM *Even ha-Ezer* ch. 42 (1936), discussed by FREIMAN, *supra* note 33, at 393–94; YOSEF E. HENKIN, PERUSHEY IBRA vol. 5 ch. 24 (1925) (postponed *get* + conditional marriage), discussed in Adam Mintz, *A Courageous Proposal: The First Heter Agunah in America*, 4 JEWISH ORTHODOX FEMINIST ALLIANCE JOURNAL. 14 (2007), www.jofa.org/sites/default/files/uploaded_files/10002_u/1270-bqsl99671.pdf. For the most recent rabbinical-academic suggested combination of three possible solutions, conditional marriage + annulment + preparing the *get* at the betrothal, or alternatively, by a postponed *get*, *see* ELIEZER BERKOVITS, CONDITIONALITY IN MARRIAGE AND DIVORCE (1967) (Heb.); Michael J. Broyde, *A Proposed Tripartite Prenuptial Agreement to Solve the Agunah Problem: A Solution without Any Innovation*, 20 JEWISH L. ASS'N STUD 1 (2010); YEHUDAH ABEL, CONFRONTING "IGGUN": A COMBINATION OF THREE POSSIBLE SOLUTIONS TO THE PROBLEM OF THE CHAINED WIFE IN JEWISH LAW (2011), http://static1.1.sqspcdn.com/static/f/784513/25919453/1422985190550/Abel+Confronting+Iggun.pdf?token=tK3STQaHp6%2FfzT8q2PqKF%2FkTCMM%3D. For an evaluation of Broyde's proposal, see Yehudah Abel, *Comments on R. Broyde's Tripartite Agreement* (Working Papers of the Agunah Research Unit, July 2009), www.manchesterjewishstudies.org/publications/, www.mucjs.org/Broyde.pdf; JACKSON ET AL., *supra* note 2, passim.

scholars[113] not to rely solely on only one possible halakhic solution to the *agunah* problem but to combine several solutions. The reason is to convince the rabbinic authorities, who easily find the various pitfalls in any given solution, that taken together, these combined solutions can completely overcome the pitfalls or at least significantly mitigate them. Our discussion of temporary marriage may perhaps add another layer to the discourse on the desirable combined solution to the *agunah* problem, adding this possible contractual solution to the other possible solutions, such as annulling the *kiddushin*, *kefiyat get* (coercing the divorce), preparing the *get* at the betrothal/a postponed *get*, and so on.

[113] *See* the Manchester Analysis's suggested combined solution in JACKSON ET AL., *supra* note 2, at 195–211 (conditional marriage + annulment + kefiyat *get*); AVISHALOM WESTREICH, NO-FAULT DIVORCE IN JEWISH TRADITION 94–95 (2014) (Heb.) (kefiyat *get* + annulment), www.idi.org.il/media/3742181/the_right_to_divorce.pdf.

5

Toward Establishing Halakhic Parenthood by Agreement?

The notion of establishing a parent–child relationship based upon the intent of the parties who are involved in the production of the child is alien to Jewish thought.[1]

INTRODUCTION

The traditional Jewish family structure, like all other theological family structures, consists of a horizontal relationship between spouses and a vertical relationship between parent and child. In the previous chapters of this book, I discussed extensively the various dispositive contractual aspects of the spousal relationship. In this final chapter of the book, I discuss the dispositive elements of the parent–child relationship. It is worth noting at the outset the acute normative gap between these two similar but different relationships; whereas private ordering is feasible in the spousal relationship, in the parent–child relationship, it is far more complicated. This is generally the case in all legal systems and particularly in the Jewish (halakhic) legal system.

In a spousal agreement, we are dealing with two sovereign adults who have the legal capacity to negotiate their monetary relationship and all other dispositive elements of their status as a married couple. In stark contrast, the parent–child agreement primarily concerns the child, who is obviously the subject of that arrangement. Should children be bound by that agreement? Or are they only

[1] Chaim Povarsky, *Regulating Advanced Reproductive Technologies: A Comparative Analysis of Jewish and American Law*, 29 U. Tol. L. Rev. 409, 428 (1998). For a similar but milder statement that "Halakha has not granted legal validity to the ... parental relations constituted by human commitment," see Noam J. Zohar, Alternatives in Jewish Bioethics 81 (1997); this option "hasn't been discussed in Jewish legal sources ... Jewish law does not traditionally recognize the establishment of parental status by intent in any form," see Pamela Laufer-Ukeles, *Gestation: Work for Hire or the Essence of Motherhood? A Comparative Legal Analysis*, 9 Duke J. Gender L. & Pol'y 91, 104 (2002).

third-party beneficiaries to the parental agreement, thus remaining free to claim their rights while totally ignoring their parents' agreement? Furthermore, children are often minors who cannot consent to their parents' agreement, as they lack the legal capacity to do so. In the vast majority of jurisdictions, a parental agreement should be inspected in light of the best interests of the child (BIC), which means that any contract that might damage the BIC should be invalid.[2] How can we validate these private agreements if we do not ensure that they are not detrimental to the BIC and do not deprive the child of any rights and interests?

The legality and enforceability of any specific parental contractual stipulation, such as who should supply the child's food and basic needs, who should decide where and what he or she will learn, which medical treatments he or she will receive, and so on, is problematic in light of the above-mentioned shortcomings of the parent-child agreement. Clearly, any agreement for establishing the legal parenthood of individuals who will be determined as a child's legal parents, fulfill his or her various needs, and receive the various parental rights is much more complicated, since its implications are dramatically far-reaching for the child, his or her parents, and society as a whole.[3] Nonetheless, such parental agreements, which I define as determining legal parenthood by agreement (DLPBA), are slowly but surely becoming more prevalent, nuanced, and detailed in modern times due to today's greater social openness and the rapid biomedical developments in the field of reproduction.

As I have elaborated in some of my previous research, the last few decades have witnessed dramatic changes in the institutions of family and parenthood. If, in the past, the family was strongly influenced by the bionormative[4] theological family structure and defined as a pair of heterosexual parents living together under one roof along with their children, sociological changes have led to a rapid and extreme transformation in the definitions of family, marital relations, parenthood, and the relationship between parents and children. Furthermore, biomedical procedures, such as artificial insemination, sperm/ova/zygote donation, and surrogacy, which have been described by scholars as a "revolution" and as the "Wild West of American medicine," have separated marital relations and fertility.[5]

[2] For the centrality of the BIC in the American legal system as the main factor for validating any parental agreement, at least as it regards child custody, see Restatement (Second) of Contracts § 191 (1981). For practical implementation and an academic discussion of this article, see, respectively, Com. ex rel. Strunk v. Cummins, 258 Pa. Super. 326 (Pa. Super. 1978); Jeffrey A. Parness, *Parentage Prenups and Midnups*, 31 GA. ST. U. L. REV. 343, 345 n.11 (2015).

[3] For the importance and consequences of establishing legal parenthood, see Yehezkel Margalit, *To Be or Not to Be (A Parent)? – Not Precisely the Question; The Frozen Embryo Dispute*, 18 CARDOZO J.L. & GENDER 355, 361–63 (2012).

[4] For this term, see Katharine K. Baker, *Bionormativity and the Construction of Parenthood*, 42 GA. L. REV. 649, 653–54 (2008).

[5] Yehezkel Margalit, *Bridging the Gap between Intent and Status: A New Framework for Modern Parentage*, 15(1) WHITTIER J. CHILD & FAM. ADVOCACY 1 (2016); Povarsky, *supra* note 1, at 409–11.

Thus, today, the traditional family structure has lost much of its strength, and greater emphasis has been placed on individual autonomy and choice and on the individual's legitimate ability to DLPBA.[6] This departure from theological marriage and parenthood, coupled with the inability of traditional parentage models to satisfactorily address the realities of modern parenthood, requires increased reliance on private ordering to determine legal parenthood. This process has already begun to some extent: in order to bridge the gap between evolving social and technological norms and prevailing normative laws, individuals have sought to privately regulate their familial relationships by private agreements and contracts.[7] This trend will likely continue in the future as the diversity and complexity of the methods for creating a family and/or producing a child increase.[8]

Following the brief discussion above of the sociological and biomedical background for the increasing proliferation of these arrangements and agreements, and exploring the troubling civil aspects of DLPBA, I wish to examine specific problematic halakhic angles of this issue. As can be deduced from the discussions in the previous chapters of this book, the halakhic conceptualization of spousal relations is a rigid status that derives directly from the nearly absolute obligation to marry.

6 For the growing acceptance of DLPBA in recent decades, see Margalit, *supra* note 3, at 358–61. For leading articles that maintain that, in the modern era, intentional parenthood is the best model for determining legal parenthood, particularly in the context of reproductive technology, see John L. Hill, *What Does It Mean to Be a "Parent"? The Claims of Biology as the Basis for Parental Rights*, 66 N.Y.U. L. REV. 353, 413–20 (1991); Alexa E. King, *Solomon Revisited: Assigning Parenthood in the Context of Collaborative Reproduction*, 5 UCLA WOMEN'S L.J. 329, 367–99 (1995); Perri Koll, *The Use of the Intent Doctrine to Expand the Rights of Intended Homosexual Male Parents in Surrogacy Custody Disputes*, 18 CARDOZO J.L. & GENDER 199, 223–24 (2011); Jesse M. Nix, *"You Only Donated Sperm": Using Intent to Uphold Paternity Agreements*, 11 J.L. & FAM. STUD. 487, 494 (2009); Jason Oller, *Can I Get That in Writing?: Established and Emerging Protections of Paternity Rights* [In re K.M.H., 169 P.3d 1025 (Kan. 2007)], 48 WASHBURN L.J. 209, 220–23, 235–37 (2008); Dara E. Purvis, *Intended Parents and the Problem of Perspective*, 24 YALE J.L. & FEMINISM 210, 227–53 (2012); Marjorie Maguire Shultz, *Reproductive Technology and Intent-Based Parenthood: An Opportunity for Gender Neutrality*, 1990 WIS. L. REV. 297, 321–98 (1990); Andrea E. Stumpf, *Redefining Mother: A Legal Matrix for New Reproductive Technologies*, 96 YALE L.J. 187, 192–208 (1986); Katherine M. Swift, *Parenting Agreements, the Potential Power of Contract, and the Limits of Family Law*, 34 FLA. ST. U. L. REV. 913, 930–57 (2007); Deborah H. Wald, *The Parentage Puzzle: The Interplay between Genetics, Procreative Intent, and Parental Conduct in Determining Legal Parentage*, 15 AM. U. J. GENDER SOC. POL'Y & L. 379, 388–89 (2007); Catherine Villareale, *The Case of Two Biological Intended Mothers: Illustrating the Need to Statutorily Define Maternity in Maryland*, 42 U. BALT. L. REV. 365 (2013); Mary Patricia Byrn & Erica Holzer, *Codifying the Intent Test*, 41 WM. MITCHELL L. REV. 130 (2015); Heather Kolinsky, *The Intended Parent: The Power and Problems Inherent in Designating and Determining Intent in the Context of Parental Rights*, 119 PENN ST. L. REV. 801 (2015).

7 *See* Linda D. Elrod, *A Child's Perspective of Defining a Parent: The Case for Intended Parenthood*, 25 BYU J. PUB. L. 245 (2011), and for a lengthier discussion, see YEHEZKEL MARGALIT, DETERMINING LEGAL PARENTAGE BY AGREEMENT (2011) (Heb.).

8 Yehezkel Margalit, *Artificial Insemination from Donor (AID) – From Status to Contract and Back Again?*, 21(1) BOSTON U. J. SCI. & TECH. L. 69, 70 (2015).

Therefore, any contractual stipulation or even a complete explicit contract in this regard would be void, as it falls under the category of "one who stipulates about what is written in the Torah." The same would apply to the parent-child relationship because of the first commandment, both chronologically and in importance, to be fruitful and multiply.[9]

Thus, *prima facie*, *halakhah* leaves no room for any private ordering of the parent-child relationship because of this relationship's rigid halakhic status,[10] and any private agreement to change any of its implications is rejected from the outset, particularly when the parent's identity is established by DLPBA. Before trying to find tools for implementing this normative model wholly or partially, I begin the discussion with a review of the old, traditional halakhic modes of determining parenthood in the most common scenarios of the ancient era – a coitally produced child and adoption. As in all other faiths and civil jurisdictions, the halakhic ramifications of determining parenthood are enormous and far-reaching. The determination that a child is Jewish (and therefore, for example, entitled to Israeli nationality under Israeli law) is based on matrilineal descent, whereas his or her status of *Kohen* (priest), Levite or Israelite is passed down patrilineally.[11]

A man who is defined as the legal father of a child must assume several Jewish and civil parental obligations.[12] In addition to fulfilling the first commandment of procreation, the Babylonian Talmud, Tractate *Kiddushin* states that the father is obligated to circumcise his son, and if the son is the mother's first born, redeem him as part of the *pidyon haben* ritual, teach him Torah and a profession, assist him in getting married, and – according to another opinion – even teach him to swim. In addition, he must maintain him, shelter him, and supply all his other needs. The child, on his part, must respect and obey his father and mother, is prohibited from hitting and cursing them, must mourn them when they die, and has the right to

[9] For more about this commandment, see Laufer-Ukeles, *supra* note 1, at 120–22; David M Feldman, Birth Control and Jewish Law: Marital Relations, Contraception, and Abortion as Set Forth in the Classic Texts of Jewish Law 46–50 (1968).

[10] It should be noted that although the secular phrase status is very important and prevalent, it is also very amorphous and difficult to define precisely because it is used in different legal fields and contexts. For its basic meanings, see Karelton C. Allen, *Status and Capacity*, 46 Law Q. Rev 277 (1930); Manfred Rehbinder, *Status, Contract and the Welfare State*, 23 Stan. L. Rev. 941 (1971); Ronald H. Graveson, Status in the Common Law 33–54 (1953). For a discussion of legal parenthood as a modern status that enables individuals to privately determine who will be regarded as the legal parent(s) of the conceived child, see Margalit, *supra* note 8, at 94–96; Margalit, *supra* note 5, at ch. 4.4.

[11] For more on the importance of Jewish blood lines, see Pamela Laufer-Ukeles, *The Lost Children: When the Right to Children Conflicts with the Rights of Children*, 8 L. & Ethics Hum. Rts. 219, 245 (2014). For the vast influence of Jewish law on Israeli civil law and for a criticism of this interplay, see Ruth Zafran, *Whose Child Are You? The Israeli Paternity Regulation and Its Flaws*, 46 Hapraklit 311 (2003) (Heb.).

[12] Avraham Steinberg, Encyclopedia of Jewish Medical Ethics: A Compilation of Jewish Medical Law on All Topics of Medical Interest vol. 2, 772–74, s.v. "Parents" (Fred Rosner trans. 2003); ibid, vol. 3, 775–82, s.v. "Paternity."

inherit them.[13] Before exploring the extent to which *halakhah* is unique in its approach of establishing legal parenthood almost exclusively by the "natural order," I wish to briefly review the basic approach of many, if not all, other legal systems, which determine it solely by law. This major disparity is not a modern one but dates back to ancient times, when *halakhah* stood alone in stark contrast to Roman law and its derivative – common law.

In ancient Roman law, the husband/father was the head of the family (*patria potestas* [Latin: power of a father]). His wife and children were his property, and he alone decided who was to be regarded as his legal child and thus inherit him and who would not be defined as his legal child, even if the child was his own biological son. In other words, the father had the social and legal power to adopt a child and define that child as his legal child and successor.[14] Later on, this approach of determining legal parenthood by law rather than biology and/or genetics was adopted by Roman law's successors, mainly common law,[15] Christian law,[16] and Islamic law.[17] In its new guise, any child conceived out of wedlock, even when there was no explicit betrayal in the sexual act, was defined as a bastard and illegitimate, as the child was not part of a legally intact marriage (*filius nullius* [Latin: "child of nobody"]). This child was indeed a child of nobody, for his or her biological father and mother were not recognized as his or her legal parents, and the child was thus deprived of all his or her basic needs and rights, most importantly the right to maintenance and ability to inherit.[18]

[13] *See* BT *Kiddushin* 29a. For an extensive discussion of some key parental obligations and rights, see Israel Z. Gilat, Family Law – The Relations between Parents and Children – Alimony, Financial Responsibilities, Custody and Education (2000) (Heb.). For the general parent-child relationship, see Benzion Schereschewsky, Family Law in Israel 351–442 (4th ed., 1993) (Heb.).

[14] For this notion, see John Crook, *Patria Potestas*, 17(1) The Classical Quarterly (New Series) 113 (1967); Herbert F. Jolowicz & Barry Nicholas, A Historical Introduction to the Study of Roman Law 118 (1972); Walter Kirkpatrick Lacey, "*Patria Potestas*" in The Family in Ancient Rome: New Perspectives 121 (Beryl Rawson ed., 1987).

[15] *See generally* Harry D. Krause, Illegitimacy: Law and Social Policy (1971); Jenny Teichman, Illegitimacy: An Examination of Bastardy (1982). For a discussion of illegitimacy from a Jewish perspective, see Povarsky, *supra* note 1, at 424–30.

[16] *See* John Witte, The Sins of the Fathers: The Law and Theology of Illegitimacy Reconsidered ch. 1 (2009); Merry Wiesner-Hanks, Christianity and Sexuality in the Early Modern World: Regulating Desire, Reforming Practice (2010).

[17] *See generally* Ebrahim Moosa, *The Child Belongs to the Bed: Illegitimacy and Islamic Law*, in Questionable Issue: Illegitimacy in South Africa (Sandra Burman & Eleanor Preston-Whyte eds., 1992); Mudasra Sabreen, *Parentage: A Comparative Study of Islamic and Pakistani Law*, 1(2) Frontiers of Legal Research 21 (2013). To obtain a sense of the extent to which this problem is still relevant today, see Christian Reus-Smit, *International Crises of Legitimacy*, 44 Int'l Pol. 157 (2007) and the following articles dealing with modern aspects of it: Symposium: *The New "Illegitimacy": Revisiting Why Parentage Should Not Depend on Marriage*, 20 Am. U. J. Gender Soc. Pol'y & L. 347–740 (2012).

[18] *See* William Blackstone, Commentaries on the Laws of England 459 (1962); Richard H. Helmholz, *Support Orders, Church Courts, and the Rule of Filius Nullius: A Reassessment of*

1 DETERMINING HALAKHIC PARENTHOOD IN THE ANCIENT ERA

1.1 *Coitally Produced Child*

Normatively speaking, if a child is born into an intact marriage in which his or her two parents are Jewish and married to one another, the child is considered their legal child,[19] he or she can marry any Jewish person, and he or she has all of the obligations and rights that pertain to both parents. But if the child is born to parents who could not be married at the time of his or her conception, because their marriage was prohibited by the Torah and would be regarded as invalid according to *halakhah*, or alternatively, when a married woman has sexual relationships with another Jew, the offspring is regarded as a *mamzer* (bastard).[20] It should be noted that the *mamzer* remains the legitimate child of his or her parents (as opposed to being regarded as an illegitimate child in other religions and legal systems) and therefore still has the right to be maintained by them, to carry their family name, and to inherit from them after their death. A son and all his descendants, however, cannot marry a Jewish woman unless she herself is a *mamzer* or proselyte. If a child is born to a single mother who is legally able to be married to the father but did so only after the child was conceived, the child is halakhically legitimate, as he or she was born to married parents, and he or she does not face the stigma of bearing the status of *mamzer*.[21] In the latter scenario of a single mother, where the putative father denies his paternity, there are no halakhic constraints to proving the genetic connection by means of a paternity test.

Similarly, there is no validity to any private agreement between the parents to release the man from his paternity, even if they signed a contract to the effect that he is not to be regarded as the halakhic father of the conceived child. But, in the case of a married woman, where there is concern that any inquiry into the true genetic connection may result in the possibility that the child will be labeled a *mamzer*, extensive halakhic efforts are made to avoid this conclusion in order to preserve the child's basic right not to suffer the stigma of being labeled a *mamzer*.[22]

the Common Law, 63 VA. L. REV. 431 (1977); Mary K. Kisthardt, *Of Fatherhood, Families and Fantasy: The Legacy of Michael H. V. Gerald D.*, 65 TUL. L. REV. 585, 587–95 (1991).

19 For an elaboration of this issue, see Pinhas Shifman, *The Status of the Unmarried Parent in Israel Law*, 12 ISR. L. REV. 194, 194–95 (1977); Ruth Halperin-Kaddari, *Redefining Parenthood*, 29 CAL. W. INT'L. L.J. 313, 316–17 (1999).

20 *See* Ben Zion Schereschewsky, "*Mamzer*" in THE PRINCIPLES OF JEWISH LAW 435–38 (Menachem Elon ed., 1975); Laufer-Ukeles, *supra* note 11, at 242–45. For the concept and importance of purity and holiness that should be part of the conjugal relationship, see Povarsky, *supra* note 1, at 413–16. For a social anthropological criticism of the politics of *mamzerut*, see SUSAN M. KAHN, REPRODUCING JEWS: A CULTURAL ACCOUNT OF ASSISTED CONCEPTION IN ISRAEL 78–80 (2000).

21 *See* Ben Zion Schereschewsky, "Parent and Child" in THE PRINCIPLES OF JEWISH LAW 424–29 (Menachem Elon ed., 1975) and more generally, SCHERESCHEWSKY, *supra* note 13, at 352–66.

22 For the difference between determining legal paternity when the child is born to a single mother and to a married mother, a difference that is well-rooted also in Israeli civil law; *see*

This religious-civil desire to avoid declaring a child a bastard in the Jewish-Israeli context is reflected in some of Israel's civil laws as well as in Israel's Population Registry Law, 5725–1965 § 22, which dictates that, "Save under a judgment of a competent civil or religious court, a man shall not be registered as the father of the child of a woman who had been married to another man within 300 days prior to the date of the birth of the child."[23] The meaning of this legislation is that under such circumstances, legal paternity cannot be registered in Israel's population registry following a declaration of the parties due to the halakhic problem of being regarded a *mamzer*. In this unique case, only a court decree may permit this registration, taking into consideration, among other things, the BIC and the far-reaching Jewish and civil consequences of such a problematic registration.[24]

Similarly, and more uniquely to Israeli civil law, is concern over the possibility of bastardy should paternity tests be conducted on a regular basis for minors, whether Jewish, Christian, or Muslim.[25] That is the reason why the Genetic Information Law, 5761–2000, following its amendment in 2008, states that a paternity test is allowed only by court order. A paternity test may be conducted only after receiving explicit permission from the child's chief religious authority and reaffirmation by the attorney general, ensuring that there is no fear of bastardy in this case, which would obviously be detrimental to the BIC and which was bitterly criticized in the scholarly literature.[26] As can be deduced from the above discussion, the rule of thumb in *halakhah*, and subsequently in Israeli civil law,[27] is that legal paternity is determined almost solely on the basis of genetics and the natural order, without taking into account the legal definition of the parents' marital status. Of course, one

Ruth Zafran, *More Than One Mother: Determining Maternity for the Biological Child of a Female Same-Sex Couple – the Israeli View*, 9 GEO. J. GENDER & L. 115, 119 n.13 (2008). For parallel secular efforts not to define a child as illegitimate, as the marital presumption, see Traci Dallas, *Rebutting the Marital Presumption: A Developed Relationship Test*, 88 COLUM. L. REV. 369 (1988); Theresa Glennon, *Somebody's Child: Evaluating the Erosion of the Marital Presumption of Paternity*, 102 W. VA. L. REV. 547 (2000).

23 www.israellawresourcecenter.org/israellaws/fulltext/populationreglaw.htm.

24 *See* Zafran, *supra* note 22, at 153–54.

25 For a secular Israeli call to conduct paternity tests on a regular basis to avoid any ambiguity concerning the putative father's identity, see Talia Agmon, *Genetic Testing of Children – Why Not? Questions Regarding the Legislation on Genetic Testing of Children in Israel*, 6 L. & BUS. 295 (2007) (Heb.).

26 For the English version of the law, but unfortunately without the relevant 2008 amendment no. 3, see www.jewishvirtuallibrary.org/jsource/Health/GeneticInformationLaw.pdf. *See also* Shahar Lifshitz, *Neither Nature nor Contract: Toward an Institutional Perspective on Parenthood Essay*, 8 L. & ETHICS HUM. RTS. 297, 305 (2014). For such criticism, see Ruth Zafran, *If It Ain't [Completely] Broke, Don't Fix It: Determining Paternity According to the Genetic Information Law (Amendment no. 3), 2008*, 3 HUKIM – THE ISRAELI JOURNAL OF LEGISLATION 191 (2011) (Heb.).

27 For this contention concerning the Israeli system's rule of thumb, see Zafran, *supra* note 22, at 118–19; Laufer-Ukeles, *supra* note 1, at 104–05.

of the major exceptions to this is the fear of the *mamzer* status, as explained above, in addition to other social-halakhic exceptions, as I explore in Section 4.[28]

1.2 *Adoption*

Adoption, one of the most well-known parent–child relationships, is deeply rooted in ancient common law and is still prevalent today. Judaism's attitude toward adoption is ambivalent at best and hostile at worst.[29] This ambivalence has its roots in biblical sources, where there are many verses in both the Pentateuch and the Prophets that can be interpreted as referring to a form of adoption, but all are so vague as to be unreliable for serving as a cornerstone for any ancient recognition of this legal mechanism.[30] Even later on, in the Tannaitic and Amoraic literature, only *aggadic* and non-halakhic sources endorse the adoption of a Jewish child by a foreign Jewish couple. For example, there is a *midrash* about a guardian who married off the female orphan he raised as his own child. When asked her father's name, for recording in her marriage contract, she remained silent for a while and then replied, "he that brings up a child is called a father, not he that begets."[31]

Adoption involves three groups of people – the adopted child; the adopting parents, who may be infertile and this is their last opportunity to become parents; and the natural parents, who often decide to give away their own child because of economic constraints. But, practically speaking, throughout the ages, the only factor that Jewish halakhic authorities have taken into account in deciding whether to

[28] For a brief discussion of those halakhic exceptions that ignore the basic theme of nature and genetics as the sole factor in establishing legal paternity, see Michael Corinaldi, *The Legal Status of a Child Born of Artificial Means from a Sperm Donor or an Egg Donor*, 18–19 SHNATON HA-MISHPAT HAIVRI 295, 304–08 (1992–94) (Heb.); ZOHAR, *supra* note 1, at 69–71, 74–76, who even concluded that "the affirmation of biological parenthood and the concomitant invalidation of parenthood by consent reflect a value-commitment rather than an inevitable necessity"; ZOHAR, ibid, at 82; MARGALIT, *supra* note 7, at 250–52.

[29] For the extent to which, even in 2015, adoption was still common and relevant, see the following seminal studies published in that year alone: HEIDI SCHWARZWALD ET AL., INTERNATIONAL ADOPTION AND CLINICAL PRACTICE (2015); BRIAN MILNE, RIGHTS OF THE CHILD: 25 YEARS AFTER THE ADOPTION OF THE UN CONVENTION (2015); KERRY O'HALLORAN, THE POLITICS OF ADOPTION: INTERNATIONAL PERSPECTIVES ON LAW, POLICY AND PRACTICE (2015); OPEN SOURCE SYSTEMS: ADOPTION AND IMPACT: 11TH IFIP WG 2.13 INTERNATIONAL CONFERENCE, OSS 2015 (Ernesto Damiani et al. eds., 2015).

[30] For a detailed discussion of those verses, see ENCYCLOPAEDIA JUDAICA, s.v. "adoption," www.jewishvirtuallibrary.org/jsource/judaica/ejud_0002_0001_0_00486.html. For a more general description of various biblical parent–child relationships, see JOSEPH FLEISHMAN, PARENT AND CHILD IN ANCIENT NEAR EAST AND THE BIBLE (1999) (Heb.); ibid, FATHER-DAUGHTER RELATIONS IN BIBLICAL LAW (2011).

[31] Ex. Rab 46:5. And similarly "Whoever brings up an orphan in his home, it is as though he gave birth to him," BT *Sanhedrin* 19b. *See also* MICHAEL GOLD, AND HANNAH WEPT: INFERTILITY, ADOPTION, AND THE JEWISH COUPLE 153–61(1988).

authorize an adoption has been the BIC.[32] If the BIC requires that a child be removed from his or her natural home – that is, when a child has been orphaned or abandoned or neglected by his or her natural parents – he or she may be adopted by others. The child was never treated as goods to be handed from his or her parents to others but rather as an independent, autonomous person whose natural or adoptive parents have the duty, and not the right, to care for him or her and fulfill all his or her needs. Even after the child is adopted by others, his or her natural and legal relationship with his or her natural family is never actually abolished.[33]

Even a superficial glance at the Jewish literature that deals with adoption clearly shows the extent to which Judaism prefers natural parenthood and genetic lineage over any social and/or psychological parenthood of adoptive parents.[34] In social or psychological parenthood, an individual can be determined as a legal parent despite not being the biological parent of the child. While some halakhists give some sort of recognition to this institution,[35] it is safe to assume that the vast majority reject such recognition and hold that "adoption is not known as a legal institution in Jewish law."[36] That is because in Jewish law, and therefore also in Israeli civil law,[37] legal parenthood is defined as natural parenthood, and no implied or explicit agreement,

[32] For the superiority of this doctrine in secular law and in Jewish law, see, respectively, Joseph Goldstein et al., Before the Best Interests of the Child (1979); ibid, Beyond the Best Interests of the Child (1980); ibid, The Best Interests of the Child: The Least Detrimental Alternative (1996); Michael J. Broyde, *Child Custody in Jewish Law: A Pure Law Analysis*, www.jlaw.com/Articles/childcus2.html; Yehiel S. Kaplan, *Child Custody in Jewish Law: From Authority of the Father to the Best Interest of the Child*, 24(1) J.L. & Religion 89 (2008/2009). For reservations with regard to this theme in the Jewish context, see Israel Z. Gilat, *Is the "Benefit of the Child"a Major Criterion According to Jewish Law in a Parental Conflict of the Child?*, 8 Bar Ilan L. Stud. 297 (1990) (Heb.). For the interplay between this doctrine and the religion of the adopted child, see Laura J. Schwartz, *Religious Matching for Adoption: Unraveling the Interests Behind the "Best Interests" Standard*, 25 Fam. L.Q. 171 (1991); Daniel Pollack et al., *Classical Religious Perspectives of Adoption Law*, 79 Notre Dame L. Rev. 693 (2004).

[33] For a fuller discussions of Jewish adoption by legal scholars and rabbinic authorities, see, respectively, Schereschewsky, *supra* note 13, at 414–24; Nili Maimon, Adoption of Children: Legal Principles 510–89 (1994) (Heb.); Elyakom Dvorks, On Your Adopted Child: Child Adoption in the Halakha Perspective (2005) (Heb.).

[34] In the modern context, the doctrine of social and/or psychological parenthood is used in order to establish or terminate legal parenthood and/or resolve any dispute with the natural parents over child custody. *See* Carolyn Curtis, *The Psychological Parent Doctrine in Custody Disputes between Foster Parents and Biological Parents*, 16 Colum. J.L. & Soc. Probs. 149 (1980); Vanessa L. Warzynski, *Termination of Parental Rights: The "Psychological Parent" Standard*, 39 Vill. L. Rev. 737 (1994); Peggy Cooper Davis, *The Good Mother: A New Look at Psychological Parent Theory*, 22 N.Y.U. Rev. L. & Soc. Change 347 (1996).

[35] *See* Mordechai HaCohen, Halachot and Halichot 155–80 (1975) (Heb.); Maimon, *supra* note 33; Dvorks, *supra* note 33.

[36] *See* Encyclopaedia Judaica, *supra* note 30; Gold, *supra* note 31, at 157; Laufer-Ukeles, *supra* note 1, at 104, 122–23.

[37] For a list of several prominent Israeli Supreme Court verdicts that support this contention, that legal parenthood is defined as natural parenthood, see Lifshitz, *supra* note 26, at 299 n.5.

or even a judicial decree and legislation, can change this axiom.[38] The only possible recognition in adoption is the recognition, to varying degrees, of the new relationship as additional and supplemental to the still-existing natural lineage, but not fully replacing it.[39]

What is crucial for the continuation of our discussion is the fact that even those who hold that adoption cannot sever the adopted child's natural lineage with his or her natural parents are likely to agree that there is enough room in *halakhah* for regarding the adoptive parents as at least "semi-parents." There is a possible Talmudic precedent for a legal guardian (*apotropos*)[40] to be recognized as the child's legal parent. This legal recognition involves many parental obligations and rights that are similar to those of the natural parents, as I discuss again in the conclusion of this chapter. Another option for granting recognition to adoptive parents is to entrust the administration of the child's property to the adopter, which places the child in the same position as the adopter's natural children, and includes his or her right to be maintained by the heirs after the adopter's death. It should be emphasized that the latter option is relevant only as regards monetary aspects, whereas the first includes a wider range of parental responsibilities, such as taking responsibility for the child's physical and mental welfare.[41]

It is worth noting that the age-old traditional approach of *halakhah* that it is possible to divorce your spouse by mutual agreement but it is impossible to "divorce" your child has been adopted in the modern era by some legal secular thinkers.[42]

38 That is the reason why Israel's 1981 Adoption of Children Law § 16 defines the adoption relationship as "the adoption ends the obligations and rights between the adopted child and his parents and the rest of his family and the authority given to them over him." This means that the adoption law does not permanently and totally terminate the natural lineage of the adopted child's natural family and does not establish a full and new relationship with his or her adoptive family, due to *halakhah*'s basic premise that at the end of the day, the new lineage cannot fully substitute the natural one. For an overview of Israeli adoption regulations and the massive influence of Judaism on it, see, respectively, Zafran, *supra* note 22, at 131–35; Laufer-Ukeles, *supra* note 1, at 104, 123–28.

39 Michael Corinaldi, Staus, Family and Succession Laws: Between Religion and State 25–26 (2004) (Heb.), and more extensively Mark Goldfeder, *The Adoption of Children in Judaism and in Israel; A Conceptual and Practical Review*, 22 Cardozo J. Int'l & Comp. L. 321 (2014); Alex J. Goldman, Judaism confronts contemporary issues 63–73 (1978); Meyer Steinberg, Responsum on Problems of Adoption in Jewish Law (1969).

40 BT *Bava Kama* 39a–40a, 44b; BT *Bava Metzia* 38a, 39a–b, 42b; BT *Bava Batra* 42a, 131b–132a. For the institution of the apotropos in Jewish law, see Ben Zion Schereschewsky, "*Apotropos*" in The Principles of Jewish Law 219 (Menachem Elon ed., 1975); Charla Murakami, *Parent-Child Relations: A Comparison of Jewish and California Law*, 1 U.C. Davis J. Int'l L. & Pol'y 107, 109–15 (1995); Kenneth B. Orenbach, *The Religiously Distinct Director: Infusing Judeo-Christian Business Ethics into Corporate Governance*, 2 Charlotte L. Rev. 369, 403–04 (2010).

41 For an overview of these two options, see Encyclopaedia Judaica, *supra* note 30. For the first option, see Laufer-Ukeles, *supra* note 1, at 104, 124.

42 For a unique secular exception and for the option of divorcing one's parents, see Kingsley v. Kingsley, 623 So. 2d 780 (Fla. Dist. Ct. App. 1993).

For example, one radical feminist maintains that the vertical parent–child relationship should be regarded as the pillar of the modern family because the horizontal spousal relationship has become too weak and shaky as a result of the skyrocketing divorce rate. Alternatively, there is the child-centered approach, whereby the BIC rather than parental rights should be the central factor in day-to-day family life.[43]

2 DETERMINING HALAKHIC PARENTHOOD IN THE MODERN ERA

2.1 *General*

The Jewish nation as a whole, and Israeli society in particular, hold childbearing in high esteem for historical, religious, demographic, and security reasons.[44] To begin with, this is the first biblical commandment for every Jew, and the Talmud states that the messiah will come when all the unborn souls are born.[45] The tragedy of the Holocaust, which destroyed a third of the Jewish nation, the fragile and problematic security and demographic situation in the Middle East, where the Jewish state is surrounded by enemy states that have repeatedly gone to war against it, coupled with the Israeli-Palestinian conflict, create a strong desire in Jewish and Israeli society to "fill the void."

The above phenomenon has been referred to as Jewish and Israeli pronatalism – that is, the encouragement of procreation, childbearing, and an emphasis on the advantages of raising children.[46] Moreover, since procreation is one of the central Jewish commandments and a socio-religious taboo, the other side of the coin is the sad situation of infertile individuals or couples. Numerous articles and books have been written about the complex and sensitive status of those who are infertile and how to overcome it.[47] The cry of the barren biblical Rachel to the patriarch Jacob,

43 See, respectively, MARTHA A. FINEMAN, THE NEUTERED MOTHER, THE SEXUAL FAMILY, AND OTHER TWENTIETH CENTURY TRAGEDIES (1995); Barbara B. Woodhouse, *Hatching the Egg: A Child-Centered Perspective on Parents' Rights*, 14 CARDOZO L. REV. 1747, 1754–71 (1993).

44 *See* STEINBERG, *supra* note 12, vol. 2, 586–92, s.v. "Fundamental Principles of Jewish Law in Relation to Technological Advances." For the general Jewish ethic, especially concerning childbirth, see, respectively, ibid, vol. 2, 380–89, s.v. "Jewish Ethics"; vol. 1, 166–94, s.v. "Child Birth."

45 *See* BT *Niddah* 13b.

46 For this notion and for a survey of its main reasons and ramifications, see, respectively, Yeheakel Margalit, *Scarce Medical Resources – Parenthood at Every Age, in Every Case and Subsidized by the State?*, 9 NETANYA ACADEMIC LAW. REV. 191, 193–207 (2014) (Heb.), www.netanya.ac.il/Schools/LawSchool/Journal/Documents/Yehezkel-Margalit.pdf; Laufer-Ukeles, *supra* note 11, at 220–24, 234–40.

47 *See* Gideon Weitzman, *The Helakhic Status of an Infertile Couple*, 23 TCHUMIN 223 (2003) (Heb.); ibid, *Give Me Children or Else I Am Dead: Orthodox Jewish Perspectives on Fertility*, in FAITH AND FERTILITY: ATTITUDES TOWARDS REPRODUCTIVE PRACTICES IN DIFFERENT RELIGIONS FROM ANCIENT TO MODERN TIMES 205 (Eric Blyth & Ruth Landau eds., 2009); RICHARD V. GRAZI, BE FRUITFUL AND MULTIPLY: FERTILITY THERAPY AND THE JEWISH TRADITION (1994); ibid, OVERCOMING INFERTILITY (2005).

"give me children, or I shall die," which the sages interpreted to mean that a childless person is accounted as blind and even dead, has echoed down through the generations, and it is only now that advanced biomedical innovations offer some comfort for those in this situation.[48]

While clearly the advent of "new" assisted reproduction technologies (ART) has successfully solved many fertility problems, these technologies have also threatened and even endangered the Jewish bionormative perceptions of proper and desired spousal and parental structures.[49] When you unravel the Gordian knot that used to exist between marriage, sexuality, and procreation, and add a third player to the dual spousal conjugal relationship – such as a sperm and/or ova donor and/or a surrogate mother – the necessity for marrying decreases.[50] I argue later on that at the end of the day, this is the real reason why some halakhists have strongly opposed ART, even in the very justified scenario of using the husband's sperm to artificially inseminate his wife.

2.2 *Artificial Insemination by Husband*

The most prevalent, and seemingly less controversial and simplest ART, is the use of the husband's sperm to impregnate his wife. Generally speaking, there are a variety of types of artificial insemination.[51] The artificial insemination process involves the injection of sperm into a woman's cervix. The procedure may be done either by a licensed physician in an official medical facility or by the woman at home. Homologous insemination occurs when the husband donates the sperm that is injected into his wife. Homologous insemination is alternatively known as artificial insemination by the husband (AIH). It has been applied successfully since at least the eighteenth century.

From the early 1930s, the possibility that a woman could be fertilized not in the "old-fashioned way" ushered in a new era in which thousands of children were born

48 *See*, respectively, Genesis 30, 1; BT *Nedarim* 64b. *See also* Gideon Weitzman, *Technology in the Service of the First Mitzvah*, 6 ḤAKIRAH, THE FLATBUSH J. JEWISH L. & THOUGHT 259 (2008).

49 For a discussion of this threat and the general interplay of ART and the "traditional" and "new" family, see, respectively, Radhika Rao, *Assisted Reproductive Technology and the Threat to the Traditional Family*, 47 HASTINGS L.J. 951 (1996); John A. Robertson, *Assisted Reproductive Technology and the Family*, 47 HASTINGS L.J. 911 (1996); *Developments in the Law: IV. Changing Realities of Parenthood: The Law's Response to the Evolving American Family and Emerging Reproductive Technologies*, 116 HARV. L. REV. 2052 (2003).

50 *See generally* Jonathan B. Pitt, *Fragmenting Procreation*, 108 YALE L.J. 1893 (1999); Deborah H. Wald, *The Parentage Puzzle: The Interplay between Genetics, Procreative Intent, and Parental Conduct in Determining Legal Parentage*, 15 AM. U. J. GENDER SOC. POL'Y & L. 379 (2007). For the Jewish perspective on fragmenting sex and procreation and for a feminist critique of it, see RONIT IRSHAI, FERTILITY AND JEWISH: FEMINIST PERSPECTIVES ON ORTHODOX RESPONSA LITERATURE 25–200, 203–75 (Joel A. Linsider trans., 2012).

51 *See* Brent J. Jensen, Comment, *Artificial Insemination and the Law*, 1982 BYU L. REV. 935, 935–37 (1982).

by this procedure. It is most relevant when the husband's sperm is medically problematic or when he must undergo medical treatment that will impair or carry a risk of impairing his ability to procreate.[52] Although this simple technology, *prima facie*, does not involve any particular ethical or legal problems, in the conservative Victorian era, it was regarded as adultery and the child was stigmatized as a bastard or illegitimate. Slowly but surely, the approach to this procedure changed, and today all societies recognize that its advantages outweigh its disadvantages.[53]

Thus, unless there is reason to suspect that the husband's sperm will be mixed with, or intentionally or even unintentionally replaced by, someone else's sperm, it should be permitted. Nonetheless, the Catholic Church is its strongest opponent, maintaining that any human involvement in the most intimate and divine process of procreation is prohibited. It views any such human involvement as "playing God" and hubris and demands that it be completely banned.[54] This stringent Catholic approach toward ART has been regarded by some as naturalism – that is, that a human being may not interfere in the divine desire and destiny that a given believer will or not have children.

One of the most fascinating halakhic aspects of this issue is the old, traditional approach of dealing with the status and consequences of a child who was conceived in noncoital reproduction. There is a discussion in the Talmud of the possibility of a virgin conceiving after bathing in a bathtub in which a man had previously ejaculated.[55] Similarly, there is a parallel *aggadic* source that states that Ben-Sira was simultaneously the son and the grandson of Jeremiah, as his daughter was impregnated by Jeremiah's sperm after he was forced to ejaculate in the water of a bathhouse.[56] Later on, in the thirteenth century, Peretz ben Elijah of Corbeil, in his halakhic work *Haggahot Semak*, cautions a married woman not to lie on the bedsheets of a man who is not her husband, for fear that the man may have ejaculated on them. The reason was that if she became pregnant, no one would know that the fetus is not that of her husband, and there is concern that the child

[52] *See* Steinberg, *supra* note 12, vol. 1, 58–73, s.v. "AIH"; Daniel B Sinclair, Jewish Biomedical Law. Legal and Extra-Legal Dimensions 68–76 (2003).

[53] For a description of the shift from regarding this procedure as problematic and worthy of rejection to more accepted and legitimate, see Wilfred J. Finegold, Artificial Insemination (1964); Gaia Bernstein, *The Socio-Legal Acceptance of New Technologies: A Close Look at Artificial Insemination*, 77 Wash. L. Rev. 1035 (2002); Margalit, *supra* note 8, at 77–80.

[54] *See* U.S. Catholic Conference, Congregation for the Doctrine of the Faith, Instruction on Respect for Human Life in Its Origin and on the Dignity of Procreation, Donum Vitae (1987), and more briefly, Shultz, *supra* note 6, at 329–30. For the approach of Islamic law, which generally permitted AIH with certain precautionary measures, similar to the Jewish approach, see Vardit Rispler-Chaim, Islamic Medical Ethics in the Twentieth Century 18–27 (1993).

[55] *See* BT *Hagigah* 14b–15a.

[56] *See* Joshua H. Lipschutz, *To Clone or Not to Clone – A Jewish Perspective*, 25 J. Med. Ethics 105 (1999); Daniel B. Sinclair, *Assisted Reproduction in Jewish Law*, 30 Fordham Urb. L.J. 71, 79 n.31 (2002).

might marry his biological sister.[57] It may be deduced from these more or less reliable sources that even though a child is conceived by the father's sperm in noncoital reproduction, he or she is nonetheless regarded as the father's legitimate child, probably in every respect.

This old and deep-rooted halakhic tradition fits the basic natural order that a child is the legal son of his or her biological progenitor.[58] While some halakhists even hold that the father fulfills his biblical, or at least rabbinic, obligation to procreate[59] via artificial means, a minority of rabbinic authorities still argue that a child conceived by artificial means, such as AIH, should not be treated as the biological child of his or her father.[60] There are a number of formalistic justifications for this determination,[61] but I would argue that they are based on meta-halakhic[62] considerations rather than hard-core *halakhah*. These considerations incline toward some form of Christian naturalism, or soft naturalism,[63] and they conceptualize ART as a threat to the Jewish bionormative family structure, therefore even prohibiting AIH, the simplest form of such artificial treatments.

One of the most effective theological methods for reinforcing the prohibition against artificial treatments and maintaining the concept of naturalism, which prohibits procreation by non-natural means, is to define this procedure as illegitimate. One of the main ramifications of this sad conclusion is that the conceived child is defined as an orphan, or "a child of no one," and is not the legitimate child of his or her biological progenitors. One of the most important conclusions to be drawn

[57] *See* Povarsky, *supra* note 1, at 430–31.

[58] This is also common sense and is well accepted in other jurisdictions. See Povarsky, *supra* note 1, at 435 ("in cases of AIH [artificial insemination by the husband] no question of paternity has ever been raised in American law").

[59] For a discussion of this, see Povarsky, *supra* note 1, at 436–37. For a general scholarly discussion of fulfilling this commandment by means of the various ART procedures, see IRSHAI, *supra* note 50, at 25–52.

[60] This is in addition to other possible halakhic problems concerning the prohibition of destruction of the seed; *see* FELDMAN, *supra* note 9, at 109. For a recent academic discussion of the relevancy and meaning of this prohibition in the various ART procedures, see Ronit Irshai, *ARTs and the Prohibition of Seed Destruction: Three Methods in the Modern Psika*, 7 IDENTITIES 21 (2015) (Heb.). There are additional concerns of replacing the husband's sperm with someone else's sperm and turning childbearing into a "mechanical" act, as claimed in IMMANUEL JAKOBOVITS, JEWISH MEDICAL ETHICS: A COMPARATIVE AND HISTORICAL STUDY OF THE JEWISH RELIGIOUS ATTITUDE TO MEDICINE AND ITS PRACTICE 248–49 (1959). For addressing and refuting all the above-mentioned concerns, *inter alia*, because of the husband's intention to procreate and not to discard his sperm, see SINCLAIR, *supra* note 52, at 69–76.

[61] For summarizing these justifications, see CORINALDI, *supra* note 39, at 81–82.

[62] For a discussion of this notion, see Alexander Kaye, *Eliezer Goldman and the Origins of Meta-Halacha*, 34.3 MODERN JUDAISM 309 (2014) and the references enumerated previously in Chapter 3 of this book, at n.26.

[63] For the notion of halakhic naturalism and for casting doubt on whether *halakhah* does indeed channel parenthood into a true natural order, see ZOHAR, *supra* note 1, at 69–78; SINCLAIR, *supra* note 52, at 68–76.

from this discussion is that *halakhah* should apply its capacity to disengage itself from its basic approach – that a child is defined as his or her parents' child only if the child is the parents' biological child – in view of other halakhic considerations. In Section 4, I discuss some additional halakhic exceptions to the natural order.

2.3 *Artificial Insemination by Donor*

When artificial insemination involves using a donor's sperm without the woman having a sexual relationship with the donor, it is referred to either as heterologous insemination or artificial insemination by donor (AID).[64] This procedure is performed when the husband is infertile for physiological or psychological reasons. Some halakhic authorities even sanction this procedure in the case of single or lesbian women, or when sperm enhancement/eugenics is necessary.[65] While AID is the most common ART procedure, it perhaps constitutes the most direct and troubling conflict between the secular and halakhic concepts of who should be recognized as the legal father of the conceived child.

I believe that this conflict is the reason why in modern-day Israel, AID regulation remains the only law concerning the determination of legal parenthood that is lacking, after the 1996 surrogacy law and the 2010 eggs donation laws were enacted.[66] The background for this inevitable clash between *halakhah* and Israeli civil law is the fact that, on the one hand, according to civil law, the entire point of AID legislation is to release the sperm donor from any parental obligations and rights. This release occurs at the expense of transferring the donor's legal fatherhood to the husband of the inseminated woman, who intended and agreed, essentially, to become the legal father of the resulting child. *Halakhah*, on the other hand, clings to its fundamental notion of natural parenthood, which means that an agreement between two people cannot change the basic concept that legal fatherhood is determined according to the biological father.[67]

64 *See* Browne Lewis, *Two Fathers, One Dad: Allocating the Paternal Obligations between the Men Involved in the Artificial Insemination Process*, 13 Lewis & Clark L. Rev. 949, 956–58 (2009). For a more comprehensive definition of the various artificial insemination procedures, see Goldman, *supra* note 39, at 74–86.

65 *See* Steinberg, *supra* note 12, vol. 1, 58–73, s.v. "AIH."

66 *See* Surrogate Motherhood Agreements (Approval of Agreement and Status of the Newborn), 5756–1996, www.health.gov.il/LegislationLibrary/Poriut_05.pdf (Heb.); Egg Donation, 5770–2010, www.knesset.gov.il/privatelaw/data/18/3/289_3_2.rtf (Heb.).

67 *See* Laufer-Ukeles, *supra* note 1, at 130–31 ("Most significantly, despite decades of use in Israel, a national law has not been passed in Israel to regulate AID due in part to significant objection to such a procedure by the Jewish law authorities in Israel."). For a description of this inevitable clash, see Zafran, *supra* note 22, at 121–23; Pinhas Shifman, *Establishing Parenthood for a Child Born through Artificial Insemination*, 10 Hebrew U. L.J. 63, 65–67 (1980) (Heb.); Corinaldi, *supra* note 28. For aspects of the erosion of natural parenthood in AID, see Lifshitz, *supra* note 26, at 306–10.

There is an extensive early discussion about whether the above procedure renders the resulting child a *mamzer*. The dispute is rooted in the interpretation given to the somewhat vague biblical prohibition of placing a man's seed in the womb of another person's wife. The verse states, "And you shall not lie carnally for seed with your neighbor's wife."[68] It is unclear whether this prohibition is due to the illicit sexual relationship that traditionally precedes the placing of a stranger's seed in a married woman's womb or whether the issue is the problematic outcome of placing a man's seed in a strange woman, even without engaging in any prohibited sexual intercourse. The clear distinction between these two interpretations finds expression in modern ART, in which a stranger's sperm can be placed in the cervix of the donee without their engaging in any problematic sexual relationship.[69] In his stringent approach, Yoel Teitelbaum regards this as adultery per se, and therefore, like any other adulterous relationship, it is totally prohibited. According to Moshe Feinstein's lenient approach, on the other hand, as long as there is no prohibited relationship between the donor and the donee, the method does not pose any particular halakhic problem; the resulting child can marry any Jewish person, and this artificial means has no negative implications for him or her.[70]

I now focus on the major dilemma of who is to be regarded as the legal father of the conceived child. Should it be the sperm donor, as prescribed by natural lineage,[71] or are there perhaps other halakhic considerations that can change this determination, such as, on the one hand, conferring legal fatherhood on the donee's husband or, on the other hand, releasing the donor from his legal paternity, thus leaving the child without any legal father? The vast majority of halakhists maintain that paternity should be determined by the natural order in the AID context as well, thus making the sperm donor the legal father of the resulting child in all respects.[72] This dichotomous determination produces two additional major problems.

Practically speaking, the sperm donor's anonymity calls into question the legitimacy of the conceived child, as there is no guarantee that the donor himself is not a *mamzer*, in which case the resulting child will also be stigmatized as such. Moreover, since the donor's identity is unknown, the conceived child is defined as a *shtuki*, or a "possible *mamzer*." On the one hand, a *shtuki* is prohibited from

68 Leviticus 18:20. For an overview of the possible interpretations of this prohibition, see Sinclair, *supra* note 56, at 82–83.

69 For a discussion of the claim that most sources endorse the first interpretation, see MENACHEM ELON, JEWISH LAW CASES AND MATERIALS 626 (1999). For the disturbing consequences of the latter interpretation, see Laufer-Ukeles, *supra* note 11, at 246–47.

70 For a summary of these arguments as well as for a review of the other halakhic justifications for prohibiting this practice, see Povarsky, *supra* note 1, at 422–34; Sinclair, *supra* note 56, at 77–94.

71 For summing up the views of those authorities who claim that the sperm donor should be regarded as the legal father of the child in all respects, see Povarsky, *supra* note 1, at 436–37.

72 Others contend that legal fatherhood is determined only for stringent considerations ("*lechumra*"), such as the prohibition against biological siblings marrying, and not for rights, such as inheritance rights. *See* the sources listed in SINCLAIR, *supra* note 52, at 90 nn. 81–82.

marrying a spouse *mamzer* since he or she himself/herself might not be a *mamzer*; on the other hand, he or she cannot marry a "regular" spouse, as there is a chance that he or she may indeed be a *mamzer*. The only option available to him or her is to marry a spouse who has converted to Judaism.[73] In addition, there is the problem of unintentional incest. If the sperm donor donated his sperm to a number of sperm banks, there is the possibility that a brother might unwittingly marry his sister, not knowing that they are biological siblings.[74] This problem is far more serious in Israel, in which there are only seventeen accredited sperm banks in the entire country.[75]

These two major problems can be resolved by more careful and thorough regulation of the entire sperm donation process. Maintaining adequate records and/or conducting accurate registries that list and document the identities of both donors and donees will go far to alleviate these two grave concerns. It should be noted that in 2010, Israel enacted a new Egg Donation Law that launched the establishment of a complete confidential registry with the identifying information of both egg donors and donees in order to avoid any problems of *mamzerut*.[76] In my opinion, this constitutes the first urgently required step in resolving the drawbacks of donating anonymous gametes. There is no choice but to allow a representative of the rabbinical courts to access this registry before any artificially conceived child marries, to ensure that incest does not occur.[77]

Alternatively, an even better – but very surprising and even ironic – solution is to use the sperm of non-Jewish donors. There is a halakhic fiction of nullifying the seed of a gentile, which means that, halakhically, a Gentile donor's sperm and descendants are not regarded as belonging to him. The outcome of this astonishing determination is that biological siblings born from a Gentile's sperm are not defined as siblings, and thus there is no problem of incest in the unlikely eventuality that they should marry. Similarly, there is no problem of the child being a *mamzer* or a *shtuki*,

[73] For the concept of *shtuki*, see SCHERESCHEWSKY, *supra* note 13, at 357; KAHN, *supra* note 20, at 55; Laufer-Ukeles, *supra* note 11, at 244–45. For the assertion that the majority of halakhists hold that AID is prohibited for a married woman and that there is no authoritative opinion that permits using the sperm of a Jewish donor, see Laufer-Ukeles, *supra* note 1, at 130–31.

[74] *See* my previous caveat that AID should be completely abolished if it turns out that it has marked negative effects on the children conceived by these artificial means. Such halakhic problems can fuel this cry; *see* Margalit, *supra* note 8, at 99–100.

[75] For this data and for a list of the recognized sperm banks in Israel up to July 2015, see www.health.gov.il/Subjects/Med_Inst/Sperm_Bank/Documents/sperm_banks_Israel.pdf. I was told recently by one of the Israel's foremost IVF experts that while there is no official regulation of the sperm donation process, there is a new nonofficial self-regulation ethic that restricts the possible number of donations to only two to three live births from the same donor.

[76] For those two suggestions, see, respectively, SINCLAIR, *supra* note 52, at 90; Laufer-Ukeles, *supra* note 11, at 249–51.

[77] For the media news that the Israeli Health Ministry Regulations from 2008 – Guidelines for the Administration of Sperm Donation of the Ministry of Health, Nov. 8, 2007 (to be effective June 1, 2008) (Heb.), to some extent contemplated these problems, see Laufer-Ukeles, *supra* note 11, at 251 n.137.

as those problems relate only to Jewish sperm.[78] In 2015, an Israeli rabbinical court rendered an explicit ruling that a child who was artificially conceived with non-Jewish sperm is to be regarded as a legitimate child and the child is even eligible to marry a priest (*Kohen*).[79]

But let us return to the dilemma at hand. Are there any halakhic considerations that could change the determination that the sperm donor should be regarded as the legal father of the resulting child? Let us recall those halakhic authorities, mentioned above in the discussion of AIH, who argue that the artificialness of the process should change the basic approach of *halakhah* to natural parenthood and the conceived child should not be determined as the legal child of his or her biological progenitor. That should apply in the case of AID as well, where the "donor" "donated" his sperm and received full payment in return for his "donation."[80] Thus, philosophically and halakhically, the donor has abandoned his sperm and has in fact disconnected himself from his genetic material, which therefore is no longer considered his, and the resulting child is no longer to be treated as his child for all intents and purposes.[81]

The most interesting and important discussion, however, revolves around the possibility of *halakhah* conferring, to varying degrees, legal fatherhood on the donee's husband. If we could find accepted halakhic tools in this regard, we would be able to resolve, if even partially, the major problem of bridging the gap between the secular and religious conceptions of who should be determined as the legal father of the conceived child. This conferring of legal fatherhood on the donee's husband is, of course, a very problematic option, as, *prima facie*, it contradicts the natural order of determining legal fatherhood. This option was considered decades ago in the Haifa rabbinical court.[82] In that AID case, the court ruled that the donee's

78 For discussing the advantages and disadvantages of this determination, see Laufer-Ukeles, *supra* note 11, at 252.

79 See Rabbinical Court (Askelon) 1051202/1 Anonymous (unpublished, 1.11.15), available at www.daat.ac.il/daat/psk/psk.asp?id=1278.

80 In Israel, the average payment for a single sperm donation is approximately NIS 700–50, the equivalent of $180 each.

81 *See* Moses Maimonides, The Guide of the Perplexed 1:72 (Chaim Rabin trans., 1995); Mordechai Halperin, *The Definition of Parenthood and the Right to Find Biological Roots* in Moral Dilemmas in Medicine 161, 167 (Raphael Cohen-Almagor ed. 2002) (Heb.); Menachem M. Kasher, *Artificial Insemination*, 1 Noam 125, 125–26 (1958) (Heb.). For a summary of this point, see Corinaldi, *supra* note 39.

82 Rabbinical Court (Haifa) Anonymous v. Anonymous (unpublished, 21.07.77), discussed in CA 449/79 Salame v. Salame PD 34(2) 779, 782 (1980) (Heb.). Unfortunately, this unique precedent was later overruled on appeal, *inter alia*, on the grounds of semi-adultery. *See* High Rabbinical Court (Jerusalem) App. 49/5745 of 4 Tevet, 5746 (unpublished, 1986). For discussions of this problematic ruling, see Pinhas Shifman, *Family Law in Israel: The Struggle between Religious and Secular Law*, 24 Isr. L. Rev. 537, 543–44 and especially n. 31 (1990); Laufer-Ukeles, *supra* note 1, at 130–31. It is pity that the long-term consideration of discouraging couples from using AID overrode the short-term consideration of providing child maintenance, which badly affected the BIC.

husband had agreed to his wife's insemination and was therefore obligated to pay the resulting child's support, because by agreeing to the insemination, he became a guarantor (*arev*) of the donee and must therefore pay the child's maintenance.

It should be emphasized that the most important AID ruling of Israel's civil Supreme Court was based on the precedent of the above rabbinical court's decision to obligate the donee's ex-husband to continue paying child support even after they had separated because of his initial oral agreement.[83] Based on this precedent, one may again deduce that *halakhah* has its own tools for deviating from the natural order of bestowing legal paternity purely on the grounds of genetics and for recognizing, to varying degrees, the donee's husband, even if only for monetary purposes, as I explore more extensively in Section 5. As mentioned earlier, in Section 4 I list some additional circumstances in which *halakhah* deviated from natural to intentional parenthood as a basis for supporting this essential compromise between the civil and religious legal systems.

2.4 *Egg Donation*

Egg donation is intended to enable women who are unable to conceive with their own ova, but can gestate a fetus to term, to give birth to children by receiving egg donations from other women. In assisted reproduction, egg donation typically involves in vitro fertilization (IVF) technology, whereby the eggs are fertilized in a laboratory with the husband's sperm or with donated sperm. After fertilization, the fertilized egg is implanted in the womb of either the donee or a surrogate mother. The typical donation is a commercial one in which an anonymous donor agrees that, for monetary consideration, her ovum may be used by an anonymous donee. The donee is the gestational mother but not the genetic mother.[84] Nowadays, the use of egg donations has become very common and is employed in a variety of circumstances: married couples; lesbian couples, where one spouse donates her egg to her female partner, and after the egg has been fertilized by a donor's sperm, this partner carries the fetus to term; disabled single women who wish to bring a child into the world, using a triple donation – egg, sperm, and surrogacy.

The Latin dictum *mater est quam gestatio demonstrat* (motherhood is demonstrated by gestation)[85] traditionally expressed the fact that in the past, before the advent of ART, the three basic compontents of motherhood – the genetic contribution, the gestational contribution, and the social/psychological contribution – overlapped

[83] Salame v. Salame, ibid. For a discussion of this precedent, see Lifshitz, *supra* note 26, at 299 n.10. and more extensively Amos Shapira, *Normative Regulation of Reproductive Technologies in Israel*, 13 Nova L. Rev. 609, 611–12 (1989).

[84] *See* Steinberg, *supra* note 12, vol. 2, 571–86, s.v. "IVF." *See also* Rabbinical Court (Tel Aviv) 1049932/8 Anonymous v. Anonymous (unpublished, 20.07.2016).

[85] *See* Rita D'alton-Harrison, *Mater Semper Incertus Est: Who's Your Mummy?*, 22(3) Med. L. Rev. 357 (2014).

in the same woman. This axiom was so strong that legislators and courts have assumed that the woman who gives birth is obviously always the mother of the conceived child in all the above aspects of motherhood, and there was no need for this axiom to be anchored in either legislation or a judicial decree.[86] But the first test-tube baby, Louise Brown, who was born in northern England in 1978, and the advent of egg donations unraveled this Gordian knot into its three basic components and totally blurred this simple working premise.[87] Today, the dilemma of who should be determined the legal mother of a child conceived by egg donation has become a very concrete, sensitive, and confusing issue. Should the egg donor be regarded as the legal mother due to her enormous influence on the child's genetic makeup and perhaps even on his or her behavioral character,[88] or should the gestational mother be regarded as the legal mother as a result of her critical contribution in bearing the child to term and her massive influence on him or her during the pregnancy?[89]

Despite this acute and confusing dilemma, and despite the great similarity between egg donation and sperm donation in terms of the mechanism they use and their merits and drawbacks, egg donation has not generated much intensive discussion in the contemporary scholarly literature.[90] In my opinion, this is either because this dilemma has merged with the broader and more complicated issue of establishing legal motherhood in surrogacy or perhaps because, since it is similar to sperm donation, the accepted conclusions for determining the legal parent can be

86 *See* U.S. Congress, Office of Technology Assessment, Infertility: Medical and Social Choices 282 (1988); Unif. Parentage Act § 3, 9B U.L.A. 287, 298 (1973) (hereinafter UPA).

87 For what is perhaps Judge Marianne O. Battani's most well-known statement – "We really have no definition of 'mother' in our law books. . . . 'Mother' was believed to have been so basic that no definition was deemed necessary" – see Smith v. Jones, No. 85-53201401 (Mich. Cir. Ct. Wayne County March 14, 1986), discussed in Scott B. Rae, *Parental Rights and the Definition of Motherhood in Surrogate Motherhood*, 3 S. Cal. Rev. L. & Women's Stud. 219, 223 (1994).

88 For the reason to prefer the genetic contribution over the gestational contribution, see Richard F. Storrow, *Parenthood by Pure Intention: Assisted Reproduction and the Functional Approach to Parentage*, 53 Hastings L.J. 597, 603–22 (2002); Rae, ibid, at 225–31, and more extensively, Yehezkel Margalit, *The Rise, Fall and Rise Again of the Genetic Foundation for Legal Parentage Determination*, 3 J. Health L. & Bioethics 125 (2010) (Heb.), http://papers.ssrn .com/sol3/papers.cfm?abstract_id=2232721.

89 For legislative, judicial and academic references that endorse the gestational component, see, respectively, UPA 201(a)(1), 9B U.L.A. 309 (2001); Andres A. v. Judith N., 591 N.Y.S.2d 946, 948 (NY Fam. Ct. 1992); George J. Annas, *Redefining Parenthood and Protecting Embryos: Why We Need New Laws*, 14 Hastings Ctr. Rpt. 5 (1984); Marshall H. Klaus, Maternal-Infant Bonding 1–15 (1976); Anne Goodwin, *Determination of Legal Parentage in Egg Donation, Embryo Transplantation, and Gestational Surrogacy Arrangements*, 1992 Fam. L.Q. 275 (1992).

90 For the lack of any comprehensive discussion of this dilemma, see Lynn M. Squillace, *Too Much of a Good Thing: Toward a Regulated Market in Human Eggs*, 1 J. Health & Biomed. L. 135 (2005); Kenneth Baum, *Golden Eggs: Towards the Rational Regulation of Oocyte Donation*, 2001 BYU L. Rev. 107, 123 (2001), and more extensively Anne Schiff Reichman, *Solomonic Decisions in Egg Donation: Unscrambling the Conundrum of Legal Maternity*, 80 Iowa L. REv. 265 (1995).

applied in the above circumstance as well.[91] In stark contrast to the paucity of the discourse in academic circles, the Jewish legal literature contains several relevant Talmudic discussions dating back to the fifth century. Thus, the determination of who should be regarded as the legal mother can be deduced only from several related, theoretical, and mainly *aggadic* sources. For example, the Talmud states that there are three partners in the creation of a fetus – the Almighty and the two parents. While the Almighty supplies the spirit, the father supplies the semen of the white substance, out of which all the white organs – "the child's bones, sinews, nails, the brain in his head and the white in his eye" – are formed, and the mother supplies "the semen of the red substance out of which are formed the child's skin, flesh, hair, blood and the black of his eye." This means that the mother's contribution to the resulting child's makeup is similar to the father's and thus grants her legal motherhood.[92]

On the other hand, there are halakhic sources that tend to recognize the gestational rather than the genetic mother as the preferred legal mother. The Talmud relates to Mordechai who took Esther as his foster daughter and inquires into the meaning of the redundancy in the verse, "For she had neither father nor mother and when her father and mother died." On the surface, the verse appears to be telling us twice that Esther was orphaned from both parents. What is the meaning of this repetition? "Rav Aha said: When her mother became pregnant with her, her father died; when she was born, her mother died." Rashi explains that "When her mother became pregnant, her father died – leaving her fatherless from the time it would have been fit to call him 'father'. And when her mother bore her, she died – and was not (ever) fit to be called 'mother.'"[93] In other words, Esther was "totally" orphaned: from the very first moment that she could have had a father – the conception – he passed away, and from the very moment that she could have had a mother, the mother too died. Literally, this means that while conception determines halakhic fatherhood, gestation establishes motherhood.[94]

91 *See* Margalit, *supra* note 7, at 49–52.

92 *See* BT *Niddah* 31a. The conclusion that the parallel genetic raw material of both the mother and the father should be the main factor in establishing halakhic parenthood was supported by important contemporary *poskim*, such as Shlomo Goren, The Laws of Medicine: Halachic Investigations into Medical Topics 176–77 (2001) (Heb.).

93 *See*, respectively, Esther 2, 7; BT *Megillah* 13a; Rashi, ibid. It should be noted that this conclusion is not entirely logical, as the redundancy can easily be explained as simply providing the accurate timing of when she was taken to her foster home, which was when her father and mother died.

94 For a fuller discussion of the various Talmudic sources, such as the plant grafting case; a fetus is part of its mother's body; the twin brothers case; the *aggadaic* tale concerning the interchanged fetuses, the fetus' ownership and inheritance rights etc., see Povarsky, *supra* note 1, at 463–80; Laufer-Ukeles, *supra* note 1, at 107–10. For the inevitable conclusion that there is no definite consensus in the Talmud as to who should be regarded as the legal mother, see Ezra Bick, *Ovum Donations: A Rabbinic Conceptual Model of Maternity*, in Jewish Law and the New Reproductive Technologies 83, 89 (Emanuel Feldman & Joel B. Wolowelsky eds.,1997)

After the advent of IVF and the birth of the first test-tube baby, the halakhic discourse became far more extensive. Until these amazing biomedical innovations made their appearance, there had been no dilemma whatsoever, as all three maternal components completely overlapped. It was only with the advent of IVF, egg donation, and surrogacy that, for the first time in Jewish history, halakhic authorities had to confront a situation wherein the genetic component had been separated from the gestational one. One of the key characteristics of Jewish law is the major importance of halakhic tradition, and in these new circumstances, it was sorely missing. Moreover, even *halakhah*'s traditional adherence to the natural order was confusing in this dilemma, as what is the natural order in this case – the gestational or the genetic component? In this circumstance, natural lineage is thus blurry and useless. Furthermore, due to the far-reaching ramifications of the legal determination of halakhic maternity, coupled with the halakhic and sociological sensitivities of this issue, all of the options for determining halakhic maternity are open. Until recently, it was commonly assumed that the majority of halakhic decisors regarded the gestational mother as the legal mother[95] and only a minority held the genetic mother to be the legal mother.[96]

In recent years, however, there has been a distinct shift in this regard, and today the opposite is true – the majority of halakhic decisors lean toward defining the genetic rather than the gestational mother as the legal mother. Furthermore, according to two minority opinions, both mothers should be regarded as the legal

("were there to exist absolutely no Talmudic guidance for our question, neither in halakhic or aggadic sources"); Laufer-Ukeles, *supra* note 1, at 105 ("there is no official singular ruling on the matter that can be derived from the Talmud").

95 For an exhaustive overview of the different opinions updated to 2010 that reach this conclusion, see MARGALIT, *supra* note 7, at 244–45; SINCLAIR, *supra* note 52, at 103 n.126. *See also* the following definitive conclusion from almost 15 years ago: "Jewish law, for the most part, has endorsed the criteria of birth as the defining factor of motherhood," Laufer-Ukeles, *supra* note 1, at 94. For several seminal English and Hebrew sources that endorse the gestational mother as the legal mother, see, respectively, Michael J. Broyd, *The Establishment of Maternity and Paternity in Jewish and American Law*, 3 NAT'L JEWISH L. REV. 117, 131–40 (1988); Ezra Bick, *Ovum Donations: A Rabbinic Conceptual Model of Maternity*, 28 TRADITION 28 (1993) (Bick, *supra* note 94) and the other sources listed in Laufer-Ukeles, *supra* note 1, at 105 n.106; SINCLAIR, *supra* note 52, at 103–06. For a more specific discussion of distinguishing parturition from gestation and which one is the superior factor in determining the gestational mother as the legal mother, see, respectively, Povarsky, *supra* note 1, at 461 n.277; J. David Bleich, *In Vitro Fertilization: Questions of Maternal Identity and Conversion*, in JEWISH LAW AND THE NEW REPRODUCTIVE TECHNOLOGIES 46, 49–52 (Emanuel Feldman & Joel B. Wolowelsky eds., 1997).

96 For the sources that endorse determining the genetic mother as the legal mother, see GOREN, *supra* note 92; Povarsky, *supra* note 1, at 482 ("By contrast, the genetic factor is absolutely clear and definite, creating the strongest biological bond between the genetic mother and the child. A mother's parent–child relationship is most likely based upon a clear and definite factor."). *See also* Gedalia Orenstein, *In Vitro Fertilization – Lineage of the Child and Fulfilling the Mitzvah of Procreation*, 24 TECHUMIN 156, 159 (2004) (Heb.). For other Hebrew sources that endorse determining the genetic mother as the legal mother, see Laufer-Ukeles, *supra* note 1, at 106–07 especially n.107.

mother – the concept of dual maternity.[97] Others argue that neither should be designated the legal mother, due to the artificial nature of the process, which means that at least officially, the conceived child is orphaned from both parents.[98] I myself am not aware of any similar halakhic shift in such a short period of time, especially with regard to an issue that is so sensitive and important. Thus, there appears to be no agreed-on determinative factor in establishing halakhic maternity. This indeterminate situation produces two important and intertwined observations for the continuation of our discussion:

1. The fact that there is no clear determination as to who should be recognized as the legal mother makes it much easier to confer halakhic validity on a surrogacy agreement. This is because it is less problematic to transfer halakhic maternity from the gestational mother to the intended mother, who is also the genetic mother, as both of them may be determined the legal mother, than it is to make the dichotomous determination that only the gestational mother can be recognized as the legal mother, where she, and not the genetic mother, is the only one who can be determined as such.
2. Since there are two possible factors in establishing legal maternity – genetic and gestational – there is more room for applying my normative model of DLPBA in determining halakhic maternity. Therefore, for a better understanding of the possible implications of determining maternity, I now explore the surrogacy arrangement and how the concept of intentional parenthood is applied in transferring legal motherhood from the gestational mother to the genetic mother.

2.5 *Surrogacy*

One of the most ancient and reliable sources that document the practice of surrogacy is the Bible. In the era of the patriarchs and matriarchs, it was common

97 For this unique notion of Jewish dual maternity, see David J. Bleich, *In Vitro Fertilization: Questions of Maternal Identity and Conversion*, 25 TRADITION 82 (1991) (Bleich, *supra* note 95, at 46); ibid, CONTEMPORARY HALAKHIC PROBLEMS 4, 237, 238–42 (1998), mentioned in SINCLAIR, *supra* note 52, at 99 n.111. For a discussion and refutation of this conclusion, see, respectively, SINCLAIR, *supra* note 52, at 106–08; Povarsky, *supra* note 1, at 481–82 ("In the absence of evidence, this theory cannot be considered in determining a mother's parental status under Jewish law"). See also Rabbinical Court (Beer Sheva) 1031698/1 Anonymous (unpublished, 01.09.15).

98 *See, e.g.*, the following harsh statement – "Even for a creature such as this that is the object of our discussion, that is formed and takes shape in a place where there is no relation [and likewise in this context, where the entire pregnancy was conceived in a test tube, as if the child is an orphan from both father and mother] and it pertains even more so to our case," ELIEZER Y. WALDENBERG, RESP. TZITZ ELIEZER vol. 15 ch. 45 (1984); Yitzhak A. Liebes, *Regarding Limb Transplants*, 14 NOAM 28 (1971) (Heb.). For the history of this statement, see Laufer-Ukeles, *supra* note 1, at 106 n.108. For a broader exploration and a refutation of this stringent approach, see SINCLAIR, *supra* note 52, at 95–102.

for the mistress of the house to give her female slave to her husband for the purpose of having the conceived child regarded as that of the mistress. This arrangement was practiced by both barren and fertile women, as demonstrated in the cases of Sara and Hagar, and Leah, Rachel, and their maidens, Bilhah and Zilpah.[99] Whereas Sara and Rachel were infertile and were compelled to use their slaves in order to procreate, Leah also gave her slave to her husband, despite being fertile and bearing children of her own. That the mistress, and not the slave, was recognized as the legal mother can be deduced from the fact that it was the former rather than the latter who named the resulting offspring.[100]

In the modern era, surrogacy basically means that the surrogate mother receives a fertilized ovum from the intended parents and, through a surrogacy agreement, agrees to carry the fetus to term and hand the child over to the intended parents immediately after the delivery. There are two types of surrogacy – traditional and gestational. In traditional surrogacy, "the surrogate mother provides two components of motherhood – the genetic material of the ovum and the gestational contribution."[101] "The gestational surrogate provides only one component of motherhood: the gestational contribution." Both types of surrogacies may be either commercial or altruistic. In commercial surrogacy, monetary consideration generally incentivizes the surrogate mother. In altruistic surrogacy, the surrogate mother is generally motivated by a desire to help desperate infertile couples.[102]

Following our discussion on egg donation, above, the main halakhic issue in a typical gestational surrogacy is who should be designated the legal mother – the intended mother, who is also the genetic mother, or the surrogate mother because of her gestational contribution. There are numerous other halakhic-ethical issues in

[99] *See* Genesis 16:1–4; 30:1–13. For a summary of these biblical surrogacy stories, see JULIA J. TATE, SURROGACY: WHAT PROGRESS SINCE HAGAR, BILHAH, AND ZILPAH! (1994). For the claim that the story of Sara and Hagar is actually the first story of a cross-border reproduction service, see Daphna Hacker, LEGALIZED FAMILIES IN THE ERA OF BORDERED GLOBALIZATION ch. 4 (2017).

[100] As was claimed by PINHAS SHIFMAN, FAMILY LAW IN ISRAEL vol. 2, 158 n.74 (1989) (Heb.). But, of course, this conclusion is problematic, as the notion of biology, with regard to both genetics and gestation, and the surrogate mother's contribution, was not known in the ancient era. Moreover, in any event the fact that the maid is her master's possession infers that even her child belongs to them and not to her. For a more general rejection of the analogy between modern surrogacy and the biblical stories, and for the claim that biblical surrogacy bears little resemblance to contemporary surrogacy arrangements, see Richard Storrow, *"The Phantom Children of the Republic": International Surrogacy and the New Illegitimacy*, 20 AM. U. J. GENDER SOC. POL'Y & L. 561, 609 (2012).

[101] Yehezkel Margalit, *In Defense of Surrogacy Agreements: A Modern Contract Law Perspective*, 20 WM. & MARY J. WOMEN & L. 423, 426 (2014); *see also* Dominique Ladomato, *Protecting Traditional Surrogacy Contracting through Fee Payment Regulation*, 23 HASTINGS WOMEN'S L.J. 245, 247 (2012).

[102] Yehezkel Margalit, *From Baby M to Baby M(anji): Regulating International Surrogacy Agreements*, 24(1) J.L. & POL'Y 41, 44–45 (2016).

these sensitive and complicated arrangements. First and foremost is the legality, validity, and enforceability of these agreements. Other halakhic-ethical issues include lack of concern for the husband's "procreational infidelity" and the endorsement of male reproductive freedom; termination of the parent–child relationship; transferability of custody rights; a nonproprietary agreement; "baby selling"; enforceability of an illegal act; neglect of duties by the surrogate mother; and execution of a transaction regarding an object not yet in existence.[103] Last but not least, even if we validate the surrogacy arrangements, there is an acute need to take necessary precautionary measures to protect the surrogate mother from any unwarranted inducement, coercion, exploitation, and so on, in addition to other intrinsic internal contractual problems, such as the unequal power of the contracting parties; change of heart; and changed circumstances.[104]

A general criticism expressed by modern feminists and scholars is that *halakhah* is more concerned with enabling the male intended parent to procreate than with the welfare and interests of the female surrogate mother.[105] They reinforce their criticism by comparing this issue with sperm donation: whereas halakhically it is almost impossible to transfer legal fatherhood from the donor to the donee's husband, there is no problem with transferring legal motherhood in the case of surrogacy. They claim that this may be understood as giving preference to the male fulfillment of the obligation to procreate over the welfare and the vulnerability of the surrogate mother.[106] In my opinion, the main issue was, and remains, the determination of who should be regarded as the legal mother of the resulting child, due to the far-reaching ramifications of this determination. The claim that *halakhah* has no concern for the welfare and interests of the surrogate mother is oversimplistic and an overgeneralization. A recently published article explored all possible explanations

[103] *See*, respectively, ZOHAR, *supra* note 1, at 80; Povarsky, *supra* note 1, at 449–58.

[104] For an exploration of these problems and a refutation of them one by one following modern contract theory, see Margalit, *supra* note 101.

[105] For an up-to-date overview of this critique, see IRSHAI, *supra* note 50, at 264–68, and more generally Ronit Irshai, *Public and Private Rulings in Jewish Law (Halakhah): Flexibility, Concealment, and Feminist Jurisprudence*, 3(1) J.L., RELIGION & STATE 25 (2014); ibid, *Toward a Gender Critical Approach to the Philosophy of Jewish Law (Halakhah)*, 26(2) J. FEMINIST STUD. IN RELIGION 55 (2010); INBAR REVEH, FEMINIST REREADINGS OF RABBINIC LITERATURE (Kaeren Fish trans., 2014). For the statement that generally there is a shift in *halakhah* concerning IVF and surrogacy from moral rejection to qualified legal acceptance, see SINCLAIR, *supra* note 52, at 103.

[106] This is the essence of the critical article by Laufer-Ukeles, *supra* note 1, at 94 ("identifying the birth mother as the legal mother has not prevented a number of prominent Jewish law authorities from condoning gestational surrogate motherhood agreements . . . sublimating the woman's rights for the sake of the biological father and his wife . . . ignore the rights of the surrogate mothers because of patriarchal considerations."). *See also* her more recent writings, at Laufer-Ukeles, *supra* note 11, at 238 ("The importance of genetic reproduction outweighed according to such scholars [important Rabbinical authorities –Y. M.] the woman's legal status as mother").

of why *halakhah* seems to be silent regarding protecting the interests of the surrogate mother, but ignoring these issues was not one of the reasons given.[107]

Moreover, the comparison between sperm donation and surrogacy, and the subsequent criticism, may be justified with regard to the earlier determination by the majority of *poskim* (halakhic decisors) that the surrogate mother should be recognized as the legal mother. However, in view of the above-mentioned shift in the majority opinion of contemporary halakhic authorities that the intended genetic mother should be designated the legal mother, it is far less problematic to transfer legal motherhood from the surrogate mother to the intended mother, as quite often the intended and the genetic mothers are the same. This conclusion is logical because, in the vast majority of cases, this woman is also married to the intended and genetic father, which means that, in fact, the two intended parents are the genetic parents.

Therefore, *a priori*, there is no particular problem in determining the intended parents, who in most cases are also the genetic parents, as the legal parents of the resulting child. In my opinion, and as I explained briefly at the end of the previous subsection, since there is no definitive halakhic determination as to who should be designated the legal mother in cases of IVF and surrogacy, there is more room for applying DLPBA as a means of recognizing the intended and genetic mother as the legal mother due to her initial agreement to serve as the legal mother of the conceived child. This enables both of the intended parents to fulfill, to varying degrees, their halakhic obligation to procreate and to receive their parallel civil parental rights.

3 DETERMINING HALAKHIC PARENTHOOD IN THE FUTURISTIC ERA

The history of biomedical innovations clearly demonstrates the speed with which yesterday's science fiction has become today's reality and how current complicated dilemmas, such as how to determine the legal parenthood of artificially conceived children, will be dwarfed by much more confusing and challenging futuristic dilemmas. In the previous section on establishing legal maternity, I explored how the halakhic natural order of motherhood determination becomes blurred when the genetic and the gestational components are separated. Presumably, such issues will become far more complicated in the foreseeable future when we are confronted with the newest advanced biomedical developments.[108] Whereas in an article written in 2010, I explored the rise, fall, and rise again of the genetic component in determining legal parentage, in 2014, in light of recent innovations, I presented a comprehensive

[107] *See* Yuval Cherlow, *Protection of the Surrogate Mother – Ethics, Law and Halacha*, 4 J. HEALTH L. & BIOETHICS 80 (2011) (Heb.).

[108] For some future directions of *halakhah* concerning cloning, cytoplasmic transfer, nuclear transfer, and oocyte cryopreservation, see Joel B. Wolowelsky & Richard V. Grazi, *Future Directions*, in RICHARD V. GRAZI, OVERCOMING INFERTILITY 425–40 (2005).

elaboration of the recent fall of the genetic component as the most clear-cut, solid, and easily proven component.[109] I summarized it as follows:

> [T]hese innovations require a more nuanced view of the roles of biology and intent in determining parentage. For example, where a child is created by way of complex genetic engineering, resulting in a child who possesses genetic material from several individuals, there is little guidance in the law as to whether biology should trump intent, which of the genetic contributors should be deemed parents, and how to delineate the various rights and obligations of the parties.[110]

The inadequacy of natural order is obvious in multiple parentage scenarios[111] – when conception can be engineered[112] from more than two parents, and even up to six different genetic male donors – or conversely, when it can be engineered from male

[109] *See*, respectively, Margalit, *supra* note 88; Yehezkel Margalit & John Loike, *The New Frontier of Advanced Reproductive Technology: Reevaluating Modern Legal Parenthood*, 37 Harvard J.L. & Gender 107 (2014).

[110] Margalit & Loike, ibid, at 111.

[111] On February 3, 2014, it was announced in England that for medical purposes, it would be permitted to produce a child from three different genetic donors, see Ritesh R Jaiswal, *Three Parent IVF/Three Parent Baby*, The Science, 19.02.15, http://thescience.co.in/tag/three-parents-ivf/. For an academic discussion of this option, see Nancy E. Dowd, *Multiple Parents/Multiple Fathers*, 9 J.L. Fam. Stud. 231 (2007); Melanie B. Jacobs, *Why Just Two? Disaggregating Traditional Parental Rights and Responsibilities to Recognize Multiple Parents*, 9 J.L. Fam. Stud. 309 (2007); Tali Marcus, *It Takes (Only) Two to Tango? Recognizing More than Two Parents for One Child*, 44 Hebrew U. L.J. 415 (2014) (Heb.); Padmini Cheruvu, *Three-Parent IVF and Its Effect on Parental Rights*, 6 Hastings Sci. & Tech. L.J. 73 (2014); Jacques Cohen & Mina Alikani, *The Biological Basis for Defining Bi-Parental or Tri-Parental Origin of Offspring from Cytoplasmic and Spindle Transfer*, 26(6) Reproductive BioMedicine Online 535 (2013), www.sciencedirect.com/science/article/pii/S147264831300134X; Michael Legge et al., *Numerical Identity: The Creation of Tri-Parental Embryos to Correct Inherited Mitochondrial Disease*, 126(1385) New Zealand Med. J. (Online) 71 (2013). The option of designating more than two parents for a given child has been accepted in several leading rulings around the world. For cases of two legal fathers and one mother, see Smith v. Cole, 553 So. 2d 847 (La. 1989); State on behalf of J.R. v. Mendoza, 240 Neb. 149 (Neb. 1992) ; T.D. v. M.M.M., 730 So. 2d 873 (La. 1999); In re Nicholas H., 28 Cal. 4th 56 (Cal. 2002); In re Jesusa V., 32 Cal. 4th 588 (Cal. 2004); J.R. v. L.R., 386 N.J. Super. 475 (N.J. 2006). For cases of two mothers and one father, see LaChappelle v. Mitten, 607 N.W.2d 151, 160 (Minn. Ct. App. 2000); A.A. v. B.B., [2007] 220 O.A.C. 115, P 14 (Can.); Jacob v. Shultz-Jacob, 923 A.2d 473 (Pa. Super., 2007); (Tel Aviv family court)37745-03-14 Nili in re the Minors A. and B. V. Alon (not published, 27.04.14) (Heb.).

[112] For the most recent updates in this field, see Ayala Ochert, *HFEA Grants Permission to Genetically Edit Human Embryos*, BioNews 837, 01.02.16; Antony Blackburn-Starza, *Germline in the Sand: The Ethics and Law of Engineering the Embryo*, BioNews 836, 25.01.16; Jess Buxton, *Genome Editing and CRISPR: The Science of Engineering the Embryo*, BioNews 835, 18.01.16; Sarah Pritchard, *Why the UK Should Be Leading the Discussion on Embryo Engineering*, BioNews 834, 11.01.16. For a discussion of possible artificial reproductive materials, such as "artificial ovaries" and "synthetic genomes," see, respectively, Yehezkel Margalit & John Loike, *Follicular Transplants and Motherhood* (unpublished manuscript, on file with author); Kristine S. Knapland, *Synthetic Cells, Synthetic Life, and Inheritance*, 45 Val. U. L. Rev. 1361 (2011). For the various halakhic aspects of engineered people, see Michael J. Broyde, *Genetically Engineering People: A Jewish Law Analysis of Personhood*, 13 St. Thomas L. Rev. 877 (2001).

or female genetic contributions, using an artificial womb rather than a human womb.[113] Alternatively, the option of human reproductive cloning[114] makes it possible to create a child with the genetic contribution from one gender, without using any seed or ovum. But, even in current advanced biomedical practice, the insufficiency of the natural order is clear in dealing with ovary transplantation,[115] mitochondrial donation/replacement,[116] stem cell technology, and uterine transplantation.

[113] *See* Jessica H. Schultz, *Development of Ectogenesis: How Will Artificial Wombs Affect the Legal Status of a Fetus or Embryo?*, 84 Chi.-Kent L. Rev. 877 (2010); Gregory Pence, *What's So Good about Natural Motherhood? (In Praise of Unnatural Gestation)*, in Ectogenesis: Artificial Womb Technology and the Future of Human Reproduction 77, 82 (Scott Gelfand & John R. Shook eds., 2006) and all the other articles in this book; Hyun Jee Son, *Artificial Wombs, Frozen Embryos, and Abortion: Reconciling Viability's Doctrinal Ambiguity*, 14 UCLA Women's L.J. 213 (2005). For the halakhic perspective, see Fred Rosner, *In Vitro Fertilization, Surrogate Motherhood, and Sex Organ Transplants Symposium: Reproductive Rights*, 25 Creighton L. Rev. 1669, 1677–87 (1991–92).

[114] For a general *halakhah* discussion of this technology, see Steinberg, *supra* note 12, vol. 2, 509-20, s.v. "Human Cloning"; Michael Broyde, *Cloning People: A Jewish Law Analysis of the Issues*, 30 Conn. L. Rev. 503 (1998); Elliot N. Dorff, *Human Cloning: A Jewish Perspective*, 8 S. Cal. Interdisc. L.J. 117 (1998); Dena S. Davis, *Religious Attitudes toward Cloning: A Tale of Two Creatures*, 27 Hofstra L. Rev. 509 (1999); Stephen J. Werber, *Cloning: A Jewish Law Perspective with a Comparative Study of Other Abrahamic Traditions*, 30 Seton Hall L. Rev. 1114 (2000); Jessica S. Sackin, *The Halakhic/Constitutional Argument for Human Reproductive Cloning in America*, 7 Geo. J.L. & Pub. Pol'y 627 (2009); Lipschutz, *supra* note 56.

[115] *See* Sherman J. Silber, *Judaism and Reproductive Technology*, 156 Cancer Treat Res. 471 (2010); Zvi Ryzman, *A Halachic Discussion of Ovarian Transplants* (2009), http://olamot.net/sites/default/files/ratz_katzvi/pdf/SHL_MMR.pdf; Edward Reichman, *The Halakhic Chapter of Ovarian Transplantation*, 31(1) Tradition 31 (1998); Richard V. Grazi & Joel B. Wolowelsky, *On Foetal Ovary Transplants* 40 Le'ela (1995), www.daat.ac.il/daat/english/ethic/transplants_1.htm. *See also* in the following Hebrew articles: Zvi Ryzman, *Ovary Transplantion – Is It Forbidden as Sterilization?*, 31 Techumin 38 (2011); Gideon Weitzman, *Ovary Transplantion in Halachic Perspective*, 31 Techumin 48 (2011).

[116] For recent academic articles discussing this issue, see Masahito Tachibana et al., *Towards Germline Gene Therapy of Inherited Mitochondrial Diseases*, 493(7434) Nature 627 (2013), www.nature.com/nature/journal/v493/n7434/abs/nature11647.html; Caroline Jones & Ingrid Holme, *Relatively (im)Material: mtDNA and Genetic Relatedness in Law and Policy*, 9:4 Life Sci., Soc'y & Pol'y (2013), http://link.springer.com/article/10.1186/2195-7819-9-4#page-1; Rebecca Dimond, *Social and Ethical Issues in Mitochondrial Donation*, 115(1) Br. Med. Bull. 173 (2015), http://bmb.oxfordjournals.org/content/115/1/173.short - corresp-1. For the few halakhic sources discussing the issue, see J. David Bleich, *Mitochondrial DNA Replacement: How Many Mothers*, 48(4) Tradition (2015); the responsum of Asher Weiss concerning triple parent IVF following mitochondrial DNA replacement that was posted at http://en.tvunah.org/2013/12/29/triple-parent-ivf/. Whereas J. David Bleich maintains that *post factum*, the question of whether the birth mother should be recognized as the sole halakhic mother or whether the child has multiple mothers remains a matter of significant dispute, Asher Weiss argues that there is no doubt that the woman who donates the germ line and not the one who donates the mitochondrial DNA should be regarded as the legal mother. It should be noted that an Israeli expert committee, the Mor-Yossef Commission, arrived at a similar conclusion, that due to the minute influence of mitochondrial DNA on a fetus's genetic makeup, the former woman rather than the latter one should be determined as the legal mother. *See* The Israeli Ministry of Health, The Public Commission for Revision of the Legislative Regulation of Fertility and Childbearing in Israel 41–42 (2012), www.health.gov.il/PublicationsFiles/BAP2012.pdf (Heb.).

In all these cases, the natural is no longer "natural," and relying solely on the genetic, or even the gestational, component can easily lead to different and sometimes even contradicting conclusions as to who should be regarded as the legal parent. I am confident that the following conclusion, written almost one-and-a-half decades ago with regard to the dilemmas raised by AIH, AID, IVF, and surrogacy, is far more applicable to upcoming biomedical challenges: "In the biomedical context, however, the fast pace of scientific technological development has produced a situation in which there is simply not enough purely legal material upon which to base halakhic decisions."[117] Therefore, I feel confident that implementing my normative model, DLPBA, may be very helpful also to halakhic authorities in establishing or determining legal parenthood, as they struggle to discover what the "natural" order should be in these imminent breathtaking developments. As I concluded previously,

> Examining the crucial role of intent where a child has multiple biological parents demonstrates that validating the intent of the parties should play a larger role in the more common surrogacy context of three biological parents. . . . [W]e argue that, where the biological paradigm is insufficient . . . [t]he benefits of using contractual/intentional parenthood in traditional ART are also present in the context of advanced ART.[118]

4 ADDITIONAL HALAKHIC EXCEPTIONS TO NATURAL LINEAGE

In the previous section, I explored the inadequacy and insufficiency of both the genetic and gestational halakhic natural order as the sole means for establishing legal parenthood. I therefore suggested adding DLPBA to the equation to assist *poskim* to reconceptualize the "natural order" in confronting futuristic complicated dilemmas and challenges. In Section 5, I elaborate on how *halakhah* can adopt my innovative proposal by moving from the traditional and "natural" order of establishing legal parenthood toward a more nuanced, sensitive, and delicate order that involves some aspect of intentional parenthood

But first, I briefly explore some additional halakhic exceptions to the natural order besides the above main exception of an artificially conceived child, especially one born by means of AID,[119] who, according to some *poskim*, is not recognized as the legal descendant of his or her progenitors despite the fact that their reproductive material brought him or her into the world.[120] The unique exceptions presented

[117] Sinclair, *supra* note 52, at 112.
[118] Margalit & Loike, *supra* note 109, at 138.
[119] *See, e.g.*, Kasher, *supra* note 81. For a summary of this issue, see Corinaldi, *supra* note 39, at 81; Yosi Green, Procreation in the Modern Era: Legal and Halachic Perspectives 155–58 (2008) (Heb.).
[120] *See, e.g.*, the following Hebrew articles: Yaakov Ariel, *Artificial Insemination and Surrogacy*, in Collection of Essays: Medical Ethics and Jewish Law 171 (Mordechai Halperin & Yeruchim Primer eds., 1996); Moshe Sternbuch, *Test-Tube Baby*, 8 Bi'Shvilei Ha'Refuah

below[121] demonstrate the extent to which *halakhah* has its own devices for ignoring natural-biological reality and uses various halakhic-sociological justifications to determine that other persons are the legal parents of a given child. In my opinion, if *halakhah* wishes to retain its massive influence and, more importantly, its relevance in this steadily and rapidly developing field, the already existing exceptions are of great importance for building the required legal infrastructure and for answering the urgent need for finding halakhic precedents for any new halakhic issue.

4.1 *The Jewish Presumption of Paternity*

As in Christianity and Islam, there is a presumption in *halakhah* that any child conceived in an intact marriage is the legal child of the husband. The reason behind this well-known marital presumption of the husband's paternity in *halakhah* was to protect the BIC and his or her welfare from the harsh consequences of being labeled an illegitimate child or *mamzer*.[122] The presumption that, statistically, a child is conceived by the husband and not as a result of infidelity is well-rooted in the Amoraic period in the Talmud and also in the authoritative halakhic codices and is particularly difficult to negate. This presumption is so strong that halakhically it is applied also in the case of a mother who is a prostitute, where it is reasonable to assume that the father of her child is one of her clients. But if she was "too involved" in sexual relationships with her clients instead of her husband, there is no choice but to realize that it is impossible that the child still be assumed to be the biological child of her husband, and the child is labeled an illegitimate child/*mamzer*.[123] This presumption is a good illustration of my claim that given a good halakhic-sociological

29, 30 (1987); Ezra Bick, *Surrogate Motherhood*, 7 TECHUMIN 266, 270 (1986). *See also* TEHILA BEERI, A SOLUTION TO THE "MAMZER" PROBLEM AFFORDED BY RECENT MEDICAL ADVANCES 86–88 (MA thesis, 2005); Tehila Beeri-Alon, *Revisiting Some Halakhic Fundamental Principles for Solving the Mamzer Problem in Light of Recent Medical Advances*, 26 SHNATON HA-MISHPAT HAIVRI 43 (2009–11).

[121] For an initial and partial overview of those exceptions, see ZOHAR, *supra* note 1, at 69–71, 74–76; Corinaldi, *supra* note 28, at 304–08; and more extensively MARGALIT, *supra* note 7, at 250–52 and all the references listed there.

[122] For a discussion of the marital presumption, see *supra* notes 20–22 and accompanying text. For a discussion of the presumption of the husband's paternity, see Paula Roberts, *Truth and Consequences: Part I. Disestablishing the Paternity of Non-Marital Children*, 37 FAM. L.Q. 35 (2003); Diane S. Kaplan, *Why Truth Is Not a Defense in Paternity Actions*, 10 TEX. J. WOMEN & L. 69 (2000); Brenda J. Runner, *Protecting a Husband's Parental Rights When His Wife Disputes the Presumption of Legitimacy*, 28 J. FAM. L. 115 (1989–90); Linda L. Chezem & Sarah L. Nagy, *Judicial Abrogation of a Husband's Paternity: Can a Third Party Seek to Establish Paternity over a Child Born into a Marriage while That Marriage Remains Intact*, 30 IND. L. REV. 467 (1997).

[123] For a summary of the sources dealing with these presumptions, see SCHERESCHEWSKY, *supra* note 13, at 360–62; TALMUDIC ENCYCLOPEDIA vol. 1, 5–16 (Shlomo Zevin et al. eds., 1978); TALMUDIC ENCYCLOPEDIA vol. 24, 131–48 (Shlomo Zevin et al. eds., 1999). *See also* Rabbinical Court (Haifa) 1087096/1 Anonymous (unpublished, 12.12.16).

justification, *halakhah* can depart from its traditional reliance on the natural order and totally ignore genetic truth and biological reality in order to achieve a much more desirable and less harsh determination.

4.2 *Annulment of the Lineage of Gentile Sperm*

As mentioned earlier,[124] there are distinct advantages to using Gentile rather than Jewish sperm in order to avoid problems of incest and "possible mamzer"/*shtuki* status.[125] *Halakhah* does not validate intermarriage with a non-Jew. Moreover, in intermarriage, the child resulting from the conjugal relationship is not defined as the legal offspring of the father but only of the mother. Thus, if the father is Jewish and the mother is not, the child, because of being regarded as the child of the mother, is defined as a non-Jew; vice versa, if the mother is Jewish and the father is not, again the child is not recognized as the child of the Gentile father.

This determination ignores natural reality and halakhically annuls the Jewish child's genetic lineage from the non-Jewish father due to a fictional determination in which the Torah "forfeits" the semen of a Gentile and, from the perspective of Judaism, his offspring are not defined as his legal children.[126] One scholar recently noted that this principle is applied also in the context of adoption, where many *poskim* indicate a clear preference for adopting non-Jewish babies over Jewish babies, for fear of incest, which could lead to *mamzerut*.[127] I myself am not aware of this preference. Moreover, this preference for Gentile sperm or a Gentile child contradicts one of Judaism's most basic principles – preserving the Jewish bloodline.[128]

4.3 *Annulment of Lineage in a Proselyte*

Like the principle discussed in the previous subsection, halakhic annulment of a Gentile's genetic lineage also occurs when he or she converts to Judaism. The Talmud states several times that a proselyte is like a newborn, thus completely

[124] *See supra* notes 78–79 and accompanying text.

[125] For the endorsement of using non-Jewish sperm and egg donors, see Laufer-Ukeles, *supra* note 11, at 252–53.

[126] For a summary of this issue, see SCHERESCHEWSKY, *supra* note 13, at 357–59; CORINALDI, *supra* note 39, at 82.

[127] *See* Laufer-Ukeles, *supra* note 11, at 245 n.123, citing Michael Gold, *Adoption as a Jewish Option*, www.adopting.org/jewish.html; Bayla Sheva Brenner, *Filling the Void: Creating Jewish Families through Adoption*, http://ou.org.s3.amazonaws.com/pdf/ja/5766/spring66/FillingVoid .pdf.

[128] For this notion of preserving the Jewish bloodline, see Shlomo Z. Auerbach, *Artificial Insemination*, 1 NOAM 145, 166 (1958) (Heb.). For a discussion of this issue, see Povarsky, *supra* note 1, at 413–16; Zvi Ryzman, A *Halachic Discussion*, *supra* note 115, at 7–8; Laufer-Ukeles, *supra* note 11, at 245–51. For considering the problem that the resulting child will have a legal mother but not a father, see GREEN, *supra* note 119, at 169–70.

severing all of his or her former familial relationships despite the fact that the biological relationships still exist.[129] Therefore, according to the Written Law, after his or her conversion, a proselyte can even marry his or her parent or sibling, and he or she does not inherit his or her biological parents. But the Oral Law restricts these two problematic consequences, as it is unfitting that what is prohibited before his or her conversion – incest – is permitted afterward. For similar reasons, it is unfitting to prevent him or her from inheriting his or her biological parents. With the exception of these two situations, the convert is totally severed from all his or her previous familial relationships. Once again, *halakhah* totally ignores the natural order because of other important halakhic-sociological reasons.[130]

4.4 *Annulment of Lineage in Posthumous Procreation*

Posthumous procreation has recently become more common,[131] at least in Israel, where it is possible to make a "biological will" to ensure posthumous use of one's sperm.[132] There is even a precedent for fertilizing a deceased woman's ovum with the sperm of her living husband and using a surrogate mother to bring their child into the world.[133] This posthumous practice may, on the one hand, be humanity's

[129] *See, e.g.*, BT *Yevamot* 22a, 62b, 97b, and parallels. For a discussion in the halakhic codices, see MAIMONIDES, *Issurei Biah* 14:11; *Shulhan Arukh, Yore Dea 269:10*. For a theoretical explanation of this rebirth that severs all previous familial relationships after the conversion, see Bleich, *supra* note 95, at 49–50; Laufer-Ukeles, *supra* note 1, at 107.

[130] *See* BT *Yevamot* 97b; MAIMONIDES, *Ishut* 15:6; *Shulhan Arukh, Even ha-Ezer* 1:7; TALMUDIC ENCYCLOPEDIA vol. 6, 259–62 (Shlomo Zevin et al. eds., 1954) (Heb.); Aharon Lichtenstein, *On Conversion*, 23(2) TRADITION 1 (1988); ZVI ZOHAR & AVRAHAM SAGI, GIYUR VEZEHUT YEHUDIT 227–48 (1994) (Heb.).

[131] For an overview of this issue and its problematic secular and religious angles, see, respectively, GREEN, *supra* note 199, at 331–36, 399–419. For a discussion of the halakhic aspect, see also Povarsky, *supra* note 1, at 437–40. For Hebrew sources that address the issue, see Gideon Weitzman, *Taking Sperm from an Unconscious Husband*, 25 TCHUMIN 59, 63 (2005); Yigal Shafran, *Postmortem Fatherhood*, 20 TECHUMIN 347 (2000); Yaakov Ariel et al., *Postmortem Sperm Procurement – Juridical and Halachic Aspects*, 139 HAREFUAH 331 (2000); Moshe Hershler, *Test-Tube Babies According to Halakha*, 4 HALAKHA & MED. 90, 92 (1985); ibid, *Test-Tube Babies According to Halakha*, 1 HALAKHA & MED. 307, 316 (1980).

[132] For an update on research conducted in Israel in this field, see Yael Hashiloni-Dolev, *Posthumous Reproduction (PHR) in Israel: Policy Rationales Versus Lay People's Concerns, a Preliminary Study*, 39(4) CULTURE, MEDICINE, AND PSYCHIATRY 634 (2015). For the notion of a biological will, see Irit Rosenblum, *The Biological Will – A New Paradigm in ART?*, NEW FAMILY ORG. (Feb. 25, 2013), www.newfamily.org.il/en/4905/the-biological-will%E2%84%A2-%E2%80%93-a-new-paradigm-in-art/; ibid, *Being Fruitful and Multiplying: Legal, Philosophical, Religious, and Medical Perspectives on Assisted Reproductive Technologies in Israel and Internationally*, 36 SUFFOLK TRANSNAT'L L. REV. 627 (2013). *See also* Lifshitz, *supra* note 26, at 313, 330.

[133] This is the story of Nissim Ayish, who fulfilled his late wife's wish to become a mother two years after she died from a deadly tumor, as published online, by David Regev, *Woman's Dream to Have Child Fulfilled after Death*, YNET MAGAZINE 06.14.11, www.ynetnews.com/articles/0,7340,L-4081456,00.html.

ultimate answer to the inevitability of an imminent death, but, on the other hand, may also create a nightmare.[134] The various socio-ethical dilemmas of "planned orphanhood"[135] and the "non-identity problem,"[136] and whether and how to evaluate the BIC of the resulting child, are beyond the scope of this book.

I will just briefly review the opinions of *poskim* who maintain that any child created after his or her progenitor's death may not be regarded as the deceased's legal child, despite the strong connection the genetic reality and natural order create between the child and his or her genetic parent.[137] The vast majority of halakhists adhere to the natural order and maintain that the conceived child is still the legal child of the deceased, even though the child was conceived after the parent's death. But, there are some prominent *poskim* who argue that in this unique scenario, the child is not defined as the legal child of his or her progenitor, at least for stringent considerations (*lechumra*) because the child was born to a dead person and by artificial means. This is yet another halakhic exception to the natural order, where *halakhah* ignores genetic reality in favor of other considerations.[138]

[134] *See, e.g.*, Devon D. Williams, *Over My Dead Body: The Legal Nightmare and Medical Phenomenon of Posthumous Conception through Postmortem Sperm Retrieval*, 34 CAMPBELL L. REV. 181 (2012); Itai Apter & Nurit Inbal, *Posthumous Insemination – A Nightmare or a Dream Come True? – Following the Attorney General's Directive* 1.2202, A(1) LAWATCH 11 (2004) (Heb.).

[135] *See* Ruth Landau, *Planned Orphanhood*, 49(2) SOCIAL SCIENCE AND MEDICINE 185 (1999); Asa Kahser, *"Planned Orphanhood": The Balanced Picture*, in MORAL DILEMMAS IN MEDICINE 161 (Raphael Cohen-Almagor ed., 2002) (Heb.).

[136] For a discussion of this challenging issue, see I. Glenn Cohen, *Beyond Best Interests*, 96 MINN. L. REV. 1187 (2012); ibid, *Regulating Reproduction: The Problem with Best Interests*, 96 MINN. L. REV. 423 (2011); ibid, *Intentional Diminishment, the Non-Identity Problem, and Legal Liability*, 60 HASTINGS L.J. 347 (2008); James Woodward, *The Non-Identity Problem* 96(4) ETHICS 804 (1986).

[137] For legislation suggesting that if the sperm of a deceased person is used without his explicit agreement, he is not regarded as the legal father of the child, but if he agreed, he is defined as the child's legal father, which strongly supports my normative model of DLPBA, see UPA § 707 ("If an individual who consented in a record to be a parent by assisted reproduction dies before placement of eggs, sperm, or embryos, the deceased individual is not a parent of the resulting child unless the deceased spouse consented in a record that if assisted reproduction were to occur after death, the deceased individual would be a parent of the child."). *See also* Margalit, *supra* note 3, at 376–77. For the centrality of intentional parenthood in the context of posthumous conception, see Anne Reichman Schiff, *Arising from the Dead: Challenges of Posthumous Procreation*, 75 N.C. L. REV. 901 (1997); Gail A. Katz, *Parpalaix c.* CECOS: *Protecting Intent in Reproductive Technology*, 11 HARV. J.L. & TECH. 683 (1998); Ruth Zafran, *Dying to Be a Father: Legal Paternity in Cases of Posthumous Conception*, 8 HOUS. J. HEALTH L. & POL'Y 47, 74–76 (2007); Raymond C. O'Brien, *The Momentum of Posthumous Conception: A Model Act*, 25 J. CONTEMP. HEALTH L. & POL'Y 332, 371–75 (2009); Amanda Horner, *I Consented to Do What?: Posthumous Children and the Consent to Parent After-Death*, 33 S. ILL. U. L.J. 157 (2008).

[138] *See* the various writings in Hebrew by Shaul Israeli, such as 4 RESP. BEMAREH HABAZAK ch. 228–29 (2001); ibid, vol. 3 ch. 226 (1998); ibid, RESP. HAVUT BENJAMIN ch. 107 (1992); ibid, *Fatherhood by Artificial Means*, 33 TORAH SHE-BE'ALPE 41 (1992). *See also* Yossi Green, *Post*

4.5 *Annulment of Lineage When the Heir Murders the Decedent*

Perhaps one of the most well-known Jewish moral dicta is the rhetorical question, "Would you murder and also inherit?"[139] This was the cry of Elijah the Prophet in the name of the Almighty against Ahab, King of Israel, who wrongfully killed a man just to inherit his vineyard, which was adjacent to Ahab's own land. The Talmud brings a difference of opinion between the sages on this matter: Did Ahab attempt to inherit the man based on the general public law that if a man is killed by the king, the king inherits his possessions? Or, as R. Yehuda claims, since Ahab was his relative, did Ahab intend to inherit him based on private law but was stopped by Elijah's moral claim, which may indicate that this Jewish ethic was well accepted in the ancient world?[140] The question of whether an heir who murders his or her decedent should be disqualified from inheriting him or her is hotly debated in Judaism. The vast majority of opinions contend that the biological relationship overrides the problematic deed. Thus, Menachem Porush, one of the most well-known ultra-orthodox members of Israel's parliament, argued that this despicable murderer may be punished by imprisonment but cannot be prevented from inheriting the deceased, as a halakhic inheritance is neither a right nor a privilege but an automatic process that we cannot stop.

In addition, Yitzchak Zilberstein, one of the most prominent *poskim* of modern medical *halakhah*, stated explicitly in a responsum that a physician who injected his wife with an overdose of medication in order to kill her is still permitted to inherit her. Lastly, according to Eliav Shochetman and Yosef Rivlin, two leading professors of Jewish and civil law, the murderer may be punished by being deprived of the inheritance, but according to *halakhah* he or she is still fully entitled to inherit the deceased.[141] But, a more challenging and important opinion for our discussion is a ruling by a minority of *poskim* that the moment the son kills the deceased, he immediately ceases to be his biological, and therefore also his halakhic, son, which prevents him from being the beneficiary. This is a unique and most interesting departure from genetic truth in favor of socio-ethical-legal considerations. These *poskim* are following an earlier and much better-known exception concerning an apostate, who according to some prominent halakhists loses his inheritance rights

Modern Procreation by Means of IVF and Ibum and Haliza, 2 Netanya Academic College L. Rev. 207, 219–28 (2002) (Heb.).

139 I Kings 21:19. This principle is embedded in article 5 of Israel's 1965 Inheritance Law. *See also* Shmuel Shilo, Commentary to the Succession Law, 1965 vol. 1, 59–77 (1992) (Heb.).

140 *See* BT *Sanhedrin* 48b; Tosafot, ibid 20b, s.v. "King is permitted."

141 *See*, respectively, the following Hebrew sources: 42 Knesset Reports 958 (1965), http://m.knesset.gov.il/pages/default.aspx; Itzhak Zilberstein, Chashukei Chemed on Tractate Bava Metzia 189–91 (2009); Eliav Shochetman, *Would You Murder and Also Inherit?*, 302 Weekly Parasha, Bereshit (2008), www.daat.ac.il/mishpat-ivri/skirot/302-2.htm; Yosef Rivlin, Inheritance and Wills in Jewish Law 124 (1999).

upon his renunciation of Judaism.[142] This principle can be implemented in our context,[143] not simply as a punishment or fine, but by annulling the murderer's status as the biological son of the deceased.[144]

5 HALAKHIC PARENTHOOD AND INTENTIONAL PARENTHOOD – CAN THEY BE RECONCILED?

In the previous sections, I explored the application of the traditional halakhic natural order as the basis for establishing legal parenthood, which, *prima facie*, does not allow for any deviation from it to other models, such as the social and/or psychological parenthood model, and in particular when the alternative is intentional parenthood. In Section 1, I enumerated the two main methods for establishing halakhic parenthood in ancient times – a coitally produced child and adoption. I discussed how, in both cases, the natural order is sometimes totally blurred. For example, the Jewish presumption of paternity, discussed in subsection 4.1, favors the principle of BIC by masking the truth that the child is actually not the "legitimate" child of the father and ignoring the fact that, by definition, the child is *mamzer*. In the case of adoption, the urgent need to "fill the void" and find caring parents for the hundreds of thousands of Jewish children orphaned in the Holocaust and in other catastrophes and disasters that have plagued the Jewish people has forced Judaism to accept adoption as a legitimate option. In these two scenarios, *halakhah* explicitly deviates from its principle of the basic natural order because of other important socio-halakhic justifications, *inter alia*, recognizing, even if only to varying degrees, the social and/or psychological parenthood of the adopting parents.

As I have elaborated in several articles, I believe that both the presumption of paternity and adoption in particular, and the social and/or psychological parenthood model in general, are examples of implementing intentional parenthood. The presumption of paternity is a fictional presumption that the husband of a woman who

[142] *See* the following sources in Hebrew: OTZAR HAGEONIM, KIDDUSHIN TRACTATE vol. 9, 32–33 (responsa of Rav Tzedek Gaon) (Benjamin M. Levin ed., 1928); ZERACH WARHAFTIG, ZRICHAT HASHANI ON TRACTATE SANHEDRIN 169–70 (1973), who maintained that this should be the destiny of any husband who betrayed his wife.

[143] *See* the following sources in Hebrew: YISSACHAR TAMAR, ALEY TAMAR ON SEDER NEZIKIN, TRACTATE MAKOT 208 (1983); YOSEF ROZIN, TZAFNAT PANEACH, *Matnot Aniim* 4:10 p. 108 (1979); YEHOSHUA EHRENBERG, RESP. DVAR YEHOSHUA vol. 1 ch. 100 (1998); ZERACH WARHAFTIG, ZRICHAT HASHANI ON TRACTATE MAKOT 205 (1973); ZVI YEHUDA BEN YAAKOV, RESP. MISHPATECHA LEYAKOV vol. 2 ch. 23 (1997).

[144] *See* the following sources in Hebrew: AVRAHAM Y. BORNSTEIN, SANHEDRI KTANA ON TRACTATE SANHEDRIN 48b p. 150 (1980); AVRAHAM PRICE, MISHNAT AVRAHAM ch. 929 (1954); AARON TEOMIM, BIGDEI AARON 41 (1987); Hillel Posek, 114 HAPOSEK a-748 (1950); AVRAHAM SHADMI, DIVREI AVRAHAM vol. 2 pp. 92–93 (1968). For a summary of these opinions, see Yaakov Shapira, *And Again, Would You Murder and Also Inherit?*, 374 WEEKLY PARASHA, Pinchas (2010), www.justice.gov.il/Units/MishpatIvri/Gilyonot/374.doc and more extensively, YOSEF RIVLIN, MISHNAT HANAKHALOT: THE LAW OF INHERITANCE AND WILLS 104–15 (2015) (Heb.).

conceives a child is the legal father of that child, even if the father is not biologically related to the child.[145] This presumption, at its core, is based on a broader societal presumption that it is the intention of the husband of a married woman who conceives a child to serve as the legal father of that child and to provide for the child financially.[146] This presumption demonstrates that throughout history, the natural order was often subordinate to other considerations, including intention, in determining legal parentage. Similarly, social and/or psychological parenthood is based primarily on the intention and express or implied agreement of an individual to accept legal parentage.[147] One underpinning of ascribing parental status to an individual acting as a de facto parent is the implicit understanding that, by his or her actions, the individual has demonstrated an intent and capacity to become a legal parent. Thus, even unintentionally, *halakhah* applied intentional parenthood in the ancient era, to varying degrees.

With regard to the modern era, I discussed in section 2 the difficulty of applying the natural order to current biomedical innovations, as illustrated in the case of AID, where the identity of the genetic donor is unknown and there is no way of compelling him to fulfill his parental obligations. There is thus no choice but to recognize the donee's husband, wholly or partially, as the legal parent of the conceived child. As I have explained in depth elsewhere, the entire AID process will work effectively only if we implement DLPBA to enhance and not damage the rights and welfare of the contracting parties. This will allow the sperm donor to opt out of legal paternity and the donee's husband to opt in to this paternity solely by virtue of their reciprocal initial intention and agreement to respectively disconnect from and connect to the resulting child.[148] But, far more problematic is the extreme blurring of the natural order in determining legal maternity in ovum donation, IVF, and surrogacy, where "natural" maternity is unbundled into its smaller and more basic natural genetic and gestational components. Even if we wished to adhere to the natural order for determining halakhic parenthood, which of the two components is superior for establishing legal maternity? And how exactly does surrogacy work, if not by validating the initial agreement of DLPBA to transfer legal maternity from the surrogate mother to the intending mother?

In the futuristic era, as I argued in Section 3, the natural order will be totally confusing, inadequate, and insufficient. Is a cloned child the child of his or her progenitor? Is the child the progenitor's "long extension" of life and/or is he or she actually a duplication of the progenitor? Or his or her (twin) brother or sister? Or perhaps

[145] *See* Rachel L. Kovach, *Sorry Daddy – Your Time Is Up: Rebutting the Presumption of Paternity in Louisiana*, 56 Loy. L. Rev. 651 (2010) (for the problematic aspects of a modern adhering to this legal fiction).

[146] *See* June Carbone & Naomi Cahn, *Marriage, Parentage, and Child Support*, 45 Fam. L.Q. 219, 221–28 (2011); Yehezkel Margalit, *Intentional Parenthood: A Solution to the Plight of Same-Sex Partners Striving for Legal Recognition as Parents*, 12 Whittier J. Child & Fam. Advoc. 39, 55–57 (2013); Margalit, *supra* note 5, at ch. 4.1.

[147] Katharine K. Baker, *Bargaining or Biology? The History and Future of Paternity Law and Parental Status*, 14 Cornell J.L. & Pub. Pol'y 1, 31–38 (2004).

[148] *See* Margalit, *supra* note 8.

the clone is not a human being at all and does not have any lineage?[149] In addition, the numerous exceptions to the determination of parenthood based on the traditional natural order, mentioned earlier, clearly demonstrate *halakhah*'s capacity to ignore the genetic component in favor of other components for establishing legal parenthood, if there are important-enough justifications. Thus, it is imperative, and useful even in and of itself, and especially in view of future biomedical innovations, to add intentional parenthood to the process of establishing legal parenthood in order to help the "natural order" survive all of these major changes. It is only the more flexible characteristics of DLPBA that can help us to understand correctly the initial intentions and agreements of the individuals involved in the process of producing a child.

In the absence of a clear halakhic consensus as to whether the genetic mother or the gestational mother is to be recognized as the legal mother, it may be possible, even halakhically, to differentially determine legal maternity in the various contexts where this determination is required, based on the initial intentions and agreement of the contracting parties.[150]

But, *halakhah* is very slow to respond, for several reasons, and its most basic principle of the natural model for establishing legal parenthood is unlikely to undergo a rapid change. I also do not anticipate my normative model being accepted in its entirety in the foreseeable future. Therefore, I conclude this chapter by suggesting that we borrow some useful existing halakhic devices that may facilitate the acceptance of my perspective and enable my model to be applied, even if only partially. First, intended parents can be recognized as legal parents through adoption.[151] There is an animated documented history of rabbinical courts issuing "adoption decrees" to settle the various parental obligations adopting parents undertake when they adopt a child.[152] Alternatively, the intended parents may be

[149] *See, e.g.*, the following sources in Hebrew: Zvi Ryzman, *Is a Cloned Kohen Permitted to Recite the Kohen's Blessing?*, http://olamot.net/sites/default/files/ratz_katzvi/pdf/-_32.pdf; Yair Shiber, *The Halakhic-Legal Status of a Living Being Born by Genetic Cloning*, 16 Bekhol Derakhekha Daehu, Journal of Torah and Scholarship 45 (2005), and more extensively, Jonathan Razyel, Genetic Cloning – A Jewish Perspective: A Collection of Essays (2004).

[150] For this challenging call, see Avishalom Westreich, *Changing Motherhood Paradigms: Jewish Law, Civil Law, and Society*, 28 Hastings Women's L.J. 97 (2017). For a previous calls to reconcile *halakhah* with secular Israeli law, see Ruth Zafran, The Right of Offspring to Seek Out Their Biological Parents 104–10 (Doctoral dissertation, 2004) (Heb.); Shifman, *supra* note 100, at 25–27, and more extensively, Michael Corinaldi, *On the Question of Legal Parentage in Israel (Children Born through an Artificial Birth Technique)*, in An Unusual Pregnancy: A Multi-Disciplinary Study of In Vitro Fertilization 137 (Shulamit Almog & Avinoam Ben-Zeev eds., 1996) (Heb.). For a discussion of whether it is possible to reconcile *halakhah* and secular Israeli law at least in the AID case, for paying the parental obligation of maintenance, see Green, *supra* note 119, at 124, 131.

[151] As discussed, for example, in the surrogacy context, see Povarsky, *supra* note 1, at 450–51, 455–58; Laufer-Ukeles, *supra* note 1, at 115–16, 128, 134 ("Jewish law should at least . . . establishing an obligatory adoption procedure after the child is born, in which the mother [gestational surrogate –Y. M.] can freely waive her parental duties and rights.").

[152] *See* Corinaldi, *supra* note 150, at 153; Corinaldi, *supra* note 28, at 326; and the following references in Hebrew: Maimon, *supra* note 33, at 555–62, and more extensively, Ido Divon, *The Obligation of an Adopting Father to Pay the Child Support Due to His Undertaking*, 9 Dinei

defined as the conceived child's legal guardians (*apotropos*), which gives them (almost) all parental rights and obligations.[153]

Similarly, and at least for the purpose of obligating them to carry out their various parental obligations, particularly maintenance,[154] it is possible to adopt the above-mentioned solution offered in 1977 by one of Israel's rabbinical courts. As mentioned earlier, the Haifa district rabbinical court compelled a sperm donee's husband to pay child support for the resulting child because, by his explicit or implied agreement to his wife's impregnation, he became her guarantor (*arev*).[155] The court explained that the husband was obligated to pay child support based upon the principle of guarantee. In consenting to his wife's AID procedure, the husband implicitly guaranteed all of her expenses in raising the child, including paying for the child's support. This principle can be extended to other parental obligations and can be applied to other ART contexts.[156] Lastly, even if a husband is not officially obligated by *halakhah* to pay child support to his wife, he can be obligated to pay it as charity (*tzedakah*).[157] This is a moral obligation that throughout the ages has

ISRAEL 184 (1978–80). For the importance of signing a written adoption agreement at the outset of the adoption, see Shlomo Dichovsky, *The Parental Obligation to Support Adoptive Children*, 15 TECHUMIN 278 (1995).

153 *See supra* note 40 and accompanying text. *See also* the following references in Hebrew: SCHERESCHEWSKY, *supra* note 13, at 425–46; YAAKOV REINITZ, THE GUARDIAN OF ORPHANS IN JEWISH LAW (Doctoral dissertation, 1984); ibid, *Appointing a Female Apotropos*, 4 BAR ILAN L. STUD. 167 (1986); ibid, *The Apotropos of Orphans Who Are Supported by the Owner*, 1 BAR ILAN L. STUD. 219 (1980); Simcha Assaf, *Appointing Women as Apotropos*, 2 JEWISH L. 75 (1927).

154 It is worth noting that the sources and the precise extent of the parental obligation to pay child support are ambiguous and therefore hotly debated. For the leading halakhic references, see GILAT, *supra* note 13 and the references listed ibid, at 155 n.1. *See also* in the following sources in Hebrew: Elimelech Westreich, *The Legal-Historical Sources of the Parents Obligation to Maintain Their Children*, 19 DINEI ISRAEL 161 (1997); HILEL HAVSHOSH, CHILD SUPPORT: PARENTAL OBLIGATIONS, JEWISH LAW (2004); Zerach Warhaftig, *To the Sources of the Obligation of Child Support*, 1 TECHUMIN 255 (1980); MOSHE S. HACOHEN, THE JEWISH LAW OF CHILD MAINTENANCE PAYMENTS – ITS FORMATION, DEVELOPMENT AND CIRCUMSTANCES (Doctoral dissertation, 1998).

155 For scholarly articles discussing the suggestion of obligating the husband as a guarantor, see Itamar Warhaftig, *The Legal Validity of Reliance on Oral Promise in Jewish Law*, 2 BAR-ILAN L. STUD. 45, 77 n.212 (1982) (Heb.); BARUCH KAHANA, GUARANTEE LAW 517 in the appendix to note 71, letter 22 (1991) (Heb.).

156 *See* the references listed in *supra* note 82 and accompanying text. This interesting ruling was first mentioned by Yosi Green, *Artificial Insemination (AID) in Israeli Court Judgments and Legislation*, 5 ASSIA 125, 132–34 (1986) (Heb.) and was discussed also by Povarsky, *supra* note 1, at 444–46; Corinaldi, *supra* note 39, at 101. For additional supporting rabbinical court rulings, see Shiber, *supra* note 149, at 34.

157 For a discussion of this option concerning the husband, see Menashe Shawa, *Maintenance of Minor Children in Jewish and Positive Law*, 13 JEWISH L. ASS'N STUD. 289 (2002) and the following references in Hebrew: Yizhak Indig, *The Problem of Support of a Child Born of Artificial Insemination*, 2 DINEI ISRAEL 83 (1971); SCHERESCHEWSKY, *supra* note 13, at 387; Shlomo Dichovsky, *Child Support – A Special Enactment in Charity Laws*, 16 TECHUMIN 87 (1996). For a summary of this issue, see Corinaldi, *supra* note 150, at 152–54.

become a binding legal duty. On November 30, 2015, this binding legal duty was expanded by the Chief Rabbinate of Israel also to women,[158] and it can be applied even if, formalistically, the intended parents are not the legal parents.[159]

[158] For a secular call based on halakhic sources for a more egalitarian obligation of child custody, see Yoav Mazeh, *The Religious Law of Child Support, the Supreme Court's Case-Law and the Practice of Courts: Between Myth and Reality* 4–18 HAIFA L. REV. (forthcoming, 2018) (Heb.), http://papers.ssrn.com/sol3/papers.cfm?abstract_id=2556149.

[159] *See* www.daat.ac.il/he-il/mishpat_ivri/maamraim/hachlata.htm?printview=true. For earlier sources in Hebrew dealing with obligating a woman to pay child support, see Gedalia Axelrod, *The Obligation of the Mother in Paying Her Child Support*, 4 SHURAT HADIN 66 (1998); Yaakov Bazak, *The Obligation of the Mother to Share the Child Support in Jewish Law*, 32 HAPRAKLIT 357, 361–64 (1979–80); Theodor Oryn, *Remarks on the Duty of the Mother to Participate in the Maintenance of Her Child*, 34 HAPRAKLIT 308 (1982); Zeev Ferber, *The Mother Sharing in Paying Child Support*, 27 TECHUMIN 273 (2007); Michael Corinaldi, *Should Equality Be Implemented in the Laws of Parents and Children*, 2 KIRYAT HAMISHPAT 131, 152 (2002); SCHERESCHEWSKY, *supra* note 13, at 372 n.7.

Epilogue

This book explored the potential influence of halakhic contract law on halakhic family law in both spousal and parent–child relationships. I opened the discussion with the subject of privately regulating conjugal relations, treating these as an absolute legal "debt" that must be "paid" at clear, rigid, and fixed times. As a consequence, there is no way to circumvent it, since it is a biblical obligation, and therefore any attempt to circumvent it contractually is restricted, as it is "the stipulation of anybody who stipulates against what is written in the Torah." Nevertheless, an in-depth and thorough rereading of the halakhic literature throughout the generations, including both the Tannaitic and Amoraic literature, and particularly the Palestinian Talmud and the medieval literature, yielded a far more complex picture – that there is enough halakhic room for such private regulation.

This was the essence of Chapter 1, "Regulating Marital Relations between Spouses by Consent," in which I explored, first and foremost, the public regulation of conjugal relations, as it is comprehensively regulated in *halakhah*. I enumerated the various binding aspects of the *onah* obligation, which suggests that the halakhic obligation is inflexible, deriving from the status of marriage as a religious institution. This approach would *prima facie* block any possibility of private contractual arrangements. Thus, I built the legal infrastructure for exploring the halakhic possibility to practically use one of the available contractual devices as a possible solution for the heart-wrenching case of the *agunah*. Therefore, I discussed the halakhic sources that endorse the usage of some contractual tools. These various contractual devices are available for a couple married according to the law of Moses and Israel (*kedat Mosheh veYisrael*) who ask to waive this intimate obligation/right. Such deviation from public regulation of conjugal relations may be achieved by the wife's renouncing of her *onah* rights or receiving permission to violate her *onah* right.

Following this explanation, I explored in Chapter 2, "'Freedom of Contract' in Jewish Family Law – The Differences between the Babylonian and Palestinian Talmuds," how that the Palestinian Talmud not only occasionally endorses more freedom of contract regarding privately regulated conjugal relations, but also has a more comprehensive and systematic perspective. Consequently, the husband may impose stipulations on or nullify not only his *onah* obligation, but also various spousal monetary obligations such as his obligation to pay the basic *ketubah* sum and his right to inherit his deceased wife's estate. The main goal of this chapter was to address from a dogmatic as well as a historic perspective that the Palestinian Talmud's "hate clause" – "if he grows to hate her or she grows to hate him" – is not merely a monetary stipulation, but also a condition that seeks to enable the wife to demand a divorce if she so desires.

In Chapter 3, "Is There Really No Conditional Marriage?," I sought to overcome the two main halakhic obstacles to using contractual mechanisms as a possible viable solution to the problem of the *agunah*. Many halakhic authorities have claimed throughout the generations that any such contractual devices, such as conditional marriage, should be rejected from the outset, since this would be "one who stipulates about what is written in the Torah" and due to the well-known Talmudic dictum "there is no conditional marriage." I argued that any halakhic marriage was actually a conditional marriage; therefore, if the sages are not satisfied with any given marriage, they can retroactively nullify it, as was extensively argued by several *rishonim* (early halakhic authorities) and Talmudic scholars.

Similarly, in Chapter 4, "Temporary Marriage – A Possible Solution to the Problem of the *Agunah*?," I reexamined the possibility of imposing a stipulation in the marriage contract that it would only be a temporary marriage, as is reflected, in my opinion, in the Babylonian Talmud. I explored the deep and precise meaning of the cry by important Babylonian *amoraim* "Who will be mine for a day?" that appears twice in the Babylonian Talmud. I claimed that there are possible common roots for temporary marriage and Shi'ite temporary marriage in ancient Persian law.

Finally, in Chapter 5, "Toward Establishing Halakhic Parenthood by Agreement?," I examined the public regulation of determining halakhic parenthood – both fatherhood and motherhood. The most challenging aspect of this proposal was the necessity of deviating from rigid public regulation that adheres in almost every instance to natural lineage, by private agreement. I explored some halakhic exceptions to the natural order, recognized by *halakhah* for several reasons. I claimed that those exceptions serve as the legal infrastructure for moving more generally from the traditional and "natural" order of establishing legal parenthood toward a more nuanced, sensitive, and delicate order that involves some aspect of intentional parenthood.

Following over a decade of research in this field, from both the halakhic and the civil perspectives, I would suggest that contract law is becoming more and more prevalent and important for family law. Thus, contractual devices and doctrines are slowly but surely penetrating, influencing, and shaping familial arrangements, both in the spousal relationship and in the parent–child relationship. Obviously, today's greater social openness, rocketing divorce rates, and rapid biomedical developments in the field of reproduction enable the increased reproduction of children in "nontraditional" families. Accordingly, the acute need for private regulation of those familial relations is accelerating. I am confident that the increasingly intensive discussions in the field of civil law regarding private regulation of spousal and parental arrangements, both in the breakdown of the traditional family and in nontraditional families, will step by step penetrate the halakhic realm. Likewise, the intensive spread of academic discourse concerning the acute necessity of increased private regulation of Jewish family and calls to use the various available contractual devices, *inter alia*, to promote the status of the wife will increasingly render those agreements as acceptable among Jewish communities across the globe.

This book has explored how the discourse in this regard is more of a political issue than a purely halakhic issue, as ideological concerns prevent the practical application of important contractual devices for the modern Jewish family. Thus, I argued that this is the reason why the Israeli rabbinical authorities and courts are slow to accept potential contractual solutions, the first and foremost of these being prenuptial agreements. These agreements are primarily intended to reduce the number of cases of a husband who refuses to give his wife a *get*. That can be achieved by imposing monetary fines on a recalcitrant husband (or wife) to prevent the partner opposing the divorce from hindering the other partner from going through with the divorce. Nonetheless, the strong resistance to such agreements arises on grounds that they are halakhically problematic, but I argued that they are based on meta-halakhic considerations rather than on hardcore *halakhah* concerns. In stark contrast to the Israeli official Rabbinate Authority, in the United States, the usage of prenuptial agreements is increasing. Moreover, the Rabbinical Council of America and the halakhic authorities in the Yeshiva University strongly support the validity of these agreements and advise couples not to get married without signing one.

There is evidence that the problem of *agunah* does not arise among couples who have signed prenuptial agreements before they married. Globalization and the ease with which people can move from one residence to another means that we are witness to an increase in the number of couples where at least one of them either lived or lives in the present out of Israel. Moreover, in recent years there has been an increase in couples who immigrate from the diaspora to Israel – but who nevertheless have married prior to their arrival outside Israel – who ask to get divorced in front of one of the Israeli rabbinical courts. It is likely that slowly but surely, similarly to any other Jewish custom (*minhag*), the more prevalent these agreements become, the more halakhic discussion will arise and the more they are likely to be accepted. The intensity and recurrence with which these agreements are being encountered will eventually force the modern halakhic authorities, first in the diaspora and later in Israel, to recognize and validate them even if just *post factum* (*bediavad*) rather than in advance (*lechatchila*).

It is hoped that one day the acute necessity of using contractual devices and doctrines suggested in this book will increasingly penetrate the circles of halakhic authorities, *poskim*, and *dayyanim*. Then, it is hoped that the theoretical conclusions of this book and its proposed practical initial outlines of the limits of the "freedom of contract" available to spouses who marry according to the law of Moses and Israel will be very useful for them.

Bibliography

JEWISH SOURCES

Bible

Genesis 16:1–4; 30:1–13; 21–22, 38:15.
Esther 2:7.
Leviticus 18:20.
I Kings 21:19.
Deuteronomy 23:18; 24:1.
THE NEW JPS TRANSLATION (2d ed., 1999).
Mark 10:9.

Mishnah

Baba Batra 8:5.
Keritot 3:9.
Ketubot 1:2; 4:1; 4:6–7; 5:1–2; 5:6; 7:7; 8:3; 8:4; 9:1.
Kiddushin 1:1; 2:2; 2:3; 2:5; 3:2; 3:3; 3:6.
Yevamot 14:1.

Tosefta

Baba Metziah 3:21; 11:23.
Ketubot (Lieberman edition) 1:4; 4:7; 7:8; 12:1.
Kiddushin (Lieberman edition) 2:5; 3:4–5; 3, 6–8; 4:9; 4:10–13.

TALMUDS

Palestinian Talmud

Baba Batra 10:1 (17c); 8:5; 8:8 (16c).
Baba Metzia 1:8 (7d–8a); 7:7 (11:c).

Eruvin 3:5 (21b).
Gittin 1:1 (43b); 7:6 (49a).
Ketubot 1:1 (25a); 1:2 (25b); 1:4 (25c); 3:5 (27d); 4:8 (28d); 4:8 (29a); 5:2 (29d); 5:5 (30a); 5:8 (30b); 7:6; 7:7 (11c); 7:9 (31c); 8:11 (32b); 9:1 (32d); 9:9 (33c); 9:10 (32d).
Kiddushin 1:1 (58a); 1:2 (59c); 1:3 (60a); 2:2 (62c); 2:3 (62c); 2:4 (62c); 2:5 (62c); 3:1 (32a); 3:2 (63d); 3:3 (64b); 3:5 (64b); 3:6 (64b); 3:7 (64b).
Megillah 1:9 (71c).
Nedarim 10:4.
Shevuot 6:6 (37b).
Yevamot 4:12 (6b); 8:3 (9c); 13:11 (36b); 13:14 (14a); 15:3 (13d); 15:3 (14d).

Babylonian Talmud

Baba Metzia 17a; 17b–18a; 20b–21a; 38a; 39a–b; 42b; 51b; 94a; 104a.
Bava Batra 8b; 42a; 126b; 130a; 131b–132a.
Bava Kama 39a–40a; 44b; 89a–b.
Eruvin 22a.
Gittin 6b; 49b; 79b; 84b; 90a.
Hagigah 14b–15a.
Ketubot 2a; 3b; 5a; 7a; 16b; 29b; 39b; 51a; 52b–53a; 54a; 54b; 56a; 57a; 57b–58b; 62a; 62b–63a; 71b; 72b; 73b–74a; 74b; 82b; 89a–b; 110b.
Kiddushin 10b–11a; 13a; 19b; 29a; 48b; 49b; 50a; 60b; 63a; 64a.
Megillah 13a.
Nedarim 15b; 29b; 64b; 81b.
Niddah 13b; 31a.
Sanhedrin 19b; 29b; 31b; 48b.
Sotah 7b.
Yevamot 18b; 22a; 37b; 62b; 88b; 89a; 94b; 97b; 107a.

MIDRASH

Halakhic *midrash* on Deuteronomy 24:1.
Midrash Bereshit (Genesis) Rabbah.
Midrash Exodus Rabbah 46:5.
MIDRASH TEHILLIM 59:3.
YALKUT SHIMONI, Prov., § 958.
YALKUT SHIMONI, Samuel 2.

HALAKHIC CODICES

Maimonides

Ishut 6:9–10; 10:7; 12:1–2; 12:6; 15:1; 15:6.
Issurei Biah 14:11; 21:11–12, 28.
Laws of Divorce 1:1–2; 10:21.

Tur

Tur, Orach Chaim 240:1.
Tur, Hoshen Mishpat 29:12.
Tur, Even ha-Ezer 76.

Beit Yosef

Even ha-Ezer 69:1–7; 118; 157:4–5.

Shulhan Arukh

Yore Dea 269:10.
Even ha-Ezer 1:7; 2:10; 25:8; 38:5; 66:9; 69:1; 69:6; 76:6; 119:1.

RESPUNSA

Alfasi, Yizhak Ben Yaakov, Resp. Rif (1969).
Alshakar, Moshe Ben Yizhak, Resp. Maharam Alshakar (1959).
Babad, David M. Manish, Resp. Havatzelet Hasharon *Even ha-Ezer* (1931).
Ben Yaakov, Zvi Yehuda, Resp. Mishpatecha Leyakov vol. 2 (1997).
Berab, Yaakov ben Moshe, Resp. Mahari Berab (1988).
Berlin, Chaim, Resp. Nishmat Hayyim (2008).
Berlin, Naftali Z., Resp. Meshiv Davar (1968).
Breisch, Mordechai Yaakov, Resp. Chelkat Yaakov *Even ha-Ezer* (1951).
Chaim Ben Izhak, Or Zarua, Resp. Maharah Or Zarua (1960).
Cohen, Shlomo ben Israel, Resp. Binyan Shelomo *Even ha-Ezer* vol. 2 (1992).
David Ben Haim, Resp. ha-Radakh (2008).
David ben Shlomo, Ibn Zimra (Radbaz), Resp. Ha-Radbaz vol. 3 (1950).
Doran, Shlomo ben Simeon, Resp. Rashbash (1968).
Duran, Shimon ben Tzemach, Resp. Tashbetz vol. 1–2 (1998).
Ehrenberg, Yehoshua, Resp. Dvar Yehoshua vol. 1 (1998).
Eiger, Akiva, Resp. Teshuvot Hadashot *Even ha-Ezer* (2002).
Eilenberg, Yissachar, Resp. Beer Sheva (2004).
Emden, Yaakov B., Resp. She'elat Ya'abez vol. 2 (2004).
Etinger, Mordechai Z., Resp. Maamar Mordechai (1968).
Ettinger, Yitzhak, Resp. Mahariya ha-Levi (1970).
Feinstein, Moshe, Resp. Iggrot Moshe *Even ha-Ezer* vol. 1, 4 (1959).
Franco, Rahamim Y., Resp. Shaare Rahamim *Even ha-Ezer* vol. 1–2 (2009).
Graubart, Judah L., Resp. Havalim Baneimim vol. 2 (1975).
Grodzenski, Chaim Ozer, Resp. Ahiezer *Even ha-Ezer* vol. 1 (1960).
Hadaya, Ovadia, Resp. Yaskil Avdi (1931).
Haim Ben Itzhak of Volozhin, Resp. Hut ha-Meshulash vol. 3 (1882).
Hazan, Elijah B., Resp. Taalumot Lev vol. 3 (1903).
Hazan, Yosef, Resp. Hikrey Lev *Even ha-Ezer* vol. 7 (1998).
Horowitz, Aryeh L. Ben Isaac, Resp. Harei Besamim vol. 2 (1984).
Isaiah the Elder of Terani (Rid), Resp. Ha-Rid (1967).
Ishmael ben Avraham, Yizhak, Resp. Zera Emet vol. 2 (1786).
Israeli, Shaul, Resp. beMareh haBazak vol. 3–4 (2001).
Resp. Havut Benjamin (1992).
Karo, Yosef, Resp. Avkat Rokhel (1960).
Klein, Menashe Ben Eliezer, Resp. Mishne Halakhot vol. 4 (1970).
Kook, Avraham Y., Resp. Ezrat Cohen *Even ha-Ezer* (1985).
Landau, Haim Yehezkel ben Yehuda, Resp. Shivat Ziyyon (1881).
Landau, Yehezkel ben Yehuda, Resp. Noda Beyhudah *Even ha-Ezer* 1st ed. (1880).

Landsofer, Yonah, Resp. Me'il Tzedakah (1968).
Levi Ben Yaakov, Haviv , Resp. Maharlbah (1865).
Lifshitz, Israel, Resp. Or Israel (1770).
Makovsky, Zvi, Resp. Yehave Daat (1935).
Mizrachi, Eliyahu ben Avraham, Resp. Maim Amukim vol. 2 (1970).
Mizrahi, Nissim H. M., Resp. Admat Kodesh *Even ha-Ezer* vol. 1 (1991).
Moshe ben Yitzhak, Resp. Maharam Mintz (1991).
Natanson, Yosef S., Resp. Shoel Umeshiv 3d ed. vol. 3 (1973).
early ed. vol. 1–2 (1993).
2d ed. (1964).
4th ed. vol. 3 (1973)
Nissim ben Reuven, Girondi (the Ran), Resp. ha-Ran (1950).
Ovadia, Yehoshua, Resp. Yismah Levav *Even ha-Ezer* (1998).
Perlemuter, Avraham Z. ben Eliezer, Resp. Damesek Eliezer *Even ha-Ezer* (1905).
Rabbeinu Asher, Resp. ha-Rosh (1954).
Rizikov, Menachem, Resp. Shaarei Shamayim *Even ha-Ezer* (1936).
Samuel ben Moshe, de Medina, Resp. Maharashdam *Even ha-Ezer* (1959).
Sasson, Aaron ben Yosef, Resp. Torat Emet (2006).
Seigel, Yehoshua ben Moshe Y., Resp. Oznei Yehoshua vol. 1 (1914).
Shlomo ben Avraham, ben Aderet (Rashba), Resp. Rashba vol. 3–5, 6 (1958).
Resp. Teshuvot HaRashba HaHadashot (2005).
Sofer, Avraham S. Ben Moshe, Resp. Ktav Sofer *Even ha-Ezer* (1960).
Sofer, Haim, Resp. Mahne Haim *Even ha-Ezer – Orach Chaim* vol. 2 (1963).
Sofer, Moshe Ben Shmuel, Resp. Hatam Sofer *Even ha-Ezer* 2 vol. 4 (1970).
Spektor, Yitzhak Elhanan, Resp. Ein Yitzhak , *Even ha-Ezer* vol. 1 (2004).
Tenenbum, Malkiel Z., Resp. Divrei Malkiel vol. 1 (1970).
Teshuvot HaGeonim (Coronel edition).
Teshuvot HaGeonim (Harkavi edition).
Teshuvot Ha-Geonim (Simcha Assaf ed., 1942).
Teshuvot Hakhmei Provence (Avraham Sofer ed., 1967).
Toledano, Yaakov M., Resp. ha-Yam ha-Gadol (1931).
Tufik, Eliyahu, Resp. Kol Eliyahu vol. 2 (1966).
Uziel, Ben-Zion M., Resp. Mishpatei Uziel *Even ha-Ezer* vol. 2, 5 (1964).
Resp. Piskei Uziel be-She'elot ha-Zman (1977).
Waldenberg, Eliezer Y., Resp. Tzitz Eliezer vol. 15 (1984).
Weil, Yaakov ben Yehuda, Resp. Mahariv (2001).
Weinberg, Yaakov, Resp. Sridei Esh vol. 1 (1961).
Wozner, Shmuel ha-Levi, Resp. Shevet ha-Levi *Even ha-Ezer* vol. 6 (2002).
Yaakov, ben Moshe, Resp. Mahari Birav (1988).
Yisrael Moshe ben Avraham, Resp. Masat Moshe vol. 1 (1998).
Yizhak, bar Sheshet, Parperet, Resp. Ribash (1546).
Yom Tov ben Avraham, Ishbili Ishbili (Ritba), Resp. Ritba (1959).
Yosef ben Meir, ibn Migash, Resp. HaRi Migash (1959).
Yosef C. ben Eliyahu, Resp. Rav Pealim *Orach Chaim* vol. 3 (1980).
Yosef, ibn Lev, Resp. Mahari ben Lev vol. 2 (1959).
Yosef, Ovadia, Resp. Yabia Omer *Hoshen Mishpat* vol. 3 (1954).
Yosef, Razin, Resp. Zafnat Pa'aneah vol. 1 (1999).

HALAKHIC BOOKS – MISCELLANEOUS

Afikei Meginim *Orach Chaim*.
AIIBISHITZ, YONATHAN, BNEI AHUVA (1965).
BEN SIMEON, RAPHAEL A., BAT NAAVAT HA-MARDUT (2000).
BENBENISHTI, CHAIM, KNESSET HA-GEDOLAH *Tur Even ha-Ezer* (1961).
BORNSTEIN, AVRAHAM Y., SANHEDRI KTANA ON TRACTATE SANHEDRIN (1980).
DINER, YOSEF Z. (RITZAD), NOVELLAE TO TRACTATE *Zebahim* vol. 4 (1999).
DISKIN, SHIMON M., MASSAT HA-MELEKH (1998).
EIGER, AKIVA, NOVELLAE TO TRACTATE *Ketubot* (1990).
Eliya Rabbah, *Orach Chaim*.
EPSTEIN, YEHIEL M., ARUKH HASHULHAN *Even ha-Ezer* (2007).
FEINSTEIN, MOSHE, DIBROT MOSHE on BT *Yevamot* (1979).
FRIEDMAN OF KARLIN, DAVID, PISKEI HALAKHOT *Hilkhot Ishut* vol. 2 (1971).
GUNZBERG, ARYEH L. BEN ASHER, SHAAGAT ARYEH (1735).
haCohen, Reem, Bade Aharon (1993).
HAI GAON, SEFER HA-SHETAROT LE-RAV HAI GAON (Simcha Assaf ed., 1930).
HAIM BEN IZHAK, OR ZARUA PISKE *Bava Metzia* vol. 3 (1862).
HAPARCHI, ASHTORI, KAFTOR VA PERACH (1994).
HELLER, ARYEH, AVNEI MILUIM (2000).
HENKIN, YOSEF E., PERUSHEY IBRA vol. 5 (1925).
HOROWITZ, AVRAHAM, KONTRAS HA-BIRURIM (1975).
HOROWITZ, PINHAS HALEVI, HAHAFLAA (1860).
HA-MAQNE *Kiddushin* (1962).
ISAAC BEN MOSHE (OR ZARUA), SEFER OR ZARUA vol. 1 (1958).
ISAAC, NUÑEZ BELMONTE, HIDUSHE SHA'AR HA-MELEKH ON TRACTATE *Kiddushin* (2000).
KAPACH, YOSEF, PERUSHE RABBENU SADYA GAON AL HA TORAH (1994).
KARELITZ, AVRAHAM Y., HAZON ISH *Nashim Hilkhot Kiddushin* (1968).
KARELITZ, AVROHOM Y. (HAZON ISH) & YAAKOV KANIEVSKY, HOLY LETTERS FROM THE OUTSTANDING RABBIS OF THE GENERATION (1968) (Heb.).
KOHUT, ALEXANDER, ARUKH HA-SHALEM (1955).
LANDAU, ELAZAR BEN ISRAEL, COMMENTARY YAD HA-MELEKH ON MAIMONIDES.
LEES, AVRAHAM (compiler) DIKDUKEI SOFRIM HA-SHALEM ON TRACTATE *Yevamot* vol. 2 (1983).
Leket Yosher, *Orach Chaim*.
LUBETSKY, YEHUDAH, EYN TENAI BENISSUIN (1930).
MAIMONIDES MOSES, THE GUIDE OF THE PERPLEXED (Chaim Rabin trans., 1995).
MEIR B. BARUCH OF ROTHENBURG (MAHARAM), SHA'AREI TESHUVOT (1891).
MEIR SIMCHA OF DVINSK, OR SAMEACH (1910).
Menachem ben Shlomo, Meiri, Bet ha-Behirah
MITCHAM, M. TIRZA, *Sefer ha-Bagrut le-Rav Shmuel ben Hofni Gaon ve-Sefer ha-Shanim le-Rav Yehuda ha-Kohen* (1999) (Heb.).
MOSHE, BEN HAVIV, GET PASHUT (1980).
MOSHE, BEN YAAKOV OF COUCY, SEFER MITZVOT GADOL.
OTZAR HAGEONIM, KIDDUSHIN – *Rosh Hashana* – *Ketubot* TRACTATE (Benjamin M. Levin ed., 1928).
OTZER HAPOSKIM vol. 1, 3–7, 13, 20 (1967).

Otzar ha-Geonim on BT Yoma
Posner, Meir, Beit Meir, *Even ha-Ezer* (2007).
Price, Avraham, Mishnat Avraham (1954).
Rabinovitz, Zeev W., Notes and Comments on Yerushalmi (1940).
Rozin, Yosef, Tzafnat Paneach (1979).
Seder Tannaim ve-Amoraim vol. 2 (1998).
Sha'ar ha-Melekh *le-Gerushin* (2006).
Shach, Elazar M. M., Avi Ezri (2d ed., 1967).
Shadmi, Avraham, Divrei Avraham vol. 2 (1968) .
Shlomo, Ganzfried, Lehem ve-simla on the *Shulhan Arukh, Yore De'ah* (1997).
Teomim, Aaron, Bigdei Aaron (1987).
The Constantinople Bet Din, Kiddushin al Tenai (1924).
Yechiel, M. Epstein, Arukh ha-Shulhan *Even ha-Ezer* (2007).
Yeshayah Aharon of Trani (Riaz), Sefer Ha-Makhria (1779).
Yizhak ben Abba Mari, Sefer Ha-Itur (Rabbi Yonah edition, 1874).
Zilberstein, Itzhak, Chashukei Chemed on Tractate Bava Metzia (2009).

VERDICTS

Rabbinical Court 056234263–21-1 Anonymous v. Anonymous, which was brought in 18 Ha-Din veha-Dayyan 12–13 (24.06.07) (2008).
High Rabbinical Court (Jerusalem) App. 49/5745 of 4 Tevet, 5746 (unpublished, 1986).
Rabbinical Court (Askelon) 1051202/1 Anonymous (unpublished, 1.11.15).
Rabbinical Court (Beer Sheva) 1031698/1 Anonymous (unpublished, 01.09.15).
Rabbinical Court (Beer Sheva) 1086905/2 Anonymous v. Anonymous (unpublished, 23.11.16).
Rabbinical Court (Haifa) 1087096/1 Anonymous (unpublished, 12.12.16).
Rabbinical Court (Haifa) Anonymous v. Anonymous (unpublished, 21.07.77).
Rabbinical Court (Tel Aviv) 1049932/8 Anonymous v. Anonymous (unpublished, 20.07.2016).
Rabbinical Court (Tel Aviv-Jaffa) 4237/1952 Anonymous v. Anonymous 1 PDR 340, 344 (unpublished, 1953).
Rabbinical Court 1064/1954, 1501/1954, Anonymous v. Anonymous, 1 PDR 257 (11.01.55).
Rabbinical Court 189/1967 Anonymous v. Anonymous, 7 PDR 83 (1 Adar Beit 1967).
Rabbinical Court 980/1967 Anonymous v. Anonymous, 7 PDR 353 (15 Tevet 1969).
Supreme Rabbinical Court appeal 120/1969 Anonymous v. Anonymous, 8 PDR 3, 9 (12 Av 1969).

BIBLIOGRAPHY – SECULAR SOURCES

Legislation

Adoption of Children Law § 16 (Isr.).
Divorce (Religious Marriages) Act 2002 Chapter 27, www.opsi.gov.uk/acts/acts2002/ukpga_20020027_en_1 (U.K.).
Divorce Act 1985 § 21.1 (Can.).
Egg Donation, 5770–2010 (Isr.).
Family Law Act 1986 §§ 2(4)–(7), 56(5)–(7) (Can. [Ontario]).
Genetic Information Law, 5761–2000 (Isr.).
Inheritance Law § 5 (Isr.).

N.Y. Dom. Rel. Law §§ 236b, 253 (McKinney 1986).
Population Registry Law, 5725–1965 § 22 (Isr.).
Restatement (Second) of Contracts § 191 (1981).
Surrogate Motherhood Agreements (Approval of Agreement and Status of the Newborn), 5756–1996, www.health.gov.il/LegislationLibrary/Poriut_05.pdf (Isr.).
The Israeli Health Ministry Regulations from 2008 – Guidelines for the Administration of Sperm Donation of the Ministry of Health, Nov. 8, 2007 (to be effective June 1, 2008) (Heb.).
Unif. Parentage Act §§ 3, 201(a)(1), 707 (1973).
Unif. Premarital Agreement Act 9c U.L.A. 39 (1983).
Unif. Premarital and Marital Agreements Act 9c U.L.A. 13 (Supp. 2014).

Verdicts

(Tel Aviv family court) 37745-03-14 Nili in re the Minors A. and B. V. Alon (not published, 27.04.14) (Heb.).
A.A. v. B.B., [2007] 220 O.A.C. 115, P 14 (Can.).
Andres A. v. Judith N., 591 N.Y.S.2d 946 (N.Y. Fam. Ct. 1992).
CA 449/79 Salame v. Salame PD 34(2) 779 (1980) (Heb.).
Casey v. Planned Parenthood, 112 S. Ct. 2791 (1992).
Com. ex rel. Strunk v. Cummins, 258 Pa. Super. 326, 392 A.2d 817 (Pa. Super. 1978).
Favrot v. Barnes, 332 So. 2d 873 (La. Ct. App. 1976).
In re Jesusa V., 32 Cal. 4th 588 (Cal. 2004).
In re Marriage of Dawley, 17 Cal. 3d 342 (1976).
In re Marriage of Vryonis, 202 Cal. App .3d 712 (Cal. App. 2 Dist., 1988).
In re Nicholas H., 28 Cal. 4th 56 (Cal. 2002).
In the Matter of the Marriage of Soleimani, 2012 WL 3729939 (Kan. Dist. Ct.).
Israeli High Court 337/62 Rizenfeld v. Jacobson, 17 PD 1009 (1963).
J.R. v. L.R., 386 N.J. Super. 475 (N.J. 2006).
Jacob v. Shultz-Jacob, 923 A.2d 473 (Pa. Super. 2007).
Kingsley v. Kingsley, 623 So. 2d 780 (Fla. Dist. Ct. App. 1993).
LaChappelle v. Mitten, 607 N.W.2d 151 (Minn. Ct. App. 2000).
Smith v. Cole, 553 So. 2d 847 (La. 1989).
Smith v. Jones, No. 85-53201401 (Mich. Cir. Ct. Wayne County March 14, 1986).
State on behalf of J.R. v. Mendoza, 240 Neb. 149 (Neb. 1992).
T.D. v. M.M.M., 730 So. 2d 873 (La. 1999).
TP (B.S.) 140/83 The State of Israel v. Amar ben Mehusan id al-Tsaria, P.M. 1986(2) 336 (1985).
Y.J. v. N.J., (1994) O.J. No. 2359.

Books

Aaron, B. Elijah of Nicomedia, *Sefer Mitzvot Gadol Gan Eden* (1972).
Abel, Yehudah, Confronting "Iggun": A Combination of Three Possible Solutions to the Problem of the Chained Wife in Jewish Law (2011).
Ahdut, Eliyahu, Ma'amad ha-Isha ha-Yehudia be-Bavel be-Tequfat ha-Talmud (PhD thesis, Hebrew University of Jerusalem, 1999) (Heb.).
al Ati, Hammudah Abd, The Family Structure in Islam (1977).
al-'Āmilī, al-Ḥurr, Wasā'il al-Sẖī'a (1288).
Al-Bahiri, Mahmoud be Ismail, Zahih Al-Bahiri: Mishkol vol. 4 (1950).

Albeck, Hanoch, Genesis Rabbah (1965) (Heb.).
Introduction to the Mishna (1959) (Heb.).
Mehkarim ba-beraita u-va-tosefta ve-yaḥasan la-talmud (1970) (Heb.).
The Six Orders of the Mishnah Seder Nashim (2d ed. 1955) (Heb.).
Albeck, Shalom, Principles of Talmudic Private Law (1994) (Heb.).
al-Darami, Abdalla ben Abdalrahman, Sanan Al-Daram vol. 2 (1966).
Alfasi, David ben Avraham, Kitab Jama al-Alfalath vol. 2 (1936–45).
al-Kirkisani, Abu Yusuf Ya'kub, Ya'qub al-Qirqisani on Jewish Sects and Christianity: A Translation of "Kitab al-anwar" Book 1 (1984).
Aranoff, Susan & Rivka Haut, The Wed-Locked Agunot: Orthodox Jewish Women Chained to Dead Marriages (2015).
Auerbach, Ephraim E., Hazal Pirkei Emunot ve-Deot (Heb.).
Baron, Salo W., A Social and Religious History of the Jews vol. 2 (1952).
Basol-Taha, Hiba, Temporary Marriage in Islam from the Perspectives of Shari'a, Civil Law and Social Norms (Arab.) (MA thesis, Bar-Ilan University, the Department of Arabic, 2008).
Beeri, Tehila, A Solution to the "Mamzer" Problem Afforded by Recent Medical Advances (MA thesis, 2005) (Heb.).
Behor, Guy, Between Vision and Reality: Law in the Arab World (2002).
Belkin, Samuel, Philo and the Oral Law: The Philonic Interpretation of Biblical Law in Relation to the Palestinian Halakah (1940).
Ben-Menahem, Hanina, Judicial Deviation in Talmudic Law: Governed by Men, Not by Rules (1991).
Berkovits, Eliezer, Conditionality in Marriage and Divorce (1967) (Heb.).
Biale, David, Eros and the Jews: From Biblical Israel to Contemporary America (1997).
Blackstone, William, Commentaries on the Laws of England (1962).
Bleich, David J., Contemporary Halakhic Problems vol. 4 (1998).
Bloch, Chaim, Veda ma-sheTashiv (1962) (Heb.).
Boteach, Shmuel, Kosher Sex (1998).
Boyarin, Daniel, Carnal Israel: Reading Sex in Talmudic Culture (1995).
Unheroic Conduct: The Rise of Heterosexuality and the Invention of the Jewish Man (1997).
Breitowitz, Irving A., Between Civil and Religious Law: The Plight of the Agunah in American Society (1993).
Browne, Edward G., A Year Amongst the Persians (1927).
Broyde, Michael J., Marriage, Divorce, and the Abandoned Wife in Jewish Law (2001).
Büchler, Adolf, Studies in Jewish History (1956).
Caetani, Leone, Annali Del'islam (1972).
Carter, George W., Zoroastrianism and Judaism (1970).
Cohen, Boaz, Jewish and Roman Law vol. 1 (1966).
Cohen, Jeremy, "Be Fertile and Increase, Fill the Earth and Master It": The Ancient and Medieval Career of a Biblical Text (1989).
Cohen, Yedidya, Enactments of the Sages Regarding Matrimonial Property vol. 1 (1997).
Cohn, Haim, Jewish Law in Israeli Jurisprudence (1968).
Corinaldi, Michael, Staus, Family and Succession Laws: Between Religion and State (2004) (Heb.).

Coulson, Noel J., A History of Islamic Law (1964).
Curzon, George N., Persia and the Persian Question vol. 1 (1996).
De Vries, Benjamin, Toldot Hahalacha Hatalmudit (1966) (Heb.).
Doi dur, Rahman I., Shari'ah: The Islamic Law (1984).
Dvorks, Elyakom, On Your Adopted Child: Child Adoption in the Halakha Perspective (2005) (Heb.).
Ellinson, Getsel, Non-Halakhic Marriage: A Study of the Rabbinic Sources (1975) (Heb.).
Elon, Menachem, Jewish Law Cases and Materials (1999).
Jewish Law: History, Sources, Principles (3d enlarged ed., 1988) (Heb.).
The Status of Women: Law and Judgment, Tradition and Transition: The Values of a Jewish and Democratic State (2005).
Englander, Yakir, Sexuality and the Body in the New Religious Zionist (2015).
Epstein, Jacob N., Introduction to Amoraitic Literature: Babylonian Talmud and Yerushalmi (1962) (Heb.).
Introduction to the Text of the Mishnah vol. 1 (2000) (Heb.).
Epstein, Louis M., The Jewish Marriage Contract (1954) (Heb.).
Ertman, Martha M., Love's Promises: How Formal & Informal Contracts Shape All Kinds of Families (2015).
Falk, Zeev W., Introduction to Jewish Law of the Second Commonwealth vol. II (1978).
Marriage and Divorce : Reforms in the Family Life of German-French Jewry (1961) (Heb.).
The Law of Marriage (1983).
Feldman, David M., Birth Control and Jewish Law: Marital Relations, Contraception, and Abortion as Set Forth in the Classic Texts of Jewish Law (1968).
Finegold, Wilfred J., Artificial Insemination (1964).
Fineman, Martha A., The Neutered Mother, the Sexual Family, and Other Twentieth-Century Tragedies (1995).
Fleishman, Joseph, Father-daughter Relations in Biblical Law (2011).
Parent and Child in Ancient Near East and the Bible (1999) (Heb.).
Fraenkel, Zecharias, Introduction to the Jerusalem Talmud (1967). (Heb.).
Frankel, David H., Studies in Saadiah Gaon's Arabic Translations 21 (MA thesis, The Ohio State University, 2012).
Frankel, Yonah, The Ways of the Midrash and the Aggadah (1991) (Heb.).
Frankel, Zechariah, Introduction to the Jerusalem Talmud (1967) (Heb.).
Freiman, Avraham C., Seder Kiddushin Venisuin Aharei Hatimat Hatalmud (1944).
Friedman, Mordechai A., Jewish Marriage in Palestine (1980).
Jewish Polygyny in the Middle Ages (1986).
Ribui Nashim be-Yisrael (1986) (Heb.).
Gafni, Isaiah, The Jews of Babylonia in the Talmudic Era (1990) (Heb.).
Gilat, Israel Z., Family Law – The Relations between Parents and Children – Alimony, Financial Responsibilities, Custody and Education (2000) (Heb.).
Gilat, Yitzhak D., Studies in the Development of the Halakha (1992).
Ginzberg, Louis, Yeruhalmi Fragments from the Genizah (1909) (Heb.).
Goitein, Shelomo D., A Mediterranean Society: The Jewish Communities of the Arab World as Portrayed in the Documents of the Cairo Geniza vol. III (1967).

Goitein, Shlomo D. & Aharon Ben Shemesh, ISLAMIC LAW IN THE STATE OF ISRAEL (1957).
Gold, Michael, AND Hannah Wept: INFERTILITY, ADOPTION, AND THE JEWISH COUPLE (1988).
Goldberg, Monique S. & Diana Villa, Za'akat Dalot: HALAKHIC SOLUTIONS TO THE AGUNOT OF OUR TIME (2006) (Heb.).
Goldman, Alex J., JUDAISM CONFRONTS CONTEMPORARY ISSUES (1978).
Goldstein, Joseph ET AL., BEFORE THE BEST INTERESTS OF THE CHILD (1979).
BEYOND THE BEST INTERESTS OF THE CHILD (1980).
THE BEST INTERESTS OF THE CHILD: THE LEAST DETRIMENTAL ALTERNATIVE (1996).
Goldziher, Ignac, INTRODUCTION TO ISLAMIC THEOLOGY AND LAW (Andras & Ruth Hamori trans., 1981).
Goren, Shlomo, THE LAWS OF MEDICINE: HALACHIC INVESTIGATIONS INTO MEDICAL TOPICS (2001) (Heb.).
Gourji, Abu'l-Qasim, TEMPORARY MARRIAGE (*Mut'a*) IN ISLAMIC LAW (1987).
Graveson, Ronald H., STATUS IN THE COMMON LAW (1953).
Grazi, Richard V., BE FRUITFUL AND MULTIPLY: FERTILITY THERAPY AND THE JEWISH TRADITION (1994).
OVERCOMING INFERTILITY (2005).
Green, Yosi, PROCREATION IN THE MODERN ERA: LEGAL AND HALACHIC PERSPECTIVES (2008) (Heb.).
Gribetz, Arthur, STRANGE BEDFELLOWS: MUTAT AL-NISA AND MUTAT AL-HAJJ: A STUDY BASED ON SUNNI AND SHII SOURCES OF TAFSIR, HADITH AND FIQH (1994).
Griffini, Eugenio, CORPUS IURIS DI ZAYD IBN 'ALF (1919).
Gulak, Asher, LEGAL DOCUMENTS IN THE TALMUD IN LIGHT OF GREEK PAPYRI AND GREEK AND ROMAN LAW (edited and supplemented by Ranon Katzoff, 1994) (Heb.).
OTZAR HA-SHETAROT (1926).
Hacker, Daphna, LEGALIZED FAMILIES IN THE ERA OF BORDERED GLOBALIZATION Ch. 4 (2017).
Hacohen, Aviad, THE TEARS OF THE OPPRESSED: AN EXAMINATION OF THE AGUNAH PROBLEM: BACKGROUND AND HALAKHIC SOURCES (2004).
HaCohen, Mordechai, HALACHOT AND HALICHOT (1975) (Heb.).
HaCohen, Moshe S., THE JEWISH LAW OF CHILD MAINTENANCE PAYMENTS – ITS FORMATION, DEVELOPMENT AND CIRCUMSTANCES (Doctoral dissertation, 1998) (Heb.).
Haeri, Shahla, LAW OF DESIRE: TEMPORARY MARRIAGE IN SHI'I ISLAM (1989).
Halevy, Isaac, DOROT HARISHONIM (1967) (Heb.).
Halivni, David, SOURCES AND TRADITIONS: A SOURCE CRITICAL COMMENTARY ON SEDER NASHIM (1968) (Heb.).
Halperin-Kaddari, Ruth, WOMEN IN ISRAEL: A STATE OF THEIR OWN (2004).
Hamilton, Alexander D., A NEW ACCOUNT OF THE EAST INDIES (1732).
Havshosh, Hilel, CHILD SUPPORT: PARENTAL OBLIGATIONS, JEWISH LAW (2004) (Heb.).
Heinemann, Yizhak, PHILONS GRIECHISCHE UND JUDISCHE BILDUNG:KULTURVERGLEICHENDE UNTERSUCHUNGEN ZU PHILONS DARSTELLUNG DER JUDISCHEN GESETZE (1932).
Hurgronje, C. Snouck, MEKKA (1888).
VERSPREIDE GESCHRIFTEN vol. 6 (1923).

Irshai, Ronit, FERTILITY AND JEWISH: FEMINIST PERSPECTIVES ON ORTHODOX RESPONSA LITERATURE (Joel A. Linsider trans., 2012).
Jachter, Chaim & Ezra Frazer, GRAY MATTER: DISCOURSES IN CONTEMPORARY HALACHAH (2000).
Jackson, Bernard S. ET AL., AGUNAH: THE MANCHESTER ANALYSIS (2011).
Jafri, Husain M., THE ORIGINS AND EARLY DEVELOPMENT OF SHI'A ISLAM (1979).
Jakobovits, Immanuel, JEWISH MEDICAL ETHICS: A COMPARATIVE AND HISTORICAL STUDY OF THE JEWISH RELIGIOUS ATTITUDE TO MEDICINE AND ITS PRACTICE (1959).
Jastrow, Marcus, A DICTIONARY OF THE TARGUMIM, THE TALMUD BABLI AND YERUSHALMI, AND THE MIDRASHIC LITERATURE (1950).
Jolowicz, Herbert F. & Barry Nicholas, A HISTORICAL INTRODUCTION TO THE STUDY OF ROMAN LAW(1972).
Kahana, Baruch, BAILMENT LAW (1998) (Heb.).
GUARANTEE LAW (1991) (Heb.).
RELINQUISHMENT IN JEWISH LAW (Doctoral dissertation, 2006) (Heb.).
Kahana, Kopel, THE THEORY OF MARRIAGE IN JEWISH LAW (1962) (Heb.).
Kahane, Yitschak Z., METHODS TO ALLOW AN AGUNAH TO MARRY (1947).
SEFER HAAGUNOT: OSEF MEKOROT IM PERUSHIM BERRUIM VEHEROT (1954).
Kahn, Susan M., REPRODUCING JEWS: A CULTURAL ACCOUNT OF ASSISTED CONCEPTION IN ISRAEL (2000).
Khomeini, Ruhollah, A CLARIFICATION OF QUESTIONS: AN UNABRIDGED TRANSLATION OF RESALEH TOWZIH AL-MASAEL (J. Borujerdi trans., 1984).
Klaus, Marshall H., MATERNAL-INFANT BONDING (1976).
Krause, Harry D., ILLEGITIMACY: LAW AND SOCIAL POLICY (1971).
Lacave, Jose L., MEDIEVAL KETUBOT FROM SEFARAD (2002).
Landau, Melanie, TRADITION AND EQUALITY IN JEWISH MARRIAGE: BEYOND THE SANCTIFICATION OF SUBORDINATION (2012).
Levy, Israel, JAHRESBERICHT DES JUDISCH – THEOLOGISCHEN SEMINARS (1895–1914) (Heb.).
Lewin, Benjamin M., GINZE QEDEM vol. 2 (1922).
Libson, Gideon, JEWISH AND ISLAMIC LAW: A COMPARATIVE STUDY OF CUSTOM DURING THE GEONIC PERIOD (2003).
Lieberman, Saul & Eliezer S. Rosenthal, YERUSHALMI NEZIQIN (2008) (Heb.).
Lieberman, Saul, HILKHOT HA-YERUSHALMI OF RABBI MOSES BEN MAIMON (1947) (Heb.).
ON THE YERUSHALMI (1929) (Heb.).
THE TALMUD OF CAESAREA (1931) (Heb.).
TOSEFTA KI-FSHUTAH: A COMPREHENSIVE COMMENTARY ON THE TOSEFTA (1973).
Lifshitz, Berachyahu, PROMISE: OBLIGATION AND ACQUISITION IN JEWISH LAW (1998).
Lifshitz, Shahar, CONTRACTUAL REGULATION OF SPOUSAL RELATIONSHIP IN CIVIL LAW (PhD thesis, Bar-Ilan University, 2002) (Heb.).
Maharezi, Aly-Ahbar, LA FAMILLE IRANIENNE (1938).
Maimon, Nili, ADOPTION OF CHILDREN: LEGAL PRINCIPLES (1994) (Heb.).
Mann, Jacob, THE JEWS IN EGYPT AND IN PALESTINE UNDER THE FATIMID CALIPHS (1920).
MARCELLINUS AMMIANUS, xiv. 4, 4.
Margalit, Yehezkel, DETERMINING LEGAL PARENTAGE BY AGREEMENT (2011) (Heb.).

PUBLIC REGULATION AND PRIVATE AGREEMENT ABOUT SPOUSAL CONJUGAL PRIVILEGES IN JEWISH LAW (LLM thesis, Bar-Ilan University, 2006) (Heb.).
Meiselman, Moshe, JEWISH WOMAN IN JEWISH LAW (1987).
Meron, Yaakov, MOSLEM LAW IN COMPARATIVE PERSPECTIVE (2001).
Milne, Brian, RIGHTS OF THE CHILD: 25 YEARS AFTER THE ADOPTION OF THE UN CONVENTION (2015).
Mir-Hosseini, Ziba, MARRIAGE ON TRIAL: A STUDY OF ISLAMIC FAMILY LAW: IRAN AND MOROCCO COMPARED (1993).
Mitteis, Ludwig & George A. Wilken, GRUNDZÜGE DER PAPYRUSKUNDE (1912).
Morier, James J., THE ADVENTURES OF HAJJI BABA OF ISPAHAN vol. 3 (1970).
Moskovitz, Leib, TERMINOLOGY OF THE YERUSHALMI: THE PRINCIPAL TERMS (2009).
Muller, Victor, EN SYRIE AVEC LES BEDOUINS: LES TRIBUS DU (1931).
Murata, Sachiko, TEMPORARY MARRIAGE IN ISLAMIC LAW (MA thesis, Divinity School, University of Tehran, 1974).
Nasir, Amal J., THE ISLAMIC LAW OF PERSONAL STATUS (1990).
Neubauer, Yaakov, THE HISTORY OF MARRIAGE LAWS IN BIBLE AND TALMUD (1994) (Heb.).
Neusner, Yaakov, A HISTORY OF THE JEWS IN BABYLONIA vol. 2 (1966).
Novak, David, HALAKHAH IN A THEOLOGICAL DIMENSION (1985).
O'Halloran, Kerry, THE POLITICS OF ADOPTION: INTERNATIONAL PERSPECTIVES ON LAW, POLICY AND PRACTICE (2015).
Olszowy-Schlanger, Judith, KARAITE MARRIAGE DOCUMENTS FROM THE CAIRO GENIZA (1998).
Petrushevsky, Il'ia P., ISLAM IN IRAN (Hubert Evans trans., 1985).
PHILO OF ALEXANDRIA, DE SPECIALIBUS LEGIBUS vol. III (1975).
Polak, Jakob E., PERSIEN: DAS LAND UND SEINE BEWOHNER: ETHNOGRAPHISCHE SCHILDERUNGEN vol. I (1865).
Porten, Bezalel, ARCHIVES FROM ELEPHANTINE (1968).
JEWS OF ELEPHANTINE AND ARAMEANS OF SYENE FIFTH CENTURY BCE (1974) (Heb.).
Post, Stephen G., ENCYCLOPEDIA OF BIOETHICS (2004).
Razyel, Jonathan, GENETIC CLONING – A JEWISH PERSPECTIVE: A COLLECTION OF ESSAYS (2004) (Heb.).
Reinitz, Yaakov, THE GUARDIAN OF ORPHANS IN JEWISH LAW (Doctoral dissertation, 1984) (Heb.).
Reveh, Inbar, FEMINIST REREADINGS OF RABBINIC LITERATURE (Kaeren Fish trans., 2014).
Riskin, Shlomo, WOMEN AND JEWISH DIVORCE: THE REBELLIOUS WIFE, THE AGUNAH AND THE RIGHT OF WOMEN TO INITIATE DIVORCE IN JEWISH LAW. A HALAKHIC SOLUTION (1989).
Rispler-Chaim, Vardit, ISLAMIC MEDICAL ETHICS IN THE TWENTIETH CENTURY (1993).
Rivlin, Yosef, INHERITANCE AND WILLS IN JEWISH LAW (1999) (Heb.).
MISHNAT HANAKHALOT: THE LAW OF INHERITANCE AND WILLS (2015) (Heb.).
Robertson, Smith William, KINSHIP & MARRIAGE IN EARLY ARABIA (1903).
Roderick, Phillips, PUTTING ASUNDER: A HISTORY OF DIVORCE IN WESTERN SOCIETY (1988).
Rose, Jenny, ZOROASTRIANISM: AN INTRODUCTION (2011).
Rosenfeld, Jennie & David S. Ribner, THE NEWLYWED'S GUIDE TO PHYSICAL INTIMACY (2011).

Rosen-Zvi, Ishay, DEMONIC DESIRES: "YETZER HARA" AND THE PROBLEM OF EVIL IN LATE ANTIQUITY (2011).

Rossini, Conti, PRINCIPI DI DIRITTO CONSUETUDINARIO DELL'ERITREA (1916).

Russell, Diana E. H., RAPE IN MARRIAGE (1982).

Satlow, Michael. L., JEWISH MARRIAGE IN ANTIQUITY (2001).

Schacht, Joseph, AN INTRODUCTION TO ISLAMIC LAW (1964).

THE ORIGINS OF MUHAMMADAN JURISPRUDENCE (1950).

Schepansky, Israel, THE TAKKANOT OF ISRAEL vol. 2 (1992).

Schereschewsky, Benzion, FAMILY LAW IN ISRAEL (4th ed., 1993) (Heb.).

Schremer, Adiel, JEWISH MARRIAGE IN TALMUDIC BABYLONIA (PhD thesis, Hebrew University of Jerusalem, 1996) (Heb.).

MALE AND FEMALE HE CREATED THEM (2003) (Heb.).

Schwarzwald, Heidi ET AL., INTERNATIONAL ADOPTION AND CLINICAL PRACTICE (2015).

Shapiro, Marc B., BETWEEN THE YESHIVAH WORLD AND MODERN ORTHODOXY: THE LIFE AND WORKS OF RABBI JEHIEL JACOB WEINBERG 1884–1966 (1999).

Sheinfeld, Avraham, TORTS (Nahum Rakover ed., 1991) (Heb.).

Shifman, Pinhas, FAMILY LAW IN ISRAEL vol. 2 (1989) (Heb.).

Shilo, Shmuel, COMMENTARY TO THE SUCCESSION LAW, 1965 vol. 1 (1992) (Heb.).

Sinclair, Daniel B., JEWISH BIOMEDICAL LAW: LEGAL AND EXTRA-LEGAL DIMENSIONS (2003).

Sindawi, Khalid, TEMPORARY MARRIAGE IN SUNNI AND SHIITE ISLAM: A COMPARATIVE STUDY (2013).

Sokoloff, Michael, A DICTIONARY OF JEWISH PALESTINIAN ARAMAIC OF THE BYZANTINE PERIOD (1990).

Sperber, Daniel, A DICTIONARY OF GREEK AND LATIN LEGAL TERMS IN RABBINICAL LITERATURE (1984).

ROMAN PALESTINE, 200–400: MONEY AND PRICES (1991).

Steinberg, Avraham, ENCYCLOPEDIA OF JEWISH MEDICAL ETHICS: A COMPILATION OF JEWISH MEDICAL LAW ON ALL TOPICS OF MEDICAL INTEREST (Fred Rosner trans., 2003).

Steinberg, Meyer, RESPONSUM ON PROBLEMS OF ADOPTION IN JEWISH LAW (1969).

Stern, Gertrude H., MARRIAGE IN EARLY ISLAM (1939).

Tamar, Yissachar, ALEY TAMAR ON SEDER NEZIKIN, TRACTATE MAKOT (1983).

Tarmadi, Abu Isa M., AL-JAMA AL-ZAHIAH SNAN AL-TARAMADI vol. 3 (1995).

Tate, Julia J., SURROGACY: WHAT PROGRESS SINCE HAGAR, BILHAH, AND ZILPAH! (1994).

Tchernowitz, Chaim, HISTORY OF HEBREW LAW (1943) (Heb.).

Teichman, Jenny, ILLEGITIMACY: AN EXAMINATION OF BASTARDY (1982).

von Kipp, Theodor & Martin Wolff, DAS FAMILIENRECHT (1923).

Warhaftig, Itamar, UNDERTAKING IN JEWISH LAW – ITS VALIDITY, CHARACTER AND TYPES (2001).

Warhaftig, Shillem, THE JEWISH LAW OF CONTRACT (1974) (Heb.).

Warhaftig, Zerach, ZRICHAT HASHANI ON TRACTATE MAKOT – SANHEDRIN (1973).

ZRICHAT HASHANI ON TRACTATE NASHIM (2000) (Heb.).

Weiss, Avraham, STUDIES IN THE LITERATURE OF THE AMORAIM (1962) (Heb.).

THE TALMUD IN ITS DEVELOPMENT (1954) (Heb.).

Weiss, Susan M. & Netty C. Gross-Horowitz, MARRIAGE AND DIVORCE IN THE JEWISH STATE: ISRAEL'S CIVIL WAR (2013).

Weitzman, Lenore J., THE MARRIAGE CONTRACT: SPOUSES, LOVERS, AND THE LAW (1987).
Westermarck, Edvard A., THE HISTORY OF HUMAN MARRIAGE (1922).
Westreich, Avishalom, NO-FAULT DIVORCE IN JEWISH TRADITION (2014) (Heb.).
TALMUD-BASED SOLUTIONS TO THE PROBLEM OF THE AGUNAH (2012).
Westreich, Elimelech, TRANSITIONS IN THE LEGAL STATUS OF THE WIFE IN JEWISH LAW: A JOURNEY AMONG TRADITIONS (2002) (Heb.).
Wiesner-Hanks, Merry, CHRISTIANITY AND SEXUALITY IN THE EARLY MODERN WORLD: REGULATING DESIRE, REFORMING PRACTICE (2010).
Wilken, George A., DAS MATRIARCHAT (DAS MUTTERRECHT) BEI DEN ALTEN ARABERN (1884).
Witte, John, FROM SACRAMENT TO CONTRACT: MARRIAGE, RELIGION, AND LAW IN THE WESTERN TRADITION (1997).
THE SINS OF THE FATHERS: THE LAW AND THEOLOGY OF ILLEGITIMACY RECONSIDERED (2009).
Wolff, Eliezer, YERUSHAT BENEI HA-ZUG BA-MISHPAT HA-IVRI VE-HA-YISRAELI (JurD thesis, Hebrew University, 1971).
Yaron, Reuven, THE LAW OF THE ELEPHANTINE DOCUMENTS (1968) (Heb.).
Zafran, Ruth, THE RIGHT OF OFFSPRING TO SEEK OUT THEIR BIOLOGICAL PARENTS (Doctoral dissertation, 2004) (Heb.).
Zohar, Noam J., ALTERNATIVES IN JEWISH BIOETHICS (1997).
Zohar, Zvi & Avraham Sagi, GIYUR VEZEHUT YEHUDIT (1994) (Heb.).
Zucker, Moshe, AL TIRGUM RASAG LA-TORAH: PARSHANUT, HALAKHA U-POLITIKA BE-TIRGUM HA-TORAH SHEL RABBI SADYA GAON: TE'UDOT U-MEHKARIM (1959) (Heb.).
BIBLICAL ENCYCLOPEDIA vol. 4 (Moshe D. Cassuto et al. eds., 1954) (Heb.).
IRAN: A COUNTRY STUDY (Helen Chapin Metz ed., 1989).
JEWISH EXPLORATIONS OF SEXUALITY (Jonathan Magonet ed., 1995).
THE PRENUPTIAL AGREEMENT: HALAKHIC AND PASTORAL CONSIDERATIONS (Basil Herring & Kenneth Auman eds., 1996).
ENCYCLOPAEDIA JUDAICA, www.jewishvirtuallibrary.org/jsource/judaica/ejud_0002_0001_0_00486.html.
SEXUALITY AND THE FAMILY IN HISTORY: COLLECTED ESSAYS (Israel Bartal & Isaiah Gafni eds., 1998) (Heb.).
TALMUDIC ENCYCLOPEDIA (Shlomo Zevin et al. eds., 1978).
WOMEN IN IRAN FROM THE RISE OF ISLAM TO 1800 (Guity Nashat & Lois Beck eds., 2003).

Articles and Chapters

Abel, Yehudah, *Comments on "'En Tenai BeNissu'in" by R. Zevi Gertner and R. Bezalel Karlinski* (Working Papers of the Agunah Research Unit, 2008), http://static1.1.sqspcdn.com/static/f/784513/11612816/1302165409993/Yehudah+Abel+Comments+by+R.+Zavi+Gertner+2008.pdf?token=KWWAVKlqn5e7bj6MB5UrhV2slUM%3D.
Comments on R. Broyde's Tripartite Agreement (Working Papers of the Agunah Research Unit, July 2009), http://static1.1.sqspcdn.com/static/f/784513/11612873/1302166102187/Yehudah+Abel+Comment+on+Dayan+Broyde%27s+Tripartite+Agreement+2009.pdf?token=KQ9J2S4rDIS%2FomB8Q2HZAygf2xs%3D.

Hafqa'ah, Kefiyyah, Tena'im (Working Papers of the Agunah Research Unit, June 2008), http://static1.1.sqspcdn.com/static/f/784513/11612810/1302165339947/Yehudah+Abel+Hafqa%27ah+Kefiyyah+Tena%27im+2008.pdf?token=c6U9xvBnSlpgv6gKGLrXyvv7sao%3D.

The Plight of the Agunah and Conditional Marriage, 1 MELILAH 31 (2005/1), http://static1.1.sqspcdn.com/static/f/784513/11612748/1302164478633/Yehudah+Abel+Plight+of+the+Agunah+and+Conditional+Marriage+2008.pdf?token=lJWm300NvHYcu700bTywo7mN668%3D.

Abramson, Shraga, *On the Takkanah of Tuletula (Toledo) Regarding the Husband's Inheritance of His Wife's Estate*, 60(2) ZION 201 (1995) (Heb.).

Agmon, Talia, *Genetic Testing of Children – Why Not? Questions Regarding the Legislation on Genetic Testing of Children in Israel*, 6 L. & BUS. 295 (2007) (Heb.).

Allen, Karelton C., *Status and Capacity*, 46 LQR 277 (1930).

Aminah, Noah, *Man Havya le-Yoma*, 81 SINAI 169 (1977).

Andaya, Barbara Watson, *From Temporary Wife to Prostitute: Sexuality and Economic Change in Early Modern Southeast Asia*, 9(4) J. WOMEN'S HISTORY 11 (1998).

Annas, George J., *Redefining Parenthood and Protecting Embryos: Why We Need New Laws*, 14 HASTINGS CTR. RPT. 5 (1984).

Apter, Itai & Nurit Inbal, *Posthumous Insemination – A Nightmare or a Dream Come True? – Following the Attorney General's Directive 1.2202*, A(1) LAWATCH 11 (2004) (Heb.).

Aranoff, Susan, *Two Views of Marriage – Two Views of Women: Reconsidering Tav Lemeitav Tan Du mi-Lemeitav Armelu*, 3 NASHIM 199 (2000).

Ariel, Shmuel, *Pilagshut ena "Haverut,"* 17 AKDAMOT 41 (2006).

Ariel, Yaakov, *Artificial Insemination and Surrogacy*, in COLLECTION OF ESSAYS: MEDICAL ETHICS AND JEWISH LAW 171 (Mordechai Halperin & Yeruchim Primer eds. 1996) (Heb.).

Ha-Pilegesh u-Ma'amadah ha-Hilkhati be-Miqra, 8 MEGADIM 57 (1989).

Ariel, Yaakov, et al., *Postmortem Sperm Procurement – Juridical and Halachic Aspects*, 139 HAREFUAH 331 (2000) (Heb.).

Arussi, Razon, *The Ethnic Factor in Rabbinical Decision-Making – (Enforcement of Divorce on the Ground of Revulsion in the Yemenite Community*, 10–11 DINÉ ISRAEL 125 (1981–83).

Assaf, Simcha, *Appointing Women as Apotropos*, 2 JEWISH L. 75 (1927) (Heb.).

Different Decrees and Customs Relating to the Husband's Right of Inheritance, 1 MADDA'EI HA-YAHUDUT 80 (1926) (Heb.).

Atlas, Samuel, *Addition to When a Man Betroths a Woman, He Does so under the Conditions Laid down by the Rabbis*, 79 SINAI 102 (1976) (Heb.).

When a Man Betroths a Woman, He Does so under the Conditions Laid down by the Rabbis, 75 SINAI 119 (1974) (Heb.).

Auerbach, Shlomo Z., *Artificial Insemination*, 1 NOAM 145 (1958) (Heb.).

Axelrod, Gedalia, *The Obligation of the Mother in Paying Her Child Support*, 4 SHURAT HADIN 66 (1998) (Heb.).

Baker, Katharine K., *Bargaining or Biology? The History and Future of Paternity Law and Parental Status*, 14 CORNELL J.L. & PUB. POL'Y 1 (2004).

Bionormativity and the Construction of Parenthood, 42 GA. L. REV. 649 (2008).

Baker, Mark, *The Voice of the Deserted Jewish Woman, 1867–1870*, 2(1) JEWISH SOCIAL STUD. 98 (1995).

Bass, David, *Contracts According to Din Torah*, 1 KETER 17 (1996).

Baum, Kenneth, *Golden Eggs: Towards the Rational Regulation of Oocyte Donation*, 2001 BYU L. REV. 107 (2001).

Bazak, Yaakov, *The Obligation of the Mother to Share the Child Support in Jewish Law*, 32 HAPRAKLIT 357 (1979–80) (Heb.).

Beeri-Alon, Tehila, *Revisiting Some Halakhic Fundamental Principles for Solving the Mamzer Problem in Light of Recent Medical Advances*, 26 SHNATON HA-MISHPAT HAIVRI 43 (2009–11) (Heb.).

Bernstein, Gaia, *The Socio-Legal Acceptance of New Technologies: A Close Look at Artificial Insemination*, 77 WASH. L. REV. 1035 (2002).

Bick, Ezra, *Ovum Donations: A Rabbinic Conceptual Model of Maternity*, in JEWISH LAW AND THE NEW REPRODUCTIVE TECHNOLOGIES 83 (Emanuel Feldman & Joel B. Wolowelsky eds., 1997).

Ovum Donations: A Rabbinic Conceptual Model of Maternity, 28 TRADITION 28 (1993).

Surrogate Motherhood, 7 TECHUMIN 266 (1986) (Heb.).

Bix, Brian, *Bargaining in the Shadow of Love: The Enforcement of Premarital Agreements and How We Think about Marriage*, 40 WM. & MARY L. REV. 145 (1998).

Bleich, J. David, *A Suggested Antenuptial Agreement: A Proposal in Wake of Avitzur*, 7 J. HALACHA & CONTEMPORARY SOC'Y 25 (1984).

In Vitro Fertilization: Questions of Maternal Identity and Conversion, 25 TRADITION 82 (1991).

In Vitro Fertilization: Questions of Maternal Identity and Conversion, in JEWISH LAW AND THE NEW REPRODUCTIVE TECHNOLOGIES 46 (Emanuel Feldman & Joel B. Wolowelsky eds., 1997).

Mitochondrial DNA Replacement: How Many Mothers?, 48(4) TRADITION (2015).

Survey of Recent Halakhic Periodical Literature: Kiddushei Taut: Annulment as a Solution to the Agunah Problem, 33 TRADITION 90 (1998).

Blumberg, J., *Munahim Mishpati'im Aravi'im mi-Dine ha-Kinyan be-Geonim uve-Rambam*, 14–15 SHNATON HA-MISHPAT HA-IVRI 61 (1988–89) (Heb.).

Borten, Laurence Drew, *Sex, Procreation, and the State Interest in Marriage*, 102(4) COLUMBIA L. REV. 1089 (2002).

Boyle-Lewicki, Edna, *Need World's Collide: The Hudad Crimes of Islamic Law and International Human Rights*, 13 N.Y. INT'L L. REV. 43 (2000).

Breault, Adam M., *"Onan's Transgression": The Continuing Legal Battle over Prisoners' Procreation Rights*, 66 ALBANY L. REV. 289 (2002).

Breitowitz, Irving, *The Plight of the Agunah: A Study in Halacha, Contract, and the First Amendment*, 51 MD. L. REV. 312 (1992).

Brewer, David I., *Jewish Women Divorcing Their Husbands in Early Judaism: The Background to Papyrus Se'elim 13*, 92(3) HARVARD THEOLOGICAL REV. 349 (1999).

Brody, Robert, *Evidence for Divorce by Jewish Women?*, 50 J. JEWISH STUD. 230 (1999).

Is the Ketubba of Biblical or of Rabbinic Origin, NETI'OT LEDAVID: JUBILEE VOLUME FOR DAVID WEISS HALIVNI 37 (Yaakov Elman et al. eds., 2004) (Heb.).

Broyd, Michael J., *A Proposed Tripartite Prenuptial Agreement to Solve the Agunah Problem: A Solution without Any Innovation*, 20 JEWISH L. ASS'N STUD. 1 (2010).

Child Custody in Jewish Law: A Pure Law Analysis, www.jlaw.com/Articles/childcus2.html.

Cloning People: A Jewish Law Analysis of the Issues, 30 CONN. L. REV. 503 (1998).

Error in the Creation of Marriages in Modern Times under Jewish Law, 22 DINE ISRAEL 39 (English Section) (2003).

Genetically Engineering People: A Jewish Law Analysis of Personhood, 13 ST. THOMAS L. REV. 877 (2001).

Review Essay: *An Unsuccessful Defense of the Bet Din of Rabbi Emanuel Rackman: The Tears of the Oppressed by Aviad Hacohen*, EDAH J. 4:2 (2004), www.edah.org/backend/journalarticle/4_2_broyde.pdf.

Some Thoughts on New York State Regulation of Jewish Marriage: Covenant, Contract or Statute?, 5 FAM. IN LAW 55 (2011).

The Establishment of Maternity and Paternity in Jewish and American Law, 3 NAT'L JEWISH L. REV. 117 (1988).

Büchler, Adolf, *Das judische Verlobins und die Stellung der verlobeten eines Priesters im ersten unt zweiten Jahrhundert*, in FESTSCHRIFT ZU ISRAEL LEWY'S SIEBZIGSTEM GEBURTSTAG 110 (M. Brann und J. Elbogen eds., 1911).

Byrn, Mary Patricia & Erica Holzer, *Codifying the Intent Test*, 41 WM. MITCHELL L. REV. 130 (2015).

Carbone, June & Naomi Cahn, *Marriage, Parentage, and Child Support*, 45 FAM. L.Q. 219 (2011).

Cherlow, Yuval, *Protection of the Surrogate Mother – Ethics, Law and Halacha*, 4 J. HEALTH L. & BIOETHICS 80 (2011) (Heb.).

Cherry, Kristen, *Marriage and Divorce Law in Pakistan and Iran: The Problem of Recognition* 9 TULSA J. COMP. & INT'L L. 319 (2001).

Cheruvu, Padmini, *Three-Parent IVF and Its Effect on Parental Rights*, 6 HASTINGS SCI. & TECH. L.J. 73 (2014).

Chezem, Linda L. & Sarah L. Nagy, *Judicial Abrogation of a Husband's Paternity: Can a Third Party Seek to Establish Paternity over a Child Born into a Marriage while That Marriage Remains Intact?*, 30 IND. L. REV. 467 (1997).

Choueka, Aharon, *The Controversy Concerning the Takkanah of Tuletula Regarding the Husband's Inheritance of His Wife's Estate*, 68(1) TARBIZ 87 (1999) (Heb.).

Coester-Waltjen, Dagmar & Michael Coester, *Formation of Marriage in Persons and Family*, in INTERNATIONAL ENCYCLOPEDIA OF COMPARATIVE LAW vol. 4, 6 (Mary A. Glendon ed., 1997).

Cohben, Aryeh, *Giddul's Wife and the Power of the Court: On Talmudic Law, Gender, Divorce and Exile*, 9 S. CAL. REV. L. & WOMEN'S STUD. 197 (1999–2000).

Cohen, Boaz, *Conditions in Jewish and Roman Law*, in WOLFSON JUBILEE VOLUME English Section 203 (Saul Lieberman ed., 1965).

On the Theme of Betrothal in Jewish and Roman Law, 18 PROCEEDINGS OF THE AMERICAN ACADEMY FOR JEWISH RESEARCH 67 (1948).

Cohen, I. Glenn, *Beyond Best Interests*, 96 MINN. L. REV. 1187 (2012).

Intentional Diminishment, the Non-Identity Problem, and Legal Liability, 60 HASTINGS L.J. 347 (2008).

Regulating Reproduction: The Problem with Best Interests, 96 MINN. L. REV. 423 (2011).

Cohen, Jacques & Mina Alikani, *The Biological Basis for Defining Bi-Parental or Tri-Parental Origin of Offspring from Cytoplasmic and Spindle Transfer*, 26(6) REPRODUCTIVE BIOMEDICINE ONLINE 535 (2013).

Cohen, Jeremy, *Intention in Sexual Relations According to Twelfth- and Thirteenth-Century Rabbinical Opinion*, 13 TEUDAH 155 (1997) (Heb.).

Cohen, Yedidya, *The Inheritance of a Wife of Her Husband in the Communal Enactments*, 6–7 SHENATON HA-MISHPAT HA-IVRI 133 (1979–80) (Heb).

Cooper Davis, Peggy, *The Good Mother: A New Look at Psychological Parent Theory*, 22 N.Y.U. REV. L. & SOC. CHANGE 347 (1996).

Corinaldi, Michael, *On the Question of Legal Parentage in Israel (Children Born through an Artificial Birth Technique)*, in AN UNUSUAL PREGNANCY: A MULTI-DISCIPLINARY STUDY OF IN VITRO FERTILIZATION 137 (Shulamit Almog & Avinoam Ben-Zeev eds., 1996) (Heb.).

Should Equality Be Implemented in the Laws of Parents and Children?, 2 KIRYAT HAMISHPAT 131 (2002) (Heb.).

The Legal Status of a Child Born of Artificial Means from a Sperm Donor or an Egg Donor, 18–19 SHNATON HA-MISHPAT HAIVRI 295 (1992–94) (Heb.).
Crook, John, *Patria Potestas*, 17(1) THE CLASSICAL Q. (NEW SERIES) 113 (1967).
Curtis, Carolyn, *The Psychological Parent Doctrine in Custody Disputes between Foster Parents and Biological Parents*, 16 COLUM. J.L. & SOC. PROBS. 149 (1980).
Dallas, Traci, *Rebutting the Marital Presumption: A Developed Relationship Test*, 88 COLUM. L. REV. 369 (1988).
D'alton-Harrison, Rita, *Mater Semper Incertus Est: Who's Your Mummy?*, 22(3) MED. L. REV. 357 (2014).
Daudpota, U. M. & Asaf A. A. Fyzee, *Notes on Mut'a or Temporary Marriage in Islam*, 8 JBBRAS 79 (1932).
Davis, Dena S., *Religious Attitudes toward Cloning: A Tale of Two Creatures*, 27 HOFSTRA L. REV. 509 (1999).
De Seife, Rodolphe J.A., Muhammad Khalid Masud, Brinkley Messick and David S. Powers eds., *Islamic Legal Interpretation: Muftis and Their Fatwas*, 42 AM. J. LEGAL HIST. 84 (1998).
Dichovsky, Shlomo, *Child Support – A Special Enactment in Charity Laws*, 16 TECHUMIN 87 (1996) (Heb.).
The Parental Obligation to Support Adoptive Children, 15 TECHUMIN 278 (1995) (Heb.).
Dimond, Rebecca, *Social and Ethical Issues in Mitochondrial Donation*, 115(1) BR. MED. BULL. 173 (2015).
Divon, Ido, *The Obligation of an Adopting Father to Pay the Child Support Due to His Undertaking*, 9 DINEI ISRAEL 184 (1978–80) (Heb.).
Donaldson, Dwight M., *Temporary Marriage in Iran*, 26(4) MOSLEM WORLD 358 (1936).
Dorff, Elliot N., *Human Cloning: A Jewish Perspective*, 8 S. CAL. INTERDISC. L.J. 117 (1998).
Dowd, Nancy E., *Multiple Parents/Multiple Fathers*, 9 J.L. FAM. STUD. 231 (2007).
Drori, Moshe, *International Jurisdiction of the Rabbinical Courts in Israel*, 24 JUSTICE 30 (2006).
Edrei, Arye, *The beit din's prerogatives in marital law*, 21 SHNATON HA-MISHPAT HA-IVRI 1 (1998–2000) (Heb.).
Ehrenberg, Yehoshua, *Conditional Marriage*, 1 NOAM 75 (1958) (Heb.).
Ehrenreich, Moshe, *The Onah Obligation: An Ordinary Obligation or the Essence of the Marriage*, 2 HEMDAT HAARETZ 42 (2002).
Ellinson, Elyakim G., *The Concubine in the Talmudic Literature*, 73 SINAI 127 (1973).
Elman, Yaakov, *"Up to the Ears" in Horses' Necks (BM 108a): On Sasanian Agricultural Policy and Private "Eminent Domain,"* 3 JSIJ 95 (2004).
Acculturation to Elite Persian Norms and Modes of Thought in the Babylonian Jewish Community of Late Antiquity, NETI'OT LEDAVID 31 (2004).
Marriage and Marital Property in Rabbinic and Sasanian Law, in RABBINIC LAW IN ITS ROMAN AND NEAR EASTERN CONTEXT 227 (Catherine Hezser ed., 2003).
Middle Persian Culture and Babylonian Sages: Accommodation and Resistance in the Shaping of Rabbinic Legal Tradition, in THE CAMBRIDGE COMPANION TO THE TALMUD AND RABBINIC LITERATURE 165 (2007).
Returnable Gifts in Rabbinic and Sasanian Law, VI IRANO-JUDAICA 139 (2008).
Elrod, Linda D., *A Child's Perspective of Defining a Parent: The Case for Intended Parenthood*, 25 BYU J. PUB. L. 245 (2011).
Epstein, Jacob N., *Li-Seridei Ha-Yerushalmi*, 3 TARBIZ 15 (1932) (Heb.).
Notes to the Jewish-Aramaic Papyri of Aswan, in STUDIES IN TALMUDIC LITERATURE AND SEMITIC LANGUAGES vol. 1, 320 (Ezra Z. Melamed ed., 1984) (Heb.).

Sefer Ha-Ma'asim Li-Vnei Eretz Yisrael, 1 TARBIZ 40 (1930) (Heb.).

Estin Ann, Laquer, *Embracing Tradition: Pluralism in American Family Law*, 63 MD. L. REV. 540 (2004).

Evans-Grubbs, Judith, *Abduction Marriage in Antiquity: A Law of Constantine (CTh IX.24.1) and Its Social Context*, 79 J. ROMAN STUD. 59 (1989).

Falk, Ze'ev W., *Mutual Obligations in the Ketubah*, 8 JOURNAL OF JEWISH STUDIES 215 (1957).

Ferber, Zeev, *The Mother Sharing in Paying Child Support*, 27 TECHUMIN 273 (2007) (Heb.).

Fleishman, Josef, *Socio-Legal Aspects of Genesis 34*, 13 SHENATON: AN ANNUAL FOR BIBLICAL AND ANCIENT NEAR EASTERN STUDIES 141 (2002) (Heb.).

The Inheritance of a Mother's Dowry in Ancient Near East Law and in Ancient Jewish Law, 23 DINE ISRAEL 95 (2005) (Heb.).

Flusser, David & Shmuel Safrai, *In the Image of the Form of His Likeness*, in ISAAC LEO SEELIGMANN VOLUME, ESSAYS ON THE BIBLE AND THE ANCIENT WORLD vol. 2 (Hebrew Section), 453 (Alexander Rofe & Yair Zakovitch eds.,1983) (Heb.).

Fournier, Pascale, *The Erasure of Islamic Difference in Canadian and American Family Law Adjudication*, 10 J.L. & POL'Y 51 (2001).

Francus, Israel, *And Again, When a Man Betroths a Woman, He Does so under the Conditions Laid down by the Rabbis*, 77 SINAI 91 (1975) (Heb.).

Birorim and Biorim in Masechet Ketubot, 73 SINAI 24 (1973) (Heb.).

Tnai Beit Din and Maase Beit Din, 115 SINAI 148 (1995) (Heb.).

Mahloket Kadmonim Be-Din Vittur Ha-Ba'al Lareshet Et Ishto, 106 SINAI 97 (1990).

Freidenreich, David M., *The Use of Islamic Sources in Saadiah Gaon's "Tafsīr" of the Torah*, 93(3/4) JEWISH Q. REV. 353 (2003).

Friedman, Mordecai A., *Halakha as Evidence of Sexual Life among Jews in Muslim Countries in the Middle Ages*, 45 PEAMIM 89 (1991) (Heb.).

Ketubot from Eretz Israel from the Geonic Period 1 TE'UDAH 58 (1980) (Heb.).

Divorce upon the Wife's Demand as Reflected in Manuscripts from the Cairo Geniza, 4 JEWISH LAW ANNUAL 103 (1981).

On the Relationship between Karaite and Palestinian Ketubot from the Genizah, 15 TEU'-DAH 145 (1956) (Heb.).

Polygamy – New Information from the Genizah, 43 TARBITZ 166 (1974) (Heb.).

Termination of Marriage upon the Wife's Request: A Palestinian Ketubba Stipulation, 37 PAAJAR 29 (1969).

Friedman, Shamma, *A Good Story Deserves Retelling – The Unfolding of the Akiva Legend*, 3 *JSIJ* 55 (2004).

Gafni, Isaiah. M., *The Institution of Marriage in Rabbinic Times*, in THE JEWISH FAMILY: METAPHOR AND MEMORY 13 (David Kraemer ed., 1989).

Gertner, Zevi & Bezalel Karlinski, *Eyn Tenai beNissuin*, 8 YESHURUN 678 (2001).

Eyn Tenai beNissuin, 9 YESHURUN 569 (2001).

Eyn Tenai beNissuin, 10 YESHURUN 711 (2002).

Ghodsi, Tamilla F., *Tying a Slipknot: Temporary Marriages in Iran*, 15 MICH. J. INT'L L. 645 (1994).

Ghori, Safiya, *The Application of Religious Law in North American Courts: A Case Study of Muta Marriages*, 10(1) J. ISLAMIC L. & CULTURE 29 (2008).

Gilat, Israel Z., *Is the "Benefit of the Child" a Major Criterion according to Jewish Law in a Parental Conflict of the Child?*, 8 BAR ILAN L. STUD. 297 (1990) (Heb.).

Glennon, Theresa, *Somebody's Child: Evaluating the Erosion of the Marital Presumption of Paternity*, 102 W. VA. L. REV. 547 (2000).

Glicksberg, Yosef, *Conditional Marriage*, 12 TORAH SHE-BE'ALPE 134 (1970) (Heb.).

Goldfeder, Mark, *The Adoption of Children in Judaism and in Israel: A Conceptual and Practical Review*, 22 CARDOZO J. INT'L & COMP. L. 321 (2014).

Goodwin, Anne, *Determination of Legal Parentage in Egg Donation, Embryo Transplantation, and Gestational Surrogacy Arrangements*, 1992 FAM. L.Q. 275 (1992).

Goren, Shlomo, *The Ketubah in the Babylonian Talmud and in the Palestinian Talmud*, 3 TORAH SHE-BE'AL PEH 119 (1961) (Heb.).

Graham, Laura P., *The Uniform Premarital Agreement Act and Modern Social Policy: The Enforceability of Premarital Agreements Regulating the Ongoing Marriage*, 28 WAKE FOREST L. REV. 1037 (1993).

Graves, Alison E., *Women in Iran: Obstacles to Human Rights and Possible Solutions* 5 AM. U. J. GENDER & L. 57 (1996).

Grazi, Richard V. & Joel B. Wolowelsky, *On Foetal Ovary Transplants* 40 LE'ELA (1995).

Green, Yosi, *Artificial Insemination (AID) in Israeli Court Judgments and Legislation*, 5 ASSIA 125 (1986) (Heb.).

Post Modern Procreation by Means of IVF and Ibum and Haliza, 2 NETANYA ACADEMIC COLLEGE L. REV. 207 (2002) (Heb.).

Greenberg-Kobrin, Michelle, *Civil Enforceability of Religious Prenuptial Agreements*, 32 COLUMBIA J.L. & SOCIAL PROBLEMS 359 (1991).

Grinberg, Shmuel, *Interpreting Layman's Language*, 12 SINAI 346 (1947) (Heb.).

Guidice, Richard, *Procreation and the Prisoner: Does the Right to Procreate Survive Incarceration and Do Legitimate Penological Interests Justify Restrictions on the Exercise of the Right*, 29 FORDHAM URBAN L.J. 2277 (2002).

Gulak, Asher, *Deed of Betrothal and Oral Stipulation in Talmudic Law*, 3 TARBITZ 361 (1932) (Heb.).

Haeri, Shahla, *An Islamic Discourse on Female Sexuality: Temporary Marriage in Postrevolutionary Iran*, in IN THE EYE OF THE STORM: WOMEN IN POSTREVOLUTIONARY IRAN 98–114 (Mahnaz Afkhami & Erika Friedl eds., 1994).

Temporary Marriage and the State in Iran: An Islamic Discourse on Female Sexuality, 59 SOC. RES. 201 (1992).

The Institution of Mut`a Marriage in Iran: A Formal and Historical Perspective, in ISLAM CRITICAL CONCEPTS IN SOCIOLOGY vol. 3 GENDER AND THE FAMILY 154–72 (Bryan S. Turner ed., 2003).

Halperin, Mordechai, *The Definition of Parenthood and the Right to Find Biological Roots* in MORAL DILEMMAS IN MEDICINE 161 (Raphael Cohen-Almagor ed. 2002) (Heb.).

Halperin-Kaddari, Ruth, *Redefining Parenthood*, 29 CAL. W. INT'L. L.J. 313 (1999).

Halperin-Kaddari, Ruth & Yaacov Yadgar, *Between Universal Feminism and Particular Nationalism: Politics, Religion and Gender (In)Equality in Israel*, 31(6) THIRD WORLD Q. 905 (2010).

Hamoudi Haider, Ala, *Sex and the Shari'a: Defining Gender Norms and Sexual Deviancy in Shi'i Islam*, 39 FORDHAM INT'L L.J. 25 (2015).

Hasday, Jill Elaine, *Contest and Consent: A Legal History of Marital Rape*, 88 CALIFORNIA L. REV. 1375 (2000).

Hashiloni-Dolev, Yael, *Posthumous Reproduction (PHR) in Israel: Policy Rationales versus Lay People's Concerns, a Preliminary Study*, 39(4) CULTURE, MEDICINE, AND PSYCHIATRY 634 (2015).

Heffening, Willi, *Mut'a* in ENCYCLOPAEDIA OF ISLAM vol. 7, 757–59 (C.E. Bosworth et. al eds., 1960)

Helmholz, Richard H., *Support Orders, Church Courts, and the Rule of Filius Nullius: A Reassessment of the Common Law*, 63 VA. L. REV. 431 (1977).
Henkin, Yehuda H., *Aharita mi Yeshurena*, 17 AKDAMOT 33 (2006).
Her, Moshe D., *Marriage from a Socio-Economic Halakhic Perspective*, in MISHPAHOT BEIT YISRAEL 37 (1976) (Heb.).
Hershberg, A. S., *Yofya ve-Hityafuta shel ha-Isha bi-Zman ha-Talmud*, 4 HE-ATID 1 (1923) (Heb.).
Hershler, Moshe, *Test-Tube Babies According to Halakha*, 4 HALAKHA & MED. 90 (1985) (Heb.)
Test-Tube Babies According to Halakha, 1 HALAKHA & MED. 307 (1980) (Heb.).
Hill, John L., *What Does It Mean to Be a "Parent"? The Claims of Biology as the Basis for Parental Rights*, 66 N.Y.U. L. REV. 353 (1991).
Hirschberg, Haim Z., *Le-Heker Rav Sadya Gaon ve-Tequfato*, 31 TARBIZ 415 (1962) (Heb.).
Hirschfeld, H., *In the Book of Megilat Starim*, in FESTSCHRIFT ZUM SIEBZIGSTEN GEBURTSTAGE A. BERLINER'S: GEWIDMET VON FREUNDEN UND SCHULERN, the Hebrew section 46 (1903) (Heb.).
Hjerrild, Bodil, *Islamic Law and Sasanian Law*, in LAW AND THE ISLAMIC WORLD: PAST AND PRESENT 49 (Christopher Toll & Jakob Skovgaard-Petersen eds., 1995).
Hopkins, Simon, *A New Autograph Fragment of Maimonides' Hilkhot Ha-Yerushalmi*, 28 J. SEMITIC STUD. 273 (1983).
Horner, Amanda, *I Consented to Do What?: Posthumous Children and the Consent to Parent After-Death*, 33 S. ILL. U. L.J. 157 (2008).
Howard, I. K. A., *Mut'a Marriage Reconsidered in the Context of the Formal Procedures for Islamic Marriage*, XX(1) J. SEMITIC STUD. 82 (1975).
Ilan, Mordechai, *A Woman Relinquishing Her Right for Maintenance*, 3 TECHUMIN 123 (1982) (Heb.).
Indig, Yizhak, *The Problem of Support of a Child Born of Artificial Insemination*, 2 DINEI ISRAEL 83 (1971) (Heb.).
Irshai, Ronit, *ARTs and the Prohibition of Seed Destruction: Three Methods in the Modern Psika*, 7 IDENTITES 21 (2015) (Heb.).
Public and Private Rulings in Jewish Law (Halakhah): Flexibility, Concealment, and Feminist Jurisprudence, 3(1) J.L. RELIGION & STATE 25 (2014).
Toward a Gender Critical Approach to the Philosophy of Jewish Law (Halakhah), 26(2) J. FEMINIST STUD. IN RELIGION 55 (2010).
Israeli, Shaul, *Fatherhood by Artificial Means*, 33 TORAH SHE-BE'ALPE 41 (1992) (Heb.).
Jackson, Bernard S., *Agunah and the Problem of Authority: Directions for Future Research* 1 MELILAH 1, 8 (2004).
How Jewish Is Jewish Family Law?, LV/2 J. JEWISH STUD. 201 (2004).
Mishpat Ivri, Halakhah and Legal Philosophy: Agunah and the Theory of "Legal Sources," 1 JSIJ 69 (2002).
Some Reflections on Family Law in the Papyri, XIV JEWISH L. ASS'N STUD. 141 (Hillel Gamoran ed., 2002).
Jackson, Bernard S. & Avishalom Westreich, *Book Review of Aviad Hacohen, The Tears of the Oppressed, an Examination of the Agunah Problem: Background and Halachic Sources*, 17 JEWISH LAW ANNUAL 303 (2007).
Jacobs, Melanie B., *Why Just Two? Disaggregating Traditional Parental Rights and Responsibilities to Recognize Multiple Parents*, 9 J.L. FAM. STUD. 309 (2007).
Jensen, Brent J., Comment, *Artificial Insemination and the Law*, 1982 BYU L. REV. 935 (1982).

Jones, Caroline & Ingrid Holme, *Relatively (im)Material: mtDNA and Genetic Relatedness in Law and Policy*, 9:4 LIFE SCI. SOC'Y & POL'Y (2013).

Kahser, Asa, *"Planned Orphanhood": The Balanced Picture*, in MORAL DILEMMAS IN MEDICINE 161 (Raphael Cohen-Almagor ed., 2002) (Heb.).

Kaplan, Diane S., *Why Truth Is Not a Defense in Paternity Actions*, 10 TEX. J. WOMEN & L. 69 (2000).

Kaplan, Yehiel S., *Child Custody in Jewish Law: From Authority of the Father to the Best Interest of the Child*, 24(1) J.L. & RELIGION 89 (2008/2009).

Kasher, Menachem M., *Artificial Insemination*, 1 NOAM 125 (1958) (Heb.).

Katz, Gail A., *Parpalaix c. CECOS: Protecting Intent in Reproductive Technology*, 11 HARV. J.L. & TECH. 683 (1998).

Kaye, Alexander, *Eliezer Goldman and the Origins of Meta-Halacha*, 34.3 MODERN JUDAISM 309 (2014).

Khan, Shahnaz, *Race, Gender, and Orientalism: Muta and the Canadian Legal System*, 8 CAN. J. WOMEN & L. 249 (1995).

Khatib-Chahidi, Jane, *Sexual Prohibitions, Shared Space and Fictive Marriages in Shi'ite Iran*, in WOMEN AND SPACE: GROUND RULES AND SOCIAL MAPS 112 (Shirley Ardener ed., 1981).

King, Alexa E., *Solomon Revisited: Assigning Parenthood in the Context of Collaborative Reproduction*, 5 UCLA WOMEN'S L.J. 329 (1995).

Kirkpatrick Lacey, Walter, *"Patria Potestas,"* in THE FAMILY IN ANCIENT ROME: NEW PERSPECTIVES 121 (Beryl Rawson ed., 1987).

Kister, Menachem, *Kedat Moshe veYehudai: On the History of a Legal-Religious Term*, in ATARA L'HAIM: STUDIES IN THE TALMUD & MEDIEVAL RABBINIC LITERATURE IN HONOR OF PROF. HAIM ZALMAN DIMITROVSKY 202 (Daniel Boyarin et al. eds., 2000) (Heb.).

Kisthardt, Mary K., *Of Fatherhood, Families and Fantasy: The Legacy of Michael H. V. Gerald D.*, 65 TUL. L. REV. 585 (1991).

Kleinman, Ron S., *Contemporary Halakhic Decisors, Commercial Practices, and Civil Law*, 19 THE REVIEW OF RABBINIC JUDAISM 78 (2016).

Kleinman, Ron S. & Amal Jabareen, *Transfer of Ownership in E-Commerce Transactions from the Perspective of Jewish Law: In Light of Israeli and American Law*, in THE OXFORD HANDBOOK OF JUDAISM AND ECONOMICS 499 (Aaron Levine ed., 2010).

Knapland, Kristine S., *Synthetic Cells, Synthetic Life, and Inheritance*, 45 VAL. U. L. REV. 1361 (2011).

Kolinsky, Heather, *The Intended Parent: The Power and Problems Inherent in Designating and Determining Intent in the Context of Parental Rights*, 119 PENN ST. L. REV. 801 (2015).

Koll, Perri, *The Use of the Intent Doctrine to Expand the Rights of Intended Homosexual Male Parents in Surrogacy Custody Disputes*, 18 CARDOZO J.L. & GENDER 199 (2011).

Kovach, Rachel L., *Sorry Daddy – Your Time Is Up: Rebutting the Presumption of Paternity in Louisiana*, 56 LOY. L. REV. 651 (2010).

Kraus, Shmuel, *Man Havya le-Yoma*, 22 SINAI 299 (1948).

Labovitz, Gail, *Review of Melanie Landau, Tradition and Equality: Beyond the Sanctification of Subordination*, 4(1) RELIGION & GENDER 70 (2014), www.religionandgender.org/articles/abstract/10.18352/rg.9491/.

Ladomato, Dominique, *Protecting Traditional Surrogacy Contracting through Fee Payment Regulation*, 23 HASTINGS WOMEN'S L.J. 245 (2012).

Landau, Ruth, *Planned Orphanhood*, 49(2) SOCIAL SCIENCE & MEDICINE 185 (1999).

Lasker, Daniel J., *Saadya Gaon on Christianity and Islam*, in THE JEWS OF MEDIEVAL ISLAM: COMMUNITY, SOCIETY, AND IDENTITY 165 (Daniel Frank ed., 1995).
Lau, Israel M., *The Halakhic Ramifications of Sexual Relationships before Marriage*, 27 TORAH SHE-BE'ALPE 84 (1986) (Heb.).
Laufer-Ukeles, Pamela, *Gestation: Work for Hire or the Essence of Motherhood? A Comparative Legal Analysis*, 9 DUKE J. GENDER L. & POL'Y 91 (2002).
The Lost Children: When the Right to Children Conflicts with the Rights of Children, 8 L. & ETHICS HUM. RTS. 219 (2014).
Legge, Michael et al., *Numerical Identity: The Creation of Tri-Parental Embryos to Correct Inherited Mitochondrial Disease*, 126(1385) NEW ZEALAND MED. J. (ONLINE) 71 (2013).
Levin, Yael, *Freeing One Agunah is Like Rebuilding One of the Ruins of Supernal Jerusalem*, 23 DINE ISRAEL 163 (2005).
Levmor, Rachel, *Pre-Nuptial Agreements with the Aim of Preventing the Husband's Refusal to Give a Get*, 23 SHNATON HA-MISHPAT HA-IVRI 127 (2005) (Heb.).
Rabbinic Responses in Favor of Prenuptial Agreements, 42(1) TRADITION 29 (2009).
The Prenuptial Agreement for the Prevention of GET-Refusal, https://iyim.org.il/wp-content/.../07/Article-The-Prenuptial-Agreement.doc.
Lewis, Browne, *Two Fathers, One Dad: Allocating the Paternal Obligations between the Men Involved in the Artificial Insemination Process*, 13 LEWIS & CLARK L. REV. 949 (2009).
Lewis, Naphtali, Ranon Katzoff & Jonas C. Greenfield, *Papyrus Yadin 18*, 37 ISRAEL EXPLORATION J. 229 (1987).
Libson, Gideon, *Halakhah and Reality in the Gaonic Period: Taqqanah, Minhag, Tradition and Consensus: Some Observations*, in THE JEWS OF MEDIEVAL ISLAM: COMMUNITY, SOCIETY, AND IDENTITY 67 (Daniel Frank ed., 1995).
Lichtenstein, Aharon, *On Conversion*, 23(2) TRADITION 1 (1988).
Liebes, Yitzhak A., *Regarding Limb Transplants*, 14 NOAM 28 (1971) (Heb.).
Lifshitz, Berachyahu, *The Theoretical Basis of the Condition in Jewish Law*, 4 MISHPATIM 636 (1973) (Heb.).
Lifshitz, Shahar, *Neither Nature nor Contract: Toward an Institutional Perspective on Parenthood Essay*, 8 L. & ETHICS HUM. RTS. 297 (2014).
Lipkin, Benjamin, *Ius Dispositivum in Jewish Law*, 35 SINAI 111 (1954) (Heb.).
Lipschutz, Joshua H., *To Clone or Not to Clone – A Jewish Perspective*, 25 J. MED. ETHICS 105 (1999).
Lowy, Simeon, *The Extent of Jewish Polygamy in Talmudic Times*, 9 J. JEWISH STUD. 115 (1958).
Macuch, Maria, *Die Zeitehe im Sasanidischen Recht – ein Vorlaufer der shi'itischen mut'a-Ehe in Iran?*, 18 ARCHAEOLOGISCHE MITTEILUNGEN AUS IRAN 187 (1985).
Malinowitz, Chaim Z., *The 1992 New York Get Law: An Exchange*, 31(3) TRADITION 23 (1997).
Malka, David, *Hithayyavut shel ha-Isha lifne ha-Nisuin le-Kabel Get*, 8 SHURAT HA-DIN 360 (2003) (Heb.).
Marcus, Tali, *It Takes (Only) Two to Tango? Recognizing More than Two Parents for One Child* 44 HEBREW U. L.J. 415 (2014) (Heb.).
Margaliot, Reuven, *Man Havya le-Yoma*, 21 SINAI 176 (1947).
Margalit, Yehezkel, *Artificial Insemination from Donor (AID) – From Status to Contract and Back Again?*, 21(1) BOSTON U. J. SCI. & TECH. L. 69 (2015).
Bridging the Gap between Intent and Status: A New Framework for Modern Parentage, 15(1) WHITTIER J. CHILD & FAM. ADVOC. 1 (2016).

From Baby M to Baby M(anji): Regulating International Surrogacy Agreements, 24(1) J.L. & POL'Y 41 (2016).
In Defense of Surrogacy Agreements: A Modern Contract Law Perspective, 20 WM. & MARY J. WOMEN & L. 423 (2014).
Intentional Parenthood: A Solution to the Plight of Same-Sex Partners Striving for Legal Recognition as Parents, 12 WHITTIER J. CHILD & FAM. ADVOC. 39 (2013).
Marriage According to the Law of Moses and Israel – Between Family Law and Contract Law (forthcoming, 2018).
On the Dispositive Foundations of the Obligation of Spousal Conjugal Relations in Jewish Law, XVIII *JLAS* 161 (2008).
Scarce Medical Resources – Parenthood at Every Age, in Every Case and Subsidized by the State?, 9 NETANYA ACADEMIC COLLEGE L. REV. 191 (2014) (Heb.).
The Rise, Fall and Rise Again of the Genetic Foundation for Legal Parentage Determination, 3 J. HEALTH L. & BIOETHICS 125 (2010) (Heb.).
To Be or Not to Be (A Parent)? – Not Precisely the Question: The Frozen Embryo Dispute, 18 CARDOZO J.L. & GENDER 355 (2012).
Margalit, Yehezkel & John Loike, *The New Frontier of Advanced Reproductive Technology: Reevaluating Modern Legal Parenthood*, 37 HARVARD J.L. & GENDER 107 (2014).
Matsumura, Kaiponanea T., *Public Policing of Intimate Agreements*, 25 YALE J.L. & FEMINISM 159 (2013).
Mazeh, Yoav, *The Religious Law of Child Support, the Supreme Court's Case-Law and the Practice of Courts: Between Myth and Reality*, HAIFA L. REV. (forthcoming, 2018) (Heb.).
McMillen, Michael J. T., *Islamic Business and Commercial Law: Contractual Enforceability Issues: Sukuk and Capital Markets Development*, 7 CHI. J. INT'L L. 427 (2007).
Islamic Shari'ah-Compliant Project Finance: Collateral Security and Financing Structure Case Studies, 24 FORDHAM INT'L L.J. 1184 (2001).
Meislin, Bernard, *Jewish Law of Marriage in American Courts*, 11 J. FAM. L. 271 (1971–72).
Miller, Kristin J., *Human Rights of Women in Iran: The Universalist Approach and the Relativist Response* 10 EMORY INT'L L. REV. 779 (1996).
Mintz, Adam, A *Courageous Proposal: The First Heter Agunah in America*, 4 JOFA J. 14 (2007).
Moosa, Ebrahim, *The Child Belongs to the Bed: Illegitimacy and Islamic Law*, in QUESTIONABLE ISSUE: ILLEGITIMACY IN SOUTH AFRICA (Sandra Burman & Eleanor Preston-Whyte eds., 1992).
Moscovitz, Leib, *Sugyot Muhlafot in the Talmud Yerushalmi* , 60 TARBIZ 19 (1991) (Heb.).
Murakami, Charla, *Parent-Child Relations: A Comparison of Jewish and California Law*, 1 U.C. DAVIS J. INT'L L. & POL'Y 107 (1995).
Nix, Jesse M., *"You Only Donated Sperm": Using Intent to Uphold Paternity Agreements*, 11 J.L. & FAM. STUD. 487 (2009).
O'Brien, Raymond C., *The Momentum of Posthumous Conception: A Model Act*, 25 J. CONTEMP. HEALTH L. & POL'Y 332 (2009).
Oller, Jason, *Can I Get That in Writing?: Established and Emerging Protections of Paternity Rights* [In re K.M.H., 169 P.3d 1025 (Kan. 2007)], 48 WASHBURN L.J. 209 (2008).
Orenbach, Kenneth B., *The Religiously Distinct Director: Infusing Judeo-Christian Business Ethics into Corporate Governance*, 2 CHARLOTTE L. REV. 369 (2010).
Orenstein, Gedalia, *In Vitro Fertilization – Lineage of the Child and Fulfilling the Mitzvah of Procreation*, 24 TECHUMIN 156 (2004) (Heb.).
Oryn, Theodor, *Remarks on the Duty of the Mother to Participate in the Maintenance of Her Child*, 34 HAPRAKLIT 308 (1982) (Heb.).

Parness, Jeffrey A., *Parentage Prenups and Midnups*, 31 GA. ST. U. L. REV. 343 (2015).

Pence, Gregory, *What's So Good about Natural Motherhood? (In Praise of Unnatural Gestation)* in ECTOGENESIS: ARTIFICIAL WOMB TECHNOLOGY AND THE FUTURE OF HUMAN REPRODUCTION 77 (Scott Gelfand & John R. Shook eds., 2006).

Perikhanian, Anahit, *Iranian Society and Law*, 3(2) CAMBRIDGE HISTORY OF IRAN 627 (Ehsan Y. Sharter ed., 1983).

Picard, Ariel, *The Proposal of Rabbi Uzziel for Resolving the Agunah Problem*, in RABBI UZZIEL AND HIS PEERS: STUDIES IN THE RELIGIOUS THOUGHT OF ORIENTAL RABBIS TWENTIETH-CENTURY ISRAEL 230 (Zvi Zohar ed., 2009) (Heb.).

Pitt, Jonathan B., *Fragmenting Procreation*, 108 YALE L.J. 1893 (1999).

Pollack, Daniel et al., *Classical Religious Perspectives of Adoption Law*, 79 NOTRE DAME L. REV. 693 (2004).

Posek, Hillel, 114 HAPOSEK a-748 (1950).

Povarsky, Chaim, *Regulating Advanced Reproductive Technologies: A Comparative Analysis of Jewish and American Law*, 29 U. TOL. L. REV. 409 (1998).

Purvis, Dara E., *Intended Parents and the Problem of Perspective*, 24 YALE J.L. & FEMINISM 210 (2012).

Rabinovitz, Zvi M., *M. A. Friedman, Jewish Marriage in Palestine – A Cairo Geniza Study, I-II, Tel Aviv and New York* 1980–1, 55 TARBIZ 456 (1986) (Heb.).

Radzyner, Amihai, *Gittin – Mitzvot That Depend on Eretz Israel? Prenuptial Agreement for Avoiding Get Refusal: Between America and Israel* (forthcoming, 2018, on file with author).

Rae, Scott B., *Parental Rights and the Definition of Motherhood in Surrogate Motherhood*, 3 S. CAL. REV. L. & WOMEN'S STUD. 219 (1994).

Rakover, Nahum, *Coercive Marital Relations between a Man and His Wife*, 6–7 SHNATON HA-MISHPAT HA-IVRI 295 (1979–80) (Heb.).

Rao, Radhika, *Assisted Reproductive Technology and the Threat to the Traditional Family*, 47 HASTINGS L.J. 951 (1996).

Rehbinder, Manfred, *Status, Contract and the Welfare State*, 23 STAN. L. REV. 941 (1971).

Reichman, Edward, *The Halakhic Chapter of Ovarian Transplantation*, 31(1) TRADITION 31 (1998) .

Reichman Schiff, Anne, *Arising from the Dead: Challenges of Posthumous Procreation*, 75 N.C. L. REV. 901 (1997).

Reinitz, Yaakov, *Appointing a Female Apotropos*, 4 BAR ILAN L. STUD. 167 (1986) (Heb.).
The Apotropos of Orphans Who Are Supported by the Owner, 1 BAR ILAN L. STUD. 219 (1980) (Heb.).

Reus-Smit, Christian, *International Crises of Legitimacy*, 44 INT'LPOL. 157 (2007).

Richardson, Christopher F., *Islamic Finance Opportunities in the Oil and Gas Sector: An Introduction to an Emerging Field*, 42 TEX. INT'L L.J. 119 (2006).

Riskin, Shlomo, *Hafka'at Kiddushin: Towards Solving the Aguna Problem in Our Time*, 36(4) TRADITION 1 (2002).

Roberts, Paula, *Truth and Consequences: Part I. Disestablishing the Paternity of Non-Marital Children*, 37 FAM. L.Q. 35 (2003).

Robertson, John A., *Assisted Reproductive Technology and the Family*, 47 HASTINGS L.J. 911 (1996).

Rodgers-Miller, Brooke D., *Out of Jahiliyya: Historic and Modern Incarnations of Polygamy in the Islamic World*, 11 WM. & MARY J. OF WOMEN & L. 541 (2005).

Rosenblum, Irit, *Being Fruitful and Multiplying: Legal, Philosophical, Religious, and Medical Perspectives on Assisted Reproductive Technologies in Israel and Internationally*, 36 SUFFOLK TRANSNAT'L L. REV. 627 (2013).

Rosner, Fred, *In Vitro Fertilization, Surrogate Motherhood, and Sex Organ Transplants Symposium: Reproductive Rights*, 25 CREIGHTON L. REV. 1669 (1991–92).

Rostain, Tanina, *Permissible Accommodations of Religion: Reconsidering the New York Get Statute*, 96(5) YALE L.J. 1147 (1987).

Roth, Rachel, *No New Babies?: Gender Inequality and Reproductive Control in the Criminal Justice and Prison Systems*, 12 AM. U. J. GENDER SOC. POL'Y & L. 391 (2004).

Runner, Brenda J., *Protecting a Husband's Parental Rights When His Wife Disputes the Presumption of Legitimacy*, 28 J. FAM. L. 115 (1989–90).

Ryzman, Zvi, A *Halachic Discussion of Ovarian Transplants* (2009).

Ovary Transplantion – Is It Forbidden as Sterilization?, 31 TECHUMIN 38 (2011) (Heb.).

Sabreen, Mudasra, *Parentage: A Comparative Study of Islamic and Pakistani Law*, 1(2) FRONTIERS OF LEGAL RESEARCH 21 (2013).

Sackin, Jessica S., *The Halakhic/Constitutional Argument for Human Reproductive Cloning in America*, 7 GEO. J.L. & PUB. POL'Y 627 (2009).

Salaymeh, Lena, *Every Law Tells a Story: Orthodox Divorce in Jewish and Islamic Legal Histories*, 4(1) UC IRVINE L. REV. 19 (2014).

Satlow, Michael L., *Slipping Toward Sacrament: Jews, Christians and Marriage*, in JEWISH CULTURE AND SOCIETY UNDER THE CHRISTIAN ROMAN EMPIRE 65 (Richard Kalmin & Seth Schwartz eds, 2003).

Schapiro, Moshe, *Divorce on Grounds of Revulsion*, 2 DINE ISRAEL 117 (1971).

Scheiber, Alexander & Yizhak Hahn, *(Manuscript) Leaves from Se'adya's Sefer Hamizwot*, 28 TARBIZ 48 (1959) (Heb.).

Schereschewsky, Ben Zion, "*Apotropos*" in THE PRINCIPLES OF JEWISH LAW 219 (Menachem Elon ed., 1975).

"*Mamzer*" IN THE PRINCIPLES OF JEWISH LAW 435–38 (Menachem Elon ed., 1975).

"*Parent and Child*" in THE PRINCIPLES OF JEWISH LAW 424–29 (Menachem Elon ed., 1975).

Schiff Reichman, Anne, *Solomonic Decisions in Egg Donation: Unscrambling the Conundrum of Legal Maternity*, 80 IOWA L. REV. 265 (1995).

Schoenbaum, Elisha, *[on] Z. W. Falk, The Divorce Action by the Wife in Jewish Law*, 6 DINE ISRAEL 303 (1975) (Heb.).

Schremer, Adiel, *How Much Jewish Polygyny in Roman Palestine?*, 63 PROCEEDINGS OF THE AMERICAN ACADEMY FOR JEWISH RESEARCH 181 (2001).

Papyrus Se'elim 13 and the Question of Divorce Initiated by Women in Ancient Jewish Halakhah, 63 ZION 377 (1998) (Heb.)

Schultz, Jessica H., *Development of Ectogenesis: How Will Artificial Wombs Affect the Legal Status of a Fetus or Embryo?*, 84 CHI.-KENT L. REV. 877 (2010).

Schwartz, Gedalia D., Comments on the New York State "Get Law" – Jewish Law?: *Examining Halacha, Jewish Issues and Secular Law* (1994), www.jlaw.com/Articles/get_law1.html.

Schwartz, Laura J., *Religious Matching for Adoption: Unraveling the Interests Behind the "Best Interests" Standard*, 25 FAM. L.Q. 171 (1991).

Segal, Peretz, *Jewish Law during the Tannaitic Period*, in AN INTRODUCTION TO THE HISTORY AND SOURCES OF JEWISH LAW 137 (Neil S. Hecht et al. eds., 1996).

Septimus, Zvi & Lena Selaymeh, *Temporalities of Marriage: Jewish and Islamic Legal Debates*, in TALMUDIC TRANSGRESSIONS: ESSAYS IN HONOR OF DANIEL BOYARIN 201 (Ishay Rosen-Zvi et al., 2017).

Shafran, Yigal, *Postmortem Fatherhood*, 20 TECHUMIN 347 (2000) (Heb.).
Shagar, *Mitzvat Onah*, in AND HE NAMED THEM ADAM: LOVE AND RELATIONSHIPS FROM A NEW JEWISH POINT OF VIEW 193 (Zohar Maor ed., 2005) (Heb.).
Shapira, Amos, *Normative Regulation of Reproductive Technologies in Israel*, 13 NOVA L. REV. 609 (1989).
Shawa, Menashe, *Maintenance of Minor Children in Jewish and Positive Law*, 13 JEWISH L. ASS'N STUD. 289 (2002).
Shiber, Yair, *The Halakhic-Legal Status of a Living Being Born by Genetic Cloning*, 16 *Bekhol Derakhekha Daehu, Journal of Torah and Scholarship* 45 (2005) (Heb.).
Shifman, Pinhas, *Establishing Parenthood for a Child Born through Artificial Insemination*, 10 HEBREW U. L.J. 63 (1980) (Heb.).
Family Law in Israel: The Struggle between Religious and Secular Law, 24 ISR. L. REV. 537 (1990).
The New Agunah: Religious Divorce in Israel, 6 ALEI MISHPAT 27 (2007) (Heb.).
The Status of the Unmarried Parent in Israel Law, 12 ISR. L. REV. 194 (1977).
Shtober, Shimon, *Al Shte She'elot she-Hufnu el Rabenu Avraham ben ha-Rambam (referring to a slave – Pilegesh)*, 6–7 SHNATON HA-MISHPAT HAIVRI 399 (1979–80).
Shultz, Marjorie M., *Contractual Ordering of Marriage: A New Model for State Policy*, 70 CAL. L. REV. 204 (1982).
Reproductive Technology and Intent-Based Parenthood: An Opportunity for Gender Neutrality, 1990 WIS. L. REV. 297 (1990).
Sikaitis, Joline F., *A New Form of Family Planning? The Enforceability of No-Child Provisions in Prenuptial Agreements*, 54 CATH. U. L. REV. 335 (2004).
Silber, Sherman J., *Judaism and Reproductive Technology*, 156 CANCER TREAT RES. 471 (2010).
Silberg, Moshe, *Law and Morals in Jewish Jurisprudence*, 75 HARV. L. REV. 306 (1961).
Sinclair, Daniel B., *Assisted Reproduction in Jewish Law*, 30 FORDHAM URB. L.J. 71 (2002).
Soloveitchik, Yosef B., *The Marriage*, in FAMILY REDEEMED: ESSAYS ON FAMILY RELATIONSHIPS vol. 1, 31 (David Shatz & Joel B. Wolowelsky eds., 2000).
Son, Hyun Jee, *Artificial Wombs, Frozen Embryos, and Abortion: Reconciling Viability's Doctrinal Ambiguity*, 14 UCLA WOMEN'S L.J. 213 (2005).
Squillace, Lynn M., *Too Much of a Good Thing: Toward a Regulated Market in Human Eggs*, 1 J. HEALTH & BIOMED. L. 135 (2005).
Sternbuch, Moshe, *Test-Tube Baby*, 8 BI'SHVILEI HA'REFUAH 29 (1987) (Heb.).
Stigall, Dan E., *Iraqi Civil Law: Its Sources, Substance, and Sundering*, 16 J. TRANSNAT'L L. & POL'Y 1 (2006).
Storrow, Richard F., *Parenthood by Pure Intention: Assisted Reproduction and the Functional Approach to Parentage*, 53 HASTINGS L.J. 597 (2002).
"The Phantom Children of the Republic": International Surrogacy and the New Illegitimacy, 20 AM. U. J. GENDER SOC. POL'Y & L. 561 (2012).
Stumpf, Andrea E., *Redefining Mother: A Legal Matrix for New Reproductive Technologies*, 96 YALE L.J. 187 (1986).
Swift, Katherine M., *Parenting Agreements, the Potential Power of Contract, and the Limits of Family Law*, 34 FLA. ST. U. L. REV. 913 (2007).
Tachibana, Masahito et al., *Towards Germline Gene Therapy of Inherited Mitochondrial Diseases*, 493(7434) NATURE 627 (2013).
Tacy, Kimberly J., *Islamic Finance: A Growing Industry in the United States*, 10 N.C. BANKING INST. 355 (2006).

Temple, Gregg, *Freedom of Contract and Intimate Relationships*, 8 HARV. J.L. & PUB. POL'Y 121 (1985).

Tiefenbrun, Susan W., *The Semiotics of Women's Human Rights in Iran*, 23 CONN. J. INT'L L. 1 (2007).

Tikachinski, Michal & Rachel Sperber-Frankel, *Tazhiram min ha-Pilegesh*, 17 AKDAMOT 67 (2006).

Triger, Zvi H., *"A Jewish and Democratic State": Reflections on the Fragility of Israeli Secularism*, 41 PEPP. L. REV. 1091 (2014).

Freedom from Religion in Israel: Civil Marriages and Cohabitation of Jews Enter the Rabbinical Courts, 27(2) ISRAEL STUD. REV. 1 (2012).

The Gendered Racial Formation: Foreign Men, "Our" Women, and the Law, 30 WOMEN'S RTS. L. REP. 479 (2008–09).

Tzfira, Yigal, *Coercive Sexual Relationships*, 24 TECHUMIN 222 (2004) (Heb.).

Uziel, Ben-Zion M., *Man Havya le-Yom*, 99–100 HA-POSEK 1979 (1948).

Man Havya le-Yoma, 101–2 HA-POSEK 1554 (1949).

Villareale, Catherine, *The Case of Two Biological Intended Mothers: Illustrating the Need to Statutorily Define Maternity in Maryland*, 42 U. BALT. L. REV. 365 (2013).

Voinarevich, Olga, *A Fairy Tale Interrupted: The Long-Term Impacts of Child Marriage in Yemen and the Necessary Adjustments to Both Local and International Laws to Stop the Practice and to Protect Voiceless Child Brides*, 16 RUTGERS RACE & L. REV. 203 (2015).

Wald, Deborah H., *The Parentage Puzzle: The Interplay between Genetics, Procreative Intent, and Parental Conduct in Determining Legal Parentage*, 15 AM. U. J. GENDER SOC. POL'Y & L. 379 (2007).

Warhaftig, Itamar, *The Legal Validity of Reliance on Oral Promise in Jewish Law*, 2 BAR-ILAN L. STUD. 45 (1982) (Heb.).

Warhaftig, Zerach, *To the Sources of the Obligation of Child Support*, 1 TECHUMIN 255 (1980) (Heb.).

Warmflash, Lawrence M., *The New York Approach to Enforcing Religious Marriage Contracts: From Avitzur to the Get Statute*, 50 BROOK. L. REV. 229 (1983–84).

Warzynski, Vanessa L., *Termination of Parental Rights: The "Psychological Parent" Standard*, 39 VILL. L. REV. 737 (1994).

Weiss, Susan M., *Sign at Your Own Risk: The RCA Prenuptial May Prejudice the Fairness of Your Future Divorce Settlement*, 6 CARDOZO WOMEN'S L.J. 49 (1999).

Weitzman, Gideon, *Give Me Children or Else I Am Dead: Orthodox Jewish Perspectives on Fertility*, in FAITH AND FERTILITY: ATTITUDES TOWARDS REPRODUCTIVE PRACTICES IN DIFFERENT RELIGIONS FROM ANCIENT TO MODERN TIMES 205 (Eric Blyth & Ruth Landau eds., 2009).

Ovary Transplantion in Halachic Perspective, 31 TECHUMIN 48 (2011) (Heb.).

Taking Sperm from an Unconscious Husband, 25 TCHUMIN 59 (2005) (Heb.).

Technology in the Service of the First Mitzvah, 6 ḤAKIRAH, THE FLATBUSH J. JEWISH L. & THOUGHT 259 (2008).

The Helakhic Status of an Infertile Couple, 23 TCHUMIN 223 (2003) (Heb.).

Werber, Stephen J., *Cloning: A Jewish Law Perspective with a Comparative Study of Other Abrahamic Traditions*, 30 SETON HALL L. REV. 1114 (2000).

Westreich, Avishalom, *Changing Motherhood Paradigms: Jewish Law, Civil Law, and Society*, 28 HASTINGS WOMEN'S L.J. 97 (2017).

Divorce on Demand: The History, Dogmatics, and Hermeneutics of the Wife's Right to Divorce in Jewish Law, 62 J. JEWISH STUD. 340 (2011).

Hafka'at Kiddushin (Annulment of Marriage): Reexamination of an Old Debate, 27–28 SIDRA 111 (2013) (Heb.)

Annulment of Marriage (Hafka'at Kiddushin): Re-examination of an Old Debate, http://static1.1.sqspcdn.com/static/f/784513/11612805/1302165216787/Avishalom+Westreich+Annulment+of+Marriage+2008.pdf?token=76V70xZQdDv2JQcFEdSwZdowP24%3D.

Right to Divorce in Jewish Law: Between Politics and Ideology, 1 INT'L J. JURISPRUDENCE FAM. 177 (2010).

"Such Coercion Never Occurred to the Sages" (Nachmanides, Ketubot 63b) – Divorce Compulsion in the Mishnaic and Talmudic Laws of the Rebellious Wife, 25(2) BAR-ILAN L. STUD. 563 (2009).

The Wife's Right to Divorce in Jewish Law: History, Dogmatics and Hermeneutics, 62(2) J. JEWISH STUD. 340 (2011).

Tradition and Equality in Jewish Marriage: Beyond the Sanctification of Subordination by Melanie Landau (review), 28 NASHIM 147 (2015).

Umdena as a Ground for Marriage Annulment: Between Mistaken Transaction (Kiddushei Ta'ut) and Terminative Condition, 20 JEWISH L. ASS'N STUD. 330 (2010).

Westreich, Elimelech, *The Legal-Historical Sources of the Parents Obligation to Maintain Their Children*, 19 DINEI ISRAEL 161 (1997) (Heb.).

Wieder, Jeremy & Shlomo Riskin, *Hafka'at Kiddushin: A Rebuttal*, 36(4) TRADITION 37 (2002).

Williams, Devon D., *Over My Dead Body: The Legal Nightmare and Medical Phenomenon of Posthumous Conception through Postmortem Sperm Retrieval*, 34 CAMPBELL L. REV. 181 (2012).

Witte, John & Joel A. Nichols, *Marriage, Religion, and the Role of the Civil State: More Than a Mere Contract: Marriage as Contract and Covenant in Law and Theology*, 5 U. ST. THOMAS L.J. 595 (2008).

Wolowelsky, Joel B. & Richard V. Grazi, *Future Directions*, in RICHARD V. GRAZI, OVERCOMING INFERTILITY 425–40 (2005).

Woodhouse, Barbara B., *Hatching the Egg: A Child-Centered Perspective on Parents' Rights*, 14 CARDOZO L. REV. 1747 (1993).

Woodward, James, *The Non-Identity Problem* 96(4) ETHICS 804 (1986).

Zafran, Ruth, *Dying to Be a Father: Legal Paternity in Cases of Posthumous Conception*, 8 HOUS. J. HEALTH L. & POL'Y 47 (2007).

If It Ain't [Completely] Broke, Don't Fix It: Determining Paternity According to the Genetic Information Law (Amendment no. 3), 2008, 3 HUKIM – THE ISRAELI JOURNAL OF LEGISLATION 191 (2011) (Heb.).

More Than One Mother: Determining Maternity for the Biological Child of a Female Same-Sex Couple – The Israeli View, 9 GEO. J. GENDER & L. 115 (2008).

Whose Child Are You? The Israeli Paternity Regulation and Its Flaws, 46 HAPRAKLIT 311 (2003) (Heb.).

Zaksh, Nisan, *Conditional Marriage*, 1 NOAM 52 (1958) (Heb.).

Zohar, Zvi, *Halakhic Positions Permitting Nonmarital Sexual Intimacy*, 17 AKDAMOT 11 (2006).

Teshuva le-Magivim, 17 AKDAMOT 77 (2006).

Developments in the Law: IV. Changing Realities of Parenthood: The Law's Response to the Evolving American Family and Emerging Reproductive Technologies, 116 HARV. L. REV. 2052 (2003).

Responsum on Eyn Tenai BeNissuin, 8 YESHURUN 715 (2001) (Heb.).

Symposium: *The New "Illegitimacy": Revisiting Why Parentage Should Not Depend on Marriage*, 20 AM. U. J. GENDER SOC. POL'Y & L. 347–740 (2012).

Miscellaneous

Blackburn-Starza, Antony, *Germline in the Sand: The Ethics and Law of Engineering the Embryo*, BioNews 836, Jan. 25, 2016.

Buxton, Jess, *Genome Editing and CRISPR: The Science of Engineering the Embryo*, BioNews 835, Jan. 18, 2016.

Gold, Michael, *Adoption as a Jewish Option*, www.adopting.org/jewish.html.

Jaiswal, Ritesh R., *Three Parent IVF / Three Parent Baby*, The Science, Feb 19, 2015, http://thescience.co.in/tag/three-parents-ivf/.

Knesset Reports vol. 42, 958 (1965), http://m.knesset.gov.il/pages/default.aspx.

Margalit, Yehezkel & John Loike, *Follicular Transplants and Motherhood* (unpublished manuscript, on file with author).

Ochert, Ayala, *HFEA Grants Permission to Genetically Edit Human Embryos*, BioNews 837, Feb. 1, 2016.

Open Source Systems: Adoption and Impact: 11th IFIP WG 2.13 International Conference, OSS 2015 (Ernesto Damiani et al. eds., 2015).

Pritchard, Sarah, *Why the UK Should Be Leading the Discussion on Embryo Engineering*, BioNews 834, Jan. 11, 2016.

Regev, David, *Woman's Dream to Have Child Fulfilled after Death*, Ynet Magazine June 14, 2011, www.ynetnews.com/articles/0,7340,L-4081456,00.html.

Rosenblum, Irit, *The Biological Will – A New Paradigm in ART?*, New Family Org. (Feb. 25, 2013), www.newfamily.org.il/en/4905/the-biological-will%E2%84%A2-%E2%80%93-a-new-paradigm-in-art/.

Ryzman, Zvi, *Is a Cloned Kohen Permitted to Recite the Kohen's Blessing?* (Heb.), http://olamot.net/sites/default/files/ratz_katzvi/pdf/-_32.pdf.

Shapira, Yaakov, *And Again, Would You Murder and Also Inherit?*, 374 Weekly Parasha, Pinchas (2010), www.justice.gov.il/Units/MishpatIvri/Gilyonot/374.rtf.

Sheva Brenner, Bayla, *Filling the Void: Creating Jewish Families through Adoption*, http://ou.org.s3.amazonaws.com/pdf/ja/5766/spring66/FillingVoid.pdf.

Shochetman, Eliav, *Would You Murder and Also Inherit?*, 302 Weekly Parasha, Bereshit (2008), www.daat.ac.il/mishpat-ivri/skirot/302-2.htm.

The Israeli Ministry of Health, The Public Commission for Revision of the Legislative Regulation of Fertility and Childbearing in Israel (2012), www.health.gov.il/PublicationsFiles/BAP2012.pdf (Heb.).

The responsum of Asher Weiss concerning triple parent IVF following mitochondrial DNA replacement that was posted at http://en.tvunah.org/2013/12/29/triple-parent-ivf/.

U.S. Catholic Conference, Congregation for the Doctrine of the Faith, Instruction on Respect for Human Life in Its Origin and on the Dignity of Procreation, Donum Vitae (1987).

U.S. Congress, Office of Technology Assessment, Infertility: Medical and Social Choices 282 (1988).

6 Immigration Law Service 2d PSD FAM Iran, Immigration Law Service, Second Edition, February 2016 Update, Reciprocity Schedules and Country Document Finder, http://travel.state.gov/content/visas/en/fees/reciprocity-by-country/IR.html.

Index